# CLAUSEWITZ IN THE TWENTY-FIRST CENTURY

The Changing Character of War Programme is an inter-disciplinary research group located at the University of Oxford, and funded by the Leverhulme Trust.

# Clausewitz in the Twenty-First Century

*Edited by*

HEW STRACHAN AND ANDREAS HERBERG-ROTHE

**OXFORD**
UNIVERSITY PRESS

# OXFORD
### UNIVERSITY PRESS

Great Clarendon Street, Oxford OX2 6DP

Oxford University Press is a department of the University of Oxford.
It furthers the University's objective of excellence in research, scholarship,
and education by publishing worldwide in

Oxford  New York

Auckland  Cape Town  Dar es Salaam  Hong Kong  Karachi
Kuala Lumpur  Madrid  Melbourne  Mexico City  Nairobi
New Delhi  Shanghai  Taipei  Toronto

With offices in

Argentina  Austria  Brazil  Chile  Czech Republic  France  Greece
Guatemala  Hungary  Italy  Japan  Poland  Portugal  Singapore
South Korea  Switzerland  Thailand  Turkey  Ukraine  Vietnam

Oxford is a registered trade mark of Oxford University Press
in the UK and in certain other countries

Published in the United States
by Oxford University Press Inc., New York

© The several contributors 2007

The moral rights of the authors have been asserted
Database right Oxford University Press (maker)

First published 2007

All rights reserved. No part of this publication may be reproduced,
stored in a retrieval system, or transmitted, in any form or by any means,
without the prior permission in writing of Oxford University Press,
or as expressly permitted by law, or under terms agreed with the appropriate
reprographics rights organization. Enquiries concerning reproduction
outside the scope of the above should be sent to the Rights Department,
Oxford University Press, at the address above

You must not circulate this book in any other binding or cover
and you must impose the same condition on any acquirer

British Library Cataloguing in Publication Data

Data available

Library of Congress Cataloging-in-Publication Data

Clausewitz in the twenty-first century / edited by Hew Strachan and Andreas Herberg-Rothe.
p. cm.
ISBN 978–0–19–923202–4 (alk. paper)
1. Clausewitz, Carl von, 1780–1831. Vom Kriege. 2. Military art and science. 3. War. I. Strachan,
Hew. II. Herberg-Rothe, Andreas. III. Title: Clausewitz in the 21st century.
U102.C6643C545 2007
355.02—dc22                    2007014610

Typeset by SPI Publisher Services, Pondicherry, India
Printed in Great Britain
on acid-free paper by
Biddles Ltd, King's Lynn, Norfolk

ISBN  978–0–19–923202–4

1 3 5 7 9 10 8 6 4 2

# Foreword
## Clausewitz On War: *A History of the Howard–Paret Translation*

The idea of a new translation of *On War* originated in the late 1950s when Peter Paret and I were working together at King's College London. Peter was studying the connection between military and political ideas in eighteenth-century Prussia for his thesis on Yorck von Wartenburg; I was devising my first courses for the new Department of War Studies. Peter was particularly concerned with the inaccuracies and misinterpretations in the existing English translations of *On War*. I was more interested in the continuing value of the text as a didactic tool for both civilian and professional students of war—particularly its insight into the concept of 'friction' and the central importance of 'moral forces', of which, during my own military service, I had become very aware.

On returning to Princeton in 1961, Peter took up the matter with the historian Gordon Craig and the political scientist Klaus Knorr. Between them they persuaded the Princeton University Press to sponsor an ambitious project for a translation of all Clausewitz's military and political writings in six volumes, each with a separate editor and translator. A meeting of those interested took place in Berlin in June 1962, attended by Werner Hahlweg, whose edition of *On War* would provide the basis for the English translation; the American historian John Shy; Knorr, Craig, and, in addition to Peter and myself, the strategic thinker Bernard Brodie. Brodie had just published his work *Strategy in the Nuclear Age* and was particularly interested in Clausewitz's thinking about 'limited war'. Klaus Knorr and the Press were very anxious to enlist his cooperation, since they considered, quite rightly, that his name would give the project credibility with a far wider audience. A certain tension developed between the historians on the panel, who saw me as the appropriate editor for *On War*, and the political scientists and representatives of the Press, who preferred Brodie. The problem was resolved by appointing both of us. Since neither had sufficient command of German to undertake the translation, I undertook to find a professional translator, while Peter, who was virtually bilingual, would exercise a *droit de regard* over all six volumes.

I was fortunate in finding an excellent translator in Angus Malcolm. Angus was a former member of the British Foreign Office who, having recently completed a translation of Karl Demeter's *The German Officer Corps*, was broadly familiar with the subject matter. He had the further advantage of living within easy walking distance from me in London. But the work made slow progress. Malcolm and I, working in London, produced drafts that we tried to make as close to contemporary English usage as possible. We then checked these, first with Peter, who by now was teaching at the University of California; then with Brodie in Los Angeles; and finally with the Princeton University Press in New Jersey whose translators found much of the Malcolm–Howard version too colloquial for their liking: all this in an era before either fax machines or email had been invented. By 1970, the task was still not complete, and poor Malcolm died while still at work on the project.

Yet even less progress had been made on the other volumes in the projected series. In fact, none of them got off the ground at all. Understandably, Princeton University Press cancelled the original project. That *On War* survived owed much to the continuing enthusiasm and influence of Bernard Brodie— whose enthusiasm, indeed, was so great that his introductory essay swelled to such a length that much of it had to be detached and printed as a separate afterword. In 1974, Brodie persuaded the Press to sign a new contract. Peter and I then undertook a revision of the entire text, and the volume finally appeared in 1976.

Its publication was timely. The experience of the Vietnam War had interested both military leaders and political scientists in the relations between political and military leadership. The continuing menace of nuclear weapons made the distinction between 'absolute' and 'limited' war alarmingly relevant; while Clausewitz's emphasis on friction, moral forces, and leadership qualities gave him credibility with professional soldiers who might otherwise have found much of his writing either excessively abstract or out of date. It was our good fortune to be able to present his work in a text that was accessible both to military colleges and to university students.

There still remained problems of translation that we had failed to iron out. *Politik*, for example: should it be 'policy' or 'politics'? Neither carry the full grandeur of the original: both imply that soldiers were being instructed to subordinate themselves to the intrigues of mere 'politicians' and still remain a sticking point for such distinguished commentators as Sir John Keegan. 'Grand strategy', the term later popularized by Paul Kennedy, might have been better, but no English word is really appropriate. The same can be said of the word *wunderlich* which Clausewitz applied to his famous 'trinity' of government, military, and people. Earlier translators had used 'wondrous', an archaism now found only in Christian hymns describing a different kind of Trinity. But was that perhaps what Clausewitz intended? Neither 'remarkable' nor 'paradoxical' carry the full weight of the original. If I were starting over again I might settle for 'amazing'; but I am open to offers.

Michael Howard

# Contents

| | |
|---|---|
| *Foreword* | v |
| *Notes on Contributors* | xi |
| Introduction<br>Hew Strachan and Andreas Herberg-Rothe | 1 |
| 1. Clausewitz and the Dialectics of War<br>Hew Strachan | 14 |
| 2. Clausewitz and the Non-Linear Nature of War: Systems of Organized Complexity<br>Alan Beyerchen | 45 |
| 3. Clausewitz's *On War*: Problems of Text and Translation<br>Jan Willem Honig | 57 |
| 4. The Primacy of Policy and the 'Trinity' in Clausewitz's Mature Thought<br>Christopher Bassford | 74 |
| 5. The Instrument: Clausewitz on Aims and Objectives in War<br>Daniel Moran | 91 |
| 6. Moral Forces in War<br>Ulrike Kleemeier | 107 |
| 7. War as 'Art': Aesthetics and Politics in Clausewitz's Social Thinking<br>José Fernández Vega | 122 |
| 8. Clausewitz's Ideas of Strategy and Victory<br>Beatrice Heuser | 138 |
| 9. On Defence as the Stronger Form of War<br>Jon Sumida | 163 |

| | |
|---|---|
| 10. Clausewitz and Small Wars<br>*Christopher Daase* | 182 |
| 11. Clausewitz and the Nature of the War on Terror<br>*Antulio J. Echevarria II* | 196 |
| 12. Clausewitz and the Privatization of War<br>*Herfried Münkler* | 219 |
| 13. Clausewitz and Information Warfare<br>*David Lonsdale* | 231 |
| 14. Clausewitz and the Two Temptations of Modern Strategic Thinking<br>*Benoît Durieux* | 251 |
| 15. Civil–Military Relations and Democracies<br>*Wilfried von Bredow* | 266 |
| 16. Clausewitz and a New Containment: the Limitation of War and Violence<br>*Andreas Herberg-Rothe* | 283 |
| *Index* | 308 |

# Notes on Contributors

**Christopher Bassford** is Professor of Strategy at National War College, in Washington, DC. He is the author of *Clausewitz in English: The Reception of Clausewitz in Britain and America, 1815–1945* (Oxford University Press, 1994) and editor of *The Clausewitz Homepage* (http://www.clausewitz.com). He is also one of the editors of The Boston Consulting Group's business-oriented *Clausewitz On Strategy: Inspiration and Insight from a Master Strategist* (2001).

**Alan Beyerchen** teaches nineteenth- and twentieth-century German history in the Department of History at Ohio State University. He is perhaps still best known for his book, *Scientists Under Hitler*, and has published 'Clausewitz, Nonlinearity and the Unpredictability of War', *International Security*, 17 (winter 1992–3): 59–90.

**Christopher Daase** is Professor of Political Science and Chair in International Relations at the University of Munich. Previously he was Senior Lecturer at the University of Kent and Director of the Programme on International Conflict Analysis at the Brussels School of International Studies. He is author of *Kleine Kriege—Grosse Wirkung* (Small Wars—Big Effects) and has published numerous articles on international relations theory, international institutions, foreign and security policy, terrorism and related issues.

**Benoît Durieux**, a French army officer, is currently assigned to the French Joint Defence Staff as a colonel, having previously served in various units of the French Foreign Legion. In 2005, he published *Relire De la guerre de Clausewitz* (Editions Economica, Paris).

**Antulio J. Echevarria II**, a former army officer, is the Director of Research at the US Army War College. He has published numerous articles on Clausewitz and on contemporary warfare. His book, *Clausewitz and Contemporary War*, was published by Oxford University Press in 2007, and he is also the author of *After Clausewitz: German Military Thinkers before the Great War* (2000).

**Andreas Herberg-Rothe** is private lecturer in political science at the Humboldt University in Berlin. He has been an associate of the Oxford Leverhulme Programme on the Changing Character of War (2004–5) and a Visiting Fellow at the London School of Economics and Political Science (2005–6). His publications include *Das Rätsel Clausewitz* (2001), published in English as

*Clausewitz's Puzzle: The Political Theory of War* (2007), and *Der Krieg. Geschichte und Gegenwart* (2003).

**Beatrice Heuser** is director of research at the Military History Research Office of the Bundeswehr, currently seconded to the University of the Bundeswehr in Munich. After obtaining degrees in London and Oxford, she studied for her Habilitation at the University of Marburg. She has taught at the universities of Reims and Lille, and was professor of international and strategic studies in the Department of War Studies, King's College, London. Her books include *Reading Clausewitz* (2002) and *Nuclear Mentalities? Strategy and Beliefs in Britain, France and Germany* (1998). She is currently working on a book entitled *The Evolution of Strategy since Vegetius*, to be published in 2008.

**Jan Willem Honig** is Senior Lecturer in War Studies at King's College London and Professor of Strategy at the Swedish National Defence College in Stockholm. His publications on Clausewitz include, most recently, the introduction to a complete re-edition of the J. J. Graham translation for Barnes & Noble in New York, and he is the author, with Norbert Both, of *Srebrenica: Record of a War Crime* (1996).

**Ulrike Kleemeier** is a private lecturer in philosophy at the Westfälische Wilhelms-Universität in Münster. Her publications include *Gottlob Frege Kontext—Prinzip und Ontologie* (1997) and *Grundfragen einer philosophischen Theorien des Krieges. Über die Konzeptionen von Platon-Hobbes-Clausewitz* (2002).

**David J. Lonsdale** is a Lecturer in Strategic Studies at the University of Hull. He specializes in strategic theory and its application to historical and contemporary strategic settings. His publications include *The Nature of War in the Information Age: Clausewitzian Future* (2004), and *Alexander the Great: Lessons in Strategy* (2004).

**Daniel Moran** is professor of international and military history at the Naval Postgraduate School in Monterey, California. He is co-editor with Peter Paret of *Carl von Clausewitz: Historical and Political Writings* (Princeton, NJ, 1992) and author of *Wars of National Liberation* (2001).

**Herfried Münkler** is professor of political theory and the history of political ideas at the Humboldt University in Berlin. In 1992 he became a member of the Berlin-Brandenburg Academy of Science and chairman of the International Marx-Engels-Foundation, Amsterdam. His books include *Machiavelli* (1982), *Gewalt und Ordnung* (1992), *Über den Krieg* (2002), *Die Neuen Kriege* (2004), which has been translated as *The New Wars* (2005), *Der Wandel des*

*Krieges. Von der Symmetrie zu Asymmetrie* (2006), and *Empires: The Logic of World Domination from Ancient Rome to the United States* (2007).

**Hew Strachan** is Chichele Professor of the History of War at the University of Oxford, where he is also Director of the Leverhulme Programme on the Changing Character of War and a Fellow of All Souls College. He is a Life Fellow of Corpus Christi College, Cambridge, and has been a lecturer at the Royal Military Academy Sandhurst and Professor of Modern History at the University of Glasgow. His publications embrace the history of the British Army, of the First World War and the conduct of war more generally, and include *Clausewitz's 'On War': A Biography* (2007).

**Jon Sumida** is an associate professor of history at the University of Maryland, College Park, and has served as Major-General Matthew C. Horner Chair of Military Theory at the US Marine Corps University (2004–6). He has also taught at the US National War College, US Marine Corps School of Advanced Warfighting, and US Army Advanced Strategic Arts Program. His books include *In Defence of Naval Supremacy: Finance, Technology and British Naval Policy, 1889–1914* (1989) and *Inventing Grand Strategy and Teaching Command: The Classic Works of Alfred Thayer Mahan Reconsidered* (1997). His monograph, *Engaging the Clausewitzian Mind*, is in the press.

**José Fernández Vega** teaches social philosophy and aesthetics at the University of Buenos Aires. He is a tenured researcher at the Conicet, the Argentinian National Scientific Research Council, and has been a DAAD scholar at the Humboldt University in Berlin and a Fulbright scholar. His books include *Carl von Clausewitz: Guerra, politica, filosofia* (1995) and *Las guerras de la política: Clausewitz entre Maquiavelo y Perón* (Buenos Aires, 2005).

**Wilfried von Bredow** is professor of political science at Philipps-Universität, Marburg. He has written on German foreign policy, transatlantic security policy, civil–military relations, and his most recent book is *Streitkräfte in der Demokratie* (Wiesbaden, 2007).

# Introduction

*Hew Strachan and Andreas Herberg-Rothe*

Carl von Clausewitz's *On War* is the prism through which we have come to look at war. Certainly within Europe, and to an increasing extent outside as well, military commentators have used his text as a departure point at least for their questions, if not their answers. A reporter covering the war in Afghanistan after the attacks on the United States on 11 September 2001 found a copy of the Everyman edition of *On War* in an al-Qaeda safe house. His discovery was doubly significant for what follows. First, it suggests that those Western pundits who are quick to condemn Clausewitz as *passé*, relevant only to an era when European armies fought each other in 'symmetrical' conflicts, an epoch which apparently ended with the conclusion of the Cold War in 1990, may have missed the mark. Second, the section of the book marked by its terrorist reader discussed courage. It did not concern the use of war as a political instrument. There is more to Clausewitz than one oft-repeated nostrum.[1]

Because Clausewitz has provided us with so many of the conceptual tools which enable us to understand the nature of war, two things tend to happen when war displays different characteristics. First, we wonder whether Clausewitz is still relevant. Those anxious to trumpet the novelty of what is happening say that he is not. Clausewitz likened war to a chameleon, allowing for changes in its appearance, but suggesting that its underlying nature remained unchanged. His critics say that some changes can alter war's very nature, and that the nature of war today is radically different from the nature of war in Clausewitz's own time, the age of Napoleon. In other words, the changes are more fundamental than can simply be accounted for by shifting characteristics. Second, when the dust settles, Clausewitz tends to recover his standing, but he does so because his readers find fresh angles from which to approach the text. The key question that emerges from this second point is, therefore, different from that which Clausewitz's critics tend to ask. They

---

[1] Lucasta Miller, 'Bound for Glory', an interview with David Campbell, the publisher of the Everyman series, *The Guardian*, Review, 13 May 2006, p. 11.

demand, somewhat rhetorically, whether *On War* continues to have any relevance. The more revealing question, posed in a spirit of greater self-awareness, is, rather, whether the most recent and fashionable interpretation of Clausewitz remains the most relevant one. For each generation reads *On War* in the light of its own understanding of war, and so each has its own reading of Clausewitz.

There is no more telling illustration of this point than the best-known of all Clausewitz's maxims that 'war is an instrument of policy'.[2] That was not a new insight when Clausewitz penned it, and it was shared by his colleagues at the war academy in Berlin, like Otto August Rühle von Lilienstern,[3] and assimilated by his greatest rival in the world of nineteenth-century military theory, Antoine-Henri Jomini, in his *Précis de l'art de la guerre* (1838). Furthermore, this is not where the weight of *On War* lies. Clausewitz wrote much more fully and definitively about the relationship between the constituent elements of war, strategy and tactics, than he did about that between war and policy. He devoted the most extensive discussion in *On War* to the defence; he gave us concepts like 'friction', by which he meant, very loosely, 'the fog of war'; he tried to define 'military genius'; and he drew a crucial distinction between real war and 'absolute war', by which he meant war in an ideal but unrealizable form. But these are not the insights that today's journalists are referring to when they use (as they all too frequently do) the epithet 'Clausewitzian'. That is their lazy shorthand for the idea that war 'is only a branch of political activity; that it is in no sense autonomous'.[4]

The starting point for the chapters which make up this volume is the concerns of contemporary journalists, not the concerns of Clausewitz when he was writing (although the latter are certainly central to much of what follows). That means that the relationship between war and policy bulks large. It has to: the very proposition has itself come under scrutiny, and because Clausewitz himself has become so closely identified with it he has himself become a target. The case for the value of studying Clausewitz has to be restated. Self-evidently, the simplification of *On War* has had two deleterious effects. Specifically, it misrepresents the range of Clausewitz's views on the relationship between war and policy, and more generally it distorts the other messages in a book that is concerned with much more than just that relationship.

Clausewitz studies at the start of the twenty-first century confront a second and even more important challenge than that of familiarity and consequently contempt. The character of war has changed since his day, so much so that

---

[2] *On War*, VIII, 6B, p. 610.
[3] Beatrice Heuser, *Reading Clausewitz* (London, 2002), pp. 30, 44–5.
[4] *On War*, VIII, 6B, p. 605.

some commentators say that a tipping point has been reached: that its nature also has fundamentally altered. The distinction—between the character of a phenomenon and its underlying nature—is important. Clausewitz certainly allowed for the former but possibly not the latter. At the end of what is today the most widely read chapter of *On War*, book I, chapter 1, there is a passage on the so-called 'trinity'. Christopher Bassford explores its meaning more fully in his chapter of this book. The most recent English translation of the text, by Michael Howard and Peter Paret, renders its opening sentence thus: 'War is more than a true chameleon that slightly adapts its characteristics to the given case. As a total phenomenon its dominant tendencies always make war a remarkable trinity.'[5] Clearly, a chameleon remains a chameleon whatever colour it adopts for the time being. The crucial two words in the translation are 'more than', which imply that the circumstances of war can cause war to change more than its characteristics: war in other words is not like a chameleon. However, an older translation, that by O. S. Matthijs Jolles, which is more faithful to the original German, if more stilted as a result, gives: 'War is, therefore, not only a veritable chameleon, because in each concrete case it changes somewhat its character, but it is also...a strange trinity'.[6] The implication here is that war may be a chameleon after all, changing its character but not its nature, which is made up of the trinity. But neither the Howard and Paret translation nor that by Jolles captures the exact nuance of Clausewitz's original: 'Der Krieg ist also nicht nur ein wahres Chamäleon, weil er in jedem konkreten Fall seine Natur etwas ändert, sondern er ist auch seinem Gesamterscheinungen nach, in Bezeihung auf die in ihm herrschenden Tendenzen, eine wunderliche Dreifaltigkeit'.[7] The implication here is that war may indeed be a chameleon, in that it changes its nature slightly in each individual case (its 'character'), but not its nature in general, which is made up of the trinity (on which see Bassford). Thus we end up with a translation which reads: 'war is not only a true chameleon, because it changes its nature slightly in each concrete case, but it is also, in its overall appearance, in relation to its inherent tendencies, a wondrous trinity'.

In this book, there are chapters which develop both these themes. Jan Willem Honig explores the problems of translating Clausewitz, and Antulio Echevarria argues that changes in the character of war can affect its nature. In the world of social and political action, unlike that of the chameleon, comprehensive changes of character may lead to changes in nature. Echevarria's chapter concerns the impact on war's nature of what the United States has

---

[5] *On War*, I, 1, § 28, p. 89.
[6] Karl von Clausewitz, *On War*, trans. by O. J. Matthijs Jolles (Washington, DC, 1950), I, 1, § 28, p. 18.
[7] *Vom Kriege*, ed. Werner Hahlweg (19th edn, Bonn, 1980), I, 1, § 28, pp. 212–13.

identified as the 'war on terror'. If terrorism is itself war rather than one way of fighting, and if it is possible to wage a war against a means of fighting, as opposed to waging war for the purposes of prevailing over a specific enemy in the pursuit of policy goals, the nature of that war is likely to become something very different from that which Clausewitz understood by war. But that series of conditions rests on the assumption that we have started with a proper understanding of war itself. This, after all, as Bassford points out, is precisely why most people read *On War* in the first place—to understand war, not because they are particularly interested in understanding Clausewitz.

The presumption in much contemporary comment in the opening years of the twenty-first century, and even more in the governmental policies of the United States and Britain, is that the terrorist attacks of 11 September 2001 changed at least the character of war and possibly its nature. But as so often in human affairs, we are in danger of privileging the clearly definable event over longer-term currents and more gradual changes. The 9/11 attacks were certainly a defining moment in people's lives, and not just in the United States. Thanks to the real-time reporting of television, they became the sort of event which prompted individuals to locate their reactions to the news in terms which were subjective more than objective, in what they were doing and where they were as the aircraft hit the twin towers—just as people recalled where they were when they heard of their nations' entries to the First World War or what they were doing when they received the news of President J. F. Kennedy's assassination.

The 9/11 attacks may have changed the character and even the nature of war. However, much of what happened thereafter, and especially the American invasions of Afghanistan and Iraq, does not support that proposition. Armed forces were used by the United States and Britain in the pursuit of political objectives: the actions of both governments were Clausewitzian in the most hackneyed sense. Since the attacks, not least thanks to the length, bloodiness, and persistence of the fighting in Iraq and Afghanistan, and to the growing belief that war may not have delivered on the political objectives of the United States, strategic studies have become fixated with those wars—and especially the war in Iraq—as though they were the exclusive templates for war in the coming century. Striking here is the lack of perspective, which fails to look at other wars going on elsewhere in the world at the same time, or neglects to look at current events in historical context, and so does not distinguish what is really new from what seems to be new.

Clausewitz confronted the same difficulty. Having written a book which was predominantly derived from the experience of the Napoleonic Wars, and which treated them as the implicit model for the future, he suddenly realized the historical illiteracy of his methodology. He had written what aspired to be a study of war as a general phenomenon which discounted much of the evidence provided by wars before 1792, and nearly all wars before 1740. He realized, probably in 1827, that he had to have a theory of war which embraced all wars, not just some wars. In particular, he had to allow for the patterns of warfare prevailing in the eighteenth century before the French Revolution. The early Clausewitz had been caught up in the vigour of Napoleonic strategy, whose unrestrained violence had led to overwhelming victories at Austerlitz in 1805 and Jena in 1806, but the later Clausewitz was forced to reconsider the assumptions which those battles generated by the failure of the same strategy in Russia in 1812 and by Napoleon's final defeat at Waterloo. The strategy which had led to Napoleon's initial successes ultimately contributed to his downfall. Clausewitz concluded that the determination to seek battle might deliver victory in the short term but could lead to defeat in the long term, unless it was subordinated to the primacy of policy.[8]

The parallel is instructive, because in seeing 9/11 as a departure point, we have neglected the much bigger shifts which were slower in their evolution but which climaxed over a decade earlier, with the end of the Cold War. This presented a much more profound challenge to Clausewitzian assumptions. Before 1990, America's use of war was reluctant, limited, and discreet; since 1990 it has gradually shed those inhibitions. Two very obvious explanations stand out to explain that shift. The first is the absence since 1990 of any rival to match the Soviet Union (however much the rhetoric directed at al-Qaeda may suggest the contrary). The second is the diminished significance of nuclear weapons and their deterrent effect.

In 1980, with the Cold War still at its height, the Clausewitz-Gesellschaft in Germany held a conference to mark the bicentenary of Clausewitz's birth. A former inspector-general of the Bundeswehr, Ulrich de Maizière, provided the foreword to the volume of essays which resulted in *Freiheit ohne Krieg?* [Freedom without war?]. The aim of the book, he said, was to show which of Clausewitz's insights were of significance for the present. In particular, he asked whether war could still be an instrument of policy given the likelihood that any conventional conflict, at least in Europe, would escalate to a nuclear exchange. Hans Apel, the defence minister of the Federal Republic, was categorical in his response: 'war can no longer be an instrument of policy. On the contrary, military power, the instrument of policy, can only now have the task of preventing war and securing peace.'[9] The purpose of security policy was,

---

[8] Andreas Herberg-Rothe, *Clausewitz's Puzzle: The Political Theory of War* (Oxford, 2007).

[9] Hans Apel, 'Vom Kriege—Vom Frieden. Zur Sicherheitspolitik der Bundesrepublik Deutschland', in Eberhard Wagemann and Joachim Niemeyer (eds), *Freiheit ohne Krieg? Beiträge zur Strategie-Diskussion der Gegenwart im Spiegel der Theorie von Carl von Clausewitz* (Bonn, 1980), 15.

he went on, to make war pointless, not the ability to win a war. Clausewitz wrote about waging war, not about keeping the peace: in Apel's eyes he was clearly redundant. But that was not how most of the contributors saw the Cold War, not least Ulrich de Maizière himself. Clausewitz, he said (with arguable accuracy), did not regard war and peace as opposites, but saw both as subsumed within the overarching concept of policy. Therefore, he concluded, the influence of policy on military power could not be restricted to war alone, and so the atomic age, far from contradicting Clausewitz, reinforced him. The political object remained the aim and war the means, and never could the means be considered in a context divorced from the aim.[10]

*Freiheit ohne Krieg?* divided its subject matter into three categories— the relationship between war and policy; the dimensions of strategy as it affected particular armed forces (there was even a chapter on the 'validity of Clausewitz's judgments for the sphere of air and space war'); and the future of the discussion on Clausewitz. The chapters in this book, *Clausewitz in the Twenty-first Century*, are derived from a conference held in Oxford in March 2005, a year which was, as it happened, the 225th anniversary of Clausewitz's birth. The agenda which the conference confronted was very different from that faced by the Clausewitz-Gesellschaft twenty-five years before. Now Clausewitz's aphorism on the relationship between war and policy was being dismissed for very different reasons: not because war had no utility but because it was being waged for reasons that were not political or policy-driven. War, some commentators were suggesting, was no longer the province of the armed forces, but of non-state actors. Thus the question arose as to whether strategy traditionally defined (which is what most of *On War* is about) was any longer the best way of looking at what was, revealingly, no longer even called war, but armed conflict. Finally, even the third, more amorphous section of the agenda of *Freiheit ohne Krieg?* was called into question. Put bluntly, some critics doubted whether Clausewitz's *On War* any longer had a place in strategic and security studies debates. He belonged to the past, to a period that began in 1648, with the end of the Thirty Years War, when the peace of Westphalia had, or so at least international relations theorists argued, made war the business solely of the state, and ended in 1990, when states allegedly lost the monopoly on waging war.

Regardless of whether this is an accurate characterization of war between 1648 and 1990 (and most historians would argue that it is not), the question still arises as to whether Clausewitz's theory is only concerned with interstate warfare. Antulio Echevarria has stated elsewhere that 'Clausewitz's theory of war will remain valid as long as warlords, drug barons, international terrorists,

[10] Ulrich de Maizière, 'Politische Führung und militärische Macht', in ibid. 92–107.

racial or religious communities will wage war'.[11] In order to bring this position into harmony with Clausewitz's few statements concerning state policy, we must stretch his concept of politics. For Echevarria, Clausewitz understood a community as having its own political and social identity, even if it lacked statehood. Such an interpretation is consonant with Clausewitz's own interest in wars before 1648, where he specifically linked the weakness of states to 'exceptional manifestations in the art of war,'[12] and to the review of the history of war which Clausewitz provided in book VIII, chapter 3B, of *On War*, where he described 'the semibarbarous Tartars, the republics of antiquity, the feudal lords and trading cities of the Middle Ages, eighteenth-century kings and the rulers and peoples of the nineteenth century' as 'all conducting war in their own particular way, using different methods and pursuing different aims'.[13]

Clausewitz stresses that in all these cases war remains a continuation of policy by other means. In doing so, however, he suppresses the difference between the policies of states and the intentions of other communities which wage war. To aid our comprehension of Clausewitz, therefore, it makes sense to supplement the primacy of policy as a general category with the affiliation of belligerents to a warring community. If the communities are states, we can speak of politics in the modern sense; if they are ethnic, religious, or other communities, the value systems and goals of those communities (their 'cultures') are the more important factors. Although this means replacing Clausewitz's use of the term 'state' with 'warring community' or some such expression, we shall be more faithful to what he understood a state to embody. Here, as elsewhere, we can be in danger of imposing the modern understanding of a word on a Clausewitzian concept.

This is an accusation which can be levelled with particular force at three books in particular, which have challenged the primacy of *On War* in the literature on strategy: all were published before the 9/11 attacks, but after the end of the Cold War. First, in chronological sequence, was Martin van Creveld's *The Transformation of War* (the title of its American edition; *On Future War* in its British version). Extrapolating from the final section of *On War*'s book I, chapter 1, van Creveld characterized Clausewitz's view of war as 'trinitarian', and said that its three elements were the people, the army, and the government. In reality Clausewitz says that the trinity consists of 'primordial violence, hatred and enmity'; 'the play of chance and probability'; and war's 'element of subordination, as an instrument of policy, which makes it subject

---

[11] Antulio Echevarria, 'War, Politics and the RMA: The Legacy of Clausewitz', *Joint Force Quarterly*, 10 (winter 1995–6), 76–80; see also Isabelle Duyvesteyn, *Clausewitz and African Wars* (London, 1995).
[12] See Hew Strachan's chapter in this volume, p. 39.
[13] *On War*, VIII, 3B, p. 586.

to reason alone'.[14] Clausewitz then went on to identify each of these 'mainly', but not exclusively, with the people, the army, and the government. For van Creveld, 'the Clausewitzian Universe rests on the assumption that war is made predominantly by states or, to be exact, by governments'.[15] In other words, Clausewitz, the product of what van Creveld saw as a post-Westphalian world view, had no interest, despite the 'trinity', in the people and their passions. As Christopher Daase's chapter in this volume shows, van Creveld was fundamentally wrong. Clausewitz had a lively interest in the irregular forms of war which van Creveld was arguing would be the dominant forms of war in the future. *The Transformation of War* had the misfortune to come out just as a conventional conflict, the First Gulf War, was reaching its apparently triumphant conclusion. It was therefore criticized on its publication for overemphasizing the future role of guerrillas, bandits, and terrorists. From the perspective of 2005, this failing looked less egregious; what is much more worrying is its selective and misleading use of Clausewitz's writings to make its case.

Two years later, in 1993, John Keegan came at the same point from a different direction in *A History of Warfare*. 'War', he declared in the opening sentence of the book, 'is not the continuation of policy by other means.'[16] Keegan argued that war antedated the creation of states, and was the product not of policy but of culture. He went on to misrepresent *On War* in ways that were frankly wilful: 'The purpose of war, Clausewitz said, was to serve a political end; the nature of war, he succeeded in arguing, was to serve only itself. By conclusion, his logic therefore ran, those who make war an end in itself are likely to be more successful than those who seek to moderate its character for political purposes.'[17] This passage strings together three totally distinct observations, of which only the first two reflect passages in *On War*, both of which in any case are not connected in the way Keegan suggests they are. The third point dismisses entirely Clausewitz's own explicit recognition that Napoleon had overreached himself, and his own realization—made evident in his note of 1827—that any theory of war had to accommodate two sorts of war, war to overthrow the enemy, and war that is the basis for negotiation with him. Keegan was guilty, as was van Creveld, of reading *On War* through the lens of its later interpreters rather than as it was written, and of doing so for the convenience of his own argument. As a result he exaggerated Clausewitz's attention to the issue of war and policy, and distorted what *On War* has to say about the relationship between the two.

---

[14] Howard and Paret's translation: *On War*, I, 1, § 28, p. 89.
[15] Martin van Creveld, *The Transformation of War* (New York, 1991), 49.
[16] John Keegan, *A History of Warfare* (London, 1993), 3.
[17] Ibid. 22–3; for a sustained attack on Keegan, see Christopher Bassford, 'John Keegan and the Grand Tradition of Trashing Clausewitz: a Polemic', *War in History*, I (1994), 319–36.

The denouement to these trends was Mary Kaldor's *New and Old Wars: Organized Violence in a Global Era*, published in 1999. At some levels, Kaldor was a much more sophisticated and nuanced critic of Clausewitz than either van Creveld or Keegan. She began by saying that Clausewitz was fond of pointing out that 'war is a social activity',[18] an observation which goes to the heart of what exactly Clausewitz meant by policy or politics. The German word *Politik* does of course cover both, but it is also clear that Clausewitz meant different things at different points. Sometimes the context suggests that he has foreign policy in mind, at others he highlights the social upheaval of the French Revolution and its consequences for warfare. But Kaldor, like most others who comment on Clausewitz, did not pause to consider the consequences of these different interpretations. Instead she went straight on to the post-Westphalian construct which so mesmerized van Creveld and Keegan, and which involves cobbling together insights and observations in a sequence that differs from the context in which they first appear, as well as adding glosses that are contentious at best: 'Clausewitz defined war as "an act of violence intended to compel our opponent to fulfil our will",' Kaldor wrote, but then went on: 'This definition implied that "we" and "our opponent" were states, and the "will" of one state could be clearly defined. Hence war, in the Clausewitzian definition, is between states for a definable political end, i.e. state interest.'[19] Kaldor's book pivoted on her case study of the war in Bosnia-Hercegovina between 1992 and 1995. From this one example, she concluded that 'new wars' involve non-state actors, war lords, and criminals, whose aims are as often economic gain as political ends, and who can have as much interest in sustaining conflict as in concluding it. Clausewitz therefore became not the analyst of war, but the representative fall guy for 'old wars'.

The arguments advanced by Martin van Creveld and Mary Kaldor in particular raise two important questions. The first is one posed to historians. They and particularly medievalists and early modernists, in other words those who deal with European history before 1648, can easily and quickly say that there is nothing new in the phenomena which *The Transformation of War* and *New and Old Wars* describe: non-state actors, war lords, brigandage, and the interpenetration of war and crime were even more familiar then than they are now. But saying that mankind has seen all this before does not get us much further forward in terms of understanding war today, nor does it deal with the real and important issues both books raise. The challenge for the historian is to identify not continuity but change, not what is old but what is genuinely new.

---

[18] Mary Kaldor, *New and Old Wars: Organized Violence in a Global Era* (Cambridge, 1999), 13.
[19] Ibid. 15.

The second question is directed at students of Clausewitz. Too often, when Clausewitz's devotees are confronted by the sorts of challenges to their beliefs posed by van Creveld, Keegan, and Kaldor, they respond with a defence that is superficial. For example, a self-confessed Clausewitzian, Colin Gray, in a recent book on the future of war used Clausewitz to argue that 'all wars are things of the same nature', and went on to say that no war is autonomous, but is always an instrument of policy.[20] Both points are defensible and probably also right (at least in the judgement of the editors of this book), but how much does it matter that the authority for this is Clausewitz? If, for example, we believe that war is always waged to fulfil political objectives, is it any more than a truism to say so? And does it make the truism any more true if we put Clausewitz's name alongside it? This is the journalist's use of *On War*, and it is the mirror image of the uses to which the book was put by Clausewitz's critics in the 1990s. None of them needed Clausewitz to sustain their basic points. The rise of the guerrilla, the role of culture in shaping war, and the predominance of warlords were no more or less true for their being presented as part of a demolition of Clausewitz. The notion that war is a political instrument does not become either more or less true because of what Clausewitz believed about the relationship between the two.

In the introduction to his chapter in this book, Christopher Bassford identifies four approaches to the study of Clausewitz. First, 'the original intent school' are historians who focus on Clausewitz and his writings in the context of the times in which he lived and wrote. Second, 'the inspirationist school' uses Clausewitz's ideas for the objectives of political science, to provoke further thought and fresh ideas (like the relevance of *On War* to war in the air and space). Third, 'the receptionist school', also composed of historians, studies the influence of his ideas and their impact on later generations. Finally, 'the editorial school' is made up of those who wish to convey what Clausewitz really meant when he wrote as he did.

Clearly, there is no strict demarcation between these four groups, and the insights of one discipline can generate insights for another. Indeed that is the premise both of the Oxford Leverhulme Programme on the Changing Character of War and of the conference on Clausewitz in the twenty-first century which it sponsored. The programme aims to look at war in an interdisciplinary fashion, from the perspective of the historian, the philosopher, the political scientist, and the practitioner. So did Clausewitz, albeit less self-consciously. The essays which follow embrace all these disciplines and all four of Bassford's approaches.

---

[20] Colin Gray, *Another Bloody Century: Future Warfare* (London, 2005), 33, 57.

During the Cold War, the normative aspects of the early Clausewitz were toned down, particularly the visceral call to arms and deep German nationalism which he expressed in the manifesto written in February 1812 when he left Prussian service to fight for Russia against Napoleon (on which see Strachan's chapter in this book). The three books which appeared in 1976, an *annus mirabilis* for Clausewitz studies, exacerbated this problematic reading—Raymond Aron's *Penser la guerre*, Peter Paret's *Clausewitz and the State*, as well as Michael Howard and Peter Paret's translation into English. All are masterpieces, but they privilege the first of the eight books of *On War*, and in some respects treat only the first chapter of that first book as still relevant. They stressed the rationality of Clausewitz's approach, so that war could only be understood as a means to a predetermined political end, even in an era of—or because of the existence of—nuclear weapons. Aron argued that, since the nuclear destruction of the planet could not be a political purpose, war could no longer be waged, it could only be 'thought'.

The liberal reduction of Clausewitzian theory to rationality was what exposed Clausewitz to attack in the period of revolutionary change after 1989. It seemed that it was no longer applicable to new forms of autonomous violence or to other forms of action, for example by warlords. In this volume, Christopher Daase and Herfried Münkler explicitly test the value of Clausewitz's approach in areas where it is generally seen to be outdated—small wars and new forms of privatized violence. Daase frees Clausewitz's writings on small wars and his manifestos of 1812 from their normative burden and shows how useful they can be in the analysis of contemporary 'small wars'. Münkler shows how the application of Clausewitzian theory to today's 'privatized wars' presupposes a fundamental interpretive shift, which involves moving away from what Aron called the 'formula', in other words war as a continuation of policy by other means, to an explicit engagement with the 'fascinating trinity' of war. In the trinity, which Clausewitz stressed contained his actual concept of war, and which he saw as the starting point for his entire theory, he repeated the 'formula' indirectly and in a somewhat weaker form. Policy in the trinity enjoys equal status with the other two tendencies in war, with primordial violence and the interplay of probability and chance.

At the conference, it did not prove possible to reach agreement on the differentiation of the 'trinity', but it was understood as the starting point—in combination with Clausewitz's concept of friction—for a general, non-linear theory of war and violent conflict (see Alan Beyerchen's chapter). Following this interpretation, the application of Clausewitz's concepts to contemporary circumstances, which as Beatrice Heuser makes clear in relation to his concept of strategy remain tied to the events of his own times, may be less helpful than more broad propositions. Ulrike Kleemeier uses Clausewitz's concepts of bravery and the moral basis for action to outline a concept of the 'ideal soldier', who would have the qualities that would not only be required in major wars but would also make it possible to set limits to his own actions in 'low intensity conflicts'. José Fernández Vega supports Kleemeier, employing the works of Immanuel Kant and Hannah Arendt to trace Clausewitz's concept of action back to that of judgement, an indispensable concept for the use of force by modern armies.

The relevance of Clausewitz's *On War* for the analysis of contemporary conflict does not rely simply on the 'trinity' as a general theory of war. It is also the result of a fundamental re-politicization of war and violence in the Western world. Jon Sumida explains that the primacy of politics in Clausewitz's theory is directly related to the identification of defence as the stronger form of war. Referring to Clausewitz's treatment of the relationship between purpose or end and goals or aims, Daniel Moran analyses the political consequences of the way in which military strength and weakness have drifted apart in industrialized Western states. So much is this the case that American perceptions of strategy are now strikingly different from those entertained in Europe. The 'temptations' of each are explored by Benoît Durieux as he uses Clausewitz to explain the inadequacies of both. Antulio Echevarria also challenges commonly accepted interpretations by stressing that globalization and the growth of information technologies (examined in detail by David Lonsdale) have in fact made political action even more significant. Echevarria argues that the struggle against terrorism is therefore principally a struggle about the hegemony of political ideas. Agreeing with this general proposition, Andreas Herberg-Rothe draws the conclusion that Clausewitz's view of the relationship between war and policy is still valid. However, he sees the content of politics in democratic societies as quite different from the implicit assumptions of *On War*. Using this as a basis, Herberg-Rothe concludes the book by developing the idea of a new containment, a limitation of war and violence in world society as the precondition for the establishment of democratic societies and for the maintenance of civilian primacy over military affairs. Wilfried von Bredow takes up this challenge directly, commenting on the tension between societies, with their overwhelmingly civilian ethos, and the military in modern democracies.

The editors, who were also the promoters of the conference, have incurred a number of debts. Within Oxford, Dr Andrew Fairweather-Tall made all the administrative arrangements, and since the conference both editors have relied on Mrs Rosemary Mills for secretarial and administrative support. Daniel

Moran has been of immense assistance to Andreas Herberg-Rothe. However, the most important debt is to the Leverhulme Trust, which supports the Changing Character of War Programme, and also funded the conference. In particular, it enabled the Programme to bring to Oxford scholars from five different countries, so uniting those with other languages (not only English) with the users of Clausewitz's own language, German.

Over the last thirty years and more the evolution of Clausewitz studies in the two linguistic spheres has been very different. In 1952, Werner Hahlweg edited the 16th edition of *Vom Kriege* in German, and in doing so reverted to the original text of the first edition of 1832–4. During his long and distinguished career, Hahlweg also supervised a number of research students working on Clausewitz: they belonged to one or other of the historical schools identified by Bassford. In Germany, Clausewitz was not much studied in the context of political science or strategic studies, not least because strategy itself was neglected in the Federal Republic of Germany after the Second World War: it suggested that war was a viable tool of policy and so was too symptomatic of Prussian militarism. Not until after 1990 did Clausewitz studies take a new turn in Germany, above all through the work of Herfried Münkler, but also through that of his pupil, Andreas Herberg-Rothe, and of Beatrice Heuser (even if her book on Clausewitz originated while she was employed in Britain and was first published in English).

Serious study of Clausewitz in the English-speaking world was kick-started in 1976 when Michael Howard and Peter Paret translated the text used by Hahlweg. Their edition, readable and yet opinionated, immediately replaced the translations by J. J. Graham (which first appeared in 1873) and O. S. Matthijs Jolles (first published in 1943), not least because the latter had both used the text of the second German edition. Indeed, it is not too much to say that when many English-language scholars discuss *On War*, they are in reality discussing Howard and Paret's interpretation of it. Sir Michael Howard was himself present at the conference and made telling contributions, partly, but not only, in elaborating on the motives that had driven both Professor Paret and himself in their work. We are very grateful to him for contributing a foreword to this volume.

Unless otherwise made clear all translations from *On War* given in this book are from the Howard and Paret edition, and all references to the German edition are to that of Hahlweg, now in its nineteenth edition. As *On War* is available in so many different formats, references to it in what follows contain not only the page number of the edition which the individual contributor has used but also the relevant book and chapter numbers.

# 1

# Clausewitz and the Dialectics of War

*Hew Strachan*

When Carl von Clausewitz died in 1831, he was a disappointed and frustrated man. He aspired to fame, but thought he had not achieved it. In his own lifetime that was true. He may not have been the failure that in his darker moments he imagined himself to be, but he had only a walk-on part in history, not a principal role. A professional soldier, he had never been the conquering hero, and, despite becoming a major-general, he had not attained the rank which he felt he deserved.

Himself the son of an officer, he had joined the army at the age of 12 and saw active service the following year. But Prussia's leading characteristic during the wars which ravaged Europe between the French Revolution of 1789 and the final fall of Napoleon in 1815 was to steer clear of trouble. For eleven years, between 1795 and 1806, Prussia was at peace, leaving it to Austria, Britain, and Russia to confront France's aspirations to European hegemony. Most of Clausewitz's early career thus reads like the familiar stuff of peacetime soldiering: regimental duty, study at the war school, and staff appointments. But that humdrum catalogue does not do justice to the intellectual ferment which embraced Berlin, and therefore Clausewitz himself, at the turn of the eighteenth and nineteenth centuries. It also assumes that Clausewitz was a typical subaltern, caught between adolescence and adulthood in a mixture of high spirits and alcohol-induced indiscretion.

In fact Clausewitz was the mess bore. His march to maturity was fuelled by his own appetite for self-education, beginning with philosophy, and nurtured by the great military reformer Gerhard Scharnhorst, who introduced him to the study of military history—to war as it really was as opposed to war in its ideal form. Scharnhorst had been quick to recognize that the changes in warfare wrought by France since 1789—the growth in the size of its armies through conscription, the enthusiasm of soldiers who were citizens rather than pressed men—had social and political roots. The French Revolution had transformed the power of the state, enabling it to plumb its own resources and to appropriate those of others, nominally in the name of liberty, equality, and fraternity. Scharnhorst believed that if the Prussian army, the embodiment of military excellence in the eighteenth century, was to add to the laurels it had garnered in the reign of Frederick the Great (1740–86), then change would be required not only in the army itself but also in the nation as a whole. However, this was not the view of the king. Frederick William III, who ascended the throne in 1799, was more interested in uniforms and military music than in tactics and strategy: his instincts were conservative and he (justifiably) associated the actual business of war with revolution.

On 2 December 1805, Napoleon smashed the armies of Austria and Russia at Austerlitz. Prussia remained neutral. But France was not appeased by its pusillanimity. Frederick William belatedly realized that continued complaisance would not enable him to prevent the humiliation and subordination of Prussia to Napoleon, and issued the French emperor with an ultimatum. In the autumn of 1806, as Clausewitz went off to war at last, he wrote to his future wife, Marie von Brühl, with optimism. It could not have been more misplaced. On 14 October 1806, the Prussian army, and with it Prussia itself, suffered one of the most comprehensive defeats of modern times on the twin battlefields of Jena and Auerstädt. Clausewitz became a prisoner of war. His humiliation and frustration left him with a visceral hatred of all things French, even its cuisine. Still Frederick William was reluctant to embrace the full range of the reforms pressed on him by Scharnhorst and others, including a second officer who profoundly influenced Clausewitz, August von Gneisenau. Gneisenau, inspired by examples springing up elsewhere in Europe, notably but not only in Spain, advocated a war of national liberation: better to fight and go down gloriously than not to have fought at all. That was Clausewitz's view too. But in 1812 the king took Prussia in the opposite direction. He agreed to Napoleon's demand that Prussia provide a contingent for the invasion of Russia. Too junior to be able to find an honourable way out, an option made available to both Scharnhorst and Gneisenau, Clausewitz left the service in which he had been brought up, betraying his own king as he did so, and joined the Russian army. He was now fighting for Prussia's enemies in the name of German nationalism. However morally courageous his actions, they left a permanent mark on his career. Never again, at least in his own estimation, did he recover royal favour.

Germany's war of national liberation was finally kick-started not by Scharnhorst or Gneisenau but by a more conservative general, Hans von Yorck, the commander of the Prussian contingent in French service. As the shattered French army wearily retreated westwards in the winter of 1812, the Prussian contingent followed a more northily route across Lithuania towards East Prussia. Yorck negotiated the Prussians' neutrality with the Russians at the convention of Tauroggen on 30 December. Clausewitz was the intermediary. Prussia and Russia were now on the same side, and his own isolation seemed to be at an end. Nonetheless, the king could not simply forgive and forget: Clausewitz continued to wear the uniform of Russia, not Prussia, until April 1814, even though he now served alongside his fellow nationals. At first the king also condemned Yorck's actions, but in March 1813 East Prussia acted unilaterally in raising a militia or Landwehr to fight the French, and Frederick William finally fell into line, declaring war on France. The war of national liberation lost nothing in the telling, both then and throughout the life of the nation up until Prussia's final extinction in 1945. However, the years 1813–15 were not a period of unalloyed sweetness for Clausewitz. Scharnhorst died of wounds in June 1813, and Clausewitz was not present at the epochal and massive 'battle of the nations' fought over three days around Leipzig in October. The combined strength of the Austro-Russian-Prussian coalition swamped Napoleon. Nor was Clausewitz's contribution any more distinguished when Napoleon abandoned his protective custody on Elba. Serving as a corps chief of staff, he spent 18 June 1815 not at Waterloo but at Wavre, tying down a French corps and so preventing it from joining Napoleon on the main battlefield. The Prussian corps did its job, but it was severely mauled. On 19 June, as the main allied armies were advancing on Paris, Clausewitz's corps was retreating. He never fully threw off the charge of undue caution in the field.

The accusation was unjust, but incontrovertible: unjust because Clausewitz was not the field commander on that day or any other, incontrovertible because he would never again have the chance to disprove it in battle. In 1818, he became the director of the war school in Berlin. This was an administrative appointment, not an academic one. The great theorist of war taught nobody. In 1830, he was dragged out of the congenial life of the capital to take up the inspectorate of artillery in Breslau. Prussia's was not the first or only army to appoint an infantryman to a job that required the specialist skills of the gunner, but the post signalled a possible return to more active service. Revolution in Poland (then part of Russia) threatened the tranquillity of Prussia's borders. To the west France threw out the Bourbons, restored to the throne by the victorious allies, and so threatened the European peace established after Waterloo. The last French Revolution had caused major war, and that was what Clausewitz feared this time. The king, still Frederick William, ever mindful of the link between revolution and war, created an army of observation to watch the Polish situation. He gave the command to Gneisenau, and the latter asked for Clausewitz as his chief of staff. In the event, Clausewitz's most burdensome task was not to wage war but to bury his chief, who succumbed to cholera three months before Clausewitz himself. This was a life story that ended with a whimper, not a bang.[1]

---

[1] The best biography of Clausewitz is Peter Paret, *Clausewitz and the State* (Oxford, 1983).

Or so it seemed. Clausewitz never knowingly underestimated the contribution of his wife, Marie, both in stimulating his intellect and in assuaging his tensions. But if he felt disappointed in the twilight years of his life, he may unwittingly have done so. Beginning in 1832, the grieving widow set about the publication of Clausewitz's writings. It was a herculean task, whose completion outstripped her own mortal span. It embraced ten volumes, of which seven were military history but the first three were a major work of theory, called simply *Vom Kriege*, or in English *On War*. Now recognized as the most important single discussion of its subject ever written, it has assured Clausewitz a posthumous fame which has outstripped that of his mentors, Scharnhorst and Gneiseneau, and rivals even that of the 'arch-fiend' himself, the man whom Clausewitz called 'the god of war', Napoleon Bonaparte. Those years of seeming tranquillity at the war school had not been wasted. They gave Clausewitz over a decade in which to study the wars in which he had participated.

Without Napoleon, *On War* could never have been written. The book is in the first instance an exploration of war as Clausewitz had experienced it, and reflected the fact that at least the character of war, if not its underlying nature, had been fundamentally altered by Napoleon. The army of Prussia was defeated at Jena because it had remained mired in the ways of Frederick the Great. But if *On War* were only that, its fame as a book would be limited by the chronological parameters which called it into existence. Clausewitz aspired to do something altogether more ambitious: his book dealt with war more generally, and could he thought—at least according to a note he wrote on 10 July 1827—'bring about a revolution in the theory of war'.[2]

There was no sign here of the introspection and angst that characterize in particular the letters to his wife. Indeed, much of *On War* is expressed with a forthrightness that can easily be mistaken for dogma. In part that is a consequence of Clausewitz's prose style. Despite the fondness of early-nineteenth-century German for passive constructions, long sentences, and ambiguous adjectives, *On War* flashes with memorable and pithy phrases, simple and graphic, often illuminated with telling metaphors and similes. Moreover, many of these aphorisms gain in strength precisely because they state the obvious. Clausewitz tells us what we already know to be true but in ways that make the familiar fresh: as so often, brilliance lies in the eye of the beholder, as much as in the mind of the creator.

Unsurprisingly, given the sudden death of its author, *On War* contained, and continues to contain, unresolved obscurities and internal contradictions.

---

[2] Carl von Clausewitz, *On War*, edited and translated by Michael Howard and Peter Paret (Princeton, NJ, 1976), 70.

A recurring theme in Clausewitz studies, and one sustained by scholars as distinguished as Hans Delbrück (1848–1929), the German military historian, and Raymond Aron (1905–83), the French political scientist, has been to speculate what the great man would have written if he had been spared to finish the book. These speculations often say more about the preoccupations of their authors and their views of war than they do about Clausewitz and his. More importantly still, they run the risk of underestimating those very qualities that have given *On War* its durability. Clausewitz's endeavour to understand the nature of war was itself work in progress: *On War*'s vitality and longevity derive in large part from its refusal to embrace fixed conclusions. It may not be too cynical to suggest that it would never have been finished to the author's satisfaction. But there is a further and specifically historical point. We can be a great deal more certain about the trajectories of Clausewitz's thinking than the bare evidence of *On War* suggests because we possess a vast corpus of other work, much of it not published in the *Hinterlassene Werke*, the posthumous edition of his works brought out between 1832 and 1837. It remains an abiding curiosity that to this day there is no definitive edition of his entire output in any language.

The tradition of projecting on to Clausewitz what he intended to say, or might have said, began immediately after his death. Faced with a mass of papers, his grieving widow, Marie, asked her brother, Friedrich Wilhelm von Brühl, to help her prepare them for publication. He took the process a stage further when the publishers, Dümmler, brought out a second edition of the *Hinterlassene Werke* in 1853. Brühl tidied up *On War*, correcting misprints and making passages that were incomprehensible comprehensible. Most of Brühl's glosses have become part of the accepted text, though as he began the process with the first edition and we no longer possess the original manuscript from which he worked, we can now never know their extent. The major exception occurs in book VIII, which deals with war plans and is the last of *On War*, where in chapter 6B Clausewitz suggests that the commander-in-chief should be a member of the cabinet, so that he can help shape its policy in time of war, thus ensuring that the policy pursued can be in line with the nature of the war. Brühl altered the text for the second edition to imply that the commander-in-chief should play a part in all the cabinet's decisions, not just those relating to war. In the light of Germany's role in the two world wars, this passage has been associated with the growth of Prussian militarism. Both the 16th German edition (that of 1952, prepared by Werner Hahlweg) and the English translation of Michael Howard and Peter Paret, first published in 1976, reverted to the text of the first German edition.

The attention given to this textual change implies that *On War* was deeply influential in Germany, and particularly so for what it had to say about the relationship between war and policy. Neither statement is necessarily true, not least in relation to the period before the wars of German unification (1864–71). At first Clausewitz was probably better known as a military historian than as a strategic theorist. *On War* only accounted for three of the ten volumes of the *Hinterlassene Werke*, the remaining seven being studies of campaigns, principally of the Napoleonic Wars. Moreover, the 1,500 copies of the first edition had not sold out when it was overtaken by the second. In 1853, although *On War* had only just been translated into French, the principal French commentary on the book said that its reputation was declining (one might ask whether by then it had ever been in the ascendant) and that many of its judgements had been shown to be false.

The publishing history of *On War* in the forty years after 1871 presents a very different picture from that of the previous forty. As the Prussian army emerged triumphant in 1871, the other armies of Europe looked to it for emulation and inspiration. Lurking behind Prussia's battlefield success lay Helmuth von Moltke, the chief of the Prussian general staff, and lurking behind him, at least in the hagiographies peddled by Moltke's admirers, lay Carl von Clausewitz. In 1873 the premier professional journal of the day, the *Militär-Wochenblatt*, declared that Clausewitz was the first authority on military science; in 1876, in the dictionary of national biography, the *Allgemeine Deutsche Biographie*, F. von Meerheimb said that the wars of 1866 against Austria and of 1870 against France had been fought in the spirit of Clausewitz; and in 1891 Max Jähns in his three-volume history of the military sciences described Clausewitz's influence as 'almost mystical'.[3] Between 1871 and 1918, there were eleven German editions of *On War*; in 1873 J. J. Graham translated it into English (with a fresh edition of Graham's text being brought out by Colonel F. N. Maude in 1908); and Lieutenant-Colonel de Vatry produced a new French translation in 1886–9.

Linking this surge of interest to the influence of Moltke rests on an underlying paradox. *On War* is a sustained dialogue between theory and practice. Clausewitz's early self-education, the inspiration of his adolescence, had been in philosophy; he had read the works of the Enlightenment, and, for all his damning comments about certain military theorists, he was determined to write a theory of his own. Both his own experience as a soldier and military history, to which he had been introduced by Scharnhorst, were the reality checks on this inclination to abstraction. Moltke on the other hand taught his staff officers by means of war games and staff rides, not theory. They examined concrete operational problems and saw the relationship between

---

[3] For these and similar references, see Ulrich Marwedel, *Carl von Clausewitz. Persönlichkeit und Wirkungsgeschichte seines Werkes bis 1918* (Boppard am Rhein, 1978), 119–20.

strategy and tactics as a profoundly practical matter, to be learnt by applied methods. 'Successive acts of war are not premeditated acts', Moltke wrote; 'they are spontaneous, dictated by military intuition.'[4] *On War* appealed to officers before 1914 precisely because it explicitly said that theory should not accompany the general to the battlefield, that its role was educational, not prescriptive, to give insights, not to hedge the commander round with fixed solutions.[5] Moreover, Clausewitz rooted his concepts in realities, in what he called 'friction' in war, in uncertainty, chance, and morale. But the result was that pre-1914 officers rejected *On War*'s philosophical and theoretical dimensions. Moltke's most famous successor as chief of the general staff, Alfred von Schlieffen, contributed a foreword to the fifth German edition of *On War*, published in 1905, in which he commended the book in Moltkean terms, as it taught 'that every case in war must be considered and thought through according to its own characteristics', but condemned its philosophical passages as outdated.[6] Schlieffen was cited in 1908 by Major-General Hugo von Freytag-Loringhoven in his study, *Kriegslehren nach Clausewitz aus den Feldzügen 1813 und 1814*, in which he contrasted the influence on the French army of Antoine-Henri Jomini, whose writings he saw as too theoretical and abstract, with that on Germany of Clausewitz, whose reflections were grounded in experience, 'something much more worthwhile than all the truths of philosophy'.[7] In France itself, Colonel Hubert Camon said that 'Clausewitz's mistake had been to load himself up with the Hegelian system'.[8] In Britain, Spenser Wilkinson, not a soldier like the others but Oxford's first professor of military history, writing in 1891, said that the influence of Kant, which Clausewitz had imbibed through the lectures of Johann Gottfried Kiesewetter at the war school, had 'tended, perhaps, to expand the bulk than to increase the value of his treatise on war'.[9]

The result was that Clausewitz's most famous philosophical abstraction, the ideal of 'absolute war' to which wars aspired but which they never attained, was interpreted as a reality, an indication for pre-1914 writers of how war had intensified since Clausewitz's day. However, just as Clausewitz attempted to harmonize the theory of war with its true nature, so *On War* contains elements which warrant treating absolute war as a description of impending reality as well as a philosophical concept. The latter is implicit (if not directly

---

[4] Quoted by Hugo von Freytag-Loringhoven, *The Power of Personality in War* (first published 1905), as published in *Roots of Strategy*, book III (Harrisburg, PA, 1991), 270.
[5] *On War*, VIII, 1, p. 578.   [6] *Vom Kriege* (Berlin, 1905), iii–vi.
[7] Hugo Freytag-Loringhoven, *Kriegslehren nach Clausewitz aus den Feldzügen 1813 und 1814* (Berlin, 1908), 21, 151, 154.
[8] H. Camon, *Clausewitz* (Paris, 1911), 58.
[9] Spenser Wilkinson, 'Military literature', in *War and Policy* (London, 1910), 152.

defined) throughout chapter 1 of book I, on the nature of war, which has assumed canonical status because it is deemed to be the only book of *On War* which its author completed to his own satisfaction. On the other hand in book VIII, chapter 2, Clausewitz argued that the Napoleonic Wars themselves approximated to absolute war. Freytag-Loringhoven used his study of the 1813 and 1814 campaigns to conclude that 'this theory of absolute war, which holds itself free of every model and mannerism, and which was developed from the great wars at the beginning of the nineteenth century, is the everlasting service of General von Clausewitz'. It led, he argued, 'to our victories in 1866 and 1870, and it will do so again'.[10] Moreover, in book VI, on the defence, Clausewitz had suggested that the more the people and their passions were involved in wars of national defence, the more extreme those wars would be. Confronted with rampant nationalism and the widespread adoption of conscription in the wake of the Prussian victories, soldiers saw this observation as even more applicable after 1871 than it had been after 1815. Major Stewart Murray, who in 1909 wrote a commentary on Clausewitz to which Wilkinson contributed a foreword, concluded that 'To-day we may say that war takes its absolute form in the modern great national war, which is waged by each belligerent with the whole concentrated physical and mental power of the nation-in-arms'.[11]

In the years between the Franco-Prussian War and the First World War, the fact that Clausewitz was a major interpreter of the Napoleonic Wars was a reason for reading him, not dismissing him. Books III to VII of *On War*, which covered strategy, battle, military forces, the defence, and the attack, were where professional soldiers focused their attention, not on books I, II (on the theory of war), and VIII: the intervening books dealt with the business of war in the most severe and sustained wars ever suffered by Europe. Vatry began his French translation with books III to VI: he only tackled books VII and VIII after its success, and left books I and II to last. In Germany, Lieutenant-General Rudolf von Caemmerer gave separate consideration to each of the books of *On War* in his book on Clausewitz, except for books I and II, which he distilled into a number of philosophical principles. His brother officer, Freytag-Loringhoven, used *On War* as the basis for discussing the role of the commander's personality in war in *Die Macht der Persönlichkeit im Kriege* (1911), but he said nothing in that book about the relationship between the commander and the statesman or between war and policy, themes of books I and VIII.

---

[10] Freytag-Loringhoven, *Kriegslehren nach Clausewitz*, 156.
[11] Stewart L. Murray, *The Reality of War: An Introduction to 'Clausewitz'* (London, 1909), 23; see also Wilkinson, *War and Policy*, 180, 421.

Vatry explained that books III and VI contained the clearest exposition of strategic principles. However, it was exactly here that Clausewitz suffered the most sustained scholarly attack, ironically from French officers in particular. The French army, the victim of Prussian military superiority in the war of 1870–1, discovered Clausewitz in the early 1880s. Almost simultaneously, a cohort of soldier-historians, Hubert Camon, Henri Bonnal, and Jean Colin principal among them, used Bonaparte's papers to re-interpret the nature of Napoleonic warfare. The coping stone of their efforts was the way in which Napoleon had fused manoeuvre with decisive battle, principally through the execution of envelopment, or what they called *la manoeuvre sur les derrières*. Clausewitz was critical of envelopment, favouring operations on 'interior lines' (as Jomini had dubbed them), so that the army was kept concentrated and could ensure mass on the decisive point. Hubert Camon, in a study published in 1911, demonstrated that Clausewitz, though ostensibly writing about the Napoleonic Wars, had not understood Napoleon's strategy. His arguments were embraced by all the other pundits of his day, regardless of nationality, including in Germany both Rudolf von Caemmerer and Hans Delbrück. One consequence was that Clausewitz's military histories were discounted as (in Camon's words) 'studies of campaigns',[12] helpful in understanding the role of contingency and morale, but not as source-based history, and were therefore designed as support for the principal work, *On War*. In other words, they could safely be put to one side; and they were. Freytag-Loringhoven's analysis of the 1813 and 1814 campaigns in the light of Clausewitz's teaching did not refer at all to Clausewitz's own accounts of the fighting, but instead set more recent histories against the insights bestowed by *On War* itself.

Vatry was right. Most of *On War* is a study of strategy, an element in war which Clausewitz regularly and consistently defined as the use of the engagement for the purposes of the war. Tactics, he said, taught 'the use of armed forces in the engagement'.[13] Although he stressed that fighting was the heart of war, he saw battle as a means to an end, not an end in itself: its decisiveness came from its exploitation. But Camon and his contemporaries not only showed that Clausewitz had not comprehended Napoleonic strategy, they also implied that battle was itself the denouement of strategy.[14] As a result, they read Clausewitz for what he said about tactics as much as, if not more than, for what he said about strategy. This was the case even in Germany itself. One of his most sensible supporters, Rudolf von Caemmerer, wrote, 'Clausewitz lays renewed stress on the facts that tactical success on the

---

[12] Camon, *Clausewitz*, vii; also 71–3.
[13] e.g. *On War*, II, 1 is the main discussion of these points; see also III, 1, p. 177, and 10, p. 202.
[14] Camon, *Clausewitz*, 22–3.

battlefield must be the first and foremost object of all efforts, and that this success always retains its highest and utmost value under all circumstances'.[15] Caemmerer drew attention to the discussion of the battle contained in book IV and emphasized, as Clausewitz did, that the main aim of fighting was the destruction of the enemy's armed forces.[16] Similarly, Freytag-Loringhoven quoted Clausewitz entirely accurately on the use of the battle for the purposes of the war, but then discussed the 1813 campaign in terms which made it clear that what he admired about its conduct was its use of strategy to achieve decisive battle, in stark contrast to the styles of warfare waged in the eighteenth century and by Archduke Charles of Austria at the beginning of the nineteenth century.[17]

The upshot was that the distinction between strategy and tactics was fudged. Most of *On War* is a discussion of this relationship, much more so than it is a discussion of the relationship between war and policy. Clausewitz the theorist was always very conscious of the difference between strategy, which invoked the moral courage and the military genius of the commander, and tactics, which were often a matter of routine. He deliberately eschewed the words 'operations' and 'operational', the descriptors which elide strategy and tactics.[18] Obviously strategy and tactics cross over in reality, and pre-1914 commentators, conscious of how technological innovation might have changed Clausewitz's analysis of battle, were particularly keen to focus on the effects of tactical change on strategy. But the consequence was that they said his views on strategy, more than on tactics, should be revisited.[19] This confusion was what made the controversy which erupted between Schlieffen and the general staff on the one hand and Hans Delbrück on the other so heated.

The official historians of the Prussian army, writing their account of the Seven Years War (published in 1901–14), argued that the strategy of Frederick the Great was directly linked to that used by Moltke in the wars of German unification. Dubbed the strategy of annihilation or destruction ('Vernichtung' in the German, though the title 'Niederwerfungsstrategie' was also used), its chronological course from Frederick to Moltke was traced through Napoleon, not least as interpreted by Clausewitz in books III to VI of *On War*. The central themes were the use of manoeuvre to bring superior forces onto the decisive

---

[15] Rudolf von Caemmerer, *The Development of Strategical Science in the Nineteenth Century* (London, 1905), 109.
[16] Caemmerer, *Clausewitz* (Leipzig, n.d.), 95–6.
[17] Freytag-Loringhoven, *Kriegslehren nach Clausewitz*, 19–20.
[18] The use of the words associated with operations in the Howard and Paret translation is a gloss not reflected in the original German.
[19] Caemmerer, *Clausewitz*, 1.

point, so as to fight a decisive battle. The core therefore was the relationship between tactics and strategy, and indeed the elision of the two. Schlieffen's pursuit of strategic envelopment, for example, was predicated on the tactical problems of frontal attack in the face of industrialized firepower.[20]

Hans Delbrück was appalled. He saw Frederick not as pursuing decisive battle, but as avoiding it: confronted by a coalition superior in numbers and resources, he decided on a strategy of 'attrition' (Delbrück called it 'Ermattungsstrategie'). Moreover, he said that Clausewitz had acknowledged this distinction, as the note which he wrote in 1827, and which is published as an introduction to every edition of *On War*, makes clear. There Clausewitz observed that war can be of two kinds: designed either to destroy the enemy so that the victor can dictate his terms, or to achieve more limited objectives so that peace can be negotiated. Clausewitz had died before he could complete the task which he had set himself, which was to rewrite *On War* in the light of this distinction, but, Delbrück stressed, 'The "completely different nature" of these two efforts must always be separated from one another'. Therefore Delbrück made it his task to explain the difference, not least in his monumental *Geschichte der Kriegskunst im Rahmen der politischen Geschichte* (4 vols, Berlin, 1908–20).[21]

German soldiers were quick to condemn Delbrück, in a controversy which spanned the best part of three decades. They were right to say that Frederick had undertaken battles that he saw as decisive, particularly in the opening stages of the Seven Years War in 1757. Moreover, they were also right to stress that Clausewitz himself was highly critical of eighteenth-century wars, which he saw as fought in a half-hearted manner. But the truth was that each side was talking past the other. The staff officers were looking at the conduct of war where strategy and tactics intersected, and were using Clausewitz's analysis of Napoleonic warfare as their analytical framework. Delbrück was looking at the relationship between strategy and policy, using not only the note of 1827 but also the insights of book I as his basis. The officers' own divisions over how to read book VI, in which Clausewitz had contrasted defence with offence, seeing the former as the stronger means in war, albeit with a negative aim, made the point even clearer. Book VI depends on a clear conceptual grasp of the three levels of war—tactical, strategic, and political. Those who refused to accept the greater strength of the defensive conflated all three; those who

---

[20] Martin Raschke, *Der politisierende Generalstab. Der friderizianischen Kriege in der amtlichen deutschen Militärgeschichtsschreibung 1890–1914* (Freiburg, 1993).

[21] Hans Delbrück, *History of the Art of War within the Framework of Political History* (Westport, CT, 1985), vol. IV, 454; see on the controversy, Sven Lange, *Hans Delbrück und der 'Strategiestreit'. Kriegführung und Kriegsgeschichte in der Kontroverse 1879–1914* (Freiburg im Breisgau, 1995).

sided with Clausewitz on this specific issue of the defence, as Caemmerer did, distinguished between the tactical defence, the use of the counterstroke in strategy, and the political issue of national self-defence. A country defending itself from invasion could still employ the offensive tactically and even strategically, and indeed would have to if the invader was to be expelled. In sum, Schlieffen and his acolytes were thinking about operations, Delbrück about war as a whole.

Delbrück looks more modern and more liberal, because he paid more attention to the relationship between war and policy than many of his military contemporaries, but he did not have the monopoly of wisdom on Clausewitz. Not all of them ignored what Clausewitz had to say on war and policy. They just read him differently from Delbrück. Moltke said that the politician might take the lead in deciding to go to war and would resume the lead when negotiating the peace, but that he should fall silent while the war was being waged. In other words, strategy, not policy, should lead even if the strategy followed in wartime might have political implications. Freytag-Loringhoven compared Moltke's position with Clausewitz's by quoting a letter from the latter written in 1827, in which he said that policy should not demand of war things that ran contrary to war's nature.[22] Friedrich von Bernhardi, in *On War of To-Day*, published in Germany in 1912, captured Moltke's position exactly:

> If, therefore, policy pursues its purpose with due regard to the forces of the State, and in case of war determines, with the co-operation of the commander, the military object to be attained, it must, on the other hand, *never interfere in the conduct of the war itself*, and *try to prescribe the way* in which the military object shall actually be attained.... Policy and conduct of war are certainly in many respects subject to the same laws, but their procedure is totally different.[23]

Bernhardi began the next paragraph saying: 'War is a continuation of policy by *other* means'. These are Clausewitz's own words, even if not directly acknowledged by Bernhardi, from book VIII, chapter 6B, albeit with added stress on the word 'other'. Book VIII sees policy as shaping the plan but not the tactics used to implement it: war, as Clausewitz puts it in the same chapter, has its own grammar, if not its own logic. This is one reason why Clausewitz went on to argue that the commander-in-chief should be in the cabinet, so that the logic of policy could be shaped in conformity with the grammar of war—with war's true nature. The historian Gerhard Ritter, in tackling the problem of German militarism in the aftermath of the Third Reich, argued

---

[22] Freytag-Loringhoven, *Kriegslehren nach Clausewitz*, 15–16.
[23] Friedrich von Bernhardi, *On War of To-Day* (2 vols, London, 1912–13), I, p. 196; italics in the original.

its corollary, that the general should be in the cabinet so that his use of the military means could conform with the expectations of policy. He, therefore, concluded that Moltke and his inheritors had clearly departed from Clausewitz's basic views.[24] They had not; they had read the same text differently and put weight on different passages. Moltke and the Prussian general staff used Clausewitz in their battle with Otto von Bismarck; Gerhard Ritter used him in another domestic struggle, that with Adolf Hitler and the Nazis.

The First World War dealt Clausewitz a near mortal blow in Western military thought. The short-term accusation, voiced by Basil Liddell Hart, was that his pupils had put the idea of absolute war into practice with disastrous effect: this was the come-uppance of the strategy of annihilation.[25] The long-term accusation, voiced most recently by John Keegan and David Stevenson, is that this was a war without political utility.[26] This argument might be described as the come-uppance of the strategy of attrition, if it were not for the fact that as a result of the First World War attrition acquired a very different meaning from that which Delbrück had given it, becoming associated with giving battle rather than avoiding it, and with the interface between tactics and strategy, rather than that between strategy and policy. After 1918, Clausewitz suffered an eclipse in the English-speaking world from which he did not fully recover until 1976.

But we must not generalize from the reactions of Britain and the English-speaking world. In France, Pierre Lehautcourt, who wrote under the nom de plume of Général Palat, published a commentary of *On War* in 1921. He said he had drafted it in 1913; in the interim he had embarked on a fourteen-volume account of the war on the western front, but that did not lead him to withdraw his endorsement of Clausewitz. For him, Clausewitz's thought had triumphed, not succumbed, in the First World War. Palat read Clausewitz's analysis of the relationship between war and policy as one where each demanded mutual respect, not rigid subordination: the political aim was 'one of the principal elements' in considering the nature of a war, but the latter should always demand that the policy did not contradict the means which it was employing.[27] Palat's analysis focused in particular on book VI of *On War*, the discussion of defence (which is by far the longest book in *On War*, embracing about a quarter of the total matter), and also treated Clausewitz's

---

[24] Gerhard Ritter, *The Sword and the Scepter: The Problem of Militarism in Germany* (4 vols, Coral Gables, Florida, 1969–73), I, p. 195.

[25] Most fully in Basil Liddell Hart, *The Ghost of Napoleon* (London, 1933).

[26] John Keegan, *A History of Warfare* (London, 1993), 22; David Stevenson, *1914–1918: The History of the First World War* (London, 2004), xx.

[27] Général Palat, *La philosophie de la guerre d'après Clausewitz* (Paris, 1998; first published 1921), 15–16.

attention to operational matters in terms that suggested an underlying continuity between 1815 and 1918, rather than fundamental change.

For Germany, even more than France, Clausewitz remained deeply instructive. First, his description of battle in book IV, a prolonged, indecisive firefight between comparable armies, was uncannily evocative of the nature of combat on the western front, for all the impact of new technologies. Second, the experience of the war drew Clausewitz's readers to a reconsideration of books I and VIII. In August 1914, Delbrück had responded to the outbreak of war with a review of Germany's advantages over its enemies. One of these advantages was the Kaiser: Delbrück cited Clausewitz to celebrate the 'single unitary will' of the monarchy, the apex of political and military power in Germany, which he saw as guaranteeing 'the union of strategy and politics'.[28] In the event, the Kaiser failed to coordinate the civil and military authorities within Germany, and post-war critics reversed Delbrück's argument. In 1926 a retired general, Leinveber, used the German official history's volumes for 1914 to publish an analysis of the war in the light of Clausewitz. He blamed Germany's defeat on the failure to read and understand Clausewitz, whose wisdom had been fully revealed by the war. Leinveber's book drew a distinction (which was not strictly speaking Clausewitzian) between what it called 'Krieg', war in its fullest conception, embracing all the affairs of state, and 'Heereskrieg', military affairs and strategy more narrowly defined. The official history, with its focus on operational issues and its dogged determination not to address policy, perpetuated the division between 'Krieg' and 'Heereskrieg' which had fractured Germany's conduct of the war. Policy should have united the two. 'The politician', the general wrote, 'should therefore be the master-builder of the war plan.' The author, like many Germans in the 1920s, looked to one man, 'a strong character', as the person who would unite war and policy.

The failure of the Kaiser to fulfil the hopes which Germans like Delbrück had entertained in 1914 was reflected in many German diaries during the war—a wish for a single, messianic figure who would prove himself a true warlord. Leinveber revealed his right-wing credentials when he suggested that Admiral Alfred von Tirpitz, a founder of the Fatherland Party in 1916, might have been that man.[29] But a similar point was put to a more left-leaning body in the same year as the publication of Leinveber's book, when the Reichstag committee of enquiry, convened to uncover the causes of the German collapse in 1918, embraced the argument that the real causes of Germany's defeat lay with the government's failure to assert itself over the military leaders: it 'did

[28] Hans Delbrück, *Delbrück's Modern Military History*, ed. Hans Bucholz (Lincoln, Nebraska, 1997), 110.
[29] Generalmajor a. D. Leinveber, *Mit Clausewitz durch die Rätsel und Fragen, Irrungen und Wirrungen des Welkrieges* (Berlin, 1926); here 14, 18, 31, 72–7.

not recognize that, as Clausewitz expresses it, "warfare must be an instrument of policy".[30] In making many commentators more aware that war should be seen in its political context, the First World War promoted, rather than suppressed, an interest in Clausewitz. A British general writing in 1918 described *On War* as 'the Bible of the German officer and to a great extent that of the German statesman, for it is an axiom with the Germans that high policy and strategy should run hand in hand'.[31]

Germans who studied Clausewitz in 1918 and its aftermath could not but draw parallels between his experience of defeat and humiliation in 1806 and their own. In January of the war's last year, Hans Rothfels submitted his thesis at the University of Heidelberg. A study of Clausewitz before he had commenced the writing of *On War* in 1816, it explored the links between his experiences of war and the evolution of his ideas. Any obscurity in the latter, Rothfels argued, fell away when seen in the context of their time and the evolution of German thought, 'the community of blood which unites [*On War*] with the world view and policy of idealism'.[32] As this provocative choice of words suggests, Rothfels's study, though it marks the point where academic historians sunk their teeth into Clausewitz, could not at the same time disengage completely from the issues of contemporary policy. Although he and several other leading Clausewitz scholars of the interwar period, notably Herbert Rosinski, emigrated to the United States before the outbreak of the Second World War, they had opened the door on another Clausewitz, a nationalist and an exponent of what we would now call 'existential war'.

In February 1812, as Clausewitz confronted the choice between his loyalty to the king of Prussia and an incipient awareness of German national identity, between subservience to France and joining the Russian army, he penned three statements of belief (although manifestos might be a better title). These were sent to Gneisenau and were first published in the 1860s by the latter's biographer. Here, the meaning of the relationship between war and policy takes on very different connotations from that implied in the calmer and more reflective ambience of peacetime Berlin in 1827. The first statement rises to a crescendo which shows how policy does not necessarily moderate the impact of war, but—the very reverse—demands apparent self-immolation. 'I believe and confess', Clausewitz wrote, 'that a people can value nothing more highly than the dignity and liberty of its existence; that it must defend these to the last drop of its blood; that there is no higher duty to fulfill, no higher law to

---

[30] Ralph Haswell Lutz (ed.), *The Causes of the German Collapse* (Stanford, CA, 1934), 200; see also 200–1.

[31] T. D. Pilcher, *War According to Clausewitz* (London, 1918), v.

[32] Hans Rothfels, *Carl von Clausewitz. Politik und Krieg. Eine ideengeschichtliche Studie* (Berlin, 1920; reprinted 1980), viii.

obey; that the shameful blot of cowardly submission can never be erased; that this drop of poison in the blood of a nation is passed on to posterity, crippling and eroding the strength of future generations.' Clausewitz had no expectation of imminent salvation; given Napoleon's achievements on the battlefield, he—like others—could only anticipate further defeat. But that was better than not fighting at all. He believed that 'even the destruction of liberty after a bloody and honourable struggle assures the people's rebirth. It is the seed of life, which one day will bring forth a new, securely rooted tree.'[33]

In the event Prussia had recovered far faster after 1812 than Clausewitz could have dared hope. The precedent of 1813–15 was a balm for Germans savaged by the perceived humiliation of the Treaty of Versailles in 1919. Clausewitz, the nationalist and the advocate of existential war, gave legitimacy to the rhetoric of the Nazis. Hitler quoted Clausewitz in *Mein Kampf*, but as the author not of *On War* but of the creeds of 1812. What now mattered in *On War* was Clausewitz's opening definition of war, 'an act of force to compel our enemy to do our will'.[34] Moreover, Clausewitz the realist, the figure embraced by soldiers before the First World War, was increasingly ousted by Clausewitz the philosopher and theorist. Karl Linnebach, who spanned both generations as a soldier and as a student of Clausewitz, in 1936 rated *On War* as a study of political thought comparable with the works of Plato, Aristotle, Machiavelli, and Montesquieu: 'its entirety can be embraced by the concept "policy" ', he wrote.[35] In 1937, Friedrich von Cochenhausen edited an abridged edition of the text, which was prefaced by a speech from the Führer (himself the unification of political and military power, and thus the embodiment of war's subordination to policy), referring to Clausewitz but again echoing the sentiments of 1812. In 1943, Cochenhausen published a study of the 1814 campaign in France, *Der Wille zum Sieg* [the will to victory]. Like Freytag-Loringhoven in 1908, Cochenhausen did not use Clausewitz's own account of the campaign, but aimed simply to illuminate the text of *On War*, or at least certain parts of it, so that it could be recast as a unitary picture, in this case adapted not to the wars of German unification but to the circumstances in which Germany found itself after the battle of Stalingrad. Although placing the national will at the heart of his analysis, Cochenhausen did not discuss Clausewitz's passage on the trinity, with its sense that the elements in war were

---

[33] This follows the translation given in Carl von Clausewitz, *Historical and Political Writings*, edited and translated by Peter Paret and Daniel Moran (Princeton, NJ, 1992), 290; for the full texts, see Clausewitz, *Schriften—Aufsätze-Studien-Briefe*, ed. Werner Hahlweg (2 vols, Göttingen, 1966–90), I, pp. 678–751.

[34] *On War*, I, 1, p. 75.

[35] H. Franke, *Handbuch der neuzeitlichen Wehrwissenschaften* (3 vols in 4, Berlin, 1936–7), I, p. 41.

like magnetic poles, both attracted to and repelled by each other. He portrayed the people as in harmony with their leader, and then lumped leader, army, and nation together in a hierarchy. All three were united under the heading of moral forces, but moral forces were themselves portrayed as predominantly political. The inner certainty of the leader could overcome friction in war, and superior morale could triumph over superior material. Most convoluted was Cochenhausen's analysis of absolute war, a pregnant topic given Goebbels's announcement of 'total war' that same year. Cochenhausen followed the argument of the leading academic commentator on Clausewitz in Nazi Germany, the philosopher Walther Malmsten Schering, who argued that absolute war was an ideal construct, not a reality. Cochenhausen observed that the drift to the realization of absolute war was held in check not by policy constraints but by the 'psyches' of war's participants and by operational factors. Of the latter, geography was one, but so too was the length of a war, as it was made up not of a single hammer blow but of a sequence of actions separated in time and space. In book VIII of *On War*, Clausewitz's ideal campaign had been short, offensive, and sudden: length, he had argued, worked to the advantage of the defence. But in 1814, or so Cochenhausen's argument seemed to run, the length of the war enabled the leaders of both sides eventually to marshal their resources, meaning that both finally reached the state of absolute war, 'this ideal form of war's conduct'. He ended, predictably, by linking the conclusion of the Napoleonic Wars to the war then in progress, and particularly to the Russian campaign.[36]

Here German will did not prevail. The immediate effect of defeat in 1945 was to discredit Clausewitz in the other country apart from Germany where *On War* had taken greatest root in the interwar years, the Soviet Union.[37] Tsarist Russia had shown little interest in Clausewitz, but Marx and Engels both admired him. In 1915 Lenin, working in exile in the Bern state library, had read *On War*. For the Bolsheviks too, the First World War made Clausewitz's discussion of the relationship between war and policy more, rather than less, relevant, since both were means to yet another end, that of revolution. Clausewitz, particularly when studied against the background of a world war, consolidated Lenin's own awareness of the use of war for the purposes of revolution. Deeply impressed by book VIII, chapter 6B, he concluded not just that war without policy was pointless, but also that policy deepened and intensified war, rather than moderated it. 'War', he noted, and

---

[36] Friedrich von Cochenhausen, *Der Wille zum Sieg. Clausewitz' Lehre von dem Kriege innewhohnenden Gegengewichten und ihrer Überwindung, erläutert am Feldzug 1814 in Frankreich* (Berlin, 1943), especially 2–11, 28, 110.

[37] On Clausewitz's reception in Russia, see Olaf Rose, *Carl von Clausewitz. Wirkungsgeschichte seines Werkes Russland und der Sowjetunion 1836–1991* (Munich, 1995).

here he was referring to book I, chapter 1, 'appears the more "warlike", the more political it is; so the more "political", the less deep policy itself is.'[38]

When the Red Army was established after the revolution of October 1917, the commissar for war, Leon Trotsky, another who had read *On War*, found himself embroiled in two debates as to its identity and mission. One was whether revolutionary ideology should prevail over military professionalism, and whether Tsarist officers should be incorporated or rejected in the new army. Trotsky cited Clausewitz in favour of the first and more pragmatic line.[39] The other was whether a revolutionary army had by definition to adopt the offensive or whether it should first concentrate on defending the revolution at home. As with the relationship between war and policy, so with attack and defence, Lenin was very open to the interaction of the two elements in Clausewitz's thinking. He had paid particular attention to book VI of *On War*, and noted that defence against an invasion, in other words strategic defence, required an army to able to go over to the counteroffensive. 'The distinction between defence and attack', Lenin concluded, 'dissolves on foreign territory when defending your own territory.'[40]

Nowhere here was there any reflection of Clausewitz's two sorts of war, which had so fuelled Delbrück's analysis. In Britain in the 1920s, thinkers like J. F. C. Fuller and Basil Liddell Hart were looking at mechanization, at the advent of the tank and the impact of aerial bombing, as a substitute for the mass army, and as a way to bypass the stalemate and slaughter of the trenches and so limit war. In the Soviet Union, thinkers like A. A. Svechin rejected such prognostications as wishful thinking, realizing that future war would continue to exploit the state's capacity to mobilize all its resources, including manpower, and apply new technologies. The result was a unitary vision of war: 'We consider ourselves bound to Clausewitz's splendid definition of destruction', Svechin wrote in 1927, 'and it would be pitiful to replace this vivid, rich definition of destruction with some watered down concept of a half-destruction or an attritional destruction, which yields no corollaries or inferences, under the pretext that destruction in pure form is inapplicable today.'[41]

Lenin's commentaries on Clausewitz were published in 1930. Two years later a fresh Russian translation of *On War* appeared, and by 1941 it had gone

---

[38] Werner Hahlweg, 'Lenin und Clausewitz. Ein Beitrag zur politischen Ideengeschichte des 20 Jahrhunderts', in Günter Dill (ed.), *Clausewitz in Perspektive. Materialien zu Carl von Clausewitz: Vom Kriege* (Franfurt am Main, 1980), 601.
[39] Bernard Semmel, *Marxism and the Science of War* (Oxford, 1981), 69.
[40] Hahlweg, 'Lenin und Clausewitz', 614.
[41] Aleksandr A. Svechin, *Strategy*, ed. Kent D. Lee (2nd edn, first published 1927; Minneapolis, MN, 1992), 65.

through five editions. But by 1945, Clausewitz represented not only the arch-enemy, Germany, but also a strategic tradition which had failed, not once but twice. In 1946 Stalin declared *On War* to be out of date, and he was only rehabilitated in the Soviet Union a decade later, after Stalin's death and Khruschev's de-Stalinization speech to the twentieth party congress. Thenceforth, Soviet military thought grappled with the same imponderables as Western strategic thinking after the advent of nuclear weapons. Their capacity for massive destruction gave the concept of absolute war the potential for realization while increasing the pressure to ensure that it remained an ideal construct. The subordination of war to policy made even more sense given the possession of massive destructive capability, but policy best fulfilled its aims by preventing war through deterrence rather than by waging war. Deterrence was centred on war's inutility, *On War* is directed to making it useful. Logically, therefore, any arguments about the relevance of Clausewitz should have ended in 1945, with the dropping of the atomic bombs on Hiroshima and Nagasaki.

Ironically the defeat of the Nazis, and their fulfilment of the Clausewitzian image of heroic downfall, also opened the way to another interpretation of the relationship between war and policy. During the Second World War, Clausewitz had inspired the resistance to the Nazis as well as the regime's supporters. In 1942, Ludwig Beck, the chief of the general staff of the army until dismissed by Hitler in 1938 and the putative head of state if the July 1944 plot against Hitler had succeeded, engaged with the concept of total war. Erich Ludendorff, the first quartermaster general between 1916 and 1918, and a leading figure of the radical right in the 1920s, had published a book in 1935 called *Der totale Krieg*, which described how policy should be subordinated to the waging of war. In answering Ludendorff, Beck linked the idea of total war to Clausewitz, though it was not entirely clear whether he was referring to his description of absolute war or the notion of a war of annihilation. But Beck, like Delbrück, was aware that Clausewitz had allowed for other sorts of war. What happened in total war, Beck argued, was that political aims were subordinated to war aims. That was not how Clausewitz saw war, which should be subordinated to policy, which in turn could not only embrace limited aims but could also find solutions short of bloodshed. Politicians, Beck concluded, had moral obligations, as did soldiers.[42] The following year, 1943, Gerhard Ritter, in an article published in the *Historische Zeitschrift*, took these arguments one stage further. He rejected the Nazi interpretation of Clausewitz as well as the tendency for each generation to see *On War* in the light of its own times and on its own terms. Clausewitz, in Ritter's interpretation, knew

---

[42] Ludwig Beck, 'Die Lehre vom totalen Krieg', reprinted in Dill, *Clausewitz in Perspektive*, 520–41.

'absolutely nothing of a "total" conduct of war', and to use him to support such an approach was 'an inadmissible modernization of the true Clausewitz'.[43]

Beck was executed by the Nazis; Ritter survived, and his interpretation of Clausewitz, and the tradition from which he came, suffused his *magnum opus*, the four-volume *Staatskunst und Kriegshandwerk. Das Problem des Militarismus in Deutschland* (1954–68), published in English as *The Sword and the Sceptre*. His key argument was that in *On War* 'politics in no way appears as the intensifying element, but as the moderating.'[44] Ritter's interpretation has permeated most subsequent readings of Clausewitz, and it allowed *On War*'s reintegration into mainstream strategic studies in the Cold War. Liddell Hart adopted a more conciliatory tone in relation to Clausewitz in the aftermath of the Second World War, acknowledging that the notion of absolute war had been misinterpreted.[45] J. F. C. Fuller's conversion was much more wholehearted, and in *The Conduct of War 1789–1961* published in the latter year, he devoted a full chapter to Clausewitz, one he described as the most important in the book. This did not mean that he dispensed with the usual Anglo-Saxon criticisms, that Clausewitz was prolix, repetitive, confusing, and 'psuedo-philosophical', but he did feel that 'his penetrating analysis of the relationship of war and policy had never been excelled'. He went on: 'Strange to relate, its lack of appreciation was an even more potent factor in the extension of unlimited war than his absolute concept.'[46]

The coping stone to this Anglophone embrace of *On War* was the new translation in 1976 of the text—and the first of the first edition—by Michael Howard and Peter Paret. Michael Howard has described the project as 'the most rewarding work, intellectually as well as financially, that I have ever undertaken'.[47] The intellectual challenge, to which Howard and Paret rose magnificently, was to present the text in prose that was accessible and in a form that gave it an underlying unity. Indeed, it could fairly be said that *On War* now has greater coherence and readability in English than it does in its native German. Shorn of its nineteenth-century style, rid of its fondness for the impersonal passive tense, and free of its lengthier sentences, it has gained immensely in clarity. It has also gained in readers (hence Howard's reference to the financial rewards).

---

[43] P.M. Baldwin, 'Clausewitz in Nazi Germany', *Journal of Contemporary History*, 16 (1981), 19.
[44] Ibid. 19.
[45] e.g., Basil Liddell Hart, *The Defence of the West* (London, 1950), 292–4, 371.
[46] J. F. C. Fuller, *The Conduct of War 1789–1961: A Study of the Impact of the French, Industrial and Russian Revolutions on War and Its Conduct* (London, 1961), 12, 64–5.
[47] Michael Howard, *Captain Professor* (London, 2006), 203.

The timing of the Howard and Paret translation, however fortuitous, was impeccable. Battered by the experiences of Vietnam, the US Army was casting around for a fresh intellectual direction, rethinking its doctrines and using them as a means to rebuild its identity. Clausewitz's *On War*, which had never enjoyed much of an American readership before 1976, helped provide it. Book I, chapter 1 gave the soldiers a vocabulary with which to engage politicians in debate and provided the means to shape policy's use of war. Colonel Harry Summers's *On Strategy: A Critical Analysis of the Vietnam War* (1981) was the most provocative salvo in this process, describing the war as a 'tactical victory' but a 'strategic defeat'. Americans, Summers argued, understood the need to subordinate war to policy (that was an automatic by-product of democracy); what they—or rather their politicians—did not understand was war itself, the means to the political end. Summers's rebuke found its way into policy through the agency of Colin Powell, who read Clausewitz while at the US National War College. Powell was the military adviser to the Secretary of Defense Caspar Weinberger, who in 1984 enunciated the so-called 'Weinberger doctrine', setting out the terms on which the United States would henceforth use military force. In 1992, when Chairman of the Joint Chiefs of Staff, Powell articulated his own doctrine, replete—as the Weinberger doctrine had been—with Clausewitzian phraseology.[48] Powell's view was that the United States should only use force when its political objects were clear and could command public support; the force used should be overwhelming and instantaneous, not incremental and insufficient and in applying it America would have a clear exit strategy. The trouble for US policymakers between 1990 and 2003, from the end of the Cold War to the invasion of Iraq, was that many of the world's problems were not well adapted to Powell's conceptual framework. Few if any of the conflicts which occurred in the Balkans, the Middle East, or Africa justified the application of overwhelming military force, and even fewer were likely to deliver clear outcomes. The Powell doctrine, however much it appealed within the army, seemed to be a constraint on American flexibility and responsiveness, a tool inappropriate to what international relations theorists described as a post-Westphalian world. They argued that an era of national sovereignty, inaugurated in Europe in 1648 with the Peace of Westphalia, had dissolved after the end of the Cold War, in a welter of non-state actors, guerrillas, terrorists, and criminals, who thrived in failed and rogue states, and tended to use war for objects that were not the pursuit of policy by other means. Powell was not the only one who was passé; so too was Clausewitz.

---

[48] See Colin Powell with Joseph Persico, *My American Journey* (New York), 207–8.

The crisis confronted by Clausewitz studies at the beginning of the twenty-first century therefore arose in large part from the emphasis on book I, chapter 1 of *On War*, itself a direct product of the influence of the Howard and Paret translation. Here Clausewitz sees absolute war as an ideal, moderated in practice not only by its own inherent constraints but also by the fact that all wars are acts of policy. Peter Paret, not only the translator and interpreter of *On War* but also its author's principal biographer, argued that the opening chapter of *On War* was 'the best introduction' and 'the best imaginable guide' to Clausewitz's 'entire theoretical work'.[49] His case for saying this rested on an undated note, published by Marie von Clausewitz in her introduction to *On War*, in which Clausewitz says that he regards only book I, chapter 1 as finished, but that it will 'at least serve the whole by indicating the direction I meant to follow everywhere'.[50] Paret dated this note to 1830, the year in which Clausewitz was recalled to active service, and in doing so he implied that Clausewitz had not revised the rest of the text. In particular he downgraded book VIII, on war plans, the conclusion to the whole, and the place where Clausewitz sees Napoleonic warfare as approximating to absolute war and policy as having enabled that.

Paret's interpretation of Clausewitz's undated note put down a clear marker between himself and earlier scholars. Werner Hahlweg considered it to have been written in 1827, and there are good grounds for arguing that it was penned before the dated note of 10 July 1827, which says that war is of two sorts. If Hahlweg is right, then Clausewitz had the time to revise and polish much more than book I, chapter 1. If Paret is right, the reader of *On War* is confronted with the possibility that the rest of the book is of only marginal interest to the contemporary study of war. However, Paret himself suggested another answer. He believed that Clausewitz's most famous assumption, that war is nothing but the continuation of policy by other means, pervades the entire text, because it was a proposition which had its roots in his earliest reactions to war and was fully fledged by 1804–5, even before the battle of Jena. Thus for Paret, and for those who have read his rendering of it, *On War* possesses an inner unity which had escaped its earlier readers.

This is the Clausewitz which has ruled the roost in American military academies for the last thirty years, and it made sense both in the aftermath of the Vietnam War and in the later years of the Cold War. However, the challenge which this interpretation confronts has arisen not purely because of the end of the Cold War; it is more than just a generational shift. It also has scholarly roots, both in history and in political science.

---

[49] Peter Paret, *Clausewitz and the State* (Oxford, 1976), 382.    [50] *On War*, I, p. 70.

In 1989, Azar Gat published *The Origins of Military Thought from the Enlightenment to Clausewitz*, a book which had begun as a thesis supervised by Michael Howard. Gat not only supported Hahlweg's belief that the undated note was written in 1827, not 1830, he also argued that the note of 10 July 1827 represented a much more profound crisis in Clausewitz's intellectual life than Paret's argument for an underlying continuity suggested. Crudely put, Gat believed that until 1827 Clausewitz focused his efforts on late Napoleonic warfare, big battles for major political objectives, war that followed an unlimited trajectory and in which he had himself served. Then he suddenly recognized that an understanding of late Napoleonic warfare was not the same as a comprehensive appreciation of war more broadly defined. The result of this crisis, both intellectual and possibly physical, was the two notes of 1827, and book I, chapter 1. The implication of Gat's interpretation is that the bulk of *On War*, having been written before 1827, is unaffected by the core idea of war's relationship to policy.

In 2001, Andreas Herberg-Rothe made a compatible point in *Das Rätsel Clausewitz*. Clausewitz's main activity between 1823 and 1827 was not writing *On War* but writing the military history of those campaigns in which he had served—Jena in 1806, Russia in 1812, and Waterloo in 1815. As long ago as 1911, Hubert Camon warned that these should not be read as historical works in the scholarly sense, but as 'studies of campaigns':[51] they had a didactic purpose and the person they taught was Clausewitz himself. Through these he realized more fully the relationship between war and policy, as Napoleon was defeated not because he failed strategically, but because he did not adapt his strategy to the political circumstances in which he found himself. Again the consequence is a disjunction between book I, chapter 1 and much of the rest of *On War*. What Herberg-Rothe, like Gat, was arguing was that at the very least Clausewitz's attitudes to war changed over time, not only because of what happened to Clausewitz as he grew and matured, but also because war itself changed between 1792 and 1815, and even between 1804 and 1815.

Herberg-Rothe represented one by-product of the Cold War's end, a reawakening of strategic thought within Germany itself, as it emerged from the legacy of the Second World War, its repudiation of Prussian militarism, and the shadow of the United States. In the divided Germany, the East studied Clausewitz more than the West; in united Germany Clausewitz has received the most sustained attention from his homeland since 1945. Herberg-Rothe's supervisor Herfried Münkler, who has been the most prominent academic in this respect, stressed a point in *Über den Krieg: Stationen der Kriegsgeschichte im Spiegel ihrer theoretischen Reflexion* (2002) which had been neglected since the

---

[51] [Hubert] Camon, *Clausewitz* (Paris, 1911), vii.

Nazis, or at least since Carl Schmitt, that Clausewitz was the spokesman of existential war, not just of war as a political act, and that the principal source for this was not *On War*, but the 1812 manifestos. The existential nature of war gives Clausewitz's supporters the ammunition with which to respond to Martin van Creveld, John Keegan, and Mary Kaldor. The latter have targeted the instrumentalist view of war and Clausewitz's writings, as propounded by Paret (and for that matter by Raymond Aron in *Penser la guerre*, another book of 1976, which also reflected the pressures of the Cold War). They have, in Gat's and Herberg-Rothe's terms, privileged the later Clausewitz over the earlier Clausewitz, or, put another way, book I of *On War* over the rest of it.

Historiographically, therefore, interpretations of Clausewitz have differed generationally, nationally, and politically. He has appealed simultaneously, and not always for opposing reasons, to Karl Marx, Adolf Hitler, and Western liberals. These differences are of course to be explained in part by the eye of the beholder, by the fact that the ambiguities of the original text and the interpretations of its editors and translators have enabled the reader to see in *On War* that which he (or she) wishes to see. But they are also to be accounted for by Clausewitz's own methodology, and above all by his use of dialectics. None of his interpreters has necessarily misquoted him. Each generation and each national tradition which wishes to resuscitate an apparently dying Clausewitz can do so by referring to an alternative text. It is not sufficient just to say that *On War* was unfinished. Aron is wrong when he says that the logical conclusion, and the one to which Clausewitz would have come if he had reworked book VI, that on defence, is a theory of conflict resolution, and not just because *On War* is a book about war, not about peace: he is also wrong because his argument, like Paret's, suggests that Clausewitz's aim was a unitary vision. Sun Tzu's method (and perhaps the reason for the current vogue for *The Art of War*) was, as Michael Handel pointed out, to present conclusions. Clausewitz's is to achieve understanding through debate, through point and counterpoint.[52] The dialogue is continuous, and to that extent replicates Clausewitz's most important insight about the nature of war itself, that it is a reciprocal activity, where the interaction of the belligerents creates its own dynamic.[53] The fundamental dialectic of *On War*, and one which does genuinely have its roots in the year 1804–5, as it was one to which Scharnhorst introduced Clausewitz, is that between theory and reality.

Clausewitz's ambition was to establish a universal theory of war. In a note on his intentions, written in about 1818, he had said that he had begun with

[52] Michael Handel, *Masters of War: Sun Tzu, Clausewitz and Jomini* (London, 1992), 24.

[53] The most important exploration of this issue is Alan Beyerchen, 'Chance and Complexity in the Real World: Clausewitz on the Nonlinear Nature of War', *International Security*, XVII, winter 1992–3, 59–90.

'concise aphoristic chapters'. This style, found in the early pieces on strategy penned in 1804 and 1808–9,[54] reflects the fact that his intellectual awakening began with philosophy. 'But', he went on, 'my nature, which always drives me to develop and systematize, at last asserted itself here as well.... The more I wrote and surrendered to the spirit of analysis, the more I retreated to the systematic approach.'[55] Clausewitz, after all, was a teacher at various points in his career. More of it was dedicated to military education than to fighting. He may not have lectured at the Kriegsakademie when its director, but he did so in 1810–11; he was, therefore, compelled to think didactically. But Clausewitz, as the pre-1914 German military pundits appreciated, also rejected systems, saying in book VIII, chapter 1 that they must teach the general, but not accompany him to the battlefield.

The law, which provided Clausewitz with many metaphors and illustrations, provides an analogy. It works at two levels. Its theory is the basis for a judge's judgement, but the actual judgement and the sentence handed down reflect the practicalities and individual aspects of the case. Similarly, theories of war must be tested against reality. Experience without philosophy is devoid of meaning; philosophy without experience is condemned to error.

Experience appears in *On War* in two forms. The first is Clausewitz's own experience of the battlefield, which is never explicit but is continually obvious. As Gat and Herberg-Rothe have observed, *On War* is in many ways a treatise on the late Napoleonic Wars, but by 1827 Clausewitz was thinking about war in retrospect, not in terms of his own future, and from the tranquillity of his study, not from the saddle of a horse or the perspective of a corps headquarters. War changed between 1792 and 1831, and so did Clausewitz. He said different things at different times, seeing different meanings in the same events. Above all, the early Clausewitz was a practical soldier, the later Clausewitz was more of a scholar.

Following Scharnhorst's advice, Clausewitz emphasized the need to study campaigns in depth.[56] History was therefore a critical tool, negative in its application, a way of seeing how robust a theory was. Clausewitz liked at times to suggest that history led to theory,[57] not vice versa, and his campaign histories of the 1820s reinforce that impression, but it is not the one created by reading *On War* as an isolated text. In *On War*, Clausewitz advances a general proposition and then military history follows. The theory comes first, and thereafter a dialogue is opened with the theory by means of military history. 'Historical examples clarify everything', he wrote in book II, chapter 6, 'and

---

[54] Carl von Clausewitz, *Strategie aus dem Jahr 1804 mit Zusätsen von 1808 und 1809*, ed. Eberhard Kessel (Hamburg, 1937).
[55] *On War*, I, p. 63.    [56] Ibid. II, 6, p. 173.    [57] Ibid. II, 2, p. 144.

also provide the best kind of proof in the empirical sciences.'[58] The latter illuminates the former, not the other way round.

He therefore used the history that best suited his purposes. In book II, chapter 6, on historical examples, Clausewitz said that the best illustrations were the most recent, and that meant they were derived from wars after 1740. In book VIII, chapter 3B, where Clausewitz provides a potted summary of the history of warfare, he presented Napoleon as the embodiment of modern war and implied that it would be hard to turn the clock back to earlier forms of war. Thus two lines of attack against *On War* are exposed. First, how can it claim universality when it excludes most of military history? Clausewitz's note of 10 July 1827, acknowledging two types of warfare, one being a more limited, pre-Napoleonic variety, was his indirect recognition of this point. Second, and more topically, how can Clausewitz cope with the post-Westphalian order when he fails to acknowledge the pre-Westphalian order?

One answer to both questions, and particularly the second, was that Clausewitz's use of military history was much more eclectic than his self-presentation suggests. Book VI, on the defence, has to make much greater use of examples from the wars of Frederick the Great than of those from the wars of Napoleon (for all the apparent dominance of the Russian campaign). What mattered to Clausewitz was where theory led him, not a Whiggish approach to history, with its presumption in favour of progress. In book V, chapter 14, when discussing the maintenance and supply of armies, he described modern war as beginning after 1648, not after 1740, let alone 1792, and volume 9 of the *Hinterlassene Werke* went back to the Thirty Years War itself. Reviewing the campaigns of Gustavus Adolphus, whom he described in *On War* as a 'new Alexander',[59] he wrote, 'The number of small princes, who took part; the very extended theatre of war, over which all parties were scattered and intermingled; the very limited organization of the armies; weakly constituted states, which still showed the remains of feudalism and the spirit of chivalry; finally the religious aim of the war—all made possible and at the same time necessary quite exceptional manifestations in the art of war.' Clausewitz was therefore much more open to the appearance of non-state actors than his recent critics allow. Moreover, he acknowledged that 'Whoever relies purely on the perspectives of his own times is inclined to treat what is most recent as best—and he finds it impossible to deal with what is exceptional or out of the ordinary.'[60]

---

[58] Ibid. II, 6, p. 170.   [59] Ibid. VIII, 3B, p. 589.
[60] *Hinterlassene Werke des Generals Carl von Clausewitz über Krieg und Kriegführung* (10 vols, Berlin 1832–7), IX, 19, quoted in Hans Rothfels, *Carl von Clausewitz. Politik und Krieg* (Berlin, 1920), 62.

This description of the characteristics of the Thirty Years War reflects—as did his brief history of warfare in book VIII, chapter 3B, of *On War*—his conviction that social and political conditions affected the conduct of war. He was comparatively uninterested in the role of policy as a cause for war. Because for most of his working life his focus lay on the relationship between strategy and tactics, not that between war and policy, he chose to look at campaigns, not whole wars. *On War* abounds with examples from the Seven Years War and the Napoleonic Wars, but not once does its author reflect on either of the wars in the round, despite the fact that only thus can one explore their links to their causes and consequences, and so expose their relationship to policy.

The dialectical method is of course a philosophical one, and Clausewitz's fondness for it exposes his debt to the philosophers of the day, particularly Kant, as mediated by Johann Gottfried Kiesewetter, who taught him at the war school, and more contentiously Hegel, who frequented the same social circles in Berlin in the 1820s. Clausewitz was caught up in the *Sturm und Drang* movement, which marked the response of German letters to the French Enlightenment and itself bled into Romanticism. His discussion of the nature of military genius owed much to the influence of Kant, and was simultaneously Romantic, emphasizing the individual and his ability to find meaning in life through struggle. His choice of vocabulary, and particularly his use of the word *Geist*, was indicative of an intellect on a philosophical cusp. Translating *Geist* as 'spirit' places Clausewitz in the context of Romanticism; translating it as 'intellect', as Howard and Paret tend to do, places him more squarely in the more rational and deductive context of the Enlightenment. Admittedly Montesquieu, who was the only political philosopher, Machiavelli apart, whom Clausewitz cited, and who belongs firmly in the Enlightenment, also used the word 'spirit' as Clausewitz often did, to mean the spirit of an abstract institution and of a people.

Clausewitz was even less explicit in his use of philosophy as a methodology than he was in his use of military history. By damning in combative terms both Heinrich Dietrich von Bülow and Antoine-Henri Jomini, two leading military theorists of his day, he at least enabled his readers to place *On War* in the spectrum of military writing. However, even here his partiality can mislead the unwary, as he did not spell out the corollary of those attacks by acknowledging the influence of the military pundits who had exercised a positive influence on his thinking. Exactly the latter point can be made about the philosophical influences: *On War* neither names names nor is clear about when it slips from the real to the normative.

This lack of openness is a principal source of the ambiguity in the text of *On War*. Clausewitz moves back and forth between the real and the ideal, but he does not make it clear when he is doing so and in which vein he is writing. His critics—and both Martin van Creveld and John Keegan are cases in point—can take the normative Clausewitz and counter him with some, albeit selective, realities. At one level this is fair game: Clausewitz did the same thing.

Crucial examples of this approach are two central Clausewitzian concepts, the effects of whose ambiguity in the evolution of military thought have already been touched upon. War's subordination to policy is an ideal, not a reality. War can create its own dynamic, as it did in the Napoleonic Wars. The realist in Clausewitz says that there must be a continuous interchange between the politician and the general and that the latter is not always subordinate to the former as the policy has in practice to conform to what is militarily practicable. Secondly, absolute war, which for Paret and Aron is an ideal, as it was for Clausewitz by the time he came to write book I, chapter 1, is treated as realizable in book VIII; indeed, Clausewitz suggests that he had experienced absolute war.

Both these examples belong on a dialectical spectrum; so too do existential war and instrumental war. This debate between proposition and antithesis is Hegelian, only Hegel then sought resolution in synthesis. There are elements of synthesis in Clausewitz, most obviously adumbrated, if not yet fully articulated, in the note of 10 July 1827. Clausewitz proposed two forms of war, wars for territorial objectives, which result in negotiated settlements, and wars of destruction which result in a dictated peace. In the Cold War, these could be adapted to the thinking on limited and unlimited war. Both are ideals; in practice, real wars can have elements of both. Clausewitz resolved the differences between the two with the further idea that war is a political instrument. In other words, a third concept acts as a synthesis. But there are many other issues explored by Clausewitz where he leaves the reader not with a resolution, but with an inherent contradiction. Clausewitz often thought in threes, not pairs. War consists of tactics, strategy, and policy, and uses means to achieve its military aim in order to deliver a political objective. But what is evident in these threes is that each exists alongside the others, and sometimes in tension with it. Theory suggests a hierarchy; reality suggests otherwise. Economy of force, for example, cuts across the escalatory pressure to achieve the military aim of victory, while the use of excessive force may undermine the political objective—which for Clausewitz (let us be clear on this point) was peace.[61]

Time and space were central to Clausewitz's thinking, as they are to the conduct of war. For all commanders, their relationship is a dialectical one. 'One cannot conceive of a regular army operating except in a definite space', Clausewitz wrote in book I, chapter 3, 'Its importance is decisive in the highest

---

[61] On this point, see *On War*, I, 2, p. 91; VII, 5, p. 528, and 22, p. 570; VIII, 6, pp. 603–4.

degree, for it affects the operations of all forces, and at times entirely alters them.' The discussion which follows embraces the tactical importance of terrain as well as the strategic, but in books VI, on the defence, and VII, on the offensive, terrain is set more clearly in its strategic context. The whole theory of attack and defence revolves around space: the attack passes its culminating point of victory because of the length of its advance, while the defender surrenders space with a view to creating favourable conditions for the counter-attack. Terrain, however, also has a political dimension. The note of 10 July 1827 defines wars of limited aims as 'occupying some frontier districts so that we can annex them or use them for bargaining at the peace negotiations'.[62]

Space, terrain, and geography therefore contain the three elements of war—tactics, strategy, and policy—and they are at odds with time. Clausewitz argued that the attack must be swiftly executed, and his treatment of campaigns as isolated acts reinforced the presumption in favour of the idea that decisive wars are short wars. Such wars are characterized by action; their apparent opposite is peace, characterized by inaction (or at least military inaction). And yet Clausewitz observed that in the eighteenth century most wars between civilized states more often involved reciprocal observation than struggles to the death. These wars contained inaction, in defiance of war's true nature; they were characterized by pauses and spontaneous armistices, and so became protracted.

Here is a classic Clausewitzian dialectic: action against inaction, speed against delay. Much of the discussion pivots around the relationship between strategy and tactics. The central issue is the engagement: should the commander seek battle or postpone it? But it is the attacker who has an interest in speed, and it is the defender that has an interest in delay. What then happens when policy, the third element in war, is added in, alongside tactics and strategy? Does it resolve the debate, acting as a synthesis? Or is it a complication?

The fulfilment of the political objectives can be very distant in time. When Clausewitz advocated war against France in 1812, he did not envisage a quick victory; indeed, he expected the opposite, a defeat from which Prussia's honour would emerge sufficiently intact to enable its resurrection at some point far in the future. Thus even existential struggle could be instrumental and utilitarian. Therefore, the management and reconciliation of the competing pressures of time and space revolve around the balance between the military aim and the political objective. But what that exposes are two differing views of the political objective. In *On War*, Clausewitz saw the outcome of war in terms of territory won or lost: ideology was important in terms of national mobilization for war, not so much in terms of having to defeat revolutionary

---

[62] *On War*, 69.

ideas or topple absolutist monarchies. The crushing of the enemy's will was not an end in itself, but a means to achieve the military aim. Most of the wars that Clausewitz discussed (and here his recent critics are right, for all his interest in the Thirty Years War) involved nations defined by their frontiers rather than by their ethnicity, religion, or political beliefs. Although Clausewitz believed in the value of the balance of power, he did not define the external political objectives of war any more specifically, and certainly did not engage with the grandiose Wilsonian objectives associated with the United States since 1917, and sustained by George W. Bush into the twenty-first century. Precisely because the right to resort to war defined the sovereignty of the state, Clausewitz had little interest in issues of international law. Nor was he a democrat, however much he might have recognized the powerful contribution which popular passions could make to a war effort.

Ideology's function in Clausewitz's view of war is therefore domestic, as an agent for national mobilization. The French Revolution had unlocked the full strength of France the better to fight war: politics was in this sense the servant of war, and enabled it more completely to approach its absolute state, particularly if the enemy reciprocated.

The resolution of these competing forces should be the group of three for which Clausewitz has become most celebrated, the 'trinity' as described in the peroration at the end of book I, chapter 1. The three elements are primeval violence, hatred and enmity; the play of chance and probability; and policy and reason. Hegelian logic suggests that policy should be the synthesizing force in the dialectic between hatred and probability, and many recent commentators have read the text in those terms. Clearly that is one possible outcome, but it is not a necessary one, either in reality or in the ideal. The three elements jostle for primacy, Clausewitz likening them to magnets in their capacity not only to attract but also to repel. The outcome is therefore almost infinitely variable.

The trinity has become massively fashionable for Clausewitz scholars. It unites Raymond Aron (who in 1976 was among the first to emphasize its importance) and other theorists of the Cold War with those looking at the existential conflicts of today. There is something in the passage for everybody. But there is one obvious reason both for its comparative neglect before 1976 and for the burden of interpretation imposed on it since: it is very short. It occupies less than half a page of the Howard and Paret translation of over 600 pages, and it is never discussed again. In particular, it leaves open how we are to read the secondary trinity of the people, the army, and the government (the trinity which Colin Powell, Harry Summers, Martin van Creveld, and Mary Kaldor, among others, treat, in a quite shamelessly inaccurate reading of the text, as *the* trinity). Clausewitz associates passion with the people, probability with the army, and policy with the government. But how fixed did he see those linkages to be, and would he have been willing, as some are, to suggest that the people can show reason, the commander passion and the government an awareness of the play of probability?

These are important questions, but not to my mind the most intriguing. The trinity is one of the most complex and divisive aspects of Christian theology, the idea of God as three in one, Father, Son, and Holy Ghost. Clausewitz's use of the word deliberately evoked these connotations: his father may have been a soldier but his grandfather and other close relatives were Lutheran pastors. He described the trinity which made up war as 'wunderliche', as strange or even wonderful.[63] The discussion about the dialectics of war in Clausewitz tends to revolve around history and philosophy, but is religion lurking there too, buried even more deeply? Less speculatively and more immediately, however, Clausewitz's trinity points the way to the true synthesis in his argument, and that is war itself. In the hands of Napoleon, the god of war and 'the conqueror of the world', war achieved 'its state of absolute perfection'.[64] Clausewitz blasphemed for a purpose: here policy's role is not to direct war, but to serve it, to enable it to fulfil its true nature. The trinity of passion, probability, and policy, or (if you must) of people, army, and government, were united—in war.

---

[63] These are the translations of 'wunderlich' favoured respectively by O. S. Matthijs Jolles and J. J. Graham respectively. The latter might have demanded an epithet like 'wunderbar', with its connotations of 'miraculous'; in any event Howard's and Paret's original choice of 'remarkable' does not get close enough to the numinous element in the word. On the translation of this passage, see Jan Willem Honig's chapter in this book; on the trinity itself, see Christopher Bassford's chapter.

[64] *On War*, II, 5, p. 166; VIII, 2, p. 580.

# 2

# Clausewitz and the Non-Linear Nature of Warfare: Systems of Organized Complexity

*Alan Beyerchen*

One of the striking facets of the *magnum opus* of Carl von Clausewitz is his use of the terms and images which were at the forefront of research in science and technology in his day. Clausewitz may not have known much Latin or Greek—phrases from those languages are conspicuously absent from the pages of *On War*—but the dialects of science are richly represented in his work. We rather expect a military mind to know the basics of Newtonian mechanics. But we do not often think of how new were the concepts of economics formulated by Adam Smith, or how the notion of friction was beginning to find its way towards the laws of thermodynamics, or how magnetism and electricity were starting to converge. Clausewitz knowledgeably availed himself of the vocabulary of all these. He also wrote of probabilities in ways we find unremarkable, but which were mathematically literate and striking for his time. These novel ideas reflected the changed realities of the world around Clausewitz, and were as much a part of his *Weltanschauung* as the new nationalism that had transformed the military landscape and the Romanticism that was challenging Enlightenment principles.

This aspect of his thought can be approached in at least two useful ways. The first is through analysing his ideas in terms of the science and technology of the late eighteenth and early nineteenth centuries. The second is by exploring some of the newer developments in the late twentieth and early twenty-first centuries and asking how our changed thinking helps us better understand the author of *On War*. The former takes us into the realm of the clash between the Enlightened and Romanticist precepts in Clausewitz's time. The second reproduces interesting echoes of the intellectual aesthetics of that clash in today's turn from the contracted focus on linearity to an expanded opening towards non-linearity. My contention is that some of the concepts of the newly emerging non-linear sciences may help us apprehend essential elements of Clausewitz's thinking. He was not only conversant with the best science of his time, but in some arresting ways he was ahead of it. For these reasons, I propose to begin not with the science of his time, but of our own.

In 1947, an influential American produced a remarkably prescient sketch for the development of science in the last half of the twentieth century.[1] Warren Weaver was a mathematician serving as director of the Natural Sciences Division of the Rockefeller Foundation who, along with Claude Shannon, was involved with generating what came to be called information theory. In an introduction to a collection of short, public addresses by a wide variety of scientists, Weaver laid out an overview of the problems addressed by science since the age of Galileo and Newton and argued for new approaches to old problems. His thinking offers us an intriguing way to categorize the thinking of Clausewitz more than a century earlier.

Weaver's elucidation of the advances of science fell into three phases. The first stage, from the seventeenth century onwards, was the period in which physical scientists learnt how to analyse systems limited to two variables (or with minor extensions perhaps three or four), confining themselves to the problems of '*simplicity*' (Weaver's emphasis). The basic idea was to study problems in which one quantity (say, gas pressure) depends with a useful degree of accuracy on a second quantity (say, gas volume) in such a way that other factors can be treated as minor or negligible. These variables might involve complicated calculations, but by being handled as discrete the systems were inherently simple both in theory and in experiment. The forces and causal trains of events could be isolated and studied in detail. Great strides could be made in the physical sciences this way, leading scientists to understand how gravitational attraction depends on distance, or how the intensity of light varies with the distance from a source, or how electric current relates to voltage, or how steam pressure correlates to steam temperature. These advances were accompanied by practical advances in technology as well.[2]

However, Weaver pointed out that around 1900 some scientists approached nature in a profoundly different way. They increasingly drew on eighteenth- and nineteenth-century mathematical developments in probability studies. Rather than deal with only two variables (or perhaps three or four), they went to the other extreme and developed powerful statistical techniques to study problems of '*disorganized complexity*'. If classical mechanics confined itself to a single billiard ball (often a perfect sphere on a frictionless surface), then statistical mechanics worked out the rules for millions or billions of such collisions. The history of a single ball was now lost in the collisions among all the

---

[1] Warren Weaver (ed.), *The Scientists Speak* (New York, 1947), 1–13. Weaver condensed this piece as 'Science and Complexity', in *American Scientist*, 36 (1948), 536–44, and then elaborated upon it again in his introduction to *The Rockefeller Foundation Annual Report* (New York, 1958), 7–15.

[2] Weaver, *Scientists Speak*, 1–2.

balls and the side rails or among gas molecules and their container walls. But some questions could be answered with useful precision: on the average, What is the distance between collisions? How many impacts does a ball experience per second? and so on. This was possible because the exact history of each ball became swamped in the array of random activity. Problems of disorganized complexity are those with a very large number of variables in which the behaviour of the variables is erratic or perhaps unknown. Yet the average properties of the system are surprisingly orderly and can be analysed and predicted with considerable confidence. These techniques are not restricted to situations in which the individual events are well known. In fact, they apply particularly to situations in which the individual events are complicated and unpredictable. Whether dealing with life insurance expectancies, the frequency of calls in a large telephone exchange, the movement of molecules in a thermodynamic system, or the behaviour of quantum entities, statistical treatments of disorganized complexity have been highly successful. In fact, as Weaver pointed out, 'the whole question of evidence, and the way knowledge can be inferred from evidence, is now recognized to depend on those same statistical ideas, so that probability notions are essential to any theory of knowledge itself'.[3]

The new problems science was beginning to tackle after the Second World War were those, I believe, which most interested Clausewitz more than a century earlier. Weaver called them the problems of *'organized complexity'*. The importance for us was that the classical approach dealt with too few variables to offer a robust approach to war, while the later approach of statistical mechanics would deal with too many.[4] The middle ground of more than a few but less than an astronomical number is what held the attention of Weaver, and, despite his evident familiarity with both Newtonian mechanics and the emerging probability theory of his day, Clausewitz. Weaver pointed to such questions as: 'Why is one chemical substance a poison while another, whose molecules have just the same atoms but assembled into a mirror-image pattern, is completely non-toxic?.... What is a gene, and how does the original genetic constitution of a living organism express itself in the developed characteristics of the adult?.... On what does the price of wheat depend?.... With a given total of national resources that can be brought to bear, what tactics and strategy will most promptly win a war?' The key element is not merely the number of variables, but the fact that a sizeable number of variables are *'interrelated into an organic whole'*.[5] (Weaver's emphasis) This is the essential feature of most biological and social systems.

---

[3] Ibid. 5.
[4] cf. Ian Hacking, *The Taming of Chance* (Cambridge, 1990) and Lorraine Daston, *Classical Probability in the Enlightenment* (Princeton, NJ, 1988).
[5] Weaver, *Scientists Speak*, 6–7.

Such problems are organized and interactive in ways that make time-dependent patterns of interaction thoroughly pertinent. In other words, these are problems in which a system evolves and has a history that matters. Weaver's vision was that interdisciplinary teams and the emergence of the new 'electronic computing devices' would be able to tackle the problems of organized complexity, and he successfully set the Rockefeller Foundation on a course to achieve this end.[6]

The essential feature of these problems is interaction or feedback, requiring attention to the long term and the full range of behaviour of a system. The key concept is that not just the variables are time-dependent, but the parameters and relationships among the variables can evolve over time. The laws for such systems do not necessarily remain fixed, because often these systems cannot be isolated or closed from their context or environment. They are fundamentally problems of non-linearity, and I believe Clausewitz understood war as a non-linear phenomenon, aspects of which were characterized by organized complexity.

What, exactly, does 'non-linear' mean? It clearly presupposes a sense of what is 'linear'. Systems are called 'linear' if their properties are such that, when their variables are plotted against each other, their relationship generates a straight line. Linearity requires two propositions to hold. They are surprisingly straightforward, even though a technical statement of them sounds more complicated than they are: (a) changes in system output are proportional to changes in input (leading one to expect that effects should be proportional to their causes), and (b) system outputs corresponding to the sum of two inputs are equal to the sum of the outputs arising from the inputs determined discretely (meaning that the whole is exactly equal to the sum of its parts). In the first, the effect of an output is related to input by a constant, such that $f(au) = af(u)$, with constant returns to scale, so that successive increases or decreases in a cause will produce a corresponding constant, predictable increase or decrease in effects. The second indicates that we can deal with the effects of a system as a whole, or we can break it into its constituent parts and then add the effects of the parts together and arrive at the same result, so that $f(u + v) = f(u) + f(v)$. The whole is thus equal to the sum of its parts. If a system's behaviour can be described appropriately by addition, subtraction, multiplication by a constant, or integration or differentiation with respect to time, it can be thought of as linear. Pretty much *all* else is non-linear.

---

[6] Weaver, *Scientists Speak*, 8–9. For an excellent, balanced account of Weaver's role in the Rockefeller Foundation, see Robert E. Kohler, *Partners in Science: Foundations and Natural Scientists, 1900–1945* (Chicago, IL, 1991), 265–391.

There are many attractive features to linearity. Due to the structural stability of a linear system, once we know a little about it, we know a lot. Two points, after all, suffice to construct a straight line. If you understand a portion of such a system you can extrapolate with confidence how the whole will behave. Given fixed parameters (i.e. distinct and stable boundary conditions), linearity permits us to focus on consistencies and regularities and to construct discrete causal trains, allowing us to predict the behaviour of a given system. It encourages us to isolate variables in input–output pairs and disregard possible interactions and contexts. But there are limitations: linearity often restricts us to problems of simplicity or disorganized complexity.

If the appropriate mathematical representation of a system does not obey the two conditions above, the system is non-linear. If it can be broken into compartmentalized subsystems, it may be classified as linear, even if it is described by a complicated equation aggregating these parts. But if interactions or feedback or indistinct boundary conditions are irreducible features of a system under consideration, it is non-linear even if relatively simple equations can be used to describe it. Multiplying or dividing variables, raising to powers, taking roots, or integrating or differentiating with respect to variables other than time are typical non-linear operations. If these are needed to describe adequately the behaviour of a system, then compartmentalization and linear analysis can only give an approximation of the system.

The linear approximation may be good enough. And some non-linear systems (say, those described by a sine or a cosine function) are regular enough to allow also for prediction of future behaviour. The mathematicians of Clausewitz's time were highly successful in generating linearization techniques of great power. This is how mechanics, including the celestial mechanics of astronomy, was done. Linearization constituted a compelling scientific vision of abstract rationality and idealization, building upon the work of Euler, Lagrange, Laplace, Fourier, and others.[7] Linearity offers many advantages when you can get it. It offers structural stability and convenient emphasis on equilibria; it justifies scaling and compartmentalization; it legitimates simple, smooth extrapolations from current conditions and belief in successive developmental stages (i.e. compartmentalization in time). Linearity implies that, if some is good, more is better. It promises prediction—and thus control. It may be helpful to realize that all this applies not only to physical systems but also to social systems. In this vein, we should note, as

---

[7] See the essays in Tore Frängsmyr, John Heilbron, and Robin Rider (eds), *The Quantifying Spirit in the Eighteenth Century* (Berkeley, CA, 1990). Some of the implications of the approach to quantification adopted in the eighteenth century are explored in Theodore M. Porter, *Trust in Numbers: The Pursuit of Objectivity in Science and Public Life* (Princeton, NJ, 1995).

Clausewitz quite probably understood, that bureaucracy is the quintessential social linearization technique.

But linear systems are restrictive, often narrow and brittle. They are frequently not robust under the changing parameters that result from dynamic environments. They do not allow for feedback, trigger effects, or threshold events (tipping points). Control is usually at the expense of resources taken from elsewhere, and without it these systems in the real world can drift or even shift abruptly from their linear regimes of behaviour. We often design our artefacts and devices to behave as linear systems; nature seldom seems to. So many systems in mathematics and science do not fit the linear mould that the mathematician Stanislav Ulam once commented that calling systems '*non*-linear' is like calling the bulk of zoology the study of 'non-elephant animals'.[8]

Today, thanks largely to the interdisciplinary research and the electronic computing devices that animated Warren Weaver in 1947, we can examine non-linear systems in significant detail and complexity. Using supercomputers, we can move beyond the limited approach of linear analysis of the partial differential equations for a continuum field and turn to the non-linear equations that describe so many of the phenomena found in nature. Phenomena that do not offer closed-form solutions under analytical techniques can be subjected to numerical techniques that are more realistic. The use of finite differences can produce a discrete space-time lattice of events, and the computer can solve the algebraic system representing the field's values at each point in the lattice. As the spacing is reduced, the discrete solution may approach that of the continuum. A *very* large number of values for the unknown can be placed into the equations and a solution found that is approximate, but realistic for the messiness of systems of complexly intercoupled variables. A major result is that we can better perceive the way order and disorder are intertwined and deeply connected with chance.

The use of ultra-fast computer graphics also changes the way we 'see' complexity in its ubiquitous manifestations. The new non-linear sciences dealing with deterministic chaos, fractals, complex adaptive systems, solitons, instantons, and others are all driven by the advent of computers and their graphics. These fields are not fads, even if they have received the hype that shrouds any novelty in our world today. They are functions of the advent of computers, which are changing our way of seeing the world as extensively and permanently as the telescope and microscope changed the world of the

---

[8] David Campbell, 'Non-linear Science: From Paradigms to Practicalities', *Los Alamos Science*, 15 (Special Issue, 1987), 218.

seventeenth century. We have come clearly to see how little of the world is actually linear, now that we can cope with non-linearity so much better. At last we can examine the long term and full range of the behaviour of systems, a necessity if we want to understand the non-linear systems of organized complexity.

We are thus now in a better position to understand why in his own day Clausewitz rejected the Enlightenment's emphasis on finding ways to restrict phenomena and their representations to fit linear techniques. It was not that Clausewitz did not value the knowledge of what Weaver termed the problems of classical simplicity. He repeatedly emphasized that in war 'everything is very simple', even if 'the simplest thing is difficult'.[9] He did find that some relationships in war were proportional, as when he observed that the effects of victory will 'increase in proportion to the scale of victory'.[10] His attention to the varieties of a 'centre of gravity' or to 'equilibrium' in the 'dynamic law of war' indicated the importance of Newtonian mechanics in his mind.[11] Sometimes he combined these concepts with other classical images such as the convergence of the sun's rays at the focal point of a concave mirror.[12] Just as telling was his frequent use of the concept of inertia, including what he termed the 'indolent inertia of peace'.[13] It seems to me this form of thinking also played a role in one of his most adamant claims, namely that defence is the stronger form of waging war.

Yet Clausewitz found that approaching war as a problem of simplicity was insufficient. Separating human affairs from their contexts and isolating variables where they should not be isolated—Clausewitz was all in favour of isolating them when this did not destroy proper representation of the phenomenon—were characteristic of the targets in his criticism of other theorists of war. By privileging one factor or a fixed set of principles (such as numerical superiority, *matériel*, geometric configuration, or interior lines) regardless of changing context, they generated uselessly idealized rules for the conduct of war. As he wrote in book II, chapter 2, their work was inadequate, because

They aim at fixed values; but in war everything is uncertain, and calculations have to be made with variable quantities.

They direct the inquiry exclusively toward physical quantities, whereas all military action is intertwined with psychological forces and effects.

---

[9] Clausewitz, *On War*, edited and translated by Michael Howard and Peter Paret (Princeton, NJ, 1976), I, 7, p. 119. The German edition used here is *Vom Kriege*, 16th edn, edited by Werner Hahlweg (Bonn, 1952).
[10] *On War*, IV, 10, p. 256.  [11] Ibid. III, 18, pp. 221–2.
[12] Ibid. IV, 11, p. 258.  [13] Ibid. III, 5, p. 189.

They consider only unilateral action, whereas war consists of a continuous interaction of opposites.[14]

Just as important, these theories could not account for the realm of genius. A theory would also have to account for moral forces and effects, for the positive reaction and interaction that war produces, and the uncertainty of all information in the fog of war.[15]

The pervasive uncertainties in war meant that what Weaver called problems of disorganized complexity also played a role in Clausewitz's thinking. Mathematical certainties do not occur in the real world in which wars were conducted. He asserted in one famous passage,

In short, absolute, so-called mathematical, factors never find a firm basis in military calculations. From the very start, there is an interplay of possibilities, probabilities, good luck and bad that weaves its way throughout the length and breadth of the tapestry. In the whole range of human activities, war most closely resembles a game of cards.[16]

In a portion of the text addressing his concept of 'friction', he pointed out:

The military machine—the army and everything related to it—is basically very simple and therefore seems easy to manage. But we should bear in mind that none of its components is of one piece; each part is composed of individuals, ... the least important of whom may chance to delay things or somehow make them go wrong. ... This tremendous friction, which cannot, as in mechanics, be reduced to a few points, is everywhere in contact with chance, and brings about effects that cannot be measured, just because they are largely due to chance.[17]

And in yet another section, he stated, 'Circumstances vary so enormously in war, and are so indefinable, that a vast array of factors has to be appreciated— mostly in light of probabilities alone'.[18] All this sounds as if the techniques of the increasingly sophisticated probability theory of Clausewitz's day would allow calculations of tendencies to useful approximations.

Yet approaching war as a system of disorganized complexity was also insufficient for Clausewitz. Even if the probabilities could be calculated, he agreed with Napoleon that they would require the mathematical talents of a Newton or an Euler.[19] But the greater objection was that war is not only suffused with chance, it is also suffused with purposeful action on both sides, and is therefore not dominated by statistical randomness: 'In war, the will is directed

---

[14] *On War*, II, 2, p. 135; see also commentary by Paret, 'The Genesis of *On War*', p. 10, and Azar Gat, *A History of Military Thought* (Oxford, 2001), 56–137.
[15] *On War*, II, 2, pp. 136–40.   [16] Ibid. I, 1, § 21, p. 86.
[17] Ibid. I, 7, pp. 119–20.   [18] Ibid. I, 3, p. 112.
[19] Ibid. I, 3, p. 112, and VIII, 3B, 586.

at an animate object that *reacts*'.[20] Each side must also take into consideration the opponent's character, institutions, general situation, and other factors and then use the laws of probability—not to calculate odds, but to estimate the opponent's likely course of action.[21] Note in the passage above, when Clausewitz looked for an analogy with games of chance, he did not cite the random outcomes of roulette or dice. Instead, he said war resembles a game of cards, in which presumably the ability to learn the character and personal tendencies of an opponent makes the game a matter of skill as well as odds.

The predictive capacity of the sciences to handle problems of simplicity and disorganized complexity was for Clausewitz of very limited utility. But did he perceive that war might present what Weaver called problems of organized complexity? Was it his view that war as a system could not adequately be closed or isolated from its environment? Did he understand war as a non-linear phenomenon, in which the long term and full range of behaviour of a system must be studied to understand it? Did the parts matter significantly to the whole? Were the variables for him organized and interrelated, producing feedback and evolution in the system? In this short space, I can only provide suggestions towards the affirmative. Elsewhere, I have argued the case that Clausewitz viewed war as a non-linear phenomenon.[22] He paid serious and sustained attention to complexity and unpredictability (arising from interaction, friction, and chance—and the latter from statistical randomness, amplification of a microcause, and analytical myopia). He was attentive to the diversity and indistinct boundary of all relationships ('die Mannigfaltigkeit and die unbestimmte Grenze aller Beziehungen').[23] War is not just an extension of politics, despite efforts of many readers to create a linear causal train from politics to war. War cannot be abstracted from its political context, for politics gives war its genesis and sustains it. War is a subset of the political context, and Clausewitz maintained it generates feedback that may alter the context itself: 'the original political objects can greatly alter during the course of the war and may finally change entirely, *since they are influenced by events and their probable consequences*'.[24]

Systems of organized complexity involve factors that are interdependent. Over time they change in ways that affect how and even which variables interact. The exact behaviour of these systems is nearly impossible to predict,

---

[20] Ibid. II, 3, p. 149.   [21] Ibid. I, 1, § 10, p. 80.

[22] Alan Beyerchen, 'Clausewitz, Non-linearity and the Unpredictability of War', *International Security*, 17 (winter 1992–3), 59–90.

[23] *Vom Kriege*, I, 3, p. 149. 'Da hier die Mannigfaltigkeit und die unbestimmte Grenze aller Beziehungen eine grosse Menge von Grössen in die Betrachtung bringen, ...' is translated as 'Circumstances vary so enormously in war, and are so indefinable, that a vast array of factors has to be appreciated ...' in *On War*, I, 1, p. 112.

[24] *On War*, I, 1, p. 87, and I, 2, p. 92. Emphasis in the original.

because they adapt to changing conditions. Effectively, in a very real sense they make themselves up as they proceed. This is why Clausewitz was utterly right when he described war as a true chameleon, and each war as having laws peculiar unto itself.[25] This is why 'continued striving after laws analogous to those appropriate to the realm of inanimate matter was bound to lead to one mistake after another'.[26] He correctly saw war as an act of human intercourse most closely akin to commerce or politics, 'the womb in which war develops— where its outlines already exist in their hidden rudimentary form, like the characteristics of living creatures in their embryos'.[27]

For Clausewitz, the task of theory could not be prescriptive, but could serve as a heuristic guide to the self-education of the commander. The goal would be the study of ends and means, examined 'in accordance with their effects and their relationships to one another'.[28] The knowledge required was basically simple, but applying it would take a natural talent for judgement, because the difficulty of applying that knowledge increases with every step up the command hierarchy. The key would be life experience, which would 'never produce a *Newton* or an *Euler*', but might generate the 'higher calculations of a *Condé* or *Frederick*'.[29] War itself evolved over time. Clausewitz offered simulated experience in the form of military history, in which genius had clearly played its role. This would produce a limited theory of the phenomena of war, he admitted, but it would have the virtue of being realistic.[30]

One of the demands Clausewitz makes of the reader of *On War* is the same as required in today's non-linear sciences—to hold in one's mind at all times the whole and the parts. As he said in the very first paragraph of book I, in war more than any other subject, 'we must begin by looking at the nature of the whole; for here more than elsewhere the part and the whole must always be thought of together'.[31] He elaborated in book VI, chapter 27 that 'in war, more than anywhere else, there is the whole and it governs all the parts, stamps them with its character, and alters them radically'. By traversing all this long (over 400 page) way upward from the simple to the complex, he claimed to avoid the constant confusion that would arise from the 'variety of interactions' that occur in war.[32] The desire to hold everything in his mind at once was characteristic of Clausewitz's understanding of war itself and of successful commanders possessing *coup d'oeil* and determination.[33] This is also the goal of anyone trying to comprehend a system of organized complexity—although few of us would even try without the aid of computers and their graphics.

---

[25] *On War*, I, 1, pp. 80, 89.
[26] Ibid. II, 3, p. 149.
[27] Ibid. II, 3, p. 149.
[28] Ibid. II, 2, p. 143.
[29] Ibid. II, 2, p. 146.
[30] Ibid. 2, p. 144.
[31] Ibid. I, 1, §1, p. 75.
[32] Ibid. VI, 27, p. 484.
[33] Ibid. VIII, 1, p. 578.

## Clausewitz and the Non-Linear Nature of Warfare

One thing that makes Clausewitz so impressive and at times infuriatingly frustrating is that he could manage this feat on his own.

As Weaver emphasized, a fundamental characteristic of systems of organized complexity is that the variables of a system are interrelated into an organic whole. This was the type of problem presented by war, as Clausewitz recognized when he wrote:

> War should often (indeed today one might say *normally*) be conceived as an organic whole [ein organisches Ganze] whose parts cannot be separated, so that each individual act contributes to the whole and itself organizes in the central concept, ....[34]

This was all consonant with the approach to nature propounded by the Romantics. Although Clausewitz appears to have reflected Kant's view in the *Critique of Judgment* that biology could not be a science, on many occasions he echoed the *Naturphilosophie* of the time.[35]

One central concept of the sciences in the Romantic era in which Clausewitz produced his text was that of *Wechselwirkung*. This notion of interdependence or reciprocal action is scattered throughout *On War*, including in book II where Clausewitz chastised other theorists for not recognizing that 'war is a continuous interaction of opposites' ('... während der Krieg eine beständige Wechselwirkung der gegenseitigen ist').[36] Anthony Ashley Cooper, 3rd Earl of Shaftesbury, in 1711 had already laid down the claim that the interdependence of parts and whole meant neither could be understood alone. Wieland, Schiller, Mendelssohn, Lessing, Herder, and Goethe were some of the figures we know studied Shaftesbury.[37] Kant used the term in various works. Both Alexander von Humboldt and Schelling made *Wechselwirkung* an essential feature of organic wholes, and by the 1830s it was introduced into educational curricula in the new field of biology.[38] At the same time, chemistry was gelling as a science of measurable quantities rather than intangible qualities.[39]

Clausewitz did not mind appropriating from any of these fields a metaphor or analogy he thought would help make a point. *Wechselwirkung* was a concept

---

[34] Ibid. VIII, 6B, p. 607; *Vom Kriege*, VIII, 6B, pp. 891–2.

[35] For a recent treatment of *Naturphilosophie* and the romanticist approach to nature, see Robert Richards, *The Romantic Conception of Life: Science and Philosophy in the Age of Goethe* (Chicago, IL, 2002). On Kant's view of the necessity of mechanistic laws as the proper hallmark of a science, see 229–37.

[36] *Vom Kriege*, II, 2, p. 181.

[37] Gerhard Müller, '*Wechselwirkung* in the Life and Other Sciences', in *Romanticism in Science: Science in Europe, 1790–1840*, edited by Stefano Poggi and Maurizio Bossi (Dordrecht, 1994), 2.

[38] Müller, '*Wechselwirkung*', 7; see Peter Paret, *Clausewitz and the State* (Princeton, NJ, 1976), 162.

[39] See Bernadette Bensaude-Vincent, 'The Chemist's Balance for Fluids: Hydrometers and Their Multiple Identities, 1770–1810', in Frederic L. Holmes and Trevor H. Levere (eds), *Instruments and Experimentation in the History of Chemistry* (Cambridge, MA, 2000), 153–84.

emerging in philosophy, chemistry, and biology rather than physics. One of its more important holistic features was that, like Clausewitz's concept of friction, it was suffused everywhere throughout war. It, too, could not be reduced as in mechanics to a few points. Importantly for our immediate purposes, reciprocal action is a feedback effect characteristic of organized complexity.

Clausewitz's thinking was profoundly historical and organicist, seeing war in an evolutionary fashion, a chameleon that was transformed by changing political contexts and specific events.[40] He repeatedly emphasized how simple tasks in war are, but how complex the interactions, frictions, and realities become in performing them. The entities performing these tasks are human beings with moral qualities, producing an essential complexity in war.

I am not suggesting that Clausewitz prefigured our understanding of non-linear systems of organized complexity. I am suggesting that *we* can turn our intentions away from linear assumptions, expectations, and modelling to the non-linear world view of the early-nineteenth-century Romantics. We would better see the limitations in our *own* thinking. Again, the idea is not to call attention to or unpack some Clausewitzian confusion. He was pretty clear on what a theory of war could and could not mean. The way he and others understood and learnt things then has some very useful dimensions for us. There are ways in which the newest developments in the sciences are helping us reach the point Clausewitz occupied nearly two centuries ago in coping with systems of organized complexity. In some ways, we are still catching up with his lead.

---

[40] *On War*, I, 1, §28, p. 89. For some reflections on the importance of the 'chameleon' image, see Andreas Herberg-Rothe, *Das Rätsel Clausewitz* (Munich, 2001), 243–5. It is not necessary to determine whether Clausewitz was an empiricist, a rationalist, a Romantic, a historicist, or a realist. These are not incompatible, given that Clausewitz viewed himself as an eclectic synthesizer of multiple traditions, taking from each whatever he needed for his own further understanding of war. Cf. Werner Hahlweg, *Carl von Clausewitz: Soldat—Politiker—Denker* (Göttingen, 1957), 63–4.

# 3

# Clausewitz's *On War*: Problems of Text and Translation

*Jan Willem Honig*

It is well known that *On War*, Clausewitz's *magnum opus*, remained unfinished on the death of the author in November 1831. It is also well known that his wife, Marie von Brühl, with the help of Major Franz August O'Etzel and her brother, Count Friedrich Wilhelm von Brühl, delivered the text for publication between 1832 and 1834.[1] Various later editors, most notably Count Brühl in the second, 1853 edition, further tinkered with the text.[2] In 1952, Werner Hahlweg published a modern edition (the 16th) which sought to restore the original German text. However, as by that time very little of the original manuscript remained available, he essentially republished the text of the first edition.[3] Another edition, with minor corrections, followed in 1973.[4] The text of *Vom Kriege* may therefore appear to pose little of an issue. It would of course have been nice to have the whole manuscript; but, considering the vagaries of history (which included a world war in which much of the manuscript legacy of Clausewitz disappeared), we possess the best German edition possible.

---

[1] Marie thanks them in her 'Preface' to Carl von Clausewitz, *Vom Kriege*, ed. Werner Hahlweg, 18th edn (Bonn, 1973), 177 (henceforth cited as *Vom Kriege*).

[2] Werner Hahlweg, 'Das Clausewitzbild einst und jetzt, Mit textkritische Anmerkungen', in ibid. 168–72.

[3] Ibid. 165–8. Although Hahlweg suggests that there is an 'Originalmanuskript' (ix) which he would publish in volume 2 of Carl von Clausewitz, *Schriften—Aufsätze—Studien—Briefe* (Göttingen: Vandenhoeck & Ruprecht, 1990), this is somewhat misleading. In this volume, he states that 'das Druckmanuskript des Werkes "Vom Kriege" bisher nicht aufgetaucht ist' (625). Hahlweg includes some drafts and preparatory works, which he dates between 1809 and 1812 (15–99). On pp. 623–717, he introduces and publishes later 'Entwürfe, Studien, frühere Fassungen' of books I and II (and a few pages of book VIII). In addition, three chapters from book II appear which are 'virtually identical' to the first edition. These he dates, rather vaguely, from between 1816 and 1830.

[4] A 19th edition appeared in 1980 (the last Hahlweg oversaw before his death in 1989). The main text is identical to the 18th (including the pagination). It adds a new afterword and updated bibliography. As all other editions (not to mention the English translations) have a different page numbering, I will include book and chapter numbers in my references.

The English translation of *On War* also no longer appears to be an issue. Of the three major ones, the most recent, undertaken by Michael Howard and Peter Paret (based on a partial draft by Angus Malcolm), is overwhelmingly considered the best.[5] This translation has received very little criticism.[6] It has become the standard text, not only in the English-speaking world, but it is even given preferential treatment by students in countries where one might have expected the original German to remain accessible. This brings out readability as one of its key advantages over the older translations (and even the original German!). Few would claim that an equally pleasurable read is offered by the translations of Colonel J. J. Graham (first published in 1873 and republished, essentially unrevised, by Colonel F. N. Maude in 1908) and O. J. Matthijs Jolles (first published in 1943).[7] A second, less immediately obvious advantage is that Howard and Paret could base their work on the Hahlweg edition. Graham and Jolles had used, not the first, but later editions. These had introduced changes, especially on an issue that is nowadays regarded as highly significant, the relationship between the general and the cabinet.[8] So, on the face of it, there appear few reasons for looking beyond the Howard–Paret translation.

The prevailing modern understanding of Clausewitz emphasizes the consistency and coherence of his thought throughout his life. Although it is accepted that Clausewitz, towards the end of his life, wanted to embark on a revision of *On War*, Peter Paret has claimed that this 'had not implied a rejection of earlier theories—he only meant to expand and refine them'. In Paret's view, 'despite the unevenness of its execution, *On War* offers an essentially consistent theory of conflict...'.[9] This understanding pervades the Howard–Paret translation. It also underpins the Hahlweg edition. But how justified is this view? Some scepticism seems warranted when one realizes that the dominant interpretation of

---

[5] Carl von Clausewitz, *On War*, ed. and trans. Michael Howard and Peter Paret, 2nd edn (Princeton, NJ, 1984; orig. 1976) (henceforth cited as *On War*).

[6] For one of the few exceptions (tucked away in a footnote), see Martin van Creveld, 'The Eternal Clausewitz', in Michael I. Handel (ed.), *Clausewitz and Modern Strategy* (London, 1986), 49 n. 2.

[7] Given the current popularity of Clausewitz, both are again in print. The Jolles translation was republished complete (with Sun Tzu's *The Art of Warfare*) in *The Book of War* (New York, 2000). All other widely available modern reprints are based on the Graham/Maude translation/edition of 1908. The preferred modern reprint of Graham was published by Barnes and Noble (New York, 2004). Unlike most other contemporary reprints (like the Penguin and the Wordsworth), this edition is complete and includes the Graham and Maude introductions, an index, as well as Clausewitz's 'Instruction to the Crown Prince' (also included in the Hahlweg, and older, German editions). It also contains, though this is perhaps less significant, a brief introduction by this chapter's author.

[8] The most notorious passage is in *Vom Kriege*, VIII, 6B, pp. 995–6; *On War*, 608.

[9] Peter Paret, 'The Genesis of *On War*', in *On War*, 4. See also Hahlweg, 'Clausewitzbild', 34–40.

*On War* changed radically in the aftermath of the Second World War. One major 'mis'interpretation in particular was corrected. The older interpreters were charged with having fundamentally misunderstood what all modern interpreters consider to be a *Hauptthema* in Clausewitz: the view that war was a political instrument.[10] They were criticized for having espoused a 'militarist' view that had led to the pursuit of war independent of political considerations. But how was it that older interpreters of Clausewitz could so strongly have believed in a view that modern interpreters have deemed so wrong? Was this a problem of a wilfully mistaken, wrong-headed interpretation, reinforced by some of the changes Count Brühl introduced? Or were there perhaps issues in the text in general that could have given substance to this particular view?

Very few voices have been raised against the contemporary interpretation shared by Hahlweg, Howard, and Paret. In English, the only major dissenters have been the philosopher W. B. Gallie and the historian Azar Gat.[11] It is perhaps no accident that a professional philosopher was more sensitive to possible incoherence in Clausewitz and that a historian whose project focused on the development of strategic thought detected a fundamental shift in the thinker's work. Gat argued that Clausewitz, for most of his life, espoused the doctrinaire view that in war—any war—one must strive to make the enemy defenceless through decisive battle. However, Clausewitz increasingly struggled to square this cherished idea with the historical record. In near desperation, Gat claims, he resorted to the then new-fangled device of Hegelian dialectics to reconcile the prescriptive theory and the historical practice in the synthesis of war as a political instrument—but died before he could work it out properly. Gallie also emphasized the stark 'duality' of Clausewitz's thinking between political control and war's inner, escalatory nature. He judged it 'essentially unresolved'.[12]

Their concerns have barely dented the consensus that *On War* contains a coherent argument. I would argue, however, that Gallie and Gat were on to something of critical importance. Building on their work, I will consider how the dominant English translation fares with respect to the 'duality' between political control and the escalatory 'imperative of destruction'.[13] I will argue that, on the issue of political control, the translation suggests more precision and coherence than is warranted, while on the issue of the imperative of

---

[10] Hahlweg, 'Clausewitzbild', 83.
[11] W. B. Gallie, 'Clausewitz on the Nature of War', in Gallie, *Philosophers of Peace and War, Kant, Clausewitz, Marx, Engels and Tolstoy* (Cambridge, 1978), 37–65; Gallie, 'Clausewitz Today', *Archives européennes sociologiques*, 19 (1978), 143–67; Azar Gat, *The Origins of Military Thought: From the Enlightenment to Clausewitz* (Oxford, 1989). See also Jan Willem Honig, 'Interpreting Clausewitz', *Security Studies*, 3/3 (Spring 1994), 571–80.
[12] W. B. Gallie, *Understanding War* (London, 1991), 60.
[13] Gat's words: Gat, *Origins*, 200.

destruction, it blurs the original's far greater clarity, consistency, and coherence. All in all, this means that *Vom Kriege* exhibits far greater tensions than is apparent from the Howard–Paret version of *On War*.

'All translation', Peter Paret has written, 'is, in the end, interpretation.'[14] Interpretation is shaped by a complex of factors. Quite apart from the technical qualities and skills of the translators, the issues of the day, and more generally, the prevailing *mentalité* are bound to influence the translation. One could expect each of the major Clausewitz translations to reflect, in many subtle ways, the different characters of their times. To Graham, Clausewitz must have been an author who helped explain the stunning, recent German successes in the wars of German unification. In Jolles's day, he had been transformed into a representative of unpalatable German militarist success. What *Charakter der Zeit* guided Howard and Paret? First of all, they emphasize Clausewitz's modernity. Like a good modern academic, Clausewitz does not simply approach his problem—war—as a timeless issue, but in terms of method, analysis, and judgement, he strives for the most objective approach. He is remarkably 'unideological'. His political beliefs are rarely seen to intrude on his analysis and, if they do, they tend to be seen as a respectable blend of 'early liberalism and of the brand of conservatism that was rooted in the tradition of enlightened absolutism'.[15] Their Clausewitz is a man therefore whom, in critical respects, they regard as a modern contemporary; a man who speaks directly to us and who, moreover, has pertinent things to say about the major challenge of the time when the translation was made, the Cold War.

This approach, one may argue, is very much coloured by their own liberal concerns and convictions, which, it should be added, have become ingrained in the Western psyche since the Second World War. A first concern is political control over the military. A proper relationship between the civil and the military came to be seen, after 1945, as essential in combating the evil of 'militarism' that was judged to have been a major contributing factor to the horror of both world wars.[16] Democratic control of armed forces is nowadays an uncontested issue. Related to this is a second, more specific concern with the political control of war or, to be precise, with the control of the use of force. Even if the military were properly subordinated to civilian authority (as they would be in a democracy), there remained an issue with the potentially

---

[14] Carl von Clausewitz, *Historical and Political Writings*, ed. and trans. Peter Paret and Daniel Moran (Princeton, NJ, 1992), xii.

[15] Peter Paret, *Clausewitz and the State: the Man, His Theories, and His Times*, 2nd edn (Princeton, NJ, 1986), ix–x, where he reacts to C. B. A. Behrens, 'Which Side Was Clausewitz on?', *New York Review of Books* (14 October 1976), 41–4. Behrens suggested that Clausewitz was much more of a conservative political thinker than Paret claimed.

[16] This is a major concern in post-Second World War German historiography which strongly pervades Hahlweg's approach, e.g. Hahlweg, 'Clausewitzbild', 83–90.

disastrous escalation of the use of force, especially with nuclear weapons. Avoiding a nuclear holocaust was a pre-eminent *policy* concern at the time of the translation's gestation. Underlying all this, finally, is a normative conviction: war is an evil. Although it might be unrealistic to assume that war could be prevented from ever happening again, it nonetheless must be regarded as a means of last resort which may only be fought for a just political cause with the least possible force. These typical Cold War concerns cannot but have attuned the translators to a strand in Clausewitz that saw war as a reasonable, controlled instrument of policy.[17]

That Howard and Paret privilege this strand in Clausewitz can be seen in their treatment of the other, the 'imperative of destruction' strand. Let us begin with one seemingly innocuous example: the translation of the word 'Niederwerfung'. Although (as we will see in a moment), they are by no means consistent, Howard and Paret have a pronounced preference for translating this word as 'defeat'.[18] This is a defensible choice of words, but *Niederwerfung*, which literally means 'to throw down', suggests something altogether more definite and final than 'defeat'. It suggests putting an enemy in a situation from which no recovery is possible. 'Defeat', on the other hand, is more readily understood as a transitory situation, a moment in a process which, overall, is marked by both reversals and successes. One suffers, or inflicts, *a* defeat. An enemy, however, is only once 'overthrown'—to use the word by which *Niederwerfung* is traditionally translated. *Niederwerfung* became an established technical term in the German military vocabulary of the nineteenth century and first half of the twentieth century. It possessed a specific meaning, which the less decisive 'defeat' does not adequately capture: the destruction of the enemy's means of resistance, that is, his armed forces. This came to be regarded as the central aim in war. Clausewitz already understood the term as such and, indeed, he can be credited with developing the conceptual framework that explained why the enemy's *Niederwerfung* played such a singular and critical role in war. The contemporary English and French military literature assimilated the idea and translated the term, respectively, with 'overthrow' and *renversement*. One can understand the avoidance of the archaic and perhaps

---

[17] In the conference where I presented the first version of this chapter, Sir Michael Howard stated that his interest in Clausewitz was sparked, first and foremost, by Clausewitz's argument that moral factors can overcome friction, rather than by these broader concerns. Sir Michael, however, did not disagree with my contention that his *War and the Liberal Conscience* (Oxford, 1981) can be seen as a key to his *oeuvre*. Central to this work is the liberal struggle with controlling the evil of war. The political instrumentality of war is also a key theme in his introductory essay to the Clausewitz translation.

[18] This is particularly marked in book VIII, chapters 4 ('Closer Definition of the Military Objective: The Defeat [*Niederwerfung*] of the Enemy') and 8 ('The Plan of War Designed to Lead to the Total Defeat [*Niederwerfung*] of the Enemy').

also extremist term 'overthrow' in a modern translation, but it seems hard to justify if one wants to remain faithful to Clausewitz's basic ideas.

Why was the overthrow of the enemy the key aim in war and why should it be understood as the destruction of the enemy's means of resistance? Here another less violent, more modern choice of words in the Howard–Paret translation may obscure the logic. Clausewitz posits, on the first page of *On War*, that war is 'an act of force to compel our enemy to do our will'. This, if it is to be achieved, requires making him, in Howard and Paret's translation, 'powerless'.[19] The word Clausewitz uses, however, is more specific. He writes 'wehrlos' or defenceless. 'Power' suggests something broader and vaguer that may be more in tune with modern perceptions of international relations which stress the importance of power, but I would argue that Clausewitz intends to be more precise.[20] Making the enemy 'wehrlos', or 'disarming' him, is the natural aim in war, as without means of resistance the enemy has no choice but to do the victor's will. It therefore constitutes the focus of military operations, or what Clausewitz calls the *Ziel*, or military aim. Choosing 'powerless', because of its broader, more political meaning, might also easily further confuse the rigorous distinction Clausewitz makes throughout the first chapter between the political aim, or *Zweck*, and the subordinate military *Ziel*. Howard and Paret's translation does not reproduce Clausewitz's rigour: *Zweck* variously appears as aim, object, purpose, end, goal, and requirements. These translations overlap with those chosen for *Ziel*. As neither *Zweck* nor *Ziel* always appears with their clarifying adjective 'political' or 'military' (*kriegerisch*), English readers must work harder to uncover the logic than Clausewitz intended.

Clausewitz is at pains to emphasize the importance and specificity of disarming the enemy and, in this context, also repeatedly clarifies the relationship between disarmament and overthrow. On the opening page of book I, chapter 2, he writes that the aim in war is 'den Gegner niederzuwerfen, d. h. ihn wehrlos zu machen'—'to overthrow the enemy, that is, to make him defenceless'. Translating this with 'to overcome the enemy and disarm him' (90) does not quite equal the clarity of the original. Other examples of clear and consistent use of the terms abound; in the third section of chapter 3 of book I, he talks about 'Entwaffnen oder Niederwerfen des Gegners' (where the '*oder*', or 'or', must be interpreted as indicating an equivalent, not an alternative).[21] Subsequently, in the fourth section, he writes 'daß die Entwaffnung oder das Niederwerfen des Feindes, wie man es nennen will, immer das Ziel

---

[19] *On War*, I, 1, § 2, p. 75; *Vom Kriege*, 191–2.
[20] The translation is not consistent: the second occurrence in the title of § 4 'das Ziel ist, den Feind wehrlos zu machen' becomes 'The aim is to disarm the enemy' (*On War*, I, 1, p. 77). In § 11 (80), it is again 'powerless'.
[21] *Vom Kriege*, I, 1, § 3, p. 192.

des kriegerischen Aktes sein muß'—'that the disarmament or the overthrow of the enemy, call it what you will, must always be the aim of the military act'.[22] The opening sentence of book VII, chapter 3 reads: 'Das Niederwerfen des Feindes ist das Ziel des Krieges, Vernichtung der feindlichen Streitkräfte das Mittel'—'The overthrow of the enemy is the aim of war, the destruction of the enemy armed forces the means'.[23] And, finally, in the concluding book on the plan of war one reads 'daß die Niederwerfung des Feindes, folglich die Vernichtung seiner Streitkräfte das Hauptziel des ganzen kriegerischen Aktes sei'—'that the overthrow of the enemy, consequently the destruction of his armed forces is the main aim of the whole military act'.[24] One further thing is worth noting here: Clausewitz's choice of the word *Akt* (which also already appears in his definition of war: 'War is an *act* of force etc.'). The use of this word reinforces my earlier point on 'overthrow' in that overthrowing an enemy suggests a definite end result. This makes sense as part of an 'act', as this not only implies something that possesses a clear beginning, but also a clear finality. In Howard and Paret, where the word *Akt* is directly translated, it usually appears as 'action'—which is open to the same objection I raised with respect to the choice of 'defeat' instead of 'overthrow': it does not possess the same sense of defined singularity, of clear finality, of the German.

Despite a clearly consistent, coherent, and very deliberate choice of words, the Howard–Paret translation renders the quoted passages as follows (I have italicized the different translation choices for *Niederwerfung*): 'disarm or *defeat*' (p. 75); 'to *overcome* the enemy, or disarm him—call it what you will—must always be the aim of warfare' (note also the inversion!) (p. 77); 'In war, the *subjugation* of the enemy is the end, and the destruction of his fighting forces the means' (p. 526); and 'that the grand objective of all military action is to *overthrow* the enemy—which means destroying his armed forces' (p. 577). This liberal approach to translating terms is typical of the translation. Howard and Paret justify it in their introductory 'translators' note' (pp. xi–xii):

we have not hesitated to translate the same term in different ways if the context seemed to demand it.... Clausewitz himself was far from consistent in his terminology, as might be expected of a writer who was less concerned with establishing a formal system or doctrine than with achieving understanding and clarity of expression.

They quote Clausewitz himself in their support: 'Strict adherence to terms would clearly result in little more than pedantic distinctions'. Yet, as the examples cited suggest, the approach is not without problems. Readers who

---

[22] *Vom Kriege*, I, 1, § 4, p. 194. The 'wie man es nennen will' ('call it what you will') immediately after *Niederwerfen* may indicate that it was a neologism in Clausewitz's day. Note (see below) that Howard and Paret invert disarmament and overthrow.
[23] *Vom Kriege*, VII, 3, p. 875.   [24] Ibid, VIII, 1, p. 949.

wish to judge for themselves whether Clausewitz was perhaps consistent and possibly attempted to establish a formal system and doctrine face a difficult task if they can only rely on this translation. Moreover, the credibility of the approach is not helped by checking the justificatory Clausewitz quote against the German original. The original (which occurs in a chapter on 'Avantgarde und Vorposten') allows for a very different reading: 'es ist aber klar, daß man wenig mehr als eine pedantische Unterscheidung gewinnen würde, wenn man sich streng an die Worte halten wollte.'—'It is clear, however, that one would gain little more than a pedantic distinction if one were to adhere strictly to the terms.'[25] The definite article in 'die Worte' ('*the* terms') indicates what is also confirmed by a reading of the context in paragraph and chapter: that there is a specific reference to the terms under discussion, *Vorposten* and *Avantgarde*, and not necessarily to terms in general.

The fundamental logic underpinning the necessity of aiming for the enemy's disarmament follows from Clausewitz's argument that escalation (to use a modern, but for once, appropriate, term)[26] is inherent in the use of force. The employment of force by one party sets off an escalatory interaction, as the other party must use more force than the first in order to prevail; in response to which the first has no choice but to use even more force, etc. In short, a failure to attempt to out-escalate the enemy offers him an opportunity to win. Logic therefore demands that the act of war, from the moment it starts, involves an *instantaneous* discharge of violence by which the protagonists aim to make each other defenceless. Clausewitz calls this 'absolute war'. He chooses this word very deliberately. 'Absolute' indicates that this is war 'absolved', loosened, set free from reality. Absolute war is a conceptual construct and represents an ideal which can never be achieved in reality. It is important because it helps reveal the fundamental tendency which is inherent in war, but which reality obscures by imposing modifications.

What Clausewitz, in effect, sets up is a basic distinction between, as he puts it in the title of book VIII, chapter 2, 'absoluter und wirklicher Krieg', 'ideal and real war'. Many have struggled with Clausewitz's typology and have confused it with what is a different and modern typology of 'total war' and 'limited war'. They see absolute war as the same as total war. In other words, absolute war becomes, like total war, a 'real war'. This is thus logically, but also historiographically, wrong.[27] The term 'total war' as such does not appear in

[25] *Vom Kriege*, V, 7, p. 539; *On War*, p. 306.

[26] Lawrence Freedman, 'On the Tiger's Back: The Development of the Concept of Escalation', in Roman Kolkowicz (ed.), *The Logic of Nuclear Terror* (Boston, MA, 1987), 109–52.

[27] Raymond Aron, *Penser la guerre, Clausewitz*, vol. I, *L'âge européen* (Paris, 1976), 26: 'quiconque assimile guerre absolue et guerre totale, quiconque présente la guerre absolue comme un idéal à atteindre, n'interprète pas, il falsifie.' Aron refers to those who desire to make total war,

Clausewitz. It was invented towards the end of the First World War in France and popularized by the German General Erich Ludendorff in the mid-1930s. It was not an ideal, but a form of real war.[28] Although one could fit it into Clausewitz's scheme as a subcategory of 'real war', total war only approximates the absolute. The two cannot coincide. Moreover, though it is tempting to read a concept of 'limited war' into Clausewitz, again one is dealing here with a modern term in English that became popular only in the 1950s. This term also, as such, does not appear in Clausewitz and, as we will see, what could easily be regarded as an equivalent needs to be approached with careful circumspection. Howard and Paret themselves, in their writings on Clausewitz, seem unclear at times about the distinctions between these four types of war. Howard, in his little biography *Clausewitz*, opens a chapter entitled 'Limited and absolute war' as follows: 'The distinction which Clausewitz drew between "limited" and "absolute" (or "total") war....'[29] Paret, in a chapter on Clausewitz in the famous *Makers of Modern Strategy*, defines 'absolute war' as 'absolute violence ending in the total destruction of one side by the other' and immediately continues: 'The thesis of total war as the ideal war....'[30] These confusions are caused by a failure to understand properly Clausewitz's categories and the radical way in which his thinking evolves.

but the error equally applies to those who merely equate them as analytical categories. See also ibid. 409.

[28] Erich Ludendorff, *Der totale Krieg* (Munich, 1935). The first instance of the use of the term I found is in Léon Daudet, *La guerre totale* (Paris, 1918). Daudet, the editor of the royalist paper *L'Action Française*, defines total war in this polemic (8–9) as 'l'extension de la lutte, dans ses phases aiguës comme dans ses phases chroniques, aux domaines politique, économique, commercial, industriel, intellectuel, juridique et financier. Ce ne sont pas seulement les armées qui se battent, ce sont aussi les traditions, les institutions, les coutumes, les codes, les esprits et surtout les banques. L'Allemagne a mobilisé dans tous ces plans, sur tous ces points.... Elle a constamment cherché, au delà du front militaire, disorganisation matérielle et morale du peuple qu'elle attaquait.' Only some ten years later the term again appears (though without any conceptual exposition): Louis Pauly, *Occupation allemande et guerre totale, Etude de l'évolution du régime des personnes et des biens d'après l'experience de la dernière guerre* (Nancy, 1930) and Henri Lémery, *De la guerre totale à la paix mutilée* (Paris, 1931). Beatrice Heuser, *Reading Clausewitz* (London, 2002), 119, reaches the same conclusion.

[29] (Oxford: Oxford University Press, 1983), 47. See also his *War in European History* (Oxford: Oxford University Press, 1976), 96.

[30] Peter Paret (ed.), *Makers of Modern Strategy from Machiavelli to the Nuclear Age* (Princeton, NJ: Princeton University Press, 1986), 199. He does get it right in his *Clausewitz and the State*, 364–5. To be fair, in three instances Clausewitz contradicts himself and suggests that with Napoleon absolute war had become a reality (*Vom Kriege*, VIII, 2, 953, 954; VIII, 3B, 973; see also VIII, 6B, 992; *On War*, 580, 593, and 606). Quite apart from the logic developed in the first chapter, he explicitly gets it right with reference to Napoleon in VIII, 3B, 972 ('[war] hat sich seiner wahren Natur, seiner absoluten Volkommenheit sehr genähert.') and VIII, 6B, 998 (*On War*, 593 and 610). See also I, 1, 22: 'das sie [die Kriegskunst] nirgends das Absolute und Gewisse erreichen kann'.

The confusion is also reflected in the translation of *On War*. On critical points in the sections where the concept of 'absolute war' is developed, it lacks clarity. Absolute war, Clausewitz argues, could only exist in reality if three conditions could be met. First, war must be an isolated act, something that arises 'urplötzlich' without any reference to 'political life' (*Staatsleben*). The 'ur' emphasizes the primeval suddenness of the event, which is rather too lamely rendered by 'suddenly' in Howard–Paret (78). Second, war should consist of 'einem einzigen Schlag ohne Dauer', that is, 'a single blow of *no duration*'. This instanteneity, which the logic demands, is not properly reflected in translating this with 'a single *short* blow' (my italics; 79). Finally, the result of war must be 'absolute'. 'Absolute' is translated with 'final' (80), which given the immediate context is defensible, but, within the broader context of the importance Clausewitz attaches to this particular word, is more difficult to accept. Once more, the translation may suggest less logical rigour and precision than the original possesses.

Clausewitz's argument that the ideal of absolute war reveals the escalatory tendency that is inherent in 'real war' suggests that there should only be one type of real war: the one that aims at making the enemy defenceless through destroying his armed forces in decisive battle. Absolute war provided the conceptual proof that meeting this imperative was what conducting (any) real war required, and constituted its one and only guiding principle. Although Clausewitz had long recognized that political aims could vary, the strategic aim to be pursued in war with force of arms could not. In his *Strategie von 1804*, he had already stated this.[31] His personal experience of the campaign of 1806 confirmed the accuracy of the idea. The Prussians, with their limited political aims, lost the cataclysmic battle of Jena–Auerstedt because they put in the lesser military effort and were overwhelmed by the man who had understood the true, escalatory nature of war. In an earlier draft of the first chapter of *Vom Kriege*, which seems to date from the 1820s, he reaffirmed this view. At the end of the chapter, Clausewitz wrote,

We have to come back again to the general concept [*Totalbegriff*] of war, in order to give it proper emphasis, because it is the fundamental idea [*Grundvorstellung*] from which everything else follows.

With this general concept, the aim [*Ziel*] of the military act is to make the enemy defenceless. This begins with the destruction of the enemy's armed forces and ends

---

[31] See Carl von Clausewitz, *Strategie aus dem Jahr 1804 mit Zusätzen von 1808 und 1809*, ed. Eberhard Kessel (Hamburg, 1937). Paret, *Clausewitz*, 90–1, (mis)paraphrases/quotes the relevant passage to suggest that Clausewitz claims that there are two types of war. This is incorrect, Clausewitz suggests that there may be two fundamentally different political aims, but they nonetheless lead to one type of war which aims at the destruction of the enemy's armed forces. See Honig, 'Interpreting Clausewitz', 575–6 and Aron, *Penser la guerre*, I, 92.

with the overthrow of the opponent. We deliberately pause at this image because it exactly describes the concept.[32]

The same position reappears at the beginning of the two opening chapters of book VIII on the 'Kriegsplan' or 'War Plan'. As the title of the book also suggests, what one would expect, in essence, is the development of one 'war plan'.[33] This plan indeed appears in the title of *On War*'s final chapter: 'Kriegsplan, wenn Niederwerfung des Feindes das Ziel ist'—which Howard and Paret translate as 'The Plan of a War Designed to Lead to the Total Defeat of the Enemy'. Yet, as the German title implies, Clausewitz had begun to allow for more than one *Ziel*, or strategic aim, to be pursued in war.[34] This indeed emerges as a central concern of book VIII: the possibility that not all 'real wars' uniquely required a plan of overthrow. In short, Clausewitz moves from a view that sees only one strategy as appropriate in pursuit of any political aim to one that begins to see a possibility that different political aims may be expressed in a variety of strategic aims (and thus war plans). The problem that emerges is how the pursuit of a limited political aim can break the escalatory tendency which absolute war reveals. This conceptualization is not adequately captured by the common dichotomy of absolute/total war and limited war, as it fails to distinguish adequately ideal from real war, and the changing relationship Clausewitz discerns between political and strategic aims from which ultimately the conclusion emerges that there must be two types of 'real war'.

Clausewitz remains remarkably obsessed in book VIII with his original 'Grundvorstellung' of 'Niederwerfung'. He repeatedly concludes—in

---

[32] 'müssen wir wieder auf den Totalbegriff des Krieges zurück kommen, um ihn gehörig herauszuheben, weil er die Grundvorstellung ist, von der alles ausgeht. Bei diesem Totalbegriff ist das Ziel des kriegerischen Aktes den Feind wehrlos zu machen. Dies fängt an mit der Vernichtung der feindlichen Streitmassen und endigt mit der Niederwerfung des Gegners. Wir bleiben bei diesem Bilde absichtlich stehen, weil es genau den Begriff bezeichnet.' Clausewitz, *Schriften*, II, 635–6. Paret, *Clausewitz and the State*, 369, rejects the view that Clausewitz preferred 'the major, decisive battle' by quoting his statement that 'many roads lead to success' which 'do not all involve the opponent's outright defeat [*Niederwerfung*]' (369 n. 31 referring to *On War*, I, 2, p. 94; *Vom Kriege*, p. 221). But when one reads on, one finds that the chapter concludes that these many roads can turn out to be *Schleifwege*, or slippery roads (Howard and Paret have 'devious paths'), on which the *Kriegsgott* can catch the general who does not realize that the 'first-born son of war' remains 'das Bestreben zur Vernichtung der feindlichen Streitkraft' (*On War*, I, 2, p. 99; *Vom Kriege*, 229–30). Hence, 'daß also, mit einem Wort, die Vernichtung der feindlichen Streitkraft unter allen Zwecken, die im Kriege verfolgt werden können, immer als der über alles gebietende erscheint.' (ibid.)

[33] Howard and Paret translate the book's title with the plural 'War Plans'. The use of the singular in this case can be read as signifying plans in general and indeed the book offers an (incomplete) development of two types of plan.

[34] A draft of a chapter, 'Zum Kriegs-Plan mit beschränktem Ziel', which one would have expected to follow after what is now the final chapter, appears in Clausewitz, *Schriften*, II, 675–80. It however merely suggests that a limited strategic aim should only follow from limited means. There is no mention of it following from political considerations.

chapters 2, 3A and 3B—with a reaffirmation of his faith, even though the preceding argument has cast doubt on the idea. His strength of feeling is further illustrated by his choice of words for that type of war that does not follow the logic that escalation is inherent in war and that one must always aim at the enemy's overthrow. He repeatedly, and pejoratively, calls these wars a 'Halbheit' or 'Halbdinge', 'half-things' or 'halflings'.[35] The choice of words, and the fact that it appears in exactly those chapters where Clausewitz begins to see that there must be more than one aim in war, clearly suggests that he is reluctant to concede that his cherished construct of 'Niederwerfung' may not be of universal applicability. His deep-seated reservations are also revealed in the adjective he attaches to a mode of behaviour that logically should have no obvious place in war: the defence. Making the enemy defenceless requires unceasing offensive action, as any faltering or decision to defend would give the enemy an opportunity to seize the initiative and prevail. The defence he therefore calls a form of war with a 'negative' purpose, while the offence has a 'positive purpose'.

Howard and Paret soften Clausewitz's deliberately pejorative choice of words. The 'Halbdinge', these 'halflings', usually become 'half-hearted war'—which takes the sting out of it.[36] The 'negative' purpose of the defence is rendered as 'passive'—which is also less value-laden.[37] Clausewitz thus emerges in English as a more reasonable, balanced author. All in all, such translation choices mean that a particular characteristic of Clausewitz does not come

---

[35] *Vom Kriege*, VIII, 2, 953 ('Halbheit' and, referring not to war to man's character, 'Halbding'); VIII, 6A, 988 (twice *Halbheit*, once referring to the views current at princely courts) and 989 ('halbe Krieg'); VIII, 6B, 991 and 996 ('Halbding'); VIII, 8, 1004 ('Halbheit'). 'Halbding' also appears twice in the earlier chapter on that other anomaly in war, the 'Stillstand': III, 16, 409 and 410 (as well as 'halbe Politik'); and also in VI, 8, 659.

[36] *On War*, 218 (once 'tame and half-hearted' and once just 'half-hearted'; in Paret, *Clausewitz and the State*, 367, 'a fragmentary thing'), 219 ('half-hearted politics'), 604 and 613. Other choices can be found on: 387 ('mongrel affairs'); 579 (whereas in the original *Halbheit* describes a characteristic of man who does not understand war, in Howard and Paret, as 'inconsistent', it is ascribed to the situation in which he finds himself); 580 ('der Krieg zu etwas ganz anderem wird, als er dem Begriff nach sein sollte, zu einem Halbding, zu einem Wesen ohne inneren Zusammenhang': 'war turns into something quite different from what it should be according to theory—turns into something incoherent and incomplete'); 603 (once 'ambigous' and once 'half-and-half affair'); 606 ('ein Halbding, ein Widerspruch in sich': 'incomplete and self-contradictory'); 609 ('half-and-half affair'). To be fair, the Jolles translation consistently prefers 'half-hearted' (443, 444, 656, 902, 931, 932, 933, 934, 938, and 944). Graham varies his choice, but 'half-and-half' predominates (180, 395, 643, 675; but also 'shilly-shally', 181, 672; 'abnormal', 673; 'the half War', 674; 'half-measure', 679; and 'indecision', 686).

[37] e.g., *On War*, VI, 1, pp. 358 and 359. An exception is found in I, 2, p. 98: 'The effort to destroy the enemy's forces has a positive purpose and leads to positive results, whose final aim is the enemy's collapse [*Niederwerfung*].... The policy [*Bestreben*] with a positive purpose calls the act of destruction [*Vernichtungsakt*] into being; the policy [*Bestreben*] with a negative purpose waits for it.'

## Problems of Text and Translation

through as well as in the German original: his style of debating with himself and the increasing desperation, which becomes so marked in the pivotal books VI and VIII, at the problems which 'the imperative of destruction' encounters. Why does war so often come to a standstill? Why does the defence not only exist at all, but why is it such an integral mode of war? And, finally, what could break the escalatory spiral?[38]

Clausewitz considered several solutions to the problem of why not all real wars displayed ceaseless offensive activity aimed at making the enemy defenceless. Friction was one. The fallibility of human nature another. A third was inequalities in the balance of forces between belligerents. A fourth was the clever insight that without a defender deciding to resist, war (and thus the offence) would not be. In the end, however, he decided that all of these solutions were partial and of a secondary order. All featured in his final intellectual construct, but they had to cede pride of place to a new 'Standpunkt' from which a unified understanding of war could be achieved: war, as every one today can paraphrase after Clausewitz, is the continuation of...but of what exactly? policy or politics? The Howard and Paret translation makes a clear choice: war is an instrument of policy. But does the German suggest so straightforward a choice? Clausewitz actually uses the word 'Politik' (and the adjective and adverb 'politisch') in two meanings which he does not carefully disentangle. The first is in the sense of 'policy', that is, a specific course of action pursued by an authority that represents a political body, like a government. The second is in the broader sense of 'politics', that is, as the medium, the *milieu*, or the system or body (as in 'body politic'), which gives meaning to political activity and from which particular policies emerge.

Raymond Aron speaks of a 'demi-confusion' which particularly marks book VIII, chapter 6B, where Clausewitz develops the idea that war is a political instrument. Even in the conceptually most advanced first chapter of book I, Aron points out,

When [Clausewitz] writes that all-out wars, those that approximate the perfect war, are no less political than the others because politics, in the sense of opposing interests, gives it its extreme character, his thinking does not lack logic, but he only retains politics in one of its two meanings: that of objectivised socio-historical relations. When war approaches the pure and simple explosion of violence, politics in the subjective sense loses all or part of its mastery or sovereignty.[39]

---

[38] There is an undated note in which he tries to list the key questions that lead to a *Neuer Standpunkt*: Carl von Clausewitz, *Geist und Tat, Das Vermächtnis des Soldaten und Denkers*, ed. Walther Malmsten Schering (Stuttgart, 1941), 309–11.

[39] 'Quand il écrit que les guerres à outrance, proches de la guerre parfaite, ne sont pas moins politiques que les autres parce que la politique (les intérêts opposés) leur confère ce caractère extrême, il ne manque pas à la logique de sa pensée mais il ne retient qu'un des deux sens de la

70   *Jan Willem Honig*

Howard and Paret, however, are remarkably consistent in translating 'Politik' as 'policy'—including in the chapter to which Aron refers. Of the nine times the word appears in book I, chapter 1, they only once use 'politics'. They even turn the adjective 'politisch' into the noun 'policy' the five times it appears in conjunction with 'Akt', 'Handlungen', 'Instrument', and 'Werkzeug'. In book VIII, chapter 6B, 'Politik' appears forty-two times. 'Politics' is chosen only twice (including once as a translation of the oft-used phrase 'politische Verkehr'). In three cases, by choosing 'political conditions' the meaning seems to move in the direction of 'politics'. 'Policy', on the other hand, is chosen twenty-seven times. In addition, 'Politik' is translated four times as 'statesmen' and once as 'statecraft'.[40] The original term and the possible (in)consistency in usage will not be obvious to the English reader.

Sir Michael Howard reminded participants in the conference in which this chapter was first presented that Peter Paret and he had great reservations about choosing the word 'politics', as they strongly believed that this word possessed a very negative connotation in English.[41] That may be true, though it seems to apply first and foremost to understanding 'politics' in the more restricted and different meaning of the disagreeable *business* of politics. Yet, does that justify the choice of 'policy' instead? I do not here want to engage in an evaluation of each occurrence, but rather make a general point. The critical issue in Clausewitz, I have argued, is the tension, or even the contradiction, between the escalatory logic of absolute war and real war. 'Politik' is intended to resolve the contradiction (and even when one denies there is a contradiction, 'Politik' remains a critical concept in controlling war). But since we are dealing with an unfinished attempt which employs an insufficiently worked out concept, a case can be made for allowing readers as much of an opportunity to make up their own mind and not foreclosing choice by using a word that only partially

---

politique: celui des relations socio-historiques objectivées. Quand la guerre se rapproche de la pure et simple explosion de violence, l'entendement duquel relève la politique subjective perd tout ou partie de sa maîtrise ou de sa souveraineté.' Aron, *Penser la guerre*, 410. Another example can be found in the letter Clausewitz wrote to Major von Roeder on 22 December 1827, where he first writes 'Der ganze Kriegsplan geht unmittelbar aus dem politischen Dasein der beiden kriegführenden Staaten sowie aus ihren Verhältnissen zu anderen hervor.' This suggests that 'politics' broadly understood informs the plan. But then, in the same paragraph, he defines war as 'nichts als die Fortsetzung der politischen Bestrebungen mit veränderten Mitteln' (my emphasis). 'Zwei Briefe des Generals von Clausewitz. Gedanken zur Abwehr', *Militärwissenschaftliche Rundschau*, 2 (1937), Sonderheft, 6.

[40] In addition, the noun 'Politik' is turned into an adjective or adverb four times and once it is not translated; 'politische Verkehr' and 'politische Element' are also each translated once with 'policy'.

[41] This appears to be of long-standing in the English language: Graham (and also Jolles) strongly preferred 'policy'. He used 'politics' only four times (172, 381, 652 ['foreign politics'], 672), while 'policy' appears 63 times in all.

covers the meaning of the original. The context within which 'policy' appears in the English translation gives ample ground for realizing that Clausewitz has a broader concept of 'politics', and some English readers may suspect the repeated appearance of 'policy' is somewhat at odds with this context. But in choosing to translate 'Politik' the way they do, Howard and Paret make what is already a complex challenge for a reader with German even more difficult for a reader with only English.

Quite apart from offering a way of avoiding the bad word of 'politics', choosing 'policy' has other modern advantages too. It suggests that there is an immediate tool that can control war. Policy is an instrument that can make a direct difference. We tend to lionize good policy or 'statecraft', as exemplified by the US President John F. Kennedy, a true 'statesman' who averted a nuclear holocaust in the 1962 Cuban missile crisis. When wars go wrong, as with Kennedy's successor Lyndon Johnson in Vietnam, we blame bad policy over all other factors. Furthermore, in the West, we have stable, entrenched democratic political systems which are seen as an uncontroversial, unassailable 'public good'. This makes it difficult to accept that there may be instances in which democracies, because it is in their nature as political systems, can only offer bad policy options that result in bad wars. To many, Johnson's Vietnam policy appears somehow to be unrepresentative of the essentially 'good' US political system. But can wars, such as Vietnam, and also the military interventions the West has undertaken since the end of the Cold War, be convincingly understood as a simple story of the good, or bad, policies of particular governments? Surely, the answer to the question of what controls war must be sought at a level deeper than that of the surface phenomenon of policy?

The embeddedness of policy within politics suggests one reason for not wanting to push policy too far as the controlling agent of conflict and war. But even if one were to cling to this notion, there still remains an issue over how exactly policy restrains the actual use of force. How does a limited political aim overcome the escalation that Clausewitz claims is inherent in war? Conceptually, Clausewitz constructs his argument in such a way that there is no compelling, intrinsic reason for a belligerent to stick with using limited means in pursuit of a limited political aim, because all it does is offer the opponent the obvious advantage of winning through escalation. He sensed that the reason had less to do with policy and more with certain 'politische Verhältnisse', that is, political conditions or relationships. Pursuing this possible line of thought, however, leads to a more sombre reading of Clausewitz which suggests that war in the modern world is less easily controllable than an emphasis on policy might imply. It also reveals a Clausewitz who is more conservative, anti-populist, and anti-democratic than we might like.

Which 'political conditions' might be responsible for war's escalation? Clausewitz's answer is quite clear: the involvement of the people in the politics of the state, or, in a word, democracy. This is clearly implied by his famous socio-historical analysis of war which he presents in book VIII, chapter 3B. It is also suggested by the 'miraculous' trinity which appears at the end of his first chapter.[42] Here he associates the people with 'der ursprünglichen Gewaltsamkeit seines [war's] elementes, dem Haß und der Feindschaft, die wie ein blinder Naturtrieb anzusehen sind'. And although he adds that the people's emotions and 'drive' could vary in strength, there is more than a hint here that involving the people in politics and war would be an escalatory step. Escalation control should thus include keeping the people out of politics. This is indeed how Clausewitz was understood when a renewed interest in his concept of 'Politik' emerged in Germany just as the tide of total war turned against that country in 1942. People like the one-time chief of the general staff, General Ludwig Beck, and the historian Gerhard Ritter, who both became associated with the conservative opposition to Hitler, saw the democratic ideas of the French Revolution as a fatal seed that had been planted into German politics. The outgrowth had been the populist Nazi regime and, with its populism, came disastrous, all-consuming total war.[43] What they, and their fellow conspirators, favoured instead was an authoritarian political order which would again remove the people from politics. Hitler's foreign policy they never much objected to—a *Großdeutschland* was an uncontroversial demand. Their issue was with the politics which had created the Führer and his war.

Ritter's and Beck's reading of Clausewitz today represents a controversial, if not wholly discredited political view. The same applies to the 'militarist'

---

[42] Howard and Paret translate 'eine wunderliche Dreifältigkeit' with 'a remarkable trinity' (89). But since Clausewitz struggles so desperately with fitting 'Politik' into his theory, might not the idea, which appears nowhere else in his work and almost seems an afterthought in the chapter (and which anyway invokes a mystical Christian concept), have looked to him like a true miracle?

[43] For Beck, see especially his June 1942 talk 'Die Lehre vom totalen Kriege: Eine kritische Auseinandersetzung', published in Ludwig Beck, *Studien*, ed. Hans Speidel (Stuttgart, 1955), 227–58. See also the works by Klaus-Jürgen Müller, *General Ludwig Beck: Studien und Dokumente zur politisch-militärischen Vorstellungswelt und Tätigkeit des Generalstabschefs des deutschen Heeres 1933–1938* (Boppard, 1980); 'Clausewitz, Ludendorff and Beck: Some Remarks on Clausewitz' Influence on German Military Thinking in the 1930s and 1940s', in Handel (ed.), *Clausewitz and Modern Strategy*, 240–66; and 'Colonel-General Ludwig Beck, Chief of the General Staff, 1933–1938', in Müller, *The Army, Politics and Society in Germany, 1933–1945: Studies on the Army's Relation to Nazism* (Manchester, UK: Manchester University Press, 1987), 54–99. For Ritter, see his 'Die Lehre Carls von Clausewitz vom politischen Sinn des Krieges', *Historische Zeitschrift*, 167 (1942), 41–65. Ritter had corresponded with Beck on this issue: Müller, 'Clausewitz, Ludendorff and Beck', 257–58. The article later appeared in chapter 3 of the first volume of the work for which he became internationally famous, *Staatskunst und Kriegshandwerk: Das Problem des Militarismus in Deutschland* (Munich, 1954), and which appeared in English under the title *The Sword and the Sceptre*.

interpretation that saw war escaping from political oversight. Both of these 'politicized' readings can, however, find considerable support in the German text (and, in case of the latter, even without Count Brühl's changes). Howard's and Paret's liberal reading can also find support, though this is perhaps not as strong as their translation suggests. But when it comes to offering a translation of a text, translators have a special responsibility. Translations tend to exclude the detailed scholarly apparatus which, in normal academic texts, serve to allow readers to evaluate and verify independently an author's argument. Translations should therefore strive to remain as faithful as possible to the original language in order to allow readers who have no access to the original the greatest possible opportunity to reflect on the richness of interpretative possibilities the text offers. By obscuring *On War*'s coherence on *Niederwerfung* and by blurring the struggle with *Politik*, the Howard and Paret translation compromises the ability of English readers to understand properly and evaluate critically two issues which lie at the heart of Clausewitz's intellectual engagement with the problem of war. This is all the more disappointing, since these issues have remained of critical importance to this day.

To conclude, I am aware that I have made an argument that to some may seem to amount to a desire to resurrect a far less readable and accessible Clausewitz in English. Yet, that would unjustly belittle the great achievement of Michael Howard and Peter Paret and their translation, which is that, precisely by avoiding these pitfalls, they created a 'Clausewitz Renaissance'. Without their work there would not have been the extensive and lively interest in Clausewitz in the English-speaking world we have seen over the past thirty years. We would also not have had the conference on Clausewitz which occasioned the writing of this piece. And perhaps paradoxically, without the 'Clausewitz Renaissance', Clausewitz would probably no longer have attracted much interest in Germany. If anyone should feel challenged by this contribution, it is German scholars. If Clausewitz's intellectual development is, as I have suggested, much richer, more complicated, and thus even more interesting, than is commonly believed, then Germans should form the vanguard of a movement that undertakes the vital task of properly dating Clausewitz's works and systematically analysing the stages in the development of his thought.

# 4

# The Primacy of Policy and the 'Trinity' in Clausewitz's Mature Thought

*Christopher Bassford*

In this short chapter on Clausewitz's trinity, which forms the final section, section 28, of book I, chapter 1, of *On War*, I shall focus almost exclusively on the first of its five paragraphs, and concentrate on the 'primacy of policy' in Clausewitz's concept, or, rather, on the evident primacy of the *word* 'policy' over the word 'politics' in the translating of Clausewitz's own term in the original German, *Politik*. Thus I will have to leave the staggering implications of Clausewitz's choice of non-linear scientific imagery to Alan Beyerchen.[1] The two issues are not unrelated, because both turn on the interactivity of mutually dependent variables. But we can discuss the word-choice issues regarding policy, politics, and *Politik* in rather traditional terms without invoking any new cosmic paradigms.

The overarching problem with attempting any short discussion of the trinity in isolation is that however various writers may try to treat the trinity as a discrete theoretical 'nugget'—indeed, as an afterthought, a conception that allegedly popped into Clausewitz's mind in the last phases of his unfinished writing process and was never effectively incorporated into the existing body of his theory[2]—in fact, the trinity is the central concept in *On War*. I do not mean 'central' in the sense of, say, Clausewitz's concept of the inherent superiority of the defensive form of war.[3] That is, I do not argue that the trinity is Clausewitz's 'most important' concept, that the desire to convey it

---

[1] See Alan Beyerchen's chapter in this book, as well as his article, 'Clausewitz, Nonlinearity, and the Unpredictability of War', *International Security*, 17 (1992–3), 59–90.

[2] Azar Gat's discussions of the evolution of Clausewitz's thinking seems to be the source of this widespread notion; see Gat, *The Origins of Military Thought from the Enlightenment to Clausewitz* (Oxford, 1989). I have no particular opinion on his reconstruction, other than that it is largely irrelevant. Gat's obsession with the ghosts of Clausewitz's earlier conceptions, however interesting those ghosts may be in helping us understand Clausewitz's personal evolution, serves only to distort our understanding of his mature thought.

[3] See Jon Sumida's chapter in this book.

was his primary motivation in writing, or that all of his other insights flowed from this one. Rather, I mean simply that the trinity is the concept that ties all of Clausewitz's many ideas and binds them into a meaningful whole. This remains true whether Clausewitz conceived his theoretical universe with this construct in mind, or instead discovered only at the end of his efforts that the seemingly divergent roads he had been travelling all led, inexorably, to this particular intersection.

An intersection is of little significance, however, without reference to the roads that run through it, which is why a discussion of the trinity is so difficult to confine within tidy boundaries: any comprehensive examination must lead to every major issue in *On War*.

In any case, the role of the trinity within the confines of book I, chapter 1, of *On War*, which reflects Clausewitz's most mature thinking, is crucial. That chapter must be read in terms of Clausewitz's dialectical examination of the nature of war, which is very carefully structured but (purposely, I suspect) largely unmarked by clear dialectical sign posts, labelled thesis, antithesis, and synthesis,[4] or even by sections clearly devoted to one stage or the other. The trinity itself represents the synthesis of this dialectical process. In this chapter, at least, it is no afterthought, clearly being foreshadowed throughout the discussion.

As the synthesis of this dialectic, the trinity incorporates but also *supersedes* Clausewitz's antithesis, that is, the famous dictum that war is 'merely the continuation of *Politik* by other means'. That antithesis is almost always treated as if it were the pinnacle and summary of *On War*'s argument. In a sense, the trinity also *contradicts* this dictum, and in yet another sense it serves to define its key term—that is, *Politik*. Unfortunately, fundamental, seemingly irresolvable, but most often unvoiced disagreements arise the moment that word, *Politik*, and its most common English translations, 'politics' and 'policy', are introduced. So our exploration of the trinity must confront their various meanings and the confusion they create.

My approach to any issue concerning Clausewitz is an eclectic one, reflecting the wide range of correspondents I engage as editor of *The Clausewitz Homepage*.[5] These tend to fall into four broad schools:

- an 'original intent' school, primarily historians narrowly focused on Clausewitz's own influences, drives, goals, and often the presumed *limits* to his thought and perceptions in the specific context of Prussia in the

---

[4] The terms dialectic, thesis, antithesis, and synthesis appear in *On War*, respectively, one, three, four, and one time each.

[5] http://www.clausewitz.com/

periods immediately surrounding the wars of the French Revolution and Napoleon;
- an 'inspirationist' school, primarily present-minded political scientists, students of strategic affairs, and business theorists, who are interested in freely adapting Clausewitzian concepts exclusively to current issues;
- a 'receptionist' school, primarily historians who are interested in the ideas and impacts of Clausewitzian inspirationists over time; and
- an 'editorial' school—people who think they have clear ideas as to what Clausewitz 'really meant' and how to edit the rough draft Clausewitz left behind in order more faithfully to convey his concepts.

In practice, I find that most of us—however much 'purists' of one stripe or another might decry the heresies involved—tend to straddle these various schools to varying degrees, at varying times, for varying purposes. As one very bright business strategist once said to me, 'It would be nice to know what's "true", of course, but the more important question is, what is *useful*?' After all, most readers of Clausewitz are fundamentally interested not in understanding Clausewitz but in understanding war. In pursuit of the latter goal, each of the schools has a valuable contribution to make.

As a final prefatory comment, I should note a certain bias in my own thinking. This is a bias towards universalizing Clausewitz. I think it would be a good thing if the entire war-studies community could use the essentials of Clausewitzian theory as the common basis for comparative military-political studies across all human societies and history. It influences my choices in translation and in defining terms like policy and politics: We want definitions that are not confined to Prussia in the era of the French Revolution, the Westphalian-model state system, or Western civilization, as, I think, did Clausewitz.

The Howard and Paret translation of section 28 is problematic in a great many ways. My discussion here reflects an alternative translation based on a systematic comparison of all three major English translations with the German original (Box 1). My proposed corrections have been culled in many cases from the thoughts of others in this field, remain tentative, and are advanced here for the purpose of fostering debate and further progress. It should be no source of dismay to Sir Michael Howard and Peter Paret that a whole community of scholars, given *thirty years* to contemplate their translation of this particular bit of text, should have come to a greater recognition of its importance and to discern alternatives in word choice more appropriate to our emerging understanding of Clausewitz's meaning(s)—none of which would have happened without the impetus given to this field by their original efforts.

*Primacy of Policy and Trinity in Clausewitz's Thought* 77

---

Box 1. *On War*, book I, chapter 1, § 28. The Consequences for Theory (Bassford translation)

---

War is thus more than a **mere** chameleon, **because it changes its nature to some extent in each concrete case**. It is also, however, when it is regarded as a whole and in relation to the tendencies that dominate within it, a **fascinating trinity**—composed of:

*(1) primordial violence, hatred, and enmity, which are to be regarded as a blind natural force;

(2) the play of chance and probability, within which the creative spirit is free to roam; and

(3) its element of subordination, as an instrument of policy, which makes it subject to **pure reason**.

The first of these three aspects concerns **more** the people; the second, **more** the commander and his army; the third, **more** the government. The passions that are to blaze up in war must already be inherent in the people; the scope that the play of courage and talent will enjoy in the realm of probability and chance depends on the particular character of the commander and the army; but the political aims are the business of government alone.

These three tendencies are like three different codes of law, deep-rooted in their subject and yet variable in their relationship to one another. A theory that ignores any one of them or seeks to fix an arbitrary relationship among them would conflict with reality to such an extent that for this reason alone it would be totally useless.

The task, therefore, is to keep our theory [of war] **floating among** these three tendencies, **as among three points of attraction**.

What lines might best be followed to achieve this difficult task will be explored in the book on the theory of war [i.e. Book II]. In any case, **the conception of war defined here will be the first ray of light into the fundamental structure of theory, which first sorts out the major components and allows us to distinguish them from one another**.

Shown in bold are sections where this translation differs substantially from that that offered by Michael Howard and Peter Paret, in Clausewitz, *On War* (Princeton, NJ, 1976, [revised edn 1984]), p. 89.

This working translation is based on comparisons of the first edition of *Vom Kriege* (Berlin, 1832-4), and the translations into English by J. J. Graham (London, 1873), O. J. Matthijs Jolles (New York, 1943), and Michael Howard and Peter Paret (Princeton, NJ, 1976, [revised edn 1984]). It has also benefited from long-running consultations with Tony Echevarria, Alan D. Beyerchen, Jon Sumida, Gebhard Schweigler, and Andreas Herberg-Rothe.

* The elements of the trinity are enumerated here for the sake of clarity.

---

Starting with the very first sentence, we run into problems, even before the trinity itself is introduced. Evidently, Clausewitz believed that his discussion prior to this point should have prepared the reader to accept the metaphor, which he now introduces, of war as a chameleon—which I take to mean that it easily changes its superficial appearance and colour. But he also expects the reader to be prepared to understand that this metaphor, while pretty good as far as it goes,[6] is still insufficient, because war also changes in deeper ways (i.e. its 'nature') according to the circumstances of each real-world case. By dropping the initial thus, Howard and Paret separate the trinity concept from the rest of the chapter, making it appear to be a new departure.

Second, Howard and Paret turn on its head the causative explanation as to *why* the chameleon metaphor is insufficient—it describes the *chameleon* as slightly adapting *its* 'characteristics' to the given case, rather than *war*'s changing *its* 'nature' in each 'concrete case'. Third, Howard and Paret's substitution of 'characteristics' for 'nature' is understandable, since we generally think of a thing's 'nature' as being immutable. Nature is the (rather strong) word Clausewitz used, but we should accept it as standing here for something intermediate—much more consequential than the chameleon's superficial colour, but less than truly fundamental or definitive. Fourth, the Howard and Paret translation gives the impression that the trinity is being offered simply as an alternative metaphor. In truth, Clausewitz has already ceased his exploitation of the chameleon imagery. He is actually switching to a whole new metaphor, with a new structure, new entailments, and new purposes. The chameleon metaphor pointed to changes in war's appearance from case to case; the trinity addresses the underlying forces that *drive* those changes.

The next issue that arises is the very choice of the word 'trinity' (*Dreifaltigkeit*). Until recently, writers in English, at least, have largely ignored the cultural and psychological implications of this term, dripping as it is with religious implications. However, this has begun to change with the re-emergence of religion as a strategic concern, especially since the attacks of 11 September 2001. It prompts the question whether his word-choice reflects some sort of mystical streak (not necessarily Christian) in Clausewitz's personality. There are, of course, innumerable three-part theoretical constructs to which one can compare or relate Clausewitz's trinity—in, *inter alia*, Plato, St Augustine, or Darwin.[7] J. F. C. Fuller had a mystical obsession with a number of three-component constructs: 'earth, water, and air' and 'men, women, and children'—to which a sceptical J. E. Edmonds suggested adding 'coat, trousers,

---

[6] Plenty of sophisticated writers are perfectly happy with this initial metaphor: 'War is a chameleon, possessed of an infinite capacity to adapt itself to changing circumstances', Andrew Bacevich, 'Debellicised', *London Review of Books* (3 March 2005).

[7] See, for instance, Stephen Jay Gould's exegesis of the 'three central principles constituting a tripod of necessary support' for Darwinian evolutionism, in *The Structure of Evolutionary Theory* (Cambridge, MA, 2002), 11.

and boots' and 'knife, fork, and spoon'.[8] Generally, I do not find this approach a particularly fruitful avenue to understanding Clausewitz's meaning. There is no hint of religiosity or mysticism in Clausewitz's thinking. He is very much a product of the Enlightenment in that respect. And it seems pretty obvious that it was his interest in modern science that brought the three-points-of-attraction imagery of paragraphs 3 and 4 forcefully to his attention. I suspect that many of those who see the trinity as evidence of mysticism are simply people with a traditionally linear, Newtonian world view, who are baffled by Clausewitz's obsession with chance, unpredictability, and disproportionality in the cause–effect relationship. Nonetheless, one has to suspect that Clausewitz was aware of the cultural significance and power of the word. Whether he was seeking to exploit them, to defy them, or simply to have some fun with them, I have no idea.

The second problem here is the choice of modifying adjective. It seems that no modern translator is prepared to render *wunderliche* in the military context as 'wonderful' or 'wondrous'. Howard and Paret in 1976 give 'remarkable', a throw-away word of no particular significance. This was changed to 'paradoxical' in the 1984 edition, but this word seems to have no relationship to *wunderliche* and carries inappropriately negative connotations: I do not think that Clausewitz wanted to convey any implication that the elements of the trinity contradict one another either in reality or in appearance. Rather, he wants us to accept the practical reality that these dynamic forces are ever present and constantly interacting in the everyday world. But he clearly found this shifting interaction really, *really* interesting—to the point of being mesmerized by it. If that seems excessive, I suggest you actually watch the scientific demonstration he alludes to in paragraph 4 and see if you do not find the experience hypnotic. Since *wunderliche* does not lend itself to translation as hypnotic, however, I have settled on 'fascinating'.

That brings us to the list of actual elements in the trinity. Their identity will be readily evident to anyone who actually *reads* the first paragraph of his description: it is composed of: (1) primordial violence, hatred, and enmity,[9] which are to be regarded as a blind natural force; (2) the play of chance and probability within which the creative spirit is free to roam; and (3) its element of subordination, as an instrument of policy, which makes it subject to pure reason. I have little complaint about the Howard and Paret version of this list, with two important caveats. First, while we can accept 'instrument of

---

[8] [J. E. Edmonds], referring to Fuller's trinities in his review of Fuller's *Foundations of the Science of War* (London, 1926); *Army Quarterly*, 12 (1926), 165–6.

[9] Roger D. Carstens, 'Talk the Walk on Iraq', *The Washington Times*, 12 August 2002, lists these three nouns as the trinity. In this case, Carstens may simply have been a victim of his editors, but I have seen this formula elsewhere as well.

policy' here, there are factors that make this a special case. Second, Howard and Paret render *bloßen Verstande* as 'reason alone', which is for rather glaring reasons contradictory to Clausewitz's actual argument, on which more later. For convenience, this set of elements is usually labelled 'emotion, chance and reason'; sometimes 'violence/chance and probability/rational calculation'; or, even more abstractly, 'irrationality/non-rationality/rationality'.

However, this enumeration of the elements of the trinity—whichever set of words one chooses for shorthand—is not universally understood. We will save for another diatribe the odd manner in which Martin van Creveld (and, in his train, John Keegan) has built an alternative Clausewitzian universe around a creative rewriting of this list. Here we will note only that the words 'people', 'army', and 'government' appear nowhere at all in this paragraph enumerating the trinity's components.[10] Creveld's anti-Clausewitzian interpretation derives from the very much *pro*-Clausewitz work of Colonel Harry G. Summers, Jr. Prior to the American debacle in Vietnam, few thinkers writing in English had paid much serious attention to the trinity as a distinct concept. The term first achieved prominence in skewed form in Summers's influential study, *On Strategy: A Critical Analysis of the Vietnam War* (written in 1981 at the US Army War College).[11] Summers focused on a secondary set of elements that were powerfully relevant in the specific circumstances in which American military thinkers found themselves during and after the defeat in Indochina. This unarguably useful secondary trinity does indeed consist of the people, the army, and the government. Those elements appear in paragraph 3 of section 28, where they are used to illustrate and clarify the primary concept, not to define it. In America's traumatic war in Vietnam, those elements had come thoroughly unstuck from one another. Summers's interpretation of the trinity of people, army, and government was a positive doctrine, highly prescriptive: a nation could not hope to achieve victory unless these three elements were kept in balance. Howard and Paret's wording reinforced that notion with its message that 'Our task...is to develop a theory that maintains a balance between these three tendencies'.

Clausewitz, in contrast, was sceptical of any positive doctrine that was not highly context-specific. The pursuit of such a doctrine was entirely alien to his approach to theory. His trinity was descriptive, not prescriptive, and foretold

---

[10] I have written about this at length elsewhere: see especially Christopher Bassford and Edward J. Villacres, 'Reclaiming the Clausewitzian Trinity', *Parameters* (Autumn 1995).

[11] Harry G. Summers, Jr., *On Strategy: A Critical Analysis of the Vietnam War* (Novato, CA, 1982). In conversations I had with Harry in the late 1980s, I gathered that he was aware of both trinities, but he largely dismissed the trinity proper as a meaningless abstraction. In later conversations, however, it was clear that he had entirely forgotten the original formulation.

the very opposite of balance. The message of this trinity was that the relationships among his three elements were inherently unstable and shifting. What he actually said was that 'the task... is to keep our theory [of war] floating among these three tendencies', and not to try to set, or to count on, any fixed relationship among them. (*Schwebe* carries the connotation of dynamism, not equilibrium.)

We can blame Summers's confusion partly on Howard and Paret's unfortunate choice in translating Clausewitz's descriptor for the links between the elements of the trinity proper and the elements of this secondary trinity. By substituting 'mainly' for *mehr* (which I have translated as 'more'), Howard and Paret lock each of the elements of the actual trinity rather too firmly and exclusively to each of these sets of human beings—violent emotion to the people, chance and probability to the commander and his army, and rational calculation to the government. In fact, each of the three categories that constitute the actual trinity affects all of these human actors to an extent that will vary wildly among societies, over time, and across situations. The army's officers and men and the political leadership are, to varying degrees in different societies, still members of the society they rule or fight for. In almost all societies, there is a 'public', whose proportion of the population varies a great deal, that expects to play a role in rational decision-making (though sometimes the only public that counts is the population of the army itself). Commanders also indulge in rational calculation in pursuit of policy objectives. Political leaders are as often driven by personal needs as by their rational calculation of their societies' practical requirements. Events on the army's battlefields have a tremendous influence both on the people and on the political leadership, while popular and political factors, in turn, affect the army's performance. As Vietnam fades in salience, it becomes clearer that the political-structural notion of the people, army, and government—while hardly irrelevant (and America's misadventures in Iraq threaten to restore its immediate importance)—is much less than fundamental. Clearly, it is quite possible to fight and even win wars about which one's people do not give a damn, especially if that is the case on both sides, or if one side so vastly outclasses the other that victory comes quickly and relatively painlessly (e.g. the wars of Frederick the Great; Clinton in Bosnia).

It is the infinite variability among these factors and in their interaction that underlies Clausewitz's insistence on the inherent unpredictability of war. It is a classic model of Chaos, in the modern scientific sense. And in this descriptive approach, permitting infinite variability among factors that can be identified in any context, which makes the trinity such a promising basis for a comparative approach to military-political studies.

It is easy to understand why thinkers hostile to the state[12] or focused on non-state war might reject the people–army–government construct, though their fears—in some cases advocacy—of the eclipse of the state are wildly overblown. But one has to wonder whether *any* war-fighting political construct must not have analogues for each of these elements (e.g. popular base, fighters, and leadership). In any case, van Creveld's and Keegan's failure to read the actual wording of the theory they so vociferously attack, and to grasp its deep relevance to the phenomena they describe, is hard to credit.

Returning to Clausewitz's actual trinity, its first element is violence. Here, however, Clausewitz is not talking primarily about physical violence, but about violent *emotion* as a motive force. Actual physical violence can be generated by any of the elements, as Clausewitz demonstrated earlier in the chapter during his discussion of hostile *intentions*. These 'are often unaccompanied by any sort of hostile feelings'—for example, violence generated as a matter of course by the simple fact of military operations (i.e. under item 2 in the list) or as the result of rational calculation (under item 3). Thus these violent emotions need not be a motivating force behind the resort to war, but whether they are present initially, they will surely be called into being by the experience of actual violence and will affect behaviour. Let us pause to note that this first category is a product of the human mind and exists only inside individual skulls, but it is quite distinct from rational calculation.

Because reason, too, exists only inside individual skulls, let us skip the trinity's second category for the moment and go to the third, war's subordination to reason as an instrument of policy. There are four critical issues here: the meaning of reason or rationality; the manner in and extent to which war is subordinate to it; the meaning of the word *Politik* (the term that actually appears in the text here is *politischen Werkzeuges*); and the nature of that 'instrumentality'.

The only point I want to make at the moment about reason or rationality is that, like emotion, it is a product of the individual human mind, though of course it is quite different, with its properties of conscious ends–means calculation. As to war's 'subordination', we can quickly dispose of an annoying translation problem: Howard and Paret's version of this line reads that war is 'subject to reason alone'. There is no reason for the word 'alone' to be there at all, and, obviously, if war is subject to two other forces as well, it cannot be

---

[12] 'The state's most remarkable products to date have been Hiroshima and Auschwitz.... Whatever the future may bring, it cannot be much worse.' Martin van Creveld, 'The Fate of the State', *Parameters* (Spring 1996).

subject to reason 'alone'.[13] The correct translation for *bloßen Verstande* here is 'pure reason'. The 'pure' seems to serve no great purpose, other than perhaps to demonstrate how artificial it is to separate human reason from human emotion. It may also be a bow to Kant, or simply formulaic in nature, as in 'damned Yankees'.

That leaves us with the problem of *Politik*. This is a huge subject, for it encompasses the entire issue of the relationship between it and war, and accounts for the majority of debates about Clausewitz. Clausewitz, of course, never overtly defines *Politik* in any detail, and he uses the word quite freely throughout contexts wherein English speakers feel compelled to choose between 'politics' and 'policy'. Some even prefer the much more specialized term 'diplomacy', which limits the discussion to relations between organized states. That is how Antoine Henri Jomini's *Politique*, as used in his works on the conduct of war, was usually rendered into English. Clausewitz himself would probably have been comfortable with the word 'statecraft', but that term avails us no greater clarity and might even lock him exclusively into the 'state', where so many modern writers want to maroon him.

Telling students that war is an expression of X, without defining X, gets them nowhere. However, every reader and every translator has personal definitions of these terms—or, more likely, an inchoate set of definitions triggered selectively by context. Asked to define politics, most will stumble a bit and raise subjects like elections, political parties, and ideological competition. We make sharp and utterly artificial distinctions between things that are 'political' as opposed to 'social', 'religious', or 'economic'. If politics is about elections or parties, there must not be any politics in monarchies or one-party states. If various wars are really about religion, or culture, or environmental collapse, they must not be 'continuations of politics'. If 'policy' is made by the governments of states, then war as waged by non-state actors—say, tribal societies, al-Qaeda, or the Hanseatic League—cannot be a 'continuation of policy'.

During the Clausewitz conference at which this chapter was first presented, Sir Michael Howard, in his usual matter-of-fact manner, said that he and Paret actually gave no systematic thought to the choice of when and whether to use policy or politics when translating *Politik*. But he said that he was biased in favour of the word policy primarily because of its grandeur: policy is what great states do on the grand stage of history, whereas politics is a sordid process carried on incessantly, by everyone, but particularly by objectionable

---

[13] This error appears to be in part a simple mistranslation, and in part an erroneous repetition of the phrase from paragraph 4, 'government alone'. It may also reflect a general tendency by Howard and Paret to emphasize the rational elements in Clausewitz's approach.

little men called politicians, in grubby, smoke-filled back rooms. That is an interesting and revealing notion. It is, however, of no great use as a theoretical distinction. We must find a more fundamental and rigorous relationship between the two words. I do not mean to impose such a distinction, but rather to derive one from usage (and from necessity). We are looking, of course, for a universal definition that applies across cultures and time, but one not contradicted by Clausewitz's own usage. In practice, the distinctions I propose *tend* (but only that) to be consistent with the choices made in the Howard and Paret translation.

(1) *Politics and policy are both concerned with power*. Power comes in many forms. It may be material in nature: the economic power of money or other resources, for example, or possession of the physical means for coercion (weapons and troops or police). Power is just as often psychological in nature: legal, religious, or scientific authority; intellectual or social prestige; a charismatic personality's ability to excite or persuade; and a reputation, accurate or illusory, for diplomatic or military strength. Power provides the means to attack, but it also provides the means to resist attack. Power in itself is therefore neither good nor evil. By its nature, however, power must be distributed unevenly to an extent that varies greatly from one society to another and over time.

(2) *Politics is the highly variable process by which power is distributed in any society*: the family, the office, a religious order, a tribe, the state, an empire, a region, an alliance, and the international community. The process of distributing power may be fairly orderly—through consensus, inheritance, election, some time-honoured tradition, or it may be chaotic—through intrigue, assassination, revolution, and warfare. Whatever process may be in place at any given time, politics is inherently dynamic and the process is under constant pressures for change. Knowing that war is an expression of politics is of no use in grasping any particular situation unless we understand the political structures, processes, issues, and dynamics of that specific context.

I frequently hear that Clausewitzian thinking may apply to wars with political objectives (using 'war' here in a sloppy, unilateral manner) but not to wars over economic issues or with economic objectives. In fact, of course, politics and economics are hardly exclusive of one another. First, even if you treat them as two isolated phenomena, they are very similar *types* of systems. But in reality, economics is just an element of politics: if politics is the general process by which general power is distributed, economics is just a subsystem by which power specifically over material wealth is distributed. In some societies, as in command economies, there is virtually no distinction. Even in market democracies, how much of domestic 'politics' is really about the redistribution of wealth? Economic issues become 'politicized' when strictly command or market processes are perceived to be providing economic outcomes unacceptable to groups capable of responding to the inequity with other kinds of tools (i.e. 'other means', which may or may not include violence). Thus, economic objectives easily become political objectives, and these, in turn, may be translated into military objectives.

The key characteristics of politics, however, are that it is multilateral and interactive—always involving give and take, interaction, competition, and struggle. Political events and their outcomes are the product of conflicting, contradictory, sometimes cooperating or compromising, but often antagonistic forces, always modulated by chance. Outcomes are seldom if ever precisely what any individual participant desired or intended. Thus politics cannot be described as a 'rational' process (though a community may achieve considerable success in rationally designing its internal political institutions so as to civilize the process). War—like politics—is inherently multilateral, of course, though Clausewitz often uses the term sloppily in the sense of a unilateral resort to organized violence. The notion that 'politics' permeate human interactions at every level of organization is banal and mundane, since it applies to everything. Clausewitz is describing the common, everyday world we actually live in. His definitions of such pervasive realities as power and politics had better be as mundane as possible.

(3) *Policy, in contrast to politics, is unilateral and rational.* (Please do not confuse rationality with wisdom, however—there is no shortage of unwise policy out there.) Policy represents a conscious effort by one entity in the political arena to bend its own power to the accomplishment of some purpose—some positive objective, perhaps, or merely the continuation of its own power or existence. Policy is the rational and one-sided *sub*-component of politics, the reasoned purposes and actions of each of the various individual actors in the political struggle.

The key distinction between politics and policy lies in interactivity. That is, politics is a multilateral phenomenon, whereas policy is the unilateral subcomponent thereof. My ally, myself, and my enemy are all bound up together in politics, but we each have our own policies: I have my policy or policies, and strategies; my ally has his policy; as an alliance, *we* have *our* policy. My enemy also has his own policy. But though they shared the same political stage and then joined in war, Hitler and Churchill did not share a policy, and the *war* as a whole had no objects or aims at all (unless you assign some guiding teleological intelligence to the historical process, which I do not, nor did Clausewitz).

This makes policy and politics very different things—even though each side's policy is produced via internal political processes (reflecting the nested, fractal[14] nature of human political organization).[15] The dangers inherent in thinking that war is 'merely the continuation of [unilateral] policy' are obvious. They include most of what Colin Gray has listed as characteristics of American strategic culture: indifference to history, the engineering style and technical fix, impatience, blindness to cultural differences, indifference to strategy, and the evasion of politics.[16]

In general, Howard and Paret's choice of words reflects this logic, despite their strong bias towards 'policy'. Whenever the context *can* be construed as unilateral, as in the trinity discussion, we see 'policy'. But when the context is unarguably multilateral, as in Clausewitz's final and most forcefully articulated version of the concept, which appears in book VIII, chapter 6B, even Howard and Paret are forced to use 'politics' or 'political':

> We maintain, on the contrary, that war is simply a continuation of *political intercourse*, with the addition of other means. We deliberately use the phrase 'with the addition of other means' because we also want to make it clear that war in itself does not suspend political intercourse or change it into something entirely different. In essentials that intercourse continues, irrespective of the means it employs. The main lines along which military events progress, and to which they are restricted, are political lines that continue throughout the war into the subsequent peace. How could it be otherwise? Do *political relations between peoples and between their governments* stop when diplomatic notes are no longer exchanged?[17]

Thus, 'war' belongs to the larger, multilateral, interactive realm of politics. Clausewitz says so quite clearly, with so strong an emphasis on intercourse and interactivity that, ultimately, even Howard and Paret are forced to veer from their preference for 'policy'.

Within the trinity discussion itself, because the third element is war's *subordination to rationality*, it seems entirely appropriate to use the word policy in translating that particular clause. But we must always bear in mind the awkward fact that, while Clausewitz seems in this discussion to be speaking from the perspective of one side in a war [e.g. the people (singular), the government (singular), and the commander and his army (singulars)], his topic in this chapter is the nature of war, which must by definition be multilateral. The

---

[14] 'Fractal' is a term from non-linear geometry. Here, it refers to the tendency of patterns to look similar at different scales—e.g. the surface of a rock under a microscope looks rather like the face of a rock cliff or an aerial photo of a mountain range.

[15] Tactics, operations, military strategy, grand strategy, and policy are all essentially the same thing—processes of interrelating means and ends—at different scales of time, space, and numbers of people and resources involved.

[16] Colin S. Gray, 'History and Strategic Culture', in Williamson Murray, MacGregor Knox, and Alvin Bernstein (eds), *The Making of Strategy: Rulers, States, and War* (Cambridge, 1994), 592–8. I have listed six characteristics out of Gray's eight.

[17] *On War*, trans. Howard and Paret, VIII, 6B, p. 605.

clash of two rational, opposing, unilateral policies brings us into the realm of multilateral politics.

That brings us to the problem of instrumentality. Force and violence are indeed instruments, in the sense of a hand-tool or weapon, of unilateral policy. War, however, must be bi- or multilateral in order to exist. Thus, while military force may be an instrument of unilateral policy, we should see war as an 'instrument' of politics only in a very different, multilateral sense, as the market is an instrument for trade or the courtroom an instrument for litigation. This is precisely the same logic Clausewitz follows in arguing that war belongs neither to the domain of art (though he is willing to place [unilateral] strategy there) nor to the domain of science (though he places tactics there):

> [R]ather, [war] is part of man's social existence. War is a clash between major interests, which is resolved by bloodshed—that is the only way in which it differs from other conflicts. Rather than comparing it to art we could more accurately compare it to commerce, which is also a conflict of human interests and activities; and it is *still* closer to politics, which in turn may be considered as a kind of commerce on a larger scale.[18]

This is a source of much confusion, and were we able to give editorial advice to a living Clausewitz, we would have to insist that he be more consistent in distinguishing between military force as a tool or weapon of one side and war as an instrument or vehicle for multilateral interaction. Clausewitz seems simply to assume that his readers will distinguish, on the fly, whether he is speaking in the unilateral or the multilateral sense. After all, he has stressed time and again the interactive nature of war, and, of course, his own language's term *Politik* encompasses both our multilateral politics and our unilateral policy. But this casual stance results in constant confusion for the reader. This is especially true regarding the next chapter's discussion of purpose and means, which—again, assuming that war as a whole has no teleological purpose—are by nature unilateral. When we talk about a war of limited aim as opposed to a war to 'render [the enemy] politically helpless or militarily impotent',[19] obviously (to Clausewitz), these are unilateral objectives rather than types of war in a holistic sense. And they can coexist—that is, I may be fighting for limited objectives while my opponent is seeking my total destruction. If I think that my opponent's objectives and behaviour will be constrained simply because *my* objectives are limited, however, I will never understand our interaction.

The other great issue about Clausewitz's *Politik* is whether it refers only to politics among and between states or extends as well to politics internal to (or even without reference to) the state. It seems obvious that civil wars, rebellions, and revolutions—of which Clausewitz was obviously well aware, and which rather by definition take place within a single state or society—

---

[18] *On War*, II, 3, p. 149.    [19] Ibid. 69, Clausewitz's note of 10 July 1827.

are expressions of internal politics, some of it quite 'private' in nature. And certainly he was aware that the foreign policies and strategies of states are driven in very large part by the unilateral, purely internal concerns of their rulers. It is ultimately impossible to disentangle internal and external politics. In any case, *we* are well aware that war occurs even in the absence of the state. Thus there seems to be little point, and less value, to clinging to the interstate-only interpretation of the famous dictum, in terms either of Clausewitz's original intent or of our own understanding of it.

On the other hand, there is great value in recognizing that, if we are to understand and describe war in any context as an expression of politics, it is therefore necessary to understand the structure, methods, and issues of politics in that context. If the state is not part of that particular context, then we simply have to work through the implications of that fact. This, it seems fairly obvious to me, is what Clausewitz expects us to do.

We sometimes forget, of course, that Clausewitz's *magnum opus* is not about policy or politics, nor about human nature or the nature of reality, though it is a mark of the book's profundity that these matters arise immediately in any serious discussion of it. In fact, Clausewitz himself dismisses the political complexities of policy in order to focus on his true subject, the conduct of military operations:

That [policy] can err, subserve the ambitions, private interests, and vanity of those in power, is neither here nor there.... here we can only treat policy as representative of all interests of the community.[20]

There is some debate as to the reason for this avoidance. I would argue that it was an author's act of economy: one gargantuan topic at a time, please. Another view is that Clausewitz was politically cowed in the age of reaction after Napoleon's defeat. This is a bit absurd, given Clausewitz's political boldness during the later Napoleonic Wars, as well as the inflammatory character of some of his other writings. In any case, Marie's preface gives a very clear explanation of Clausewitz's determination not to publish while he was still alive, which obviated any political motives for avoiding touchy subjects.

Having treated policy and politics, we now arrive, at last, at the second element of the trinity: the play ('interplay' might be preferable) of chance and probability. I have changed the sequence in order to stress the important point that both emotion and reason are products of the human mind. In that sense, they are subjective forces. They are the internal sources of our desires and the internal governors of our efforts. While they are so different from one another that we must treat them separately, they are also intrinsically linked. There can be no 'rational' consideration of goals without taking into account the

[20] *On War*, trans. Howard and Paret, VIII, 6B, p. 606.

emotions that give rise to the goals in the first place. Can we imagine policy, politics, economics, or reproduction without fear, love, greed, lust, or hope? But the chances and probabilities of which Clausewitz speaks are *external* to human desire and intent—they represent, purely and simply, the concrete (in this sense, 'objective') reality with which the actors must cope. That reality yields to their hopes, dreams, and plans only with great resistance (friction) and at great cost to themselves in time, energy, resources, will, and, in the case of war, of blood.

This objective externality consists both of the physical world (including mountains, roads, weather, weapons, geography, demographics, technology, economics, disease vectors, and so on —in short, everything we cannot alter at once by merely wishing) *and* of the personalities, capabilities, hopes, dreams, plans, energies, resources, and will of other actors—the human ecology within which the participants' perceptions, plans, and actions must co-evolve. We tend to think first of those other actors who are our opponents. We need to think not only of our enemies and their intentions, but also of our often recalcitrant or annoyingly self-centred allies, of potentially influential neutrals, and, as Clausewitz makes clear in his discussion of friction, of those who are part of our own body politic and even of our own military machine:

> But we should bear in mind that none of [war's] components is of one piece: each part is composed of individuals, every one of whom retains his potential of friction. In theory it sounds reasonable enough: a battalion commander's duty is to carry out his orders; discipline welds the battalion together, its commander must be a man of tested capacity, and so the great beam turns on its iron pivot with a minimum of friction. In fact, it is different, and every fault and exaggeration of the theory is instantly exposed in war. A battalion is made up of individuals, the least important of whom may chance to delay things or somehow make them go wrong.[21]

Obviously, such factors are at work during the making of our policy and strategy as well. These, once produced, are unilateral, but their production is via an internally multilateral, and therefore political, process.

We have to assume that Clausewitz used these two words together for a reason. That is, 'chance and probability' are not a redundancy but, rather, two distinctly different things. Chance, in a pure sense, is arbitrary and incalculable. We can prepare for it only in a general manner. Probability, on the other hand, refers to things whose likelihood can be to some useful extent estimated. It is chance that there is a mountain range between France and Spain; it is quite a good probability that it will still be there when our armies arrive on the border. It is also chance that a copy of General Lee's order of battle should be carelessly wrapped around a bunch of cigars and lost by their owner—and still more so that the package should be found in the field, recognized, and

[21] Ibid. I, 7, p. 119.

delivered to the appropriate headquarters. What, however, is the probability that a McClellan will actually act upon such a chance windfall? We would be fools to plan on such a chance occurrence, but also fools not to have a general apparatus for making and dealing with such finds, and fools for failing to act upon one when it occurs.

In short, this last element of the trinity represents concrete reality, that is, everything outside of our own skull and its emotions and calculations. It is true that in the military conduct of war, Clausewitz's primary focus, these factors may loom largest for the commander and his army, because the number, scope, range, tempo, and sheer variety of factors shaped by chance and probability are massive at that level. But political leaders and policy-makers must deal with such factors as well. It is therefore absurd to think, or to claim that Clausewitz thought, that courage, creativity, and skill are 'mainly' requirements for military leaders.

Thus Clausewitz's trinity is all-inclusive and universal, comprising the subjective and the objective, the intellectual, the emotional, and the physical components that constitute the phenomenon of war in any human construct. It is thus a profoundly realistic concept. Understanding it as the central, connecting idea in Clausewitzian theory will help us to order the often confusing welter of his ideas and to apply them, in a useful, comparative manner, to the history of the world we live in and to its present realities. Perhaps most important, its realism will help us steer clear of the worst tendencies of theory and ideology, 'pure reason' and logic, and pure emotion. As Clausewitz himself said of his theory as a whole:

Its scientific character consists in an attempt to investigate the essence of the phenomena of war and to indicate the links between these phenomena and the nature of their component parts. No logical conclusion has been avoided; but whenever the thread became too thin I have preferred to break it off and go back to the relevant phenomena of experience. Just as some plants bear fruit only if they don't shoot up too high, so in the practical arts the leaves and flowers of theory must be pruned and the plant kept close to its proper soil—experience.[22]

But perhaps Sir Michael Howard put it best when criticizing the strategic theorists of the nuclear age:

Kahn and his colleagues... ignor[ed] all three elements in the Clausewitzian trinity: popular passion, the risks and uncertainties of the military environment, and the political purpose for which the war was fought. Their calculations bore no relation to war as mankind has known it throughout history.[23]

[22] *On War*, 61.
[23] Michael Howard, 'The Military Philosopher', *Times Literary Supplement*, 25 June 1976, 754–5.

# 5

# The Instrument: Clausewitz on Aims and Objectives in War

*Daniel Moran*

Clausewitz believed that wars were fought for objectives that arose outside the military sphere, objectives that he normally characterized as political in nature. He believed that, as a matter of historical fact, political objectives shaped the course of military operations, and also, as a matter of theoretical inference, that they should do so: that one common source of strategic failure lay in an inability properly to relate political ends to military means. He recognized that there were limits to the influence that political goals could exert: politics, he conceded in book VIII of *On War*, will not determine the posting of guards.[1] But he seems to have regarded those limits as practical or prudential, rather than as reflecting any theoretical or logical constraint. There is nothing in Clausewitz's work or method that would have prevented him from accepting that under some conditions—such as might prevail in patrolling a frontier or conducting a military occupation—political goals might well determine where guards would be posted. He certainly believed that the influence of political objectives always extended to the conduct of major operations, the raising and training of armies, and the day-to-day decisions of senior commanders.

He also believed that, among the instrumental alternatives available to political leaders, the choice of war was distinctive and fraught with peril. For Clausewitz, war's outstanding characteristic as a tool of policy lay not simply in its destructiveness, but in the violent, irrational emotions that the use of force could inspire. Such feelings threatened to alter, if not to overwhelm, two critical sets of interactions: that of ends and means, whose reconciliation was the hallmark of strategic excellence; and that of adversaries in the heat of battle. Because every act of force invited a more forceful rejoinder, the violence of war necessarily pressed against the guiding influence of putatively rational,

---

[1] Carl von Clausewitz, *On War*, ed. and trans. by Michael Howard and Peter Paret (Princeton, NJ, 1976), VIII, 6B, p. 606.

cold-blooded political objectives, sometimes lending them a shape and size quite different from what they had possessed when recourse to violence was first decided upon. Clausewitz's recognition of the centrality of this escalatory dynamic to all aspects of warfare is one of his most original contributions to military theory, and his sensitivity to it runs like a leitmotiv throughout his work.

In considering the role of aims and objectives in Clausewitz's thinking, it is essential to recognize that if he is wrong about their general salience for the conduct of war, then he is for all intents and purposes wrong about everything. Many real or alleged deficiencies of his work—his neglect of naval warfare, his indifference to technological change, his deprecation of the value of intelligence, his supposed preference for big battles and big battalions—these and similar complaints can all be set aside as parochial misreading, or contextualized with reference to historical conditions that have changed since Clausewitz wrote. But if one takes away the recursive, instrumental dialectic of ends and means that pervades all of his mature writing, there is not much left of contemporary theoretical relevance. *On War* becomes a book of purely historical interest, a voice from a remote past, when war made some kind of sense.

Or, at any rate, when it was believed to. For if Clausewitz is wrong about the significance of political objectives in war, he must be wrong in one of two ways. It is possible that the logic of ends and means really did shape the conduct of war in his day, and no longer does; in which case we are left to consider why a formerly purposeful form of human behaviour should have lost its purposive character. Alternatively, one would have to concede that war has never been anything other than a deeply atavistic form of cultural practice, whose pointlessness has been masked by superficial claims of instrumental rationality that do not withstand serious scrutiny.

Historians do not possess tools that allow us to know for sure which, if either, of these claims is true; though we are well-positioned to recognize that the second of them is very old. The suspicion that war is nothing more than an expression of the darkness in the hearts of men is central to all forms of ethically or religiously grounded passivism. It is also implicit in claims that war is merely symptomatic of some underlying social pathology—the continued preponderance, for instance, of a warrior elite, a feudal aristocracy, or an avaricious bourgeoisie. Against this, historians are obliged to weigh the apparently universal insistence, by those who have waged war, that they have done so for a reason; that they had some objective in view that caused them to take up arms in the first place. Such claims are no less ubiquitous among terrorists and revolutionary insurgents at the turn of the twenty-first century than they were among the sovereign princes of Clausewitz's day.

The proposition that times have changed, on the other hand, is one that historians are better able to address, partly because it is the sort of question that does not require a categorical answer. One does not need to believe that war has entirely lost whatever purpose it may once have possessed in order to take seriously the argument that, as a practical matter, the effective translation of political ends into military means has become more difficult as a consequence of political and social changes since Clausewitz's time; or perhaps that certain kinds of political communities are more adept than others at employing violence instrumentally in pursuit of their objectives. These are the kinds of questions that Clausewitz himself was inclined to ask. He held tight to the idea that the conduct of war at every level was permeated by politics precisely because it allowed him to understand things that otherwise made no sense: why some wars were big and others small; why some campaigns fizzled out while others were fought to the finish; why the violence of war was not instantaneous or continuous, but episodic and inconsistent; why the wars of the past differed from those he had experienced himself.

Of these, it was the first question whose resolution proved of greatest consequence in shaping Clausewitz's mature work. In a much-commented-upon note written in July 1827, Clausewitz declared his intention to revise the manuscript of *On War* in light of a newly crystallized understanding of war's 'dual nature'. Wars, he proposed, could be of two 'types' or 'kinds', depending on the character of their political objectives. One type sought 'to overthrow the enemy—to render him politically helpless or militarily impotent', whereas the other sought limited goals, such as seizing territory 'for bargaining at the peace negotiations'.[2] This insight has occasionally been represented as radically discontinuous with respect to Clausewitz's earlier thinking.[3] Clausewitz seems to have regarded it as more in the nature of an epiphany, in which a variety of threads reaching back to his earliest writings finally wove themselves into a single cord, strong enough to bear the weight of his life's work.

That wars arose from political quarrels had been a commonplace idea since long before Clausewitz was born. This proposition had literally been forged in bronze by Cardinal Richelieu, who caused the words *Ultima Ratio* ('the final argument') to be cast into the barrels of French cannon.[4] Clausewitz's contribution lay in his recognition that the controlling effect of politics on war was

---

[2] 'Note of 10 July 1827', in Clausewitz, *On War*, p. 69.

[3] See especially Azar Gat, *The Origins of Military Thought: From the Enlightenment to Clausewitz* (Oxford, 1989), 213–14. Gat considers the note of 10 July 1827 symptomatic of a 'crisis' that 'shatters Clausewitz's lifelong conception of theory'.

[4] Daniel Moran, 'Strategic Theory and the History of War', in John Baylis, James Wirtz, Elliot Cohen, and Colin S. Gray (eds), *Strategy in the Contemporary World* (Oxford, 2002; online at http://www.clausewitz.com/CWZHOME/Bibl/Moran-StrategicTheory.pdf), 1; cf. Clausewitz, *On War*, VIII, 6B, p. 605, where he declares the political origins of wars to be a familiar idea.

so pervasive as to afford a vantage point—the only one, he says—from which the entire subject could be comprehensively surveyed.[5] In his 'Observations on the Wars of the Austrian Succession', written in the early 1820s, Clausewitz was already aware that the conduct of all the belligerents had been 'saturated with politics', and that, except for Austria, none 'had interests that called for an all-out effort'; a fact that in turn explained the limited scope of the wars' major campaigns, and even the movements of minor military units.[6] When he wrote these words, Clausewitz seems to have regarded the controlling effect of politics on war as historically contingent, a reflection of 'the political nature of wars at the time'.[7] Even this circumscribed interpretation represented an advance upon more conventional theorists, for whom Napoleonic warfare appeared to be a normative standard, against which conflicts in the past were judged deficient by virtue of the failure of those who had conducted them to grasp the true principles of war. This was a point of view that Clausewitz never found very convincing. But it was only towards the end of his life, when he realized that all wars, even the most intense and encompassing, shared the same instrumental character, that he was in a position to offer a comprehensive theoretical alternative.

Clausewitz thought his insight into the dual nature of war was of practical as well as analytical value. 'Wars', he tells his readers at the outset of *On War*, 'must vary in the nature of their motives and of the situations which give rise to them', such that 'the first, the supreme, the most far-reaching act of judgment that the statesman and commander have to make is to establish by that test the kind of war on which they are embarking, never mistaking it for, nor trying to turn it into, something that is alien to its nature'.[8] The formulation could hardly be more emphatic. Yet an underlying ambivalence is apparent. Clausewitz's discussions of real military campaigns leave no doubt that war does not possess a 'dual' nature. There is no categorical barrier separating limited and unlimited war, such that one can decide at the beginning which 'kind' of war to fight. On the contrary, 'all wars are things of the *same* nature',[9] albeit one that is both 'diverse'[10] and fungible. The risk that a war begun for some modest purpose might gradually expand into one of great consequence, owing to the tendency of the belligerents to out-do each other

---

[5] Clausewitz, *On War*, VIII, 6B, pp. 605–6.

[6] Carl von Clausewitz, *Historical and Political Writings*, ed. and trans. by Peter Paret and Daniel Moran (Princeton, NJ, 1992), 21–9; quotation p. 22.

[7] Ibid. 22.

[8] Clausewitz, *On War*, I, 1, p. 88; see also the celebrated passage in book VIII, where Clausewitz advises that 'No one starts a war—or rather, no on in his senses ought to do so—without first being clear in his mind what he intends to achieve by that war and how he intends to conduct it'. Ibid. VIII, 2, p. 579.

[9] Ibid. VIII, 6B, p. 606; emphasis in the original.    [10] Ibid. I, 1, p. 87.

in their use of force, is one that is never far from Clausewitz's mind. In any case, even the apparently straightforward task of deciding at the start exactly how much one is willing to risk or suffer in order to achieve a given aim immediately involves the statesman in a host of imponderables:

> To discover how much of our resources must be mobilized for war, we must first examine our own political aim and that of the enemy. We must gauge the strength and situation of the opposing state. We must gauge the character and abilities of its government and people and do the same in regard to our own. Finally we must evaluate the political sympathies of other states and the effect the war may have on them.... Bonaparte was right when he said that Newton himself would quail before [these] problems.[11]

At a minimum, it is apparent that an effective reconciliation of ends and means was not something that could be accomplished by a 'first...act of judgment', however 'far-reaching', but required constant renegotiation. The best commander was one whose character combined the natural boldness necessary to overcome the effects of chance and 'friction' with the dispassionate judgement required continuously to recalculate the political effects of the violence that he wielded, so as to avoid the disasters that may befall those who do not know when to quit; among whom Napoleon, the greatest military genius of all, was of course the pre-eminent example.

Not the least challenge in reading Clausewitz is to recognize that, while he routinely talks in terms of polarities, his real interest always lies in the spectrum of possibilities that connects the poles. Clausewitz was loath to assert fixed relationships among the theoretical elements that interested him. Genius and friction, reason and chance, passion and prudence, attack and defence, victory and defeat—these and other, similar concepts are always in motion with respect to each other, pushing and pulling as they go. His insistence on the unvarying primacy of politics in the formation of strategy is a striking exception to this rule, which he repeats so relentlessly that one begins to suspect that some unresolved ambiguity must lurk beneath what is, for Clausewitz, an unusually adamantine theoretical surface. And indeed it does. The problem is not merely a matter of scaling one's effort to one's aims and resources, nor even of estimating how an adversary might be making the same kinds of decisions. There is also the possibility that the choice of war as such may be misguided, because the end in view contradicts the essential characteristics of the instrument itself. 'What remains peculiar to war', Clausewitz proposed, 'is simply the peculiar nature of its means'—ineluctable violence and the passions that go with it. Thus 'war in general, and the commander in

---

[11] Ibid. VIII, 3B, p. 586.

any specific instance, is entitled to require that the trend and designs of policy shall not be inconsistent with these means'.[12]

This, he concedes, is 'no small demand'. Yet one may search Clausewitz's writings in vain for an example of its actually having been made. And it is in this connection, perhaps, that even sympathetic readers of Clausewitz may wonder whether the questions that he regarded as foundational to an understanding of war are as salient today as they were in the wake of Waterloo. Even if war has not lost its purposive character; even if it is still 'about' something; even if whatever it is about can still be described in political language—it is still possible that knowing what it's about may be less useful than it once was, both analytically and operationally.

It is difficult to claim, for instance, that the choice between limited and unlimited war is the first and most far-reaching of strategic decisions under current circumstances. The proliferation of nuclear weapons has made this an easy choice, at least for those who possess them. As far as advanced societies are concerned, even wars undertaken for the complete overthrow of an opposing state are pervaded by a concern for 'economy of force', since the aim of ousting a hostile government is invariably limited by a corresponding desire to inflict as little damage as possible on the surrounding society. The contemporary prominence of such considerations has made little difference when it comes to devising military plans, because questions about the scale of effort to commit against a given objective are rarely paramount. Relative to capabilities, the effort is always small. The complaint that dogs the conduct of war in our own time is not that a given war's objectives are either too limited, or insufficiently so, but rather that they are 'unclear', which seems close to what Clausewitz had in mind when he warned against employing the instrument of war for ends that contradict its nature. This concern has gained special prominence since America's defeat in Vietnam, which has routinely been attributed to the failure of the country's political leadership to provide its armed forces with consistent and decisive political guidance. Yet American objectives in Vietnam were not, in any logical sense, especially obscure. The United States sought to establish an independent, non-communist government in the South. Whatever lack of clarity may have existed did not involve this objective, but the steps by which it could be achieved militarily. There is nothing in Clausewitz's work that would

---

[12] *On War* I, 1, p. 87. The first formulation of this idea appears in a letter from Clausewitz to a junior colleague, Karl von Roeder, which is discussed below. There Clausewitz says that 'war in its relation to policy has above all the obligation and the right to prevent policy from making demands *that are contrary to the nature of war*, to save it from misusing the military instrument from a failure to understand what it can and cannot do'. In Carl von Clausewitz, 'Two Letters on Strategy', ed. and trans. by Peter Paret and Daniel Moran, *Strategic Studies Institute Monograph* (Carlisle, PA: US Army War College, 1984; online at http://www-cgsc.army.mil/carl/resources/csi/Paret/paret.asp), 16; emphasis in the original.

have suggested, to those responsible at the time, that they were embarking on a war whose aims and objectives contradicted war's essential nature.

For Clausewitz, the paradigmatic aim of limited war, one that he regularly employed to demonstrate what he meant by the concept, was the forcible seizure of enemy territory.[13] His study of military history seemed to demonstrate that military campaigns designed with this purpose in mind were destined to end in negotiation rather than surrender. Such an inference appeared well-founded when Clausewitz made it. Yet it clearly requires that belligerents in war share a common, mutually transparent sense of how tactical results should be translated into strategic objectives and (if necessary) political concessions, which has deteriorated steadily with the passage of time. Frederick the Great came close to biting off more than he could chew in seizing Silesia from the Habsburgs in the 1740s. But even so, it was easier for him to anticipate the political consequences of his actions than it was for Bismarck to anticipate those of seizing Alsace and Lorraine, if for no other reason than because the range of people whose reactions counted politically was a lot broader in the 1870s than it had been a century earlier. Nowadays this sort of piratical opportunism is sufficiently perilous as to suggest that, far from being synonymous with limited war, war for territorial gain is virtually a recipe for *guerre à outrance*. In 1980, Iraq's newly installed President, Saddam Hussein, might well have felt himself in a position similar to that of Frederick, whose invasion of Silesia was predicated on the idea that Austria's powers of resistance had been weakened by the succession crisis that followed the death of Emperor Charles VI. Saddam viewed the recent overthrow of the Shah of Iran in similar terms: as an upheaval that had temporarily weakened a traditionally superior rival, to the point where a bold move to shift the balance back in his own favour might succeed. It was on this basis that he sent his armies across the Shatt al-Arab, the waterway that describes the southern border of Iraq and Iran, at their juncture with the Persian Gulf. Saddam's aim was to seize some especially choice tracts of oil-rich land, keep some for himself, and trade the rest back to Iran, in return for political concessions and the respect he felt he deserved. The result was a war lasting eight years, in which perhaps a million men died. And not only men, for there were numerous occasions when the Iranians did not scruple to commit their children to the fight; as, for instance, when minefields were cleared by the simple expedient of sending masses of young boys across them, each one carrying a little piece of white cloth, to symbolize his burial shroud.[14]

---

[13] 'Note of 10 July 1827', in Clausewitz, *On War*, 69; cf. 'Two Letters on Strategy', 15.
[14] Efraim Karsh, *The Iran–Iraq War, 1980–1988* (London, 2002), 62.

The difficulty that Saddam encountered in executing his predatory scheme illustrates an essential characteristic of limited war, which is that the limited nature of one's objectives must be apparent and credible to the other side. It is not enough to scale one's chosen means properly to the chosen objective, or even to estimate correctly the adversary's powers of resistance, difficult as those things might be. War cannot be limited merely by self-restraint. It also requires that military operations be conducted in a way that expresses restraint clearly enough to moderate the reactions of the opponent.[15] Saddam's seizure of the Shatt al-Arab was perceived by the Iranians as commencing an open-ended campaign to overrun and humiliate their country. Or perhaps it was merely represented to them as such by a cynical leadership, who recognized that Saddam's land-grab would afford them additional leverage with which to mobilize support for their Islamist policy, and purge the faint-hearted. We need not pause to consider which was really the case, since both possibilities are entirely characteristic of modern public life. Nor are they confined to states in the throes of revolution. The Egyptian seizure of the Suez Canal at the outset of the Yom Kippur War in 1973 was conducted by military methods that could hardly have spoken more plainly of the limited ends in view. Yet the Israeli reaction is widely suspected to have included a threat to employ nuclear weapons, and eventually created conditions that left both the United States and the Soviet Union teetering on the edge of direct military intervention.[16]

Modern war is distinguished by the scale and diversity of social resources that are mobilized on its behalf, and also by the complexity of social and political interactions that are set in motion within belligerent communities whenever they exercise, and experience, organized violence. These go substantially beyond the arousal of hostile feelings, and have proven resistant to mastery by any form of social theory. They have lent an ominous imponderability to the conduct even of limited war. Clausewitz anticipated this as a general possibility. He notes in one passage that escalation of a war begun for limited aims would be prevented 'in most cases...on account of the domestic problems it would raise'.[17] He also associated the broadening of political participation that the Revolution had brought about with an increase in the ferocity and implacability of war. But such considerations, had he chosen to pursue them, would have taken him beyond the military sphere that was his focus, and he did not explore them comprehensively. One way or another, he

---

[15] There is a lucid discussion of this requirement, and the difficulty of implementing it in practice, in James Cable, *Gunboat Diplomacy, 1919–1991* (New York, 1994), 15–64.
[16] Martin van Creveld, *The Sword and the Olive: A Critical History of the Israeli Defense Force* (New York, 1998), 217–37.
[17] Clausewitz, *On War*, VIII, 3B, p. 585.

was sure, the *Zeitgeist* would make itself felt. 'The aims a belligerent adopts', he proposed, 'must be governed by the particular characteristics of his own position; but they will [*sic*] also conform to the spirit of the age and to its general character.'[18] This is as far as Clausewitz felt able to go in analysing this aspect of his problem.

Nevertheless, Clausewitz knew that the aim of theory was not to draw a map of the unknown world, but to point us in the right direction, and it would be nonsense to suggest that his emphasis on the controlling effect of ends on means in war is no longer capable of doing this. For Clausewitz, victory and defeat are psychological facts, which the physical violence of war is intended to bring about. At a minimum, this might suggest a rule of thumb, to the effect that, the more remote, complex, subtle, or speculative are the psychological changes required in the mind of one's adversary, the more difficult it may be to bring about those changes by force. This is not a prescription that Clausewitz offers in so many words. But it would appear to be a reasonable elaboration on his insistence that the ends of policy do not contradict the nature of its most violent and unpredictable instrument.

The point is strengthened if we set Clausewitz's arguments about the primacy of politics alongside his equally persistent emphasis on the role of emotional and psychological elements in war. Their interactions were among the most likely reasons for ends and means to part company. Knowing what a war is about may be the beginning of wisdom, but it could be no more than a starting point from Clausewitz's perspective. One sees this, for instance, in a series of letters that he exchanged with a young staff officer named Karl von Roeder. The exchange occurred toward the end of 1827, a few months after Clausewitz had written the note in which he outlined his plans to revise *On War* in light of his new appreciation of war's dual nature.

Roeder wrote to Clausewitz to get his views on a staff exercise, hypothesizing war between Austria and Prussia. Clausewitz began by criticizing the problem, which had been formulated in purely operational terms. The size and deployments of the opposing forces were specified, but there was no hint of the quarrel that was supposed to be bringing them within weapons' range of each other. Without such information, Clausewitz began, it was difficult to evaluate any military plan. He then goes on to highlight some of the incongruities that arise from the failure of the exercise to specify the strategic objectives of the belligerents. Prussia's aim, since it was the side being attacked, could be presumed to be self-defence, at least initially. Austria's was mysterious, and could not be inferred from the information presented. The exercise stipulated a rough parity between Austrian and Prussian forces, which suggested to

---

[18] Ibid. VIII, 3B, p. 594.

Clausewitz that Austria's goals in going to war must be quite limited. But it also described conduct on the Austrian side that was not consistent with limited aims. Some of the operations attributed to them entailed great risk, and involved objectives that the forces specified could not have been expected to achieve.

In the end, Clausewitz advised his young colleague (somewhat dishearteningly, one imagines) that any solution Roeder might propose was destined to fail because of the underlying contradictions of the problem itself. This seemed to him especially true with respect to one of the questions Roeder was supposed to answer: what course of action, by Austria, posed the greatest danger for Prussia? This, Clausewitz says, is entirely dependent on what the Austrians were trying to achieve: 'The greatest threat for Prussia', he says, 'can only be determined if we know what the Austrian objective...will be'.[19]

All of which exemplifies Clausewitz's approach to operational analysis. Ideally, every line on the map should be related to the overall strategic objective for which the war is fought; or, at any rate, should not contradict or imperil that objective. Nevertheless, in seeking to impress upon Roeder the importance of taking political objectives fully into account, Clausewitz does not actually address the problem of why the Austrians might want to attack Prussia. On the contrary, he virtually dismisses the question, by noting that, in real life such answers can usually be inferred from what we know about the prior relationship of the belligerents. In all probability, he regarded the range of possibilities in this instance as self-evident.

In any case, rather than proceed to an analysis of current relations between the Habsburgs and the Hohenzollerns, he turns instead to an altogether different topic: the diverging personalities and circumstances of Napoleon Bonaparte and Frederick the Great. Comparisons of these two great captains in Clausewitz's day were inclined to favour Bonaparte, who raised more powerful armies, and led them to more stunning victories. But such arguments, Clausewitz declares, are of little value, and not just because they fail to notice that Napoleon ruled a country eight times larger than Frederick's. The moral basis of his rule was also different: Napoleon was 'a usurper, who had won his immense power in a kind of perpetual game of chance, and who, for the greater part of his perilous career, did not even possess an heir; while Frederick disposed of a true patrimony'. Even given identical psychological characteristics, Clausewitz says, their conduct would still have reflected the difference in the nature of the states they ruled; to which one might add that their contrasting political circumstances were themselves reflections of their personalities. A man like Frederick would scarcely have risen to the top of the

[19] Clausewitz, 'Two Letters on Strategy', 17.

heap amid the turmoil of the French Revolution; while Napoleon was no better suited to rule a small, impoverished central European kingdom than he was to be the emperor of Elba. Such considerations, Clausewitz tells Roeder, are not 'trivialities, but the *most important issues*'.[20]

Which is to say that, for Clausewitz, the question 'What is the war about?' immediately leads not to categorical answers, but to additional questions, and above all: Who is fighting? What moves them, really? One sees this in his studies of Napoleon's campaigns. Napoleon's conservative opponents, even those willing to acknowledge his military brilliance, were inclined to see him as a demonic nemesis spawned by the French Revolution. There are some passages like this in Clausewitz, too. But Clausewitz also never forgot that Napoleon was the supreme leader of France, which had been the most powerful state in Europe since long before Napoleon was born. Its expansionist ambitions had been amplified, but not fundamentally altered, by the same revolutionary forces that brought Napoleon to power. Napoleon's armies did not go to war as an expression of ideological frenzy. They fought for real strategic objectives, and the first step to resisting them was to grasp what the objectives were. But still, they were also *Napoleon's* armies, and this mattered, too. The demons were not the primary drivers of policy, but they were able to make their influence felt, sometimes decisively.

Thus, in his brilliant analysis of the campaign of 1812, Clausewitz rejected what had already become the common-place explanation for France's defeat: that Napoleon was doomed from the moment he set out to overwhelm the Russians in a single campaign. Clausewitz was not willing to settle for this. In particular, he did not settle for the unspoken assumption that caution is synonymous with safety. The safer path—by which Clausewitz meant the path most likely to achieve the political purpose of the war—was in fact the one Napoleon chose: to reach Moscow in a single leap, and hold the city hostage until the conclusion of peace. Clausewitz does not see anything implausible in this idea. Napoleon did not fail because he made some kind of logical error in the reconciliation of ends and means. In Clausewitz's judgement the end was feasible enough, and the means adequate, if barely so. No, he failed for two reasons. First, he did not anticipate the Russian reaction to his arrival outside Moscow: that they would burn the place down and defy Napoleon to do his worst. This, Clausewitz concluded, was a possibility for which there was no sure strategic solution, no alternative course of action that would have led to success. But it could only have been regarded in advance as an utterly remote possibility—it was, after all, an episode without precedent—and to that extent the burning of Moscow, and the defiance that it symbolized, were not really

---

[20] Ibid. 15; emphasis in the original.

a mistake that Napoleon could have avoided. The ruination of Napoleon's empire in the frozen steppes of Russia was simply fate, a demonstration of how the uncertainties of war can exceed the grasp of even the greatest genius.

Nevertheless, there was a second reason for Napoleon's failure, and one that could be laid squarely at his feet: he wasted him own army during his advance into Russia, and thus omitted 'one...essential consideration: *to remain strong even in Moscow*'.[21] This is the one thing Napoleon could have done differently that might have given him a chance to control the implacable Russian reaction that Napoleon himself inspired by virtue of his initial, deeply humiliating successes. And this omission Clausewitz unhesitatingly assigns not to any sort of miscalculation, but to 'the arrogant recklessness that was characteristic of him'. Which in turn leads to a typically Clausewitzian inversion, whereby Napoleon's fatal arrogance is revealed to be but one aspect of his genius. His failure was part and parcel of his success, and flowed from the same source. 'Everything he was', Clausewitz concludes, 'he owed to his daring and resolute character; and his most triumphant campaigns would have suffered the same censure as this one, had they not succeeded.'[22]

Clausewitz's treatment of Napoleon illustrates with exceptional clarity the place of strategic and military objectives in his work. It is a central concern, the starting point from which every major military problem is considered. Yet it remains one tool among others. Its analytical value can only be proportional to the moral and psychological hold that the objective has upon a belligerent: its political leadership, its people, and its armed forces. That hold, Clausewitz knew, would vary with circumstances, including the relative strength and efficiency of the political institutions that are available to mobilize support and fight the war; institutions whose purpose is precisely to subordinate private interests and values to the interests and values of the state. The strength of the grip that politics may exert on the conduct of military operations will also change as the war proceeds, and violence and suffering take their toll. But that is the risk of having chosen war as an instrument in the first place. The only point of violence and suffering in war is to change people's minds. Clausewitz would have been the first to agree that it is not always possible to anticipate the ways in which they will be changed.

In contemplating the wars of Napoleon, Clausewitz emphasized the organizing effect of political objectives on military violence. But he regularly qualified and sometimes discounted their impact in order to account for

---

[21] Carl von Clausewitz, 'The Campaign of 1812 in Russia', in *Historical and Political Writings*, 202; emphasis in the original.
[22] Ibid. 204.

the confounding effects of Napoleon's personal psychology, and also for the fact that Napoleon was the leader of a post-revolutionary government, whose unexampled military success was the chief source of public legitimacy for what Clausewitz seems to have regarded as an otherwise fragile regime. Clausewitz knew that not all governments were equally adept at translating political objectives into purposeful military action. But this was not a problem that especially concerned him. He wrote at a time when the great powers of Europe presented an unusually uniform political picture, and, as he says to Roeder, this allowed certain common characteristics to be taken for granted in practice.

Nevertheless, it is clearly wrong to claim that his work is unduly coloured by the temporary pre-eminence of the absolutist state, or that he was unaware of other political possibilities. In the same way that war is 'merely an instrument of policy', policy, he tells us, is 'merely the trustee' of all the varied interests existing within a political community.[23] Any community capable of envisioning its collective interests should be capable, in theory, of employing force to advance them. If centralized states were the characteristic political form of his day, Clausewitz believed this was because their military and political structures had proven superior to available alternatives. Weak and fragmented societies were likely to be less militarily effective than others, but that did not mean that the wars they waged lacked meaning or purpose.

Trusteeship, however, is clearly important, and the claim to exercise it cannot be taken at face value. Revolutionary and secessionist movements always present themselves as paladins of an oppressed community. Yet their relationship to that community may be overwhelmingly predatory, if not entirely imaginary. Such conditions do not necessarily deprive violence of its purposive character. They merely render its ostensible, political purposes irrelevant as a lens for judging or anticipating an adversary's actions. But Clausewitz would have said that this was equally true of Napoleon. In his final campaigns it scarcely made sense to think of him fighting for the felicity and safety of France. To do so merely introduced an additional source of strategic miscalculation: Napoleon was fighting to save himself. France had become a weapon in his hands.

Clausewitz's limited comments on medieval warfare, and a few incisive pages on what he called 'people's war', are as close as he comes to discussing what are nowadays called 'non-state actors'. He wrote little about either of these military forms, perhaps because he felt he did not know very much about them. 'People's war', as he said, seemed to him 'a phenomenon of the nineteenth century', about which no firm conclusions could yet be drawn. Though

[23] Clausewitz, *On War*, VIII, 6B, p. 606.

he does seem to have recognized that, under conditions of ultimate peril, when the future existence of the community is at stake, and all the 'trustees' are dead and gone, at such moments the conventionalized relationship of ends and means that characterized conflict between intact governments might turn into something like existential violence, intended less to achieve a political aim than to affirm a political identity:

> There will always be time enough to die; like a drowning man who will clutch instinctively at a straw, it is the natural law of the moral world that a nation that finds itself on the brink of an abyss will try to save itself by any means.
>
> No matter how small and weak a state may be in comparison with its enemy, it must not forego these last efforts, or one would conclude that its soul is dead.[24]

As far as war in the Middle Ages was concerned, he regarded it as having a diffuse and generic character, which he attributed to the fact that both combat and the ends for which it was undertaken were still shaped by the cultural preferences of a self-contained social elite, for whom war was both a political instrument and a form of personal self-expression.[25] Clausewitz regarded such conditions—the warfare of the feudal nobility on the one hand, and of the popular uprising on the other—as symptomatic of political weakness, and in the latter case of political desperation. But, with the possible exception of the striking passage quoted above, nothing that he says about them suggests that he thought they embodied any theoretical contradiction of a sort that would deprive war of its instrumental quality.

To return, then, to that seminal strategic question—what is the war about?—it is safe to say that Clausewitz's theoretical framework is able to accommodate any answer except one: 'Nothing'. If war is about nothing—if its violence cannot be related to some ulterior motive or purpose—then both historical analysis and strategic planning become, at the very least, distinctly peculiar. We get a hint of this peculiarity in the American 'global war on terror', a conflict that is thought to be distinctive by virtue of the shadowy, insubstantial nature of the terrorist opponent. No less distinctive, however, is the outlook of the United States, which is waging its war on terror without reference to any kind of strategic interaction between itself and its adversary. The perpetrators of terrorism are not conceived as having strategic objectives. Rather, they are thought to have embarked on a campaign of *non-instrumental* violence, directed against humanity as such. The United States, it is supposed, is being assailed not for what it does, or even for what it wants, but simply because of what it is.[26]

---

[24] *On War*, VI, 26, p. 483.   [25] Ibid. VIII, 3B, pp. 587–8.

[26] This point of view was anticipated, and perhaps shaped, by Samuel Huntington's influential book, *The Clash of Civilizations and the Remaking of the World Order* (New York, 1996); see also

As a consequence, it has proven extraordinarily difficult for the United States to conceive of its own conduct strategically. Having defined its enemy in purely tactical terms—and terrorism is after all nothing more than a tactic—its defensive efforts have largely been reduced to a tissue of tactical expedients. Enormous sums have been spent on 'homeland defense', with a view to making air travel safer, beefing up security at tempting targets like port facilities and power plants, and de-conflicting the responses of local police and fire departments, so as to make sure, for instance, that everyone is using the same kind of radio, in the event that someone puts poison in the town water tower. If one sets aside the United States' invasion of Iraq in 2003, whose ostensible links to Islamist terrorism have not withstood much scrutiny, American military strategy since its initial dismantlement of the Taliban regime in Afghanistan has devolved into a globalized search-and-destroy operation, whose aim is to round up and wipe out al-Qaeda and its affiliates, if need be one terrorist at a time.

No one within the American armed forces has yet complained publicly that the United States lacks a 'clear' objective in conducting its war on terror. Perhaps it is just a matter of time, or perhaps military leaders are satisfied that the current objective—a successful round-up—is clear enough. It certainly presents a compelling theory of victory to the public: the complete elimination of terrorist attacks on Americans. But it also entails considerable risk, of political disillusionment in the event of it not being achieved, and also of the likelihood that any successful attack on the United States will be perceived and experienced not as a tactical setback, but as a strategic defeat, to which a disproportionate and escalatory response may prove difficult to resist.

Clausewitz would probably have suggested that this sort of disabling, excessively self-referential perspective was itself a measure of the terrorists' success. Terroristic violence is always designed to achieve great psychological leverage through the expenditure of small amounts of force, and one sign that the leverage has been achieved is the willingness of the victim to alter its traditional habits and values in response. But beyond that it is hard to know what else Clausewitz might have had to contribute. If the war on terror is really a struggle against an adversary without a purpose—a claim whose investigation is beyond our present purpose—then in Clausewitzian terms it is war only metaphorically: like war on cancer, or crime, or poverty. The rhetoric of war is employed to mobilize support, and brush aside doubts or criticism. But that is as far as it goes. The logic of politics is no longer able to employ the grammar of war to express itself, because the mutual interaction of ends and

---

Ian Buruma and Avishai Margalit, *Occidentalism: The West in the Eyes of its Enemies* (New York, 2004).

means, and of adversaries with each other, is absent. A world in which violence is employed without reference to strategic or political ends is not one that Clausewitz envisaged. Strictly speaking, it would be a world without war—without 'final arguments', in which the ultimate instrument of politics is no longer of much use. But that does not mean that it will necessarily be a safe or easy place in which to live.

# 6

## Moral Forces in War

*Ulrike Kleemeier*

Clausewitz is well known for his maxim 'War is the continuation of policy by other means'.[1] Indeed, research on Clausewitz since the Second World War, at least in Germany, has mainly concentrated on the relationships between war and policy. (Things are slightly different in the United States.[2]) What follows draws the reader's attention to another stream of thought in the work of Clausewitz, one which is not contradictory to his views on war and policy but different.[3] The motto which dominates this line of thinking is a statement for which he is less known that 'The main sources of human action are feelings'.[4] I will elucidate Clausewitz's theory of moral forces[5] in war as it is developed in book I, chapter 3, of *On War*,[6] and also investigate the connections between Clausewitz's reflections on moral factors and his theory of friction. The

---

[1] This essay is a revised and developed version of chapter 4. 3 of my Habilitationsschrift, Ulrike Kleemeier, *Grundfragen einer philosophischen Theorien des Krieges. Platon–Hobbes–Clausewitz* (Berlin, 2002), 244 ff. The 19th German edition of *Vom Kriege*, ed. Werner Hahlweg (Bonn, 1980) has been used, and all translations are mine.

[2] See, e.g. Alan Beyerchen, 'Clausewitz, Nonlinearity, and the Unpredictability of War', *International Security*, 17, 3 (1992–3), 59–90; Jon Tetsuro Sumida, 'The Relationship of History and Theory in *On War*: The Clausewitzian Ideal and Its Implications', *Journal of Military History*, 65 (2001), 333–54.

[3] War is not only the continuation of policy by other means. According to Clausewitz, war is structured by the so-called 'trinity' which is described by Clausewitz from several points of view. One way of describing the trinity is government, armed forces, and people. Here the level of policy (government) is only one among others. See Christopher Bassford's chapter in this book.

[4] *Vom Kriege*, I, 3, p. 252.

[5] Originally I used the term 'moral virtues' instead of 'moral forces'. The word 'virtue' is not morally neutral in the widespread sense of the expression 'moral'. To say of somebody that he or she possesses certain virtues means that we praise him or her for being just or kind, etc. The term 'force' seems to be more neutral. To push matters to the extreme: perhaps a (war) criminal can have moral forces in the Clausewitzian sense. This is a very subtle question, which José Fernández Vega, among others, has put to me, and I keep changing my mind about the answers. As long as I am not sure, it is better to use the broader term 'forces', and this is also the expression employed by Michael Howard and Peter Paret in their translation of *Vom Kriege*.

[6] Clausewitz also refers to moral forces in *Vom Kriege*, III, 2–10, pp. 356–72. These considerations are taken into account here, but the principal focus is on book I.

Clausewitzian way of thinking has influenced Prussian–German conceptions of military leadership up until the present. In a sense Clausewitz outlined the paradigm of a good soldier in the Prussian–German tradition. The chapter then moves on to the possible relevance which this image of a good soldier might have for us today. My general position runs as follows. Clausewitz was not a rationalist thinker, though he is often considered as such.[7] In fact, human emotions play a role in Clausewitz's account of war which cannot be overrated. Feelings of different kinds are the very foundation on which the faculty of reason can build. His deep appreciation of the role of emotions connects Clausewitz not with Hegel and still less with Kant.[8] Instead, there are many similarities to a tradition of thinking represented by Spinoza, Hobbes, Hume, and Montesquieu. All these philosophers share the emphasis on feelings as the only source of rational activity. Clausewitz read and appreciated Montesquieu; he presumably never read Spinoza, Hobbes, or Hume, but nevertheless there are strong analogies between many of their views.

Clausewitz's theory of moral forces in war is founded on a simple observation: military action in war always faces an enormous gap between theory and practice. What seems to be very straightforward in a plan of war is difficult in reality and can often not be realized at all. Similar differences also exist in other areas like economics, policy, and everyday life. But war as the extreme form of conflict takes place in the field of mutual violence, and therefore the gap between ideas and reality is here more drastic and dramatic than in any other field of human action. As a common designation for all factors which stand between theory and practice, between plan and action, Clausewitz used the term 'friction'. He borrowed this expression from mechanics. There is a stream of frictions characterizing every war from the beginning to the end. Countless examples of friction exist. You want to cross a bridge, but the enemy has destroyed it. In normal circumstances you would take a detour, but perhaps the enemy has blocked every other way. Suddenly an ally on whom you relied leaves you in the lurch; the result may be terrible. You are in a northern country and winter is coming. Certainly, you can in principle protect yourselves even against extreme cold, but in this case the enemy will use the cold against

---

[7] See, e.g. Martin van Creveld, *The Transformation of War* (New York, 1991), 96–7 [for the German edition, *Die Zukunft des Krieges* (Munich, 1998), 104]; Gerhard Ritter, *Staatskunst und Kriegshandwerk. Das Problem des Militarismus in Deutschland* (4 vols., Munich, 1954–68), I, 210 et seq.

[8] Clausewitz was perhaps much less influenced by German Idealism than many people suppose. There is of course an influence from German Idealism, but the way Clausewitz uses its ideas is not typical, and he picks those which he considers to be important for his purposes. His ideas cannot be systematically subsumed under the heading 'idealism'. It seems to me that Clausewitz was very much aware of Kant's *Kritik der Urteilskraft*, but this does not mean that he agreed with Kantian practical philosophy. In fact, everything speaks against this.

you; he will make every effort to destroy your means of protection. One could go on like this. The main causes of extreme friction in war are twofold. First, acting in war is always acting *against* somebody in the most threatening way. At every stage of war you have to be aware of your enemy trying to harm you by taking your life. Second, human beings are fearful creatures. In particular, they are afraid of violence and violent death. Frictions result from the interplay between these factors. The most important factor is human fear. In a thought experiment you could imagine human beings who know no such feeling as fear. In this case there would still be friction, but it would be more or less meaningless. Anthropology lies at the core of Clausewitz's theory of frictions. Frictions do not develop out of nothing, but are mainly produced by human weakness. The more friction there is the more chaos dominates and this in turn widens the distance between theory and reality even more. Frictions are cumulative processes; if there is one there are likely to be others.

Here is an example: in war rumours are spread. Nobody knows if they are true. Some people tend to be anxious and fearful, and they believe only the bad ones. Others are more optimistic and believe the good ones. As a result nobody really knows what is going on. Clausewitz once said that information in war and about war is either false or contradictory and completely useless.[9] He would not have been much more positive today. Intelligence services are equipped with the latest products of computer technology, but friction is not reduced. On the contrary, in the whole flood of information made possible by technical development recipients have to choose between what is relevant and what is useless. And of course a lot of false information can be spread, sometimes intentionally. Far from being diminished, friction can be increased through technology.[10] In any event, frictions produce confusion and, following Clausewitz, one could truly say, 'there is a general named "chaos" and he is every soldier's enemy'.

In this context, it is to be noted that the English word 'war' has its origin in the old Germanic term, *werra*, which means more or less the same as 'confusion' or 'disorder'. This meaning is also present in the French *guerre* or the Spanish *guerra*. So with his concept of friction Clausewitz has grasped a central part of the traditional semantics of 'war'. This original meaning of the term 'war' has to be sharply distinguished from the content of the Latin word *bellum*. *Bellum* has always meant the same as 'violent struggle for rights'. Because the notion of right relates to law, the concept of *bellum* also belongs to the realm of law, be it natural or positive law. Of course today the meanings of *werra* and *bellum* have merged. The use of the word 'war', for example,

---

[9] See *Vom Kriege*, I, 6, pp. 258 ff.
[10] See also the contributions by Antulio Echevarria and David Lonsdale in this book.

provides a link to international law. But the semantic histories of 'war' and *bellum* are very different. In a way, they are even contradictory, because law is something conceived of as well ordered. It belongs to the nature of law both to be ordered in itself and at the same time to impose an order on human beings. In so far as 'war' originally meant precisely the same as 'disorder' we have a contrast between 'war' and *bellum*.[11] Clausewitz tells us a great deal about war but almost nothing about *bellum*.[12]

## MILITARY GENIUS: THE POWER OF BALANCE AND THE BALANCE OF POWERS

The conception of war as the paradigmatic field of friction forms the basis of Clausewitz's theory of military leadership. A military leader's quality is to be measured by his ability to display human virtues against a chaos characterized by permanent danger and violence. To achieve this, several competences are required which Clausewitz subsumed under the concept of moral forces.

On a very general level, Clausewitz describes the so-called genius for war or, as we would put it today, the ideal military leader as a *harmonious unity composed of the powers of reason and soul*, or a unity of rational and emotional capacities. This general explication is important. Clausewitz does not start by focusing on a single competence, for example a specific area of military expertise. His starting point is the *whole* person. The genius for war comprises all aspects of personality, rational as well as emotional. There are no parts of a person which do not contribute to the military genius. The employment of all human forces is still not sufficient; what is even more important is the *harmony* or *balance* of all the parts. The isolation and independent action of just one element, for example reason, would result in a thing as dysfunctional as a leg which is cut off from a living body.

This holistic conception of military genius reflects a basic fact. The fact is that soldiers in war have to accomplish the double task of risking their own lives (or the lives of subordinates) and taking other lives in certain circumstances. Therefore in borderline situations of this type the whole of

---

[11] For the difference between 'war' and *bellum*, see Peter Henrici, 'Two Types of Philosophical Approach to the Problem of War and Peace', in Peter Caws (ed.), *The Causes of Quarrel: Essays on Peace, War and Thomas Hobbes* (Boston, MA, 1989), 149–61.There is a tension and at the same time a subtle interplay between the semantics of 'war' and *bellum* in the work of Thomas Hobbes. See Kleemeier, *Grundfragen*, 135.

[12] Andreas Herberg-Rothe has pointed out that it might be constructive to combine the Clausewitzian approach to war with theories of just war. See Herberg-Rothe, *Das Rätsel Clausewitz*, pp. 240 ff.

human existence is at risk and because of this the corresponding tasks can only be fulfilled by the whole human being. In fact, Clausewitz's model of military competence is founded on the premise that military action is always action either *in* an exceptional state or *referring to* the exceptional state. People sometimes tend to ignore the truth of this premise. In Germany, for example, phrases like 'being a soldier is a profession like every other profession' have become fashionable. Declarations of this kind are false as well as dangerous. They are false because bakers, butchers, or philosophers are not expected to kill other people or be killed themselves. They are dangerous, because, if public opinion becomes accustomed to them, it will in the end not accept that it is the right and duty of soldiers under well-defined conditions to use their weapons. Of course, there is nothing against soldiers building kindergartens or helping civilians reconstruct their lives. Very conservative minds can find all this ridiculous, because they think the only job of soldiers is combat. However, that attitude is itself ridiculous in Clausewitzian terms, since it is founded on the wholly un-Clausewitzian view that military tasks can be divided from political ones. The kindergarten built by soldiers may be attacked by enemies and then it has to be defended through violence.

Clausewitz's military genius is characterized by four qualities: (*a*) totality, (*b*) holism, (*c*) vital dynamics, and (*d*) egalitarianism.[13] The genius for war represents a totality, because it comprises *all* the facets of a personality, both rational and emotional. No element of the human mind should or can avoid contributing to the whole. It becomes holistic not just because every element of the human being contributes to the whole but through the idea of balance and interaction. We confront not the mere sum of capacities, each of which could work independently of the other, but something similar to an organism. Thirdly, the genius for war is dynamic in a vitalistic sense. This can be made clear by an investigation of the term 'force' (*Kraft*). A force is not self-sufficient as a quality but has a direction it follows. Intimately connected to the idea of force are the conceptions of development and growth.[14] Finally, the genius for war is structured in an egalitarian way, because there is no mental force which is either exclusively dominant or exclusively suppressed.

---

[13] These ideas were inspired by Massimo Mori, 'Das Bild des Krieges bei den deutschen Philosophen', in Johannes Kunisch and Herfried Münkler (eds), *Die Wiedergeburt des Krieges aus dem Geist der Revolution. Studien zum bellizistischen Diskurs des ausgehenden 18. und beginnenden 19. Jahrhunderts* (Berlin, 1999), 225–40; here p. 233 f. Mori is not concerned with Clausewitz at all in this essay, but he uses the first three of the criteria and points out that they fit the Kantian notion of an organism.

[14] There is an exact analogy here between Clausewitz's theory of the genius for war and his concept of war. For Clausewitz war is not a *status*, but an *actus*. See *Vom Kriege*, I, 1, p. 191. In an analogous way the persons who wage war are not sums of static qualities, but fields of forces, although in a vitalistic, not a mechanistic, sense of force.

One seemingly peculiar thing has to be added to these remarks. Clausewitz also describes the military genius as a melancholic person.[15] Unfortunately, the word 'melancholy' has fallen out of current use. We use the clinical term 'depression' to refer to a mental illness. Depressed people are notoriously unhappy. They are unable to enjoy the pleasures of life. Instead, their mind is darkened by permanent sadness. Clausewitz is not telling us that a severely depressed state of mind is a precondition for being a good military leader. That would be farcical. Rather, he uses the expression 'melancholy' to describe people who have deep and serious feelings which develop slowly and cannot easily be overcome. Melancholic persons are distinguished from phlegmatic, choleric, and sanguine people.[16] The phlegmatic person can hardly be moved by anything; the choleric one is very easily moved, but he cannot control and balance his emotions and is successful only in the short run. Sanguine people have emotions, but these never overcome a certain modest limit. Following Clausewitz, none of these three characters is much use in war, for obvious reasons. On the other hand, the melancholic possesses everything war requires: feelings which are at the same time strong and continuous. What Clausewitz has in mind when he uses the word 'melancholy' proves to be something very different from depression. We think of depressed persons as being severely limited in their actions. A melancholic in the Clausewitzian sense is, on the contrary, someone who will act in exactly the right way, because his passions form a strong and solid foundation for action. So melancholy is not an illness at all, but a source of successful action. There is a certain ring of paradox here. On the one hand, you cannot eliminate the element of suffering from the notion of a passion (*Leidenschaft*). Having a passion, as distinct from having a spontaneous emotion or affection, means being driven by a constant and powerful mental need, and to be in permanent need of something certainly indicates suffering. On the other hand, passions can become the very basis of great actions. This is so, because passions can combine with reason in a way spontaneous feelings cannot.[17] Passions and reason share something. Passions are long-term emotions. Reason is able to think and plan in long-term ways. So the faculty of reason can be used to fulfil passions. It is this special relationship on which Clausewitz focuses. Suffering from deep and strong emotions

[15] *Vom Kriege*, I, 3, p. 243.

[16] This is only partly Clausewitz's own terminology. I take these conceptual distinctions from Kant. See Immanuel Kant, *Anthropologie in pragmatischer Hinsicht*, in *Werke in zwölf Bände*, ed. Wilhelm Weischedel, XII, p. 626 ff. The differentiation between phlegmatic, sanguine, choleric, and melancholic persons has a long tradition reaching back to Greek antiquity, and was widespread in Clausewitz's times.

[17] It is exactly the intimate connection of passions and reason which led Kant to reject passions altogether. For Kant, passions are nothing but weaknesses. Passions and human freedom are not compatible. See Kant, *Anthropologie in pragmatischer Hinsicht*, p. 599 ff.

can be turned into action through employing the intellect. The link between passion and reason is will power, which possesses both emotional and rational elements. It is will power which gives structure and direction to emotions and prevents a person from being overwhelmed by them.

Despite all their differences, melancholy and depression are linked. Just like the melancholic, the depressed person is capable of being moved in deep and serious ways. That is why a predisposition to sadness is always present in melancholy. The difference is that in depression those emotions do not produce action, because will power is almost completely lacking in the depressive state of mind. Perhaps the best way to heal a depression, according to Clausewitz, is to (re-)turn it into melancholy.

## THE FACULTY OF JUDGEMENT: VISIONS IN THE DARK

Clausewitz differentiates between several special moral forces in war. First, there is the *Takt des Urteils*, or faculty of judgement. Sometimes Clausewitz also uses the French expression *coup d'oeil*, which may indicate a more intuitive response to the battlefield, but which I see as synonymous. This is a specific form of reason described by Clausewitz as a capacity 'which even in this increased darkness is not without some traces of the inner light leading it to truth'.[18] Clausewitz refers to its results as 'flashes of lightning which arise almost unconsciously and don't develop within a long chain of thought'.[19] It is best to conceive of *coup d'oeil* as a union of feeling and reason. It is a specific kind of faculty by which truth is felt rather than deduced. It is not an analytical power but a capacity to synthesize which helps the military leader 'to become conscious of the truth as if it were a single clear thought'.[20] Although it may sound peculiar in the framework of military thought, 'intuition' is the word which best captures this power of judgement. We use exactly this term to signify mental acts which happen rapidly, are spontaneous, intimately connected with emotional life, and possess synthesizing power. Of course, this does not mean that intuitions cannot be based on experience. Presumably the opposite is the case. A completely untrained person who finds himself on a battlefield would not have constructive intuitions. But the phenomenon remains that these are insights very different from those achieved through deductive reasoning.[21]

[18] *Vom Kriege*, I, 3, p. 233.  [19] Ibid. VI, 30, p. 855.  [20] Ibid. VIII, 1, p. 951.
[21] It is a delicate philosophical question whether there are 'really' intuitions or whether we in fact infer everything we think or perceive from something else. We may have the impression that we have an intuition, but we may be in error, because we may have actually inferred from

114     Ulrike Kleemeier

Clausewitz's remarks on *coup d'oeil* are directed at the rationalist theorists of war who focused almost exclusively on a dissecting and calculating form of reason, built round long-term planning. Of course, this type of reasoning is important in the area of policy. You have to calculate means and ends; you have to make long-term plans for the post-war settlement, and so on. If you do not do this you run a high risk of losing the war. But for soldiers as themselves all this is insufficient and sometimes even unproductive. Deductive reasoning takes a long time to develop and works too inflexibly in the chaos which is war. Action in war demands a more intuitive way of thinking. Clausewitz's *coup d'oeil* is a capacity which exactly fits the demands of borderline situations. It belongs to those powers generated in some people by trouble and danger. Today the fashionable term for this sort of power is 'emotional intelligence'. Indeed, it seems to me that Clausewitz is a theorist of emotional intelligence in violent conflict. His high appreciation of emotions acts as a guiding principle through his theory of moral forces in war. Clausewitz believed that so called 'pure' reason was not an adequate instrument to master war. War in particular requires the vigilance and activity of the feelings, senses, and passions—in short the interacting effects of the whole pool of human abilities. These Clausewitzian insights have deeply influenced German conceptions of military leadership up until the present. Unfortunately, they were severely simplified by Helmuth von Moltke the elder, but that is a different matter.[22]

## SHADES OF BRAVERY: MANY WAYS TO BE COURAGEOUS

*Coup d'oeil* is not the only virtue required in war. As is to be expected Clausewitz adds *bravery* or *courage*.[23] Being a soldier, Clausewitz knew that there was

experience. This problem cannot be followed here. The American philosopher, Charles Sanders Peirce, has many sophisticated observations on this question.

[22] Moltke tended to draw sharp distinctions between reason and emotion which are completely alien to Clausewitz. In his *Verordnungen für die höheren Truppenführer* of 1869 he wrote: 'In war qualities of character are more important than qualities of reason.' The *Heeresdienstvorschrift 100/100* from 1998 uses a very similar formulation: 'Bravery, resoluteness, being able to have one's way and personal charisma often are more important than the abilities of reason' (see Christian E. O. Millotat, *Das preußisch—deutsche Generalstabssystem. Wurzeln—Entwicklung—Fortwirken* (Zürich, 2000), 148). These statements suggest that a military leader may be brave, resolute, wilful, and charismatic, while at the same time being a bit stupid. Clausewitz would never have written these sentences.

[23] Clausewitz himself mainly uses the term *Mut* and rarely the word *Tapferkeit*. I will use both as synonyms. In English *Mut* corresponds more to 'courage', whereas *Tapferkeit* is more or less equivalent to 'bravery'. So I will use both English terms as synonyms, too. I may be in error, because today *Mut* and *Tapferkeit* can have slightly different connotations. If you praise someone

more than just one kind of bravery. He distinguished between (at least) three types. The first is bravery in situations where life and body are at risk. This sort of bravery is subdivided into two categories. It can consist of mere indifference to danger, but it can also be an emotion resulting from positive motivations. Yet a third kind of bravery is resolution, a quality which refers to the inner life of a military leader.

Indifference to danger is a result of routine or habit. It is a permanent state of mind compared by Clausewitz to second nature. It is striking, and symptomatic, that Clausewitz is hardly interested in this sort of courage. On the one hand, it indicates that Clausewitz is principally concerned with military leaders, rather than with those under their command. On the other, it means that Clausewitz breaks with a certain tradition in thinking about a soldier's virtues. According to the stoic tradition, the most noble task of soldiers was to endure the danger of death and wounds, and to submit to the fate of certain death. Bravery in this framework is conceived of as an intensified ability to suffer. This kind of courage is perhaps closest to what Clausewitz calls 'indifference to danger'. Although it is secondary to Clausewitz, it is not unimportant. A person without a certain indifference to danger and other challenges would be helpless in war.[24]

Much more valuable than indifference is boldness (*Kühnheit*), a form of courage induced by positive motivations. Clausewitz refers to it as a 'creative force' (*schöpferische Kraft*).[25] Boldness enables a person not just to endure danger but to master and overcome it through acting. All of this demonstrates the new model of a soldier who acts and thinks as an individual. His primary task is not submission to a fate or to providence, but survival in even the most difficult situations. Following Clausewitz, battle and war are not mainly places of sacrifice but places of active and creative survival. I assume that this attitude has more or less gained acceptance in all modern Western armies.

As emotional sources of boldness Clausewitz counts every sort of enthusiasm, especially patriotism and ambition. In his view patriotism is more important for the rabble.[26] More striking is his estimation of ambition, which

for being *mutig* (courageous), you mean that he is risking something important. We tend to use this term to refer to an act, not to refer to being ready to suffer something. The word *Tapferkeit* can also be used to designate states of mind which enable you to suffer with honour a terrible fate like dying or being wounded.

[24] An untrained person on a battlefield will presumably have just one intuition, which is to flee. Whether this is a constructive intuition depends on your point of view.

[25] *Vom Kriege*, III, 6, p. 366.

[26] There seems to be an important difference here from the young Clausewitz who wrote the *Bekenntnisschrift* in 1812. Here Clausewitz very emotionally refers to the unity of state, nation, and the people. See for this, Herfried Münkler, 'Instrumentelle und existentielle Kriegsauffassung

he sees as the decisive stimulus for the military leader. The general must want to do things better than his comrades; he is expected to compete. The more everbody does this the more the military as a whole will profit. With ambition and competition, Clausewitz introduces 'bourgeois' ideas of efficiency into military thinking. It is evident that a military organization corresponding to these criteria cannot build on the principle of inheritance and also cannot rely on too strict hierarchies. If only aristocrats can become officers, despite the fact that some of them are silly, cowardly or lazy, efficiency is of course not guaranteed. Strict hierarchies are also obstacles to efficiency, because they do not give people enough opportunities to act and think on their own. Following Clausewitz, one could say that a military institution works best when everybody gets the chance to prove his individual efficiency. The German general staff system tried to integrate this Clausewitzian insight. Traditionally, every general staff officer had the right and even the duty to counsel his superior in the process of a military decision. He was expected to voice his opinion and argue for it, especially if it diverged from that of his superior.[27] Naturally, this presupposes superiors who are open to arguments and also subordinates who are brave enough to risk their careers. At this point military and civil virtues merge. One cannot be a good officer if one is unable to tell a superior that he is wrong. For Clausewitz, bravery comprises much more than the readiness to risk one's life. It also comprises freedom of mind and spirit, and of course freedom of speech. This is a very important point. Even today it appears to be easier for many soldiers to risk their lives following an order than to criticize their superiors.

Resolution (*Entschlossenheit*) can be described as the capacity to make decisions and stick to them. The French term Clausewitz uses for this is *courage d'esprit*.[28] *Courage d'esprit* is a special type of bravery. Unlike those already discussed it is a form of courage that deals not with danger to one's body, but with danger to one's soul. What is discussed here is an internal or mental experience. Resolution is the result of a fight against doubt or uncertainty. *Coup d'oeil* can produce insights, but these do not necessarily lead to action, because you might doubt them, and if you do you will doubt them especially in confusing situations, and according to Clausewitz war is always confusing. At this point *courage d'esprit* becomes important. It can also be characterized as the will to act in accord with the insights brought forward by *coup d'oeil*.

---

bei Carl von Clausewitz', in *Gewalt und Ordnung. Das Bild des Krieges im politischen Denken* (Frankfurt a. M., 1992), 92–110.

[27] See Millotat, *Das preußisch—deutsche Generalstabssystem*, 33 ff.

[28] Clausewitz is concerned with resolution in *Vom Kriege*, I, 3, p. 235 ff.

As with all moral forces, resolution is an amalgamation of reason and feeling. On the one hand, people without strong intellectual powers cannot be resolved, because resolution presupposes doubt, even doubt about yourself, and doubt is an act of intelligence. Silly persons may often be able to act without hesitation in situations of trouble, but they also act without much reflection and therefore without *courage d'esprit* in Clausewitz's sense. On the other hand, resolution in itself is an emotional state of mind. The will to action results from an intellectual process, but nevertheless it is a feeling. Here we again have the well-known Clausewitzian constellation: intellect as an isolated phenomenon is insufficient; it has to be combined with emotions and only then it can be transformed into action.

The concept of resolution has traditionally played an important role in Prussian–German conceptions of military leadership. In 1908, soldiers were told that it was better to do something wrong than to do nothing at all. This sounds rather dull and of course loses the richness of Clausewitz's considerations, but it is the practical meaning of resolution. It is evident that resolution can only be realized in an army as a whole if the soldier is not treated as a mere recipient of orders. You have to grant the individual a high degree of independence. This is why the Prussian–German conception of military leadership contains the principle of *Auftragstaktik*, a term that is not easily translated into English.[29] The most common translation is 'mission command'. The principle runs as follows: an order should comprise only those things a subordinate must know to achieve the ends in an independent way. This means that a soldier receives a command, but the way he wants to accomplish it is up to him. He knows the ends, but he himself is left to decide about the means. To give a simple example: you tell soldiers, 'Build a fence around this camp'. You do not tell them how much distance there should be between the poles and so on. They have to solve those problems on their own. The intention behind the principle of mission command is to give subordinates, no matter what their rank, as much scope for individual decision-making as possible. Clausewitz did not explain the principle of mission command, but nevertheless it is based on a thoroughly Clausewitzian spirit. Clausewitz's idea was that military action in war cannot and should not be prescribed in detail, because frictions set limits to every detailed plan. A military commander always has to consider the frictional character of each war. This is precisely the deeper sense of command by mission.

---

[29] See Millotat, *Das preußisch—deutsche Generalstabssystem*, 41 ff. There is a debate as to whether the principle of *Auftragstaktik* is of Prussian or Austrian origin, or whether it has its roots in the Prussian reception of the Reformation.

## SELF-CONTROL: A PASSION FOR REASON[30]

Clausewitz's list of moral forces is completed by the quality of *self-control* (*Selbstbeherrschung*). As a synonym for 'self-control', Clausewitz sometimes uses the expressions 'energy of mind' (*Gemütsstärke*) or 'energy of soul'. Self-control is the power to subordinate even intense emotions to reason or intellect. This sounds very rational. I shall show that it is not. Primacy of reason has always been demanded from soldiers, especially from military leaders. This demand mainly results from the experience that, in violent conflict, feelings like fear, confusion, or revenge can sometimes become so mighty that they tend to delay or even hinder victory. Revenge, for example, is often counterproductive, because it may provoke the enemy to resist to the bitter end. Frequently, the power of emotions conflicts with military ends. The predominance of reason was expected to solve this tension. Superficially it looks as if Clausewitz, in his description of self-control, has simply subscribed to the opinion of many others who have written on war. In fact, things are more complicated than this. It is true that the task of self-control is to subordinate strong feelings to reason. On the other hand, self-control itself is founded on a feeling of a special kind. It results from the intense mental need to act[31] as somebody who is not just driven by something but instead drives things forward. The source of self-control is nothing other than a particular form of striving for *Menschenwürde* or human dignity. But this need is of course itself an emotion, a passion in this case, and not a product of the faculty of intellect. So, once more Clausewitz points out that reason by itself is a poor thing. Reason develops its full power only through forces which lie outside itself. Because Clausewitz believed this, he also believed that, wherever reason and emotion stand against each other, reason will be the inferior part. If you want to control the very strong feelings which are inevitable in war, you can do so only by powers which are themselves located within the emotional realm. Even where Clausewitz seems to argue on rationalist lines he eventually pleads for a unity of intellect and feelings, a unity in which reason is indeed the dominating power, but this is so because sufficiently strong feelings want it to dominate and move it forward. It is at this point that the notion of honour

---

[30] I was inspired to use this title by Terence Holmes.
[31] The German term I translate as 'to act' is *wirken*. The semantics of *wirken* are ambivalent in German. On the one hand, it means the same as 'being good in impressing other people'; on the other hand, it is used as a synonym for 'acting in an effective manner'. These two meanings are of course very different. You can impress other people without acting effectively, and it is possible to do the latter without leaving any impression on others. Terence Holmes pointed out to me that Clausewitz uses *wirken* in the second sense. My original assumption was that he used it in the first meaning. The result was a much too utilitarian interpretation which I now believe to be wrong.

implicitly enters the theory of moral forces. Surprisingly, Clausewitz hardly ever uses the word 'honour' in *Vom Kriege*. In my opinion, the moral force of self-control is the main source of honour. Honour consists in the firm conviction that one has not become a victim of spontaneous emotions, but has followed one's passions in a rational way.

## CLAUSEWITZ TODAY: MODERN TIMES AND MORAL FORCES

Clausewitz outlines an image of the soldier which is highly individualistic, holistic, and deeply attached to the emotional realm of the human mind. Does all this mean anything to us today, and if so what exactly? I would like to answer this question by making three points which are deeply connected.

First, for Clausewitz moral forces are so important in war because there are so many frictions in war. Moral forces are a counterweight to friction. There is no war without friction. The current war in Iraq is a conflict full of frictions. Modern technology does not imply, or not only implies, a reduction in frictions but an increase in them. So, if Clausewitzian virtues are an adequate means to deal with friction, they are needed today even more than they were in the nineteenth century.

Second, there is a strong tendency to overrate the importance of advanced technology in war. In America military experts construct future battlefields on which there are no people, just weapons. Following Clausewitz in war, we have to deal with human beings with all their weaknesses and all their powers. This emphasis on the human dimension seems to me absolutely necessary, in order to overcome the modern illusion that in the future war will be waged by machines, not people.

Third, among the great challenges facing us today is fighting small wars against so-called 'guerrillas'. These are armed conflicts without clear fronts, wars which are not fought with collective weapons like tanks and rockets, but with Kalashnikovs, knives, machetes and rape, wars where limits between combatants and non-combatants are almost completely dissolved, wars which often seem to be completely irrational and without any political motives, wars with a great deal of primitive violence, but without battles. Clausewitzian virtues become very relevant when Western forces are involved in this kind of constellation. With all their inherent individualism, they are in a way even better designed for 'small' warfare than 'big' warfare. People are needed who possess *coup d'oeil* in situations even more confusing than traditional warfare, and also people who are able to cope and survive without receiving any orders for a long time. On the other hand, you do not of course need people who are likely to assimilate with those criminals or half-criminals they are expected to fight. What is required is a type of soldier deeply committed to Western values and at the same time able to find his way in a kind of warfare dominated not so much by *esprit de corps* as by a mixture of economic interests and seemingly irrational factors. It appears to me that Clausewitz gave us a sketch of precisely this type of soldier. Perhaps we need another Lawrence of Arabia, whom Clausewitz would have appreciated. But following Clausewitz, we are in need of many Lawrences, because just one will necessarily fail as Lawrence did. Do not count on a few individuals, but on a lot of people who act as individuals.

Finally, I would like to make some remarks on matters which Clausewitz does not talk about. Sometimes it is as enlightening to consider what an author neglects as to investigate what he does consider. There is something missing in Clausewitz's account of moral forces in war. We call it 'obedience'. Obedience has counted and still counts as a military virtue *par excellence*. But Clausewitz does not even mention obedience in book I, chapter 3 of *On War*, where he discusses moral forces. How is this to be explained? A possible answer is that Clausewitz omitted the topic, because he took it to be self-evident that an army is founded on the principle of obedience. Maybe, but I do not think so. Obedience does not fit Clausewitz's frame of thought at all. Why should anyone blessed with *coup d'oeil*, *courage d'esprit* and boldness follow orders which do not make any sense to him? Clausewitz nowhere gives us a convincing answer to this question. He did not raise the question, because he knew there *is* no convincing answer. Most soldiers are somehow subordinates. Even soldiers of the highest rank are subordinates, namely to their governments (at least in Western states). But the type of soldier Clausewitz presents to us does not have a subordinate mind. He is characterized by a vivid, independent, and wilful spirit. People like this do not tend to submit to anyone. So one might ask: the virtues stressed by Clausewitz are all very fine, but would not they destroy the military institution from within? A similar objection could be directed against Prussian–German conceptions of leadership, which are very Clausewitzian. Leaving subordinates free to make important decisions on their own is a very loose and liberal way of leading people. Is it not risky in any military organization? My answer to those objections would be: it may be risky, but it is much riskier to educate soldiers who never learn to use their brains. There have been many excellent soldiers who were disobedient. Clausewitz himself is an example. In 1812, he left his country and joined the Russian army to fight against Napoleon. You may conceive of this as high treason. Another instance is Claus von Graf Stauffenberg, who placed the bomb in Hitler's headquarters on 20 July 1944. Still another case is General Hans von Yorck who as a young man was even sentenced to imprisonment for mutiny. Later he was disobedient again; in 1812 it was his official duty to fight for the French, but he changed sides and supported the Russians against the will of his king and sovereign. Supported by Clausewitz, he entered into the agreement with the Russians known as the Convention of Tauroggen. Without Yorck (and Clausewitz) victory against Napoleon would have come much later. As these examples show, military disobedience often leads to better results than obedience. There is a story, no doubt apocryphal, that the Austrian army once went so far as to reward every soldier with the highest decoration who had acted against an order in case, by doing so, he achieved something good. There are worse things than disobedience. Perhaps there is even a culture of military disobedience, as Colonel Dupuy once said of the German general staff system.[32]

---

[32] T. N. Dupuy, *A Genius for War: the German Army and the General Staff 1807–1945* (Englewood Cliffs, NJ, 1977), 116. Andreas Herberg-Rothe has pointed out that the liberal traditions in German military leadership, especially the principle of *Auftragstaktik*, could easily result in a conflict with the primacy of policy. On similar lines Wilfried von Bredow argued that armies are not democratic institutions and that it would even be dangerous to make them democratic. These differences of opinion cannot be discussed here, because the primacy of policy is not my subject.

# 7

# War as 'Art': Aesthetics and Politics in Clausewitz's Social Thinking

*José Fernández Vega*

*The Art of War* is the translation usually given in Western languages to the title of Sun Tzu's book, the only volume on military matters which comes close to the stature of Clausewitz's *On War*, and which along with it has the privilege of being considered a perennial classic of strategy. One of the aims of this chapter is to show that Sun Tzu's title could also have been Clausewitz's choice for his own work. To that end, it will be necessary to make a philosophical detour. Focusing on the later philosophy of Kant, I intend to show the relevance that such an approach can have in dealing with contemporary issues. The overall aim of this essay is to convey the idea that Clausewitz's most essential teachings are not to be sought in any specific passage of his book, but in what I would call his method.

Even if Clausewitz's knowledge of Kantian theories was only second-hand, in *On War* he rendered both an original and highly political approach to Kant's aesthetics. An exploration of Clausewitz's creative elaboration of Kant's late work deepens our understanding of his own philosophy of war. Clausewitz understood that one could apply Kant's ideas on judgement to the study of social events, such as battles, that follow particular patterns such as works of art do. This also implies that we cannot explain society in general and exact terms, as scientists attempt in their studies of the natural world. This approach, as Clausewitz was well aware, is particularly relevant in times of crisis.

We know that *On War* has been misinterpreted many times in the past. No matter how profound those misinterpretations, most can of course still be easily corrected, but a few seem to conspire directly against the core of the book and are more difficult to remove. First, most of today's wars are civil wars. Despite the fact that the Spanish popular reaction against Napoleon aroused his interest, Clausewitz lived in a time when wars were fought between states. Second, today airspace supremacy has acquired a central role for military interventions in faraway places. These are two facts that have had a decisive influence in the context of contemporary wars and any serious study must consider them. It goes without saying that *On War* would have never been able to consider either the current crises of nation-states across entire regions of the globe or the tremendous impact of technology everywhere, including of course warfare. These are peculiar features of our 'post-heroic' epoch.

Can *On War* possibly tell us something meaningful about the reality of the world in which we live today and not just about the Napoleonic period? The political and military environment that Clausewitz studied seems to have been melted into history. Should we let *On War* disappear together with it? The answer will be 'yes' if we are unable to see in Clausewitz a political thinker instead of just a strategist. Such an answer to our question will also fit if we show neither the ability nor the desire to read *On War* as a rare political classic, instead of considering it simply as an old practical handbook or a historical source. Much of the value in Clausewitz's teachings comes from the fact that his work is a treatise trying to approach war in a broader sense, as opposed to the narrower and more familiar *military* distortions of his time (and ours).

That is why, to be able to grasp an important point arising out of Clausewitz's 'method', as I will try to do here, it will be necessary to link his thinking to some of the developments in philosophy in his own times. In the early nineteenth century, social or political sciences were not an independent cultural reference but were both linked to philosophy.

Clausewitz wrote in an undated note that he would have liked to go through his entire work *On War* to convey the strength achieved in its first pages, the only part of his treatise which he considered complete, and the most challenging for the reader.[1] Clausewitz's last wish, which he could not fulfil, was to write an even more 'philosophical' treatise than the one we know today. Paradoxically, that style, so often labelled as abstract in the past 150 years, is precisely what has protected *On War* from obsolescence, the fate suffered by most strategic treatises of its kind.

Without the theoretical ambition that characterizes Clausewitz, *On War* would not have survived the period of historic acceleration that divides us from its publication, or the complete transformation that military technology as well as international politics has undergone. That period is relatively short if it is compared to the *longue durée* of the forms that both war and society had adopted in previous centuries. Indeed, the remote 'art of war' of Sun Tzu (dating back some 2,500 years) was closer, at least in practical terms, to that

---

[1] Carl von Clausewitz, *On War*, trans. and ed. Michael Howard and Peter Paret (Princeton, NJ, 1976), 70–1.

of Clausewitz than to ours, even if ancient China did not use firearms or fight with cavalry, as was common in the nineteenth century.[2]

But, at the same time, both Clausewitz and we are children of the modern age and that implies a strong link with him and a huge distance from the universe of Sun Tzu. 'Modernity' is the cultural atmosphere that requires justifications made by means of rational arguments, but Sun Tzu could avoid arguing in such a way since his ancient Chinese culture provided a traditional intellectual frame of mind into which his thought fitted. That world was no longer Clausewitz's, and, since then, it has become even less ours because 'modernity' has become a time when cultural traditions confront increasing crisis.

It is not unreasonable to imagine that the cultural climate of so-called German idealism influenced Clausewitz in one way or another. It cannot be proved, however, that he was acquainted with the writings of Hegel, who at that time was a professor at Berlin University, despite the fact that both men lived in Berlin during the last stage of their lives and possibly saw each other at some social events (they died in exactly the same year). But there are no reasons to think that Clausewitz did not learn at least the essential of Kant's philosophy, the other great monument of the era of the idealism, though we are not entirely clear how much or even in which way Clausewitz had access to it. What we do know is that in his youth he studied logic and mathematics in the Kriegsschule of Berlin where he attended the courses of Johann G. C. Ch. Kiesewetter (1766–1819). Kiesewetter not only disseminated Kantian theories but also collaborated with Kant in Berlin in the corrections for his last major book, the *Critique of the Power of Judgement*.[3] In that work, Kant tried to offer a vision of human knowledge less dependent on the paradigm offered by physics. As a product of the Enlightenment, Kant, of course, admired science. Newtonian physics had a tremendous intellectual impact on him, but

---

[2] See Michael Handel, *Sun Tzu y Clausewitz: 'El arte de la guerra' y 'De la guerra' comparados* (Buenos Aires, 1997): most recent English edition, *Masters of War: Classical Strategic Thought* (London, 2003).

[3] Most scholars dismiss the notion that Kant had any direct or deep influence on Clausewitz (no other proof of the link exists other than that represented by Kiesewetter). They make the customary references to the impact of the *Critique of Pure Reason* or the *Anthropology* on Clausewitz, but give less attention to the *Critique of the Power of Judgement*. Peter Paret and Raymond Aron deal, but only *en passant*, with the generic influence on Clausewitz of the aesthetic thinking of the Enlightenment. Although there are other authors who have considered issues arising out of the Third *Critique* in relation to *On War*, including Alexis Philonenko, Mario García Acevedo, Azar Gat, and Werner Hahlweg, I do not know of any systematic study of the subject, apart from the contributions of Wilhem Malmsten Schering who, in the second half of the 1930s, pointed out the influence of both Kant and the aesthetic theory on Clausewitz's vision, action, and resolution (see in particular, Schering, *Die Kriegsphilosophie von Clausewitz. Eine Untersuchung über ihren systematischen Aufbau* (Hamburg, 1935)). I have tried a new approach in *Las guerras de la política. Clausewitz de Maquiavelo a Perón* (Buenos Aires, 2005).

he understood that the epistemological model it provided did not facilitate the approach to certain areas of human activity.

Science (in particular physics), stated Kant, worked mechanically, subsuming each particular phenomenon in a general law. In this way, the peculiar nature of this concrete phenomenon disappears because we only pay attention to the features that match with other cases under the same law. For instance, if a book or a stone falls to the ground, what is relevant, according to the laws of gravity that explain that fact, is the quantitative data like the height from which the fall begins or the different weights that each of those bodies have. Physics, of course, is not interested in the nature of each of those completely different objects. From, say, a cultural point of view, on the other hand, such differences would immediately come to the surface.

This way of reasoning becomes even more evident when it comes to art. Kant started the *Critique of the Power of Judgement* (or third *Critique*) by focusing on judgements about beauty, since in the aesthetic dimension the peculiarity of the objects becomes crucial. Works of art are not interchangeable, as each one possesses its own idiosyncrasy. Appreciating the beauty of a rose is not the same as the appreciation of that of a portrait (in his aesthetics, Kant emphasized the natural beauty symbolized by the rose). Each of these aesthetic experiences is unique. They cannot be reduced to a particular or common aspect that standardizes them or that simply quantifies their differences. In art, the beholder finds a peculiarity that cannot be generalized. *Werther* and *Don Quixote* are novels, but that does not tell us anything about their values, their structure, or their impact on the readers. A work of art has its own particular hierarchy and dignity, exactly as is the case for human individuals.

That is the reason why there is no 'science' of art, though Kant held that subjective judgements about beauty are not arbitrary. They aspire with some reason to be quasi-universal—or, to put it more accurately, to form judgements *as if* they were universal—since their universality is very different from the one that scientific laws enjoy. Going deeper in this direction will take us too far, and we now have to focus more on the political consequences that derive from these thoughts.

At the end of her life, in her lectures on the *Critique of the Power of Judgement*, Hannah Arendt tried to extend the scope of Kant's argumentation into the domain of politics and that of historical experience in general. Some historical facts, she noticed, have for us the value of examples, and this is exactly what happens with some masterpieces in the world of art according to Kant. These facts provide us with the schemata or formal models we then use to reflect about other phenomena, but we can never ignore the differences between the model and the fact to be explained, or reduce the distance between them to a mere question of measurement. The 'exemplary models' work *as if* (*als ob*) they were concepts for thinking, but strictly speaking they are not concepts at all. They do not create regularities or universal laws in which we can mechanically integrate a particular phenomenon, as is the case with classical physics. Hitler's dictatorship may be described as a special kind of Bonapartism, but that does not mean that Hitler and Napoleon can be put at the same level or that one can completely be understood in terms of the other. Bonapartism is an *exemplary model* that works *as if* it were a concept. It is a comparative term to support our judgement when we do not have (and cannot have) scientific laws available to clarify a situation.

The need to think from a perspective not based on laws or rules—what Kant called judging—is still more urgent in times of crisis, and what Arendt really wanted, above all, was to find a political sense in the dreadful twentieth century, the era of wars and revolutions. She believed that a series of unprecedented shocks had dismantled most of the old beliefs and aroused a strong demand for new paradigms, which a reinterpretation of the late philosophy of Kant could help to build. Clausewitz also went through an era of great transformation. For him too, turbulent times provided new visions, since all received wisdom either was shaken or collapsed. Clausewitz started to walk a path that was later followed by Arendt with greater technical skill. Such a coincidence is, of course, methodological. Needless to say, just because they referred to, or were (openly or tacitly) inspired by, the philosophy of Kant, does not imply that the thought of both Arendt and Clausewitz necessarily have many other points in common.

These preliminary explanations, though too basic, allow us better to understand what encouraged Arendt to assert that the third *Critique* is the true source of Kant's political philosophy, though it does not deal with political issues.[4] Arendt held that the role of the faculty that Kant called imagination (*Einbildung*) is the most important discovery of the third *Critique* for political theory. The imagination is crucial for our knowledge of the singular or idiosyncratic, since it is the faculty, as Arendt explained, that enables the 'representative thinking' of the observer and that contributes to the building up of schemata, forms, or exemplary models on which our power of judgement will later work. In principle, every individual is endowed with that power or faculty and it is for this reason that we are capable of passing judgements based on forms or exemplary models.

However, Kant believed that, in art, only the artist is in charge of *producing* those concrete and real forms or models by means of their work. Kant called the artist a genius (*Genie*) because he considered that the artist was endowed by Nature itself with outstanding gifts. Through his or her active or productive

---

[4] Hannah Arendt, *Lectures on Kant's Political Philosophy*, ed. R. Beiner (Chicago, IL, 1989).

innate imagination, the genius builds aesthetic real forms, that is masterpieces that inspire other artists and delight the spectators who judge them. The spectator, thus, is capable of enjoying a piece of work through judging, but only the genius can make it happen and bring it to life.

Neither in the realm of art nor in that of politics have we access to universal laws that would explain facts with accuracy, as happens in physics. The old hope of understanding society with the same precision as science shows when it explains nature was renewed by positivism in the second half of the nineteenth century. Throughout the twentieth century, it also found many supporters. But what Clausewitz (and Kant according to Arendt) tried to make clear was that this hope was unreal. The actual challenge was to understand society as a specific domain that requires an appropriate method in which chance and human freedom prevail. This is a complex task, as close to the work of science as it is to the making of aesthetic taste. My argument is that a very similar approach can be applied to the understanding of war. Clausewitz, probably following Kant in this, rejected the current idea, according to which one should choose between a strict scientific paradigm or a purely intuitive framework in order to think on social issues (like war). Taken in isolation, any one of those paradigms is one-dimensional. It generates ideological statements, rather than a reliable knowledge about a society in constant movement or conflict.

When an era pretends to possess a battery of laws applicable and accurate enough to explain the evolution of society, a crisis comes to tear down such certainty. And it is in that moment that we must resort to another kind of thinking, less pretentious and more trustworthy.

Social thinking demands flexible criteria to formulate its judgements. The imagination, which according to the Kantian use of the term is far from being the same as fantasy or simple delusions, shows all its worth when it captures the novelty of a historic moment or a concrete situation characterized, as Clausewitz said war was, by uncertainty and danger. That is why Arendt claimed that the imagination is the political faculty *par excellence* of our ability to know and to reason. Kant, in his lectures on logic, according to the transcript kept by a student, had described the tension between imagination and understanding in the following words:

The more universal the understanding is in its rules, the more perfect it is, but if it wants to consider things *in concreto* then [it] absolutely cannot do without imagination.[5]

---

[5] Henry E. Allison, *Kant's Theory of Taste. A Reading of the Critique of Aesthetic Judgement* (Cambridge, 2001), 48. This quotation, in Allison's translation, also makes reference to the role played by the imagination in scientific knowledge as such, but I prefer not to explore this complex issue here.

For the imagination is the faculty to grasp the concrete, not the general (which is an issue handled by science based on the understanding faculty that Kant had studied in his first *Critique*). Thus, politics shares with aesthetics its interest in the particular (a specific work of art, a special political circumstance or time). The imagination makes up the sensitive data taken from reality and presents a schema. This form, or model, takes the place of the concept when the latter is not possible, that is, when there are no available categories for the case or when they do not provide us with a useful notion to think *in concreto*.

Kant, as already mentioned, had pointed out a fundamental difference between the role of the observer and that of the artist. The former was in charge of reflecting and appreciating—*judging*—while the latter was 'confined' to creating by means of his or her *praxis*. In other words: the observer judges, while the artist, or genius, creates.[6] In this way, the audience judges works of art with impartiality, and creators make up pieces of work over which they possess no cognitive control. Artists do not follow any particular theory nor do they offer one for consideration; their inspiration works on a basis provided by the previous creations of their colleagues. An artist acting as Kant held he did can never have the unbiased perspective on the whole which allows proper reflection. If this is also the conclusion to Kant's political philosophy (never written as such, according to Arendt), then it is clear that there are many reasons why Clausewitz rejected such a conclusion. At this point, Clausewitz stepped back from the political implications of the third *Critique*.

The core question with which Kant confronted Clausewitz is an old topic in social and political philosophy: the relationship between theory and practice. I am not trying to suggest that Clausewitz overtly opened an argument against Kant; in fact, there is no explicit reference to him in *On War*. But in this work, a very typical Kantian word—*Kritik*—is used to designate the specific solution that the author found to overcome the gap between theory and practice, a gap especially acute in the field of strategy.[7]

Besides, another 'Kantian' word, genius (*Genie*), is also used in *On War* to name a military chief. But, according to Clausewitz, a commander-genius should be able both to act *and* to know. He is precisely the one who exercises the *Kritik*, since he must adapt the abstract conceptions of strategic theory to

---

[6] See Pierre Aubenque, *La prudence chez Aristotle* (Paris, 1963) for the ancient Greek difference between *praxis* and *poíesis*; in more recent times the use of both terms seems to have merged.

[7] Carl von Clausewitz, *Vom Kriege*, ed. W. Hahlweg (19th edn, Berlin, 1991), II, 5, p. 312; *Kritik* is the title of the whole chapter. Howard and Paret rendered it as 'Critical analysis'; see Clausewitz, *On War* (Princeton, NJ, 1976), trans. and ed. Michael Howard and Peter Paret, II, 5, 156.

the concrete challenges of the particular situation that he faces. The *Kritik* is exercised through the power of *judgement* (*Urteil* or *Takt des Urteils*, as it was also called by Clausewitz), and this is, as we have seen before, a crucial notion in the Kantian vocabulary that Clausewitz might only have known second-hand, through the teaching of Kiesewetter or from another source (in this respect we should consider more closely the philosophical and artistic interests of his wife, Marie von Brühl, not to mention her readings).

The challenges that a military chief faces force him to give quick practical answers rather than speculative and elaborated arguments. A general, though free to develop a theory, does not need to elaborate one. Nevertheless, the type of capacity that demands a practical reaction from him when confronted with a given situation, implies a similar kind of judgement to the one Kant calls aesthetic, since the understanding of a particular moment (or a given work of art), is never identical to the previous one. History contributes by offering the chief useful forms (models instead of concepts proper) to understand the present, but, even though the chief's military reaction can be inspired by examples from the past, it is always specific.

Clausewitz, as we see, uses a series of notions that have a remarkable 'family resemblance' to the idiom of Kantian philosophy, but he re-worked them in a personal way. We have already mentioned two very important concepts with an intense Kantian flavour, *judgement* and *critique*, which represent respectively the subjective and the objective side of the chief's activity. There are still other notions, such as *Takt* and *coup d'oeil*, described by Clausewitz as having similar functions to the former ones. All these terms try to designate the typical abilities of a chief or a strategist and, at the same time, they illustrate the way *On War* mediates between theory and practice.

It is important to stress that all the above-mentioned mental abilities (or faculties or powers) should not be identified with a kind of immediate or irrational intuition. On the contrary, they are cognitive and reflexive powers. The remote intellectual ancestor of this type of approximation to the link between theory and practice was what Aristotle named prudence or *fronesis*, a type of wisdom that is acquired through experience and reflection and applied to the concrete challenges our moral life confronts. In our moral life (or *praxis*), we must choose a specific and justifiable course of action; however, no science based on universal and exact laws can possibly tell us which is the best option.

Human activity is always facing different contexts that modify it. Although general values can provide some references, just or right decisions are not prescribed in any user's manual and it is impossible to deduce them automatically as though there were some kind of general formula. Since only on rare occasions have we the necessary time to think about our praxis thoroughly, we often act as guided by our *Takt*. Being an intellectual skill achieved through practice, *Takt* is what makes easier the prompting of proper reactions in the event of new and urgent situations. This mental faculty is not, then, a simple irrational impulse or the consequence of a supernatural inspiration.[8] Rather, it has to do with the reflexive experience.

I hope that I have offered some support for my initial hypothesis, which was that conducting a war for Clausewitz is an art because, in the first place, *art* is just another name for *Kritik*, that is, the power that binds together theory and practice. In the creative field, the artist through the production of new works of art connects with the tradition of preceding masters. *Mutatis mutandis*, the military strategist operates in the same way. He must bind military conceptions, which are taken either from his own experience or available theory or the study of history, together with the challenges of reality. This connection will also give impetus to theoretical renewals directed towards the understanding of his own decisions and results. This link or connection is a critical function (of the *Kritik*) and its conclusion is a judgement oriented towards a practical decision. This is the 'art' of a general according to *On War*.

The word 'art', incidentally, offers a wider semantic field. So far, we have restricted its meaning to a conventional sense, that is to say creation, production, and the bond between the theory and practice, and I shall continue to consider it in this way. During the early modern period, the Latin word *ars* gave rise to the division between *ars mechanica* and *beaux arts* as they were later called in the eighteenth century, the mechanical technique of the artisan vis-à-vis the creative talent of those capable of creating beauty and producing something new or different from the simple technical repetition of a job. The art of war, according to Clausewitz, must combine both those sides in its application. The military genius, as he understands it, may be a skilful artisan in some sense, but above all he is an artist who fulfils an intellectual function. These qualities might be summarized in the notion of political talent. What is more, this is a capacity that, as Isaiah Berlin pointed out, requires a great flair for judgement.[9] With these reflections, Clausewitz enlightens a topic which is still current: the secrets of political leadership. Much has been said about it, but the mysterious quality that revolves around its subjective origin is far from being lost.

*On War* was a landmark for modern strategy almost in the same way that the *Critique of the Power of Judgement* was a foundation stone for modern

---

[8] On the concept of *Takt* in Modernity, see Hans-Georg Gadamer, *Wahrheit und Methode* (Tübingen, 1975), 3, 12 f.

[9] Isaiah Berlin, 'Political Judgement', in *The Sense of Reality: Studies in Ideas and Their History*, ed. Henry Hardy (London, 1996), 40–53. It is curious that Berlin makes no mention of the third *Critique* in his essay.

aesthetics. At first glance both are very different pieces of work, with not much connection between them; nevertheless, their methods as well as their general conclusions have something in common. Even more basic than this is the fact that there are also some deep similarities between their respective subject matters: the strategy that thinks about war and the taste that ponders over art.

Neither art nor war is able to fit the methodological demands of science, but this does not mean that they fall into irrationalism or that it is impossible to know anything about either activity.[10] What Kant called *judgement* (as did Clausewitz) allows us to come closer to an understanding of those fields, although a precise grasp, mathematical exactitude for instance, will never be possible within them. The judgement (as power) can be acquired and will be the main virtue of any chief, who, at this point, resembles the spectator of a work of art according to Kant, or the artist himself according to other conceptions including the one Clausewitz held in opposition to Kant's.

In politics, and there is no need to stress that for Clausewitz war is a part of it, we are constantly facing what is new. That is, unprecedented factors combine in ways that simply do not recreate past circumstances. The activity of a previous genius in history is like a 'great work of art' that serves as an inspiring model for other 'artists'—military commanders. In wartime, the action of a genius, such as Napoleon, so many times mentioned in *On War*, both renews old paradigms and compels us to develop a new vision. Napoleon, according to what we read in a passage in *On War*, was worthy of the same respect due to great scientific talents. The complexities that Napoleon had to face were no less difficult. Besides, and unlike Isaac Newton or any of the other key figures of the modern scientific revolution quoted in the book, Napoleon could not rely on solving his problems just by applying mathematical tools.[11] *On War* insists on the intrinsic inaccuracy of war (and whoever thinks differently is a dogmatist) since it involves physical risk and it is subject to the incalculable reaction of moral forces. The machine of war (according to a favourite image of the Enlightenment) goes through a permanent friction (*Friktion*). With these remarks, Clausewitz distanced himself from the hyper-rationalism of the Enlightenment that had its strategic correlates (and still has).

Talented military chiefs face big theoretical challenges, though they are not necessarily builders of theories. Their supporters are their own experience, the theoretical legacy of the tradition previous to them, logical thinking,

---

[10] On what Aron calls the 'Kantian situation' of Clausewitz's theorizing, see Raymond Aron, *Pensar la guerra, Clausewitz* (2 vols, Buenos Aires, 1989; original French edition, *Penser la guerre, Clausewitz* (Paris, 1976)), I, pp. 201, 251, 257.

[11] Clausewitz, *Vom Kriege*, I, 3, p. 251, and VIII, 3B, p. 961.

and historical knowledge.[12] On this basis, and bearing in mind the concrete situation in which they find themselves, they exercise their *Takt* (or their judgement, if we want to remain faithful to the specific Kantian jargon) to take dangerous decisions surrounded, as they are, by unknown factors. The military commentator or theorist (like Clausewitz) must contribute with non-dogmatic models of understanding in order to clarify what the genius does. But the intellectual resources of the commentator are basically the same as those which assist geniuses themselves.

An important difference between the Kantian conception of genius and that of Clausewitz is that for the former the inspiration of a genius is a natural gift and an innate talent. Clausewitz does not deny that there are exceptional geniuses in history, but his political realism causes him to emphasize that a state cannot wait to be blessed by providence to entrust its defence to some extraordinary military commander. That is why it is made clear that a military 'artist' (i.e. not a genius proper) can be a product of education, training, and experience. This training, both theoretical and practical, will not necessarily create another Napoleon, but at least it will provide suitable personnel to run military operations. For Kant, on the other hand, since geniuses are never the result of learning, their talent is not transferable. While Kant anticipates an image of the artist as genius that was going soon to become very popular among romantic movements, Clausewitz seems to defend a liberal conception of the artist, for he thinks that becoming one is a process not exclusively open to innate talent. Anyone exercising herself or himself with enough discipline could develop her or his *Takt* to the point of transforming it into a sort of second nature, or into a habit of taking right decisions, something similar to what Aristotle called *fronesis*, the distinctive feature of the wise person's (*frónimos*) praxis.

To what extent are Clausewitz's theories still helpful in illuminating today's world? *On War* should no longer be considered just as a practical treatise, though there may be in it practical guidelines that are still useful. Above anything else, it is a book that includes a fruitful methodological approach. It states that strategic thinking demands an open and flexible attitude and should always be ready to react in an adequate (and, of course, rational) way to concrete challenges that will be never identical to each other. It is precisely in this sense that war is an 'art', a concept opposed to the dogmas and the determinist thinking characteristic of certain currents of the Enlightenment.

In addition to some general and interesting coincidences between Kant and Clausewitz, there are also definite divergences. Some of them are rather obvious. Kant was a professional philosopher with a very sophisticated

---

[12] This point is stressed several times in Peter Paret, *Clausewitz and the State* (Princeton, NJ, 1976).

technical lexicon, while Clausewitz was a cultured but self-taught person with a weak formal education, an amateur philosopher living in the atmosphere of a great age in Western thought. Another and for us more relevant difference between the two is evident in the different attitude that each of them held on a key question of their time (and ours): how can we achieve peace? By means of legal arguments inspired by moral beliefs, supported by institutions, and ultimately by a philosophical vision of history (as a 'liberal' Kant believed)? Or, through the political action of a state, not always peaceful or moral, as a 'realistic' Clausewitz held?

While Kant believed in the moral progress of our species, and considered that perpetual peace was the highest aim in human evolution, according to his own interpretation of history, Clausewitz showed himself in *On War* indifferent towards those values and the metaphysics of history that supported them. He simply thought that the whole subject was out of his reach and it was not part of his business as a military writer. His subject matter was war and he focused on that, not on peace.

From the very beginning of his book, Clausewitz states that he will not tackle peace-related topics. He thinks that neither international law nor the principles of ethics seem strong enough to avoid the outbreak of the war or to mitigate its development.[13] Politics is the only means, if any, that can set limits to the atrocities of the battlefield. Sometimes politics seeks to achieve its aims through war and forces it to adopt suitable forms to reach that purpose. War is like a chameleon, according to Clausewitz's famous metaphor. Depending on the circumstances, it can either turn itself into a volcanic deployment of lethal forces or reduce its energy to a minimum, getting closer to a simple diplomatic tension. The more irreconcilable political interests in conflict are, the more violent the struggle will be.

Clausewitz deeply disliked what he termed philanthropic souls (*menschenfreundliche Seelen*), those moralists who constantly try to distract our attention from war with abstract discourses. Today, in terms of international politics, we would call him a 'realist', one who thinks that violent conflicts between political entities cannot always be avoided. Some years before Clausewitz started working on his book *On War*, Kant had written the most important pacifist manifesto of modern times, *Toward Perpetual Peace* (1795). Both thinkers were worried, though from very different standpoints, about the revolutionary events in France and their consequences for Prussia and the whole of Europe. Kant's essay became a landmark for subsequent liberal doctrines. Inspired by it, they were influential in the creation of institutions such as the League of Nations and the United Nations. Kant's ideas have also given impetus to a cosmopolitan doctrine of law since the end of the Cold War.

[13] Clausewitz, *Vom Kriege*, I, 1, p. 192.

The delayed influence of Kant's essay is due to the fact that pacifism did not become a popular demand until after the First World War, when it was evident that the energies liberated by nation-states at war, technologically equipped and capable of mobilizing millions of combatants, could produce unprecedented catastrophes that could seriously affect civil life. For this reason alone, the reproach so often levelled at Clausewitz, that he is a warmonger, can be rejected as anachronistic. Kant himself wrote odd paragraphs in favour of war in his works. He considered it historically progressive and even sublime on certain occasions, though, as a moral philosopher, he simultaneously deplored it.[14]

Clausewitz, by contrast, never wrote in favour of a philosophy of war, nor did he praise the aesthetic qualities of battle. He did not think that a set of mere moral principles or legal mandates could really moderate war, let alone eradicate it. Rather, he thought that the balance of power could be the key to a more peaceful and stable situation in the Europe of his time. The balance of power which he imagined consisted of states with forces and internal political regimes that were both comparable. Therefore, they could not be radically opposed enemies, with divergent ideologies. But revolutionary France did not fit into this picture and so the balance failed.

The state was the main agent of war, and its politics imposed basic guidelines that the military chief must adapt through his judgement and imagination to the concrete conditions of the battlefield. Clausewitz was not a *militarist* thinker, but a military thinker who held that the problems of war should not be approached from an operative or speculative perspective, but rather through a political theory of war. Clausewitz urges us to think, first, in political terms, applying a flexible method with *Takt* and judgement. The art of war would not be anything without the art of the political leadership.

The basic problem with the military, therefore, cannot be restricted to a purely military perspective. True strategic thinking that includes a clear vision of the ends (*Ziele*) demands another look. Arendt emphasized that the fundamental teachings of Kant in the third *Critique* consisted of adopting an external perspective. According to Kant, the exercise of judgement demands three fundamental principles:

They are the following: 1) To think for oneself. 2). To think in the position of everyone else. 3). Always to think in accord with oneself. The first is the maxim of the *unprejudiced* way of thinking, the second of the *broad-minded* way, the third that of the *consistent* way.[15]

---

[14] Immanuel Kant, *Critique of the Power of Judgement*, trans. P. Guyer and E. Matthews (Cambridge, 2001), §28, p. 146.

[15] Ibid. § 40, p. 174.

According to the second maxim, political judgement puts us in the other person's shoes. This is also, strategically and tactically, what 'military' judgement is about. The key political question here could be posed as follows: 'what is all our fighting about?' Kant explained that he who thinks politically 'sets himself apart from the subjective private conditions of the judgement, within which so many others are as if bracketed, and reflects on his own judgement from a *universal standpoint* (which he can only determine by putting himself into the standpoint of others)'.[16] Kant also characterized these maxims as 'enlightened', or possessed 'of reason' and of 'enlarged thought'.

The intellectual capacity that Clausewitz showed in relation to the immediate conditions both of his country, Prussia, and of its political system was precisely what allowed him to understand the weaknesses of the Prussian army and the strategy it adopted to confront Napoleon. In his effort to capture the innovations that Napoleon introduced to the European battlefields of his era, Clausewitz directed his judgement above all to the social and political configuration that Napoleon represented. His *political* interpretation of Napoleon allowed him then to produce a military interpretation that was unique. This was possible because he adopted, whether or not he was familiar with Kant's third *Critique*, the maxim of the broad-minded way and thus reached a politically universal standpoint, which had huge military consequences that *On War* analysed in detail. Since Clausewitz was interested in studying a method, and not just a particular situation in his time, he succeeded in overcoming the specific crisis of his own time and gave expression to a theory of war that still has a lot to tell us.

Clausewitz realized that he would not be able to encapsulate the challenge that Napoleon represented just by applying his usual political and military ideas, or those customary in his circle. The task would be impossible if he relied on the inherited wisdom and the conventional strategic theories that were available to him. To understand his enemy, Clausewitz had first of all to go far beyond his own national context, and adopt a universal standpoint. Thus, the second fundamental principle of the judgement that Kant formulates—'to think in the position of everyone else'—also acquires a special prominence in *On War*. It is no longer a simple principle of 'shrewdness' or a common piece of advice, like 'know thy enemy', as stated by Sun Tzu or by other authors who write about strategy.

The result of this process was *On War*, a book that avoids the mere projection of the peculiar military and political conditions of Clausewitz's own time and takes an off-centre intellectual approach. Clausewitz came to an interpretation of the French Revolution which allowed him to understand what

---

[16] Ibid. § 40: p. 175; see also editorial note 13 on p. 379.

was specific to Napoleon in his conduct of war. The political interpretation preceded the purely military and so Clausewitz was capable of approaching *in concreto* these two dimensions at the same time.

The imagination, that faculty identified by Arendt as the major contribution of Kant to political philosophy, played an essential role in this operation. This was, primarily, a methodological contribution, since such a faculty does not introduce any particular content, but rather indicates a way of thinking about our reality and of being able to capture it correctly without the familiar distortions due to the narrow and limited standpoint from which we naturally tend to project our own situation onto others.

Clausewitz wrote not only a strategy book full of theoretical inspiration and even of practical suggestions that can be applied today, but also a book that goes beyond all that, representing a major contribution to Western culture. *On War* is a book about political theory, which puts forward a method; that is to say, it is not only a practical military masterpiece. We must consider Clausewitz as a forerunner of the social sciences that began to develop independently later in his own century.

As a conclusion, I would like to stress, though very briefly, the value of 'military judgement' in avoiding the perils of a new kind of militarism. If war is the continuation of politics by other means, then politics follows war too. This is something usually forgotten when we utter the famous 'slogan' of *On War*. Politics, when transformed into a war politically led, tries to reach its own ends (*Ziele*) through military means. However, when they have been achieved, another temporal sequence is opened. In other words, politics *will go on* or *re-start by other means* when overt combat ends.

So, if we adopt the point of view of the political imagination, which is that of Clausewitz, it becomes essential to ask about the policies which will be implemented once the military operations are over. Does not the West need to ask itself this essential question in relation to its current and so-called 'war on terrorism'?

We can argue whether the term 'war' is appropriate to describe the clash against terrorism or just represents a political hyperbole adopted to spread a generalized panic and so obtain the necessary consensus to back up both huge military deployments and also illegal procedures in the fight against the 'enemy'.[17] For the risks in the militarization of the 'war against terrorism' are that it will erode the war's own legitimacy when civil rights and democratic liberties are curtailed on the grounds that such steps are necessary in a struggle against an anti-democratic enemy.

---

[17] Zbigniew Brzezinski, *The Choice: Global Domination or Global Leadership* (New York, 2004), argues that terrorism is a tactic rather than an enemy proper, and therefore the United States cannot make it the centre of its strategic attention.

Another international factor promotes militarism. Today, politics seem to have lost importance relative to technology and economics. Politics are repeatedly attacked for posing an obstacle to the free movement of capital and are seen as a standing source of inefficiency, even of corruption. Social scientists have launched a debate on the end of the nation-state. Meanwhile, a third of humanity has undergone a change of political and economic regimes since the end of the Cold War, and this process has deeply affected the politicians' ability to stabilize entire regions of the planet. Countless civil wars, chronic in some regions of the world, have been the obvious result.

Violence has spread because political authority has been incapable of laying down a just, or at least legitimate, order, and this is a typical consequence of the last wave of capitalist globalization. In the end, we have inherited a world that is getting richer and richer, but leaves behind dead victims, drowned in poverty.

By putting politics aside, the West seems to be incapable of taking a 'universal standpoint'. Violence is, therefore, incomprehensible to those who demand 'security' only for themselves. It is often thought of as something either typical of insanity or characteristic of an anachronistic and inexplicable will to return to the darkest times of human history. The universal standpoint does not oblige us to justify the crimes of others, but it does help us to understand their political nature. Clausewitz, though a Prussian, was able to understand the origins and motivations of his revolutionary French enemies, and he did not stop fighting them (this does not imply, of course, that Napoleon can be compared with terrorism or that Clausewitz aligned himself with the 'right side').

The method that led to the war in Iraq was not the reflexive judgement, the *Takt*, the *Kritik*, or the universal standpoint. It was rather imperialist arrogance. The West has all the military means to crush its enemies, but it has no clear policies left to continue the military victory. The military power of the United States is in theory unbeatable; but that supremacy has not yet come up with a viable and acceptable model of society for the countries it occupies or just bombs from the air. This is a war without politics; its faculty of imagination appears to be empty. In this way, violence becomes militarized and permanent.

We are at a difficult crossroads, and also *a military one*. A political void surrounding US alternatives is clearly reflected in the military operations both in Iraq and in other parts of the world. If this description is right, though it can only be exposed schematically, what other political–military thinker is today able to offer us a broader inspiration or better interpretative clues than those offered by Clausewitz?

Translated by Carolina Piguillem

# 8

## Clausewitz's Ideas of Strategy and Victory

*Beatrice Heuser*

This chapter will tease out of Clausewitz's writings ideas which were not yet associated with the concepts of strategy and victory in his own time, but which have come to be associated with them in the light of Clausewitz's works. This may sound obscure at first, but my argument revolves around the linguistic problem of using terms today which have undergone a shift in meaning since they were first employed.

In order to explain my semantic problem, I need to borrow from literary studies. As historians of past periods inevitably noticed, the past is another country, and the words we use today in any given language have often undergone a shift in meaning from earlier uses in the 'same' language so that the language is no longer identical. It can be more treacherous to go back in time in a language one thinks one knows than to turn to a language one knows only a little, as the former is teeming with what the British (but not the French) call *faux amis*, treacherous friends which turn out to be strangers.

Key political concepts, such as *demokrateia, res publica, imperium,* and Commonwealth, have changed massively in meaning over two-and-a-half millennia. Another example might be the transformations of meaning undergone by the words and concepts associated with partisan and guerrilla warfare. *La petite guerre* started out in the eighteenth century as reconnaissance actions, sabotage and minor military operations, carried out particularly by light cavalry (*partisans*) on the fringes of a regular war, with classical battle at its centre. In the Peninsular War, *petite guerre* having been translated into Spanish as *guerrilla*, former regular soldiers carried on the struggle after the abdication of the king, but began to attract and organize peasants and other locals in their efforts to deny the French regular forces control of Spain. In the twentieth century, *guerrilla* came to mean irregular warfare, carried out by irregular soldiers or partisans, not formally in the service of any government. Monoglot Anglophones even began to use the word guerrilla, often misspelled guerilla, to mean the fighters themselves, and so introduced the tautology, guerrilla warfare.

The problem is what should we call operations conducted by, say, American farmers fighting locally in the War of Independence in the eighteenth century, when they used what Mao Zedong or Vô Nguyên Giap would have called 'guerrilla tactics' in the twentieth century. Given what the literature of the eighteenth century describes as *petite guerre*, or what the *guerrilla* of the Peninsular War meant, we cannot use either term in its contemporary sense (i.e. as it was used at the time), but, if we use it in the modern sense, as a political scientist might do, or as a historian of ideas who traces the roots of an idea, not the etymology of a word, would, we risk being anachronistic.[1]

It has often been remarked that, for today's readership, Clausewitz is more easily intelligible in Michael Howard's and Peter Paret's English translation than in the German original, for the simple reason that Clausewitz's German is obsolescent, but not obsolete. This inhibits German readers from modernizing his language, in the way one would naturally do when working with medieval or early modern German texts. But his actual use of 'international' and contemporary words like 'strategy/*Strategie*', albeit in a sense slightly different from that in which the term is widely used today, inhibits anyone from changing his language here.

Nevertheless, that is exactly what this chapter does. I shall incur the charge of writing anachronistically and ahistorically. I do not see any other option, as it is impossible for me to invent a new word and insist that the world adopt it to avoid confusion with earlier meanings of words still in usage today. Clausewitz's thoughts on the general subject are far more subtle than his simple definition of *Strategie* and his employment of *Sieg* (victory) allow, and the treasures of his ideas would not be fully mined if we imposed on ourselves the limits of a merely literal interpretation of *On War*. Indeed, it is unlikely that he would have become so famous a writer, so influential on other people's writings and minds, if there had not been more fertile ideas scattered throughout his ill-shaped work than his mere, limited, and technical definition of strategy. I shall thus try to cull from his work a definition of 'strategy' that is more compatible with the usage of the term today, and seek to explore what we can deduce from this about the concept of victory (*Sieg*), a word that is in fact used only rarely in *On War*.

---

[1] For Clausewitz's thinking on guerrilla warfare and people's uprisings, see Beatrice Heuser, 'Clausewitz und der Kleine Krieg', in *Clausewitz Mitteilungen*, 1 (2005).

## DEFINITIONS OF STRATEGY

Clausewitz defined strategy as 'the use of engagements for the object of the war'.[2]

> [W]e clearly see that the activities characteristic of war may be split into two main categories: those *that are merely preparations for war* and *war proper*. The same distinctions must be made in theory as well.
>
> The knowledge and skills involved in the preparations will be concerned with the creation, training, and maintenance of the fighting forces. It is immaterial what label we give them, but they obviously must include such matters as artillery, fortification, so-called elementary tactics, as well as the organization and administration of the fighting forces and the like. The theory of war proper, on the other hand, is concerned with the use of their means, once they have been developed, for the purposes of the war. All that it requires from the first group is the end product, an understanding of the main characteristics. That is what we call 'the art of war', in a narrower sense, or 'the theory of the conduct of war', or 'the theory of the use of the fighting forces'. For our purposes, they all mean the same thing.
>
> That narrower theory, then, deals with the engagement, with fighting itself, and treats such matters as marches, camps, and billets... It does not comprise questions of supply, but will take these into account on the same basis *as other given factors*.
>
> The art of war in the narrower sense must now in its turn be broken down into *tactics and strategy. The first is concerned with the form of the individual engagement, the second its use*. Both affect the conduct of marches, camps, and billets only through the engagement; they become tactical or strategic questions in so far as they concern either the engagement's form or its significance.[3]

Book III is actually headed 'Strategy in general', and here he writes:

> Strategy is the use of the engagement for the purpose of the war. Though strategy in itself is concerned only with engagements, the theory of strategy must also consider its chief means of execution, the fighting forces. It must consider these in their own right and in their relation to other factors, for they shape the engagement and it is in turn on them that the effect of the engagement first makes itself felt. Strategic theory must therefore study [actually: strategy must teach] the engagement in terms of its possible results and of the moral and psychological forces [*die Kräfte des Geistes und des Gemüts*] that largely determine its course.[4]

This last definition offers some potential, as I shall argue below, but let us turn first to other contemporary definitions of 'strategy'. Jomini defined strategy as:

---

[2] Carl von Clausewitz, *On War*, trans. and ed. Michael Howard and Peter Paret (Princeton, NJ, 1976), II, 1, p. 128; henceforth *On War*.

[3] *On War*, II, 1, p. 131 f., my emphasis.   [4] Ibid. III, 1, p. 177.

the art of making war upon the map, and comprehends the whole theatre of operations. Grand Tactics is the art of posting troops upon the battlefield according to the accidents of the ground, or bringing them into action, and the art of fighting upon the ground in contradistinction to planning upon a map.... Strategy decides where to act... grand tactics decides the manner of execution and the employment of the troops.[5]

Hardly more riveting stuff, this. Elsewhere Jomini wrote, 'Strategy... is the art of bringing the greatest part of the forces of an army upon the important point of the theatre of war or the zone of operations.'[6] This is very much in keeping with other writers of his era. For Heinrich von Bülow, 'Strategy is the science of military movements outside the enemy's range of view, tactics within it' (the range of view).[7] In his most famous work, *Reflections on the Art of War*, Georg Heinrich von Berenhorst only used the expression 'tactics', which he defined as including the choice of weapons:

the way of combining them; any rule, instructions and exercises for the soldier... with regard to the use of his arms, in his posture and the movement of his body,... I should like to call this elementary tactics. Tactics further means: the principles according to which a century, a cohort, a company or a battalion breaks up, moves, reconfigures...; according to which one deploys cohorts, battalions in the order of battle and lets them advance towards the enemy who is within a shot's or a throw's reach, or lets them retreat: all that pertains to the actual fight, all that will decide on a particular day, at a particular hour, that which the higher sciences of war and skills of army leadership aim for—higher in the sense that they are based on tactics. These higher sciences to me are the art of marching with the entire army or substantial parts thereof, to advance, to retreat,...; of establishing... strongholds; of choosing campsites; of using the surface of the earth according to its features; of passing streams and rivers: finally, the great art of making apposite, reliable plans and of... adapting them cleverly to new developments, or of abandoning them and replacing them with others. One could also count as [tactics] the *coup d'oeil* [*den scharfen, richtigen Blick*], quick decision-making, I count among natural and intellectual talents. Anything pertaining to small wars in the narrower sense I also count among tactics, such as the construction of a campsite.[8]

A century later, Marxist-Leninist teaching on war still defined strategy as the preparation and execution of the war as a whole and tactics as the organization and conduct of battle. The content of strategy and tactics was the

---

[5] Antoine-Henri de Jomini, *The Art of War*, trans. G. H. Mendell and W. P. Craighill (reprint, Westport, CT, 1971), 69–71.

[6] Jomini, *The Art of War*, 322.

[7] Heinrich von Bülow, *Geist des neuern Kriegssystems hergeleitet aus dem Grundsatze einer Basis der Operationen* (Hamburg, 1799), 83f.

[8] Georg Heinrich von Berenhorst, *Betrachtungen über die Kriegskunst* (reprint of the 3rd edn of 1827, Osnabrück, 1978), 7 f.

same—armed struggle.[9] This very technical definition was still remarkably close to that supplied by Clausewitz.

It also reverberates in the 1989 definition of strategy by the US Joint Chiefs of Staff: 'Strategy is the art and science of developing and using political, economic, psychological, and military forces as necessary during peace and war, to afford the maximum support to policies, in order to increase the probabilities and favorable consequences of victory and lessen the chances of defeat.'[10] But there are new elements here, which exceed Clausewitz's and his contemporaries' narrow definition of the term 'strategy'. The late Michael Handel, a highly popular teacher of generations of US officers, put it more simply and trenchantly: 'strategy is the development and use of all resources in peace and war in support of national policies to secure victory'.[11] We see in both American definitions a much wider understanding of strategy, which takes on board the nexus between policy and war as its instrument, for which Clausewitz is so famous, as for him, 'war...is an act of policy'.[12] In the same vein, Handel's British colleague, Colin Gray, opined: 'Strategy is the bridge that relates military power to political purpose; it is neither military power *per se* nor political purpose...strategy...[is] the use that is made of force and the threat of force for the ends of policy.'[13]

As Hew Strachan has ably and exhaustively demonstrated in his inaugural lecture of 2003, the term 'strategy' has undergone a shift in meaning and usage since Clausewitz was writing. Until the First World War, 'strategy' was used by most writers to mean something below politics in a hierarchy of determinants. Since then, terms like 'grand strategy' or 'major strategy' (as opposed to 'pure strategy' or 'minor strategy') have been coined, embracing the pursuit of political ends (primarily in international relations) not only with military tools but also with diplomatic, economic, or even cultural instruments. For Basil Liddell Hart, this still applied exclusively to war, while J. F. C. Fuller already saw the need to connect peace strategy with war strategy, and the Cold War with its blurred edge between war and peace finally pushed 'strategy' over the fence up to the level of politics, leading to what Strachan calls a 'conflation of strategy and politics'.[14] But the expansion of the word continued. The American political scientist Bernard Brodie, writing in the Cold War, wrote

[9] Major-General Professor Rasin, 'Die Bedeutung von Clausewitz für die Entwicklung der Militärwissenschaft', *Militärwesen* 2nd year, 3 (May 1958), 385.
[10] In Michael I. Handel, *Masters of War: Classical Strategic Thought* (2nd edn, London, 1996), 36.
[11] Ibid. 36.   [12] *On War*, I, 1, § 24, p. 87.
[13] Colin S. Gray, *Modern Strategy* (Oxford, 1999), 17.
[14] Hew Strachan, 'The Meaning of Strategy: Historical Reflections' (Inaugural Lecture, December 2003). Excerpts in *Newsletter of the University of Oxford*, 15 January 2004, and published in full as 'The Lost Meaning of Strategy', *Survival*, 47/3 (autumn 2005), 33–54.

that strategy 'is nothing if not pragmatic.... Above all, strategic theory is a theory for action.' The thinking of the American military historians, Williamson Murray and Mark Grimsley, went in the same direction: 'strategy is a process, a constant adaptation to shifting conditions and circumstances in a world where chance, uncertainty, and ambiguity dominate.'[15] And finally the British expert on strategy, Sir Lawrence Freedman, with his political science background, put it elegantly: 'Strategy is about the relationship between (political) ends and (military, economic, political etc.) means. It is the art of creating power.'[16]

Today, the advertisement of a vacant 'chair in strategy' is as likely to refer to a branch of business management as to anything military, and Clausewitz specialists can earn a fast buck by joining forces with economists. Today, governments try to develop 'strategies' for dealing with unemployment, housing shortages, and education, while every business has a business plan or 'strategy'. The conflation of strategy and politics and the vaguely synonymous use of the terms 'strategy' and 'policy' (and thus the inflation of the term 'strategy') can be deplored or criticized as unhelpful, or taken as a matter of fact and worked with. What I intend to do in this chapter is the latter, and with that in mind to re-read Clausewitz.

## DEFINITIONS OF VICTORY

But first, let us turn to the second term discussed in this chapter. How did Clausewitz define victory? *On War* does not contain a simple definition. Clausewitz implies that the achievement of the war's aims, either the disarmament of the enemy (or, as he put it elsewhere, the annihilation of his forces in battle) or alternatively the acquisition of a more limited objective, spells success, or victory. In support of the first aim, a large part of *On War* concerns the need to concentrate all efforts on casting down (*niederwerfen*) the enemy in a decisive battle, on inflicting a crushing, indeed an annihilating defeat (*vernichtende Niederlage*) by making him 'defenceless' (*wehrlos*). These passages in *On War* inspired future generations, particularly those of the militaristic late nineteenth and early twentieth centuries, in their cult of the decisive battle, the battle of annihilation, which was the hallmark of Western strategy

---

[15] Williamson Murray and Mark Grimsley, 'Introduction: On Strategy', in Williamson Murray, MacGregor Knox, and Alvin Bernstein (eds), *The Making of Strategy: Rulers, States and War* (Cambridge, 1994), 1; Williamson Murray, 'Military Culture Does Matter', *Strategic Review*, 2 (Spring 1999), 33.

[16] Lawrence Freedman, 'Strategic Studies and the Problem of Power', in Freedman, Paul Hayes, and Robert O'Neill (eds), *Strategy and International Politics: Essays in Honour of Sir Michael Howard* (Oxford, 1992), 294.

for major war until 1945 (and again in the war against Iraq in 1991).[17] On the other hand, if the war aim is limited, as he argued in book I, chapter 2, the achievement of the limited war aims constitutes a full and satisfactory victory.

However, history is full of examples of battles where defeat or victory had less to do with superiority in numbers or firepower, or clear successes in the field, than with surprise or confusion, aggravated by Clausewitz's 'fog of war'. It was a *topos* of his times that, as his French contemporary Joseph Comte de Maistre (1754–1821) had written, 'A battle lost... is a battle that one thinks one has lost.'[18] Moreover, plenty of battles, while ending in a clear-cut military victory for one side, have failed to produce a lasting peace; within a generation peace yielded to a revanchist war. The wars studied most and known best by Clausewitz, the Seven Years War and the Napoleonic Wars, provide blatant examples of this.[19] Clearly, the definition of victory as prevailing in battle is inadequate, when seen in a wider political context. But Clausewitz himself had thoughts which take us far beyond his own earlier thinking of what constituted the successful end to a war.

Another Clausewitzian idea has informed modern ideas of strategy, and that concerns his reflection on war as a contest of wills. For Clausewitz, 'War is an act of force to compel our enemy to do our will'.[20] Clausewitz describes war as a contest between two wrestlers:

Each tries through physical force to compel the other to his will; his immediate aim is to throw his opponent in order to make him incapable of further resistance. War is thus an act of force to compel our enemy to do our will.... Force—that is, physical force,...—is thus the means of war; to impose our will on the enemy is its object.[21]

In acknowledging a wide range of possible manifestations of war, and the way in which war could escalate, Clausewitz's earlier definition of war as something aimed at annihilating the forces of the enemy proved insufficient. Towards the end of his work *On War*, he seems to have understood this, and as a result attempted to come up with a wider understanding of war and its aims. From this we may deduce that the successful conclusion of a war (in other words, victory) must lie in the achievement of certain political war aims which the enemy has sought to deny. In other words, *victory is success in compelling the enemy to do our will.*

---

[17] Brian Bond, *The Pursuit of Victory: From Napoleon to Saddam Hussein* (Cambridge, 1996).
[18] Quoted in Emmanuel Terray, *Clausewitz* (Paris, 1999), 190.
[19] Something oddly enough not acknowledged by Clausewitz with respect to Napoleon, whose many victories in battle gave him few years of peace and ultimately led to a resounding defeat of his entire project.
[20] *On War*, I, 1, § 2, p. 75.    [21] Ibid. I, 1, § 2, p. 75.

But can this be accomplished through a military victory alone? Clausewitz conceded in book I, chapter 1, of *On War* that even a completed war cannot necessarily be regarded as something absolute in itself.

*In war the result is never final*
... even the ultimate outcome of a war is not always to be final. The defeated state often considers the outcome merely as a transitory evil, for which a remedy may still be found in political conditions at some later date.[22]

However, Clausewitz should not have described the search for this remedy as restricted to political measures. In book I, chapter 2, he wrote that the aim of a campaign must be to disarm the adversary's country, but added that one must distinguish in this context between 'the armed forces, the country, and the enemy's will':

The fighting forces must be destroyed: that is, they must be put in such a condition that they can no longer carry on the fight. Whenever we use the phrase 'destruction of the enemy's forces' this alone is what we mean. The country must be occupied; otherwise the enemy could raise fresh military forces. Yet both these things may be done and the war, that is the animosity and the reciprocal effects of hostile elements, cannot be considered to have ended so long as the enemy's will has not been broken: in other words, so long as the enemy government and its allies have not been driven to ask for peace, or the population made to submit.

We may occupy a country completely, but hostilities can be renewed again in the interior, or perhaps with allied help. This of course can happen after the peace treaty, but this only shows that not every war necessarily leads to a final decision and settlement. ... Be that as it may, we must always [for the purposes of the book *On War*] consider that with the conclusion of peace the purpose of the war has been achieved and its business is at an end.[23]

Clausewitz further recognized that war, this act of force, affects minds as well as bodies—here is the crucial recognition of the psychological dimension of war.[24] In the *Principles of War for the Crown Prince* (which he wrote between 1810 and 1812), Clausewitz listed the conquest of public opinion among the 'three main purposes of the conduct of war'.[25] His emphasis on the psychological dimension of war was closely connected with the involvement of the people which the French Revolution had ushered in, with the mobilization of the entire population for the war effort both in France and

---

[22] Ibid. I, 1 § 9, p. 80.  [23] Ibid. I, 2, p. 90 f.  [24] Ibid. I, 1 § 3, p. 76.
[25] 'Übersicht des Sr. Königl. Hoheit dem Kronprinzen in den Jahren 1810, 1811 und 1812 vom Verfasser erteilten militärischen Unterrichts', in Carl von Clausewitz, *Vom Kriege*, ed. Werner Hahlweg, (19th edn, Bonn, 1980, repr. 1991), 1070. These instructions to the crown prince are available in an English edition, Carl von Clausewitz, *Principles of War*, trans. and ed. Hans W. Gatzke (London, 1943).

later, as a reaction, in Prussia, and with the 'great interests' that were at stake. In this context, one must conclude that battles not only affect the balance of forces in real terms: their outcome also leaves important impressions on the participating soldiers, on the population at large and on its leadership, and on any other observers. In book IV, he explained that he thought of the 'main battle' primarily in terms of its psychological effect on the enemy ('... it should not simply be considered as a mutual murder—its effect... is rather a killing of the enemy's spirit than of his men'[26]).

Clausewitz's 'ideal' war, the war of Napoleon, differed so much from the pre-Napoleonic Wars for two reasons: one, because its political leader had unlimited war aims; and two, because he broke through the socio-economic limitations of the professional army, by drawing on conscript forces and the mobilization of the entire population, harnessing popular enthusiasm to the war effort.

In *On War*, we thus find in embryo the various elements of a concept which went beyond targeting the enemy army and aimed at changing the will of the enemy more generally: we have already noted that Clausewitz recognized the need to influence the thinking of the enemy public. A key aspect of the French revolutionary war, and of Clausewitz's *Volkskrieg* or *Volksaufstand* (people's war or insurrection, total mobilization to resist an occupant), was the involvement in warfare of the population, the people itself. These wars had shown, wrote Clausewitz, '... what an enormous contribution the heart and temper of a nation can make to the sum total of politics, war potential, and fighting strength. Now that governments have become conscious of these resources, we cannot expect them to remain unused in the future, whether the war is fought in self-defense or in order to satisfy intense ambition.'[27]

Clausewitz did not propose to fight for the hearts and minds of the people through persuasion and ideological argument: crude force, namely big, spectacular victories, and the conquest of the capital were his recipes for success.[28] It is striking how so soon after the ideological warfare of the French Revolution, so little thought was given to the need to appeal to political ideals other than crude nationalism to mobilize the population. But then Prussia was a reactionary, status quo power, which wanted to protect its monarchy against French republican ideas about equality. Clausewitz advocated *Volkskrieg*, a people's war sustained by arming the entire able-bodied male population, confident that he could build on their patriotism and monarchism, not on any promise to redistribute wealth and power. Some recognized that arming the

---

[26] *On War*, IV, 11, p. 259.  [27] Ibid. III, 7, p. 220.
[28] 'Übersicht des Sr. königl. Hoheit...' *Vom Kriege*, 1070.

people in the German-speaking lands might generate a war which would spin out of government control and so counselled against it. Others were torn.[29]

Helmuth von Moltke, the chief of the Prussian general staff in the wars of German unification (1864–71), echoed Clausewitz's language on the contest of wills in battle:

Victory in combat is the most important moment in war. It alone breaks the will of the enemy and forces him to submit himself to ours. It is not in general the conquest of a piece of land or of a strongpoint, but the destruction of the enemy's forces alone which will be decisive. This is therefore the chief objective of the operation.[30]

In France, a few years later, Ferdinand Foch (to become a general and finally, in 1918, the supreme commander of the Allied forces in the First World War) quoted to his students at the war college the words of Lucien Cardot, who had himself lectured on Clausewitz at the war college: ' "Ninety thousand vanquished men withdraw before ninety thousand victors merely because they have had enough of it, and they have had enough of it because they no longer believe in victory, because they are *demoralised*, because their *moral* resistance is exhausted" (merely *moral*: for the physical situation is the same on both sides).' Foch went on to quote de Maistre's idea that only that battle was lost that one thought lost, where de Maistre had added, 'a battle cannot be lost physically'. Foch concluded:

Therefore, [a battle] can only be lost morally. But then, it is also morally that a battle is won, and we may extend the aphorism by saying: *A battle won, is a battle in which one will not confess oneself beaten.*

... *Victory* means *will*...

In order to reach [the battle's] *end*—which is the imposing of our will on the enemy—modern war uses but one *means*: the destruction of the organised forces of the enemy.

That destruction is undertaken, *prepared*, by battle, which overthrows the enemy, disorganises his command, his discipline, his tactical connections, and his troops *as a force.*

It is *carried out* by the pursuit, in the course of which the victor utilises the moral superiority which victory provides over the vanquished, and tears to pieces, finishes

---

[29] Manfred Rauchensteiner, 'Betrachtungen über die Wechselbeziehung von politischem Zweck und militärischem Ziel', in Eberhard Wagemann and Joachim Niemeyer (eds), *Freiheit ohne Krieg? Beiträge zur Strategie-Diskussion der Gegenwart im Spiegel der Theorie von Carl von Clausewitz* (Bonn, 1980), 63 f.

[30] Großer Generalstab (ed.), *Moltkes Militärische Werke*, IV: *Kriegslehren*, Part 3 (Berlin, 1911), 6.

off, troops already demoralised, disorganised, no longer manageable—that is, forces which are no longer a force.

What we are considering now is the act of war, the means of overthrowing the enemy and of securing victory.[31]

From Clausewitz's and Foch's works, the French strategic thinker General André Beaufre deduced his own definition of strategy as 'the art of the dialectic of wills using force to resolve their conflict' in order to 'convince' the adversary 'that to engage or pursue the battle is pointless'.[32] Strategy, he wrote, is 'the art of the dialectic of force or, more precisely, the art of the dialectic of two opposing wills using force to resolve their dispute'.[33]

## How Clausewitz might have re-defined Strategy and Victory, had he completed *On War*

Gray's, Foch's, and Beaufre's definitions of strategy are Clausewitzian logic taken one step further, in times when strategy in general has been more broadly defined. Building on Clausewitz's views, they gave strategy a wider meaning in which the political aim, and the dialectic of force, of wills, are built into strategy. This is how Clausewitz himself might have re-defined strategy in the light of his own thoughts, had he had more time to revise his *magnum opus*, and had he been able to listen in on some of the discourse on strategy over the following century and a half. Like Gray, Foch, and Beaufre, who derived their thinking from a close reading of *On War*, he might himself have said that 'strategy is the use of any available instruments, up to and including the threat of force or the use of force, for the ends of policy, in a dialectic of two opposing wills, with the aim of imposing our policy and our will upon the enemy'. Concomitantly, 'victory is the successful and lasting imposition of our will upon the enemy', resulting in peace.

### THE QUEST FOR VICTORY IN HISTORY

In the light of these two different Clausewitzian interpretations of strategy, the narrow one he used himself which sees the decisive battle as the be-all and end-all of strategy, and the wider one we have derived from his later writings which

---

[31] Marshal [Ferdinand] Foch, *The Principles of War*, trans. Hilaire Belloc (London, 1918), 283, 286: his italics.
[32] Général André Beaufre, *Introduction à la stratégie* (Paris, 1963), 15 f.
[33] André Beaufre, *An Introduction to Strategy*, trans. R. H. Barry (London, 1963), 22.

would see a lasting imposition of one's will, and a lasting peace settlement, as the wider aim, let us proceed to reflect on the pursuit of victory and its inherent difficulties. The quest for victory, for the meaning and the secret of how to achieve victory, has of course been the central preoccupation of generations of strategists and philosophers from Sun Tzu to Clausewitz, from Vegetius to the political and social scientists of our own era.

Concomitant with both the narrower and the wider Clausewitzian definitions of the aims of strategy, there are two lines of thought about victory. One emphasizes that the decisive battlefield victory is the war aim; the other that a conflict can only be regarded as ended if neither side has the will and determination to resume it; in other words, if there is a lasting peace after the military operations have ended. The first led to the obsession in the nineteenth and twentieth centuries with decisive battles and battles of annihilation, the second has played an important role in thinking about crisis management. I shall argue that both are insufficient, as they do not include the vital element of a *meaningful* victory, the achievement of an enduring peace, a peace, however, which is not the peace of the graveyard, genocide, or the annihilation of the enemy.

In the light of the French revolutionary and Napoleonic Wars, Clausewitz and Jomini focused much of their writing on large battles that decided the fates of whole states for years to come. The aim of war and battle, Clausewitz wrote in *On War*, was to 'disarm' the adversary, to 'annihilate his armed forces' (book I, chapter 2). Once this was achieved, the theory ran, one would be free to dictate one's own political aims to the enemy. The political aims could range from very limited ones to very extensive ones (book VII, chapter 3), and for Napoleon they certainly included the conquest of entire countries, regime change, and the institution of new forms of government and new legislation. To reach these political aims, argued Clausewitz, one had to attack the centre of gravity, the *Schwerpunkt* of the enemy.

But what is the centre of gravity? In his instructions for the crown prince, written in 1810–12, Clausewitz had argued in a narrow military sense (matching his narrow military definition of strategy) that the way to victory lay in attacking 'one point of the enemy's position (i.e. one section of his troops— a division, a corps) and doing so with great superiority, leaving the rest of his army in uncertainty but keeping it occupied'. Even if we are in a position of numerical superiority, we 'should still direct our main attack against one point only. In that way we shall gain more strength at this point.'[34] In book VI of *On War*, he defined this in terms of mechanics, as the point where one could get most leverage, the place where most armed forces were concentrated.

---

[34] 'Über die sr. königl....', *Vom Kriege*, 1053 f.

He strongly opposed the division of an army into separate forces (e.g. for the execution of a pincer movement), except in very special conditions, as he regarded a blow with all one's might at the centre of the enemy's gravity as the key to success.[35] He defined the identification of the enemy's centre of gravity as the first task in the conception of a war plan, while the second task would be to concentrate the forces needed to strike at it.[36] The centre of gravity could be many different things—the enemy's army, his capital, or public opinion.[37] Thus, the more Clausewitz pondered on the role of intangible factors like morale, the more he moved away from analysing war as merely a function of physical factors, military balances, and the outcome of battles on the battlefield.

The first generations of Clausewitz's disciples, particularly in Prussia and Germany, did not follow him in his intellectual move away from a physical centre of gravity (in the form of the enemy's armed forces) to a metaphysical centre of gravity (in the form of public opinion, will, and morale). Instead, they homed in on the idea of the decisive battle and annihilating the enemy's forces in the field. The latter idea was fuelled by the fashion for Social Darwinism, which saw wars in terms of national survival, pitting nation against nation and race against race: the idea that one's own nation or race could only survive through a bloody struggle for survival, in which the enemy would experience terrible losses, together with the suspicion that this would also require 'the ultimate sacrifice' by many combatants on one's own side.[38] Between the Franco-Prussian War of 1870–1 and the First World War, the annihilation of the enemy came increasingly to be seen as the way to success. Whether by attrition or through elusive decisive battles, the First World War, particularly on the western front, became largely a *Materialschlacht*, a quantitative contest of weapons, munitions, and men, resulting in a mutual war of annihilation on the battlefields. For four years, no decision was reached on the western front, and the geographically and temporarily limited battles of Napoleon's campaigns, and also of Königgrätz (in 1866) or Sedan (in 1870), gave way to a continuous confrontation over four years along a frontier spanning a whole continent.

The victory finally achieved by the Western allies in the First World War allowed them to impose their will on the defeated enemies. The Versailles peace treaty with Germany, like the other peace treaties of the Paris suburbs,

---

[35] *On War*, VI, 27–8, pp. 485–7.  [36] Ibid. VIII, 9, p. 619.
[37] Ibid. VIII, 4, pp. 596 f.; see also 'Über die sr. königl....', *Vom Kriege*, 1049 f.
[38] Jehuda L. Wallach, *Das Dogma der Vernichtungsschlacht: Die Lehren von Clausewitz und Schlieffen und ihre Wirkung in Zwei Weltkriegen* (Frankfurt a.M., 1967); see also Jehuda L. Wallach, 'Misperceptions of Clausewitz's *On War* by the German Military', in Michael I. Handel (ed.), *Clausewitz and Modern Strategy* (London, 1986).

was signed in its totality, as none of the defeated powers had the leverage to exact any substantial changes. And yet the victors were soon left with a bitter taste—not only had the price of victory in the lives of their own soldiers been exorbitant, but the following two decades passed with a constant background noise of German grumbling, non-compliance with peace-treaty clauses, strikes, and growing revisionism. The victors gradually faced up to what Sally Marks has called *The Illusion of Peace*.[39] In less than the time that now stands between us and the end of the Cold War, the German republic that had grudgingly accepted its western boundaries turned into a dictatorship which loudly denounced the Versailles Treaty and rejected its obligations. As Hitler undid the Versailles settlement step by step, the value of the Allied victory that had led to an illusory peace and to German revanchism dwindled. One answer given in Britain and France was to blame the politicians for losing the peace that the generals had won; another answer was pacifism or at least pacificism.[40]

Even though the First World War was a clash of nationalisms, marked by chauvinism on all sides, its aims were still a cross between those familiar to the *anciens régimes* and those of Napoleon: some states wanted to reconquer lost territory, some merely wanted to help allies, some peoples wanted their own states or to get rid of occupying powers, and what the Germans wanted, apart from war, was probably unclear even to them. The way the war was waged economically, as contemporaries observed, was new: the industrial and economic mobilization of several of the societies involved went beyond anything that could have been possible in the pre-industrial age, and two Frenchmen, Alphonse Seché and Leon Daudet, called this phenomenon, respectively, 'totalization of the national strength'[41] and 'total war'.[42] But during this war, the differences between combatants and non-combatants were largely respected, as laid down by existing international law and as later confirmed by the Hague Conventions of 1922–3.

Erich Ludendorff's definition of 'total war', published in his famous book of 1935, was quite different. The total mobilization of the population and the economy for the war effort was present in his concepts, certainly. But his ideas far exceeded the totalization of war on one's own side. He wanted a totalization of war also with regard to the annihilation of the enemy, which must not be confined to the bloody slaughter of enemy soldiers on the battlefield. His idea of total war included the elimination of the enemy population from the

---

[39] Sally Marks, *The Illusion of Peace: International Relations in Europe 1918–1933* (London, 1976).
[40] Martin Ceadel, *Pacifism in Britain, 1914–1943: the Defining of a Faith* (Oxford, 1980).
[41] Alphonse Seché, *Les Guerres d'Enfer* (Paris, 1915), 124.
[42] Léon Daudet, *La Guerre Totale* (Paris, 1918), 8 f.

world. The enemies of his fantastically warped brain were Jews and Catholics. Ludendorff, an early supporter of the National Socialist Party, shared with Hitler a hatred of the Jews and added to it a profound disdain for all Slavs. Both defined entire populations as enemies, and Hitler and his supporters set out to annihilate or enslave them.[43]

Traces of Social Darwinism survived the First World War in other countries too. Entire cultures, like those of fascist Spain or totalitarian Italy, worshipped force and thought themselves superior to others due to their own supposed warlike natures. Strikingly, even the Western democracies continued to carry such strands of the virus. The air power strategy of Britain, under the influence of Hugh Trenchard, chief of the air staff of the fledgling Royal Air Force, aimed to defeat an enemy nation by sapping its morale through a contest in which each side bombed the other's cities. Trenchard was convinced that the British national morale was greater and that Britain would therefore win, simply because the British had a higher threshold of pain (which supposedly made them fitter for surviving such a war).[44]

The link between the ethnic-racist integrationist aims of the National-Socialist political programme and the instrument of war led to a mixture which was distinct from the mentalities prevailing in the First World War, even though that had served Ludendorff as a first field of experimentation for some of his ideas about warfare. And while acknowledging that traces of this thinking were present in other cultures, it was the Germans who truly succumbed to the disease. For Hitler, it was not only the integration of all 'Aryan' German speakers into one vast empire that became the object of his military campaigns. His aims included not only the Napoleonic one of overthrowing regimes in neighbouring countries but also that of subjecting their populations to the rule of the 'master race'. In the occupied Slav countries, the populations were integrated into Germany's war effort as slave labourers, who were often worked to death. Hitler's war on the Jews led to their systematic murder. Hitler's war of annihilation took place not only on the battlefields but also in the labour and death camps.[45]

Paradoxically, it was the United States, not Germany, which took the war in the air to its logical extreme, without being ideologically motivated to resort to mass civilian killing. That Germany did not develop the atomic bomb was no noble feat of self-denial, but due to the loss of its best scientific brains in its self-imposed purges: Jewish refugees from Nazi Germany played crucial parts

---

[43] Erich Ludendorff, *Der Totale Krieg* (Munich, 1935), transl. by Dr A. S. Rappoport as *The Nation at War* (London, 1936).

[44] Text in Charles Webster and Noble Frankland, *The Strategic Air Offensive against Germany* (London, 1961), IV, 72 f.

[45] Lucy Davidowicz, *The War against the Jews, 1933–1945* (Harmondsworth, UK, 1977).

in the development of the bomb, which some of them saw as the only way to deter German use of such a weapon (which they suspected their 'Aryan' colleagues of developing).[46] Thus a Western, democratic power ended up killing tens of thousands of undefended civilians in Hiroshima and Nagasaki, in the last, one-sided annihilation battle of the Second World War. And this battle led to unchallenged victory.

However, with this first use of nuclear weapons, Western strategists recoiled in horror from what had previously been seen as a one-way street towards a total war of annihilation. The American strategist, Bernard Brodie, wrote very shortly after the atomic bombing of Hiroshima and Nagasaki that, henceforth, such weapons could only make sense as weapons of deterrence, an idea that was shared even then by the French strategic thinker, Admiral Raoul Castex, and by some British defence planners.[47]

The paradox was, however, that in order to deter nuclear use by the adversary, one needed (or felt the need) to threaten nuclear use oneself as punishment for such use by the other side. American and NATO defence planners thus developed comprehensive planning for the use of nuclear weapons in case the USSR were to start a war against the West, and indeed, at least until the mid-1950s, aimed to 'win' such a war. While NATO documents stopped short of defining what victory would entail, US documents did not. They aimed at the occupation of the USSR and the de-Sovietification and democratization of Russia and its empire, war aims very similar to those entertained with regard to the much smaller Germany in the Second World War. Only thus, it was argued, could the threat of a Communist ideological-cum-military recovery be eradicated.[48]

Once the Soviet Union had an operational nuclear arsenal, this war aim became unacceptable, as it would have had to be bought at too high a cost: mutual nuclear destruction. NATO's Strategic Concept MC 14/2 of 1957 mentioned as aims only a 'successful conclusion' to the war,[49] or 'a termination of hostilities', a phrase which could have applied to an armistice. The best NATO could have hoped for was a restoration of the *status quo ante*.[50] By contrast,

---

[46] For the Frisch-Peierls memorandum, see Lorna Arnold (ed.), 'The History of Nuclear Weapons: the Frisch-Peierls Memorandum on the Possible Construction of Atomic Bombs of February 1940', *Cold War History*, 3 (2003), 111–26.

[47] Amiral Castex, 'Aperçus sur la bombe atomique', *Revue de Défense nationale*, 2 (October 1945); for British planners' views, Julian Lewis, *Changing Direction: British Military Planning for Post-War Strategic Defence, 1942–47* (London, 2003), 178–241.

[48] NSC 20/4, November 1948, repeated in Annex to NSC 153/1, June 1953, and in Annex to NSC 162/2, October 1953, *Foreign Relations of the United States* 1952–1954, II, 596 f., and NSC 162/2, ibid. 582.

[49] NATO MC 14/2(Revised) (Final Decision), § 5.g.

[50] NATO MC 14/2(Revised) (Final Decision), § 25; NATO MC 48/2 (Revised), § 2.

Soviet and Warsaw Pact strategy retained the old thinking about victory and decisive battle until the end of the Cold War. The terms 'annihilation of the enemy's armed forces' and 'decisive victory/defeat' abounded, language similar to that used of European operations in the Second World War, prior to the invention of nuclear weapons. Few words were wasted in Soviet writing on how to pacify the conquered countries that would be devastated at least by 'conventional' firepower, and probably also by nuclear weapons, even if these would have been targeted primarily at military installations. In Soviet military doctrine, imposing one's will on the enemy was contemplated through the use of force, and agitation, propaganda, subversion by persuasion were treated quite separately, by separate institutions. There is no sign that any war would have included elements of persuasion other than the threat and execution of nuclear strikes, and Soviet-cum-GDR influences on Western peace movements played on Western fears of nuclear war, not on any promise of political compromise or rapprochement over issues of human rights.[51] It was only in 1987 that Warsaw Pact strategy became truly defensive. Once the Warsaw Pact was disbanded, reliance on nuclear weapons as weapons to be used in war made a renaissance in the two Russian strategic concepts of 1993 and 1997. The fact that they have so far not been used (e.g. in Chechnya) may be inspired by deterrence thinking, but such thinking always has to be translated into practicable (and thus credible) preparations for nuclear use, which alone make the employment of nuclear weapons possible—and it is the latter that creates concern, not the deterrence thinking per se (if that is what it is).

The paradox of deterrence—the need to plan for the use of nuclear weapons in order to frighten the enemy away from using them in the first place—haunted Western planners as well, even after NATO's early turn towards the defensive. At the end of the 1970s, in the wake of the defeat in Vietnam and widespread despondency among the American military, a group of American and British civilian strategists came up with the concept of 'war-fighting deterrence', which aimed not at deterrence by threat of intolerable punishment, or even at deterrence by denial of any gains in a war. In a famous article of 1979, one of the groups, the same Colin Gray whose Clausewitzian definition of strategy we have already quoted above, called for a new theory of victory in the context of nuclear war.[52] He argued that the enemy had to be made to believe that the United States could win even a nuclear war, which would lead to 'deterrence by anticipation of US victory'. This, in his view, had to imply not only minimizing losses on one's own side, but also

---

[51] Michael Ploetz, *Ferngelenkte Friedensbewegung? DDR und UdSSR im Kampf gegen den NATO-Doppelbeschluß* (Münster, 2004).

[52] Colin S. Gray, 'Nuclear Strategy: The Case for a Theory of Victory', *International Security*, 4 (1979), 54–87.

annihilation—of the enemy's armed forces, to some extent, but mainly of the enemy's leaders.[53] Changing the enemies' minds by eliminating their leading elite was arguably foreshadowed in Clausewitz's recognition that a rebel leader might be the 'centre of gravity' of the enemy, whom one might have to eliminate. Gray's thinking can be said to have had an impact on US policy, in the form of the Presidential Decision PD 59, the National Security Decision Document NSDD 13, and the procurement of precision-guided nuclear weapons under Presidents Carter and Reagan.[54] The underlying nuclear strategy was apparently not formally abrogated before November 1997. While it is said to have contained leadership-'decapitation' options, the Reagan strategy seems to have aimed at enabling American (NATO) forces to survive several nuclear exchanges, with the intention of achieving military victory over the Warsaw Pact.[55] Both postures, Gray's decapitation posture and the Reagan administration's survival-of-nuclear-exchanges posture, were acclaimed as more robust and more effective deterrents than previous strategies, which had signalled Western timidity in the handling of nuclear weapons. The USSR, the 'nuclear warfighters' argued, would be tempted to exploit such hesitancy. These strategies adopted rather limited concepts of victory, though admittedly set within the overall aim of deterrence. They aimed at influencing the enemy's will through his view of whether (nuclear) war was a potentially lucrative option. They did not, however, in any way contribute to a stable peace, that is a peace which neither side seeks to upset if the opportunity presents itself. In no way did they address the underlying causes of East–West tension.

The Conference on Security and Cooperation in Europe, by contrast, did just this. It tried to provide common grounds for mutual security, while establishing rules for the respect for human rights on both sides of the Iron Curtain. The Helsinki Final Act led to the possibility of inspecting gaols in Eastern Europe and reporting on human rights abuses. It established de facto mutual guarantees for existing frontiers, with the result that since 1975 no claims have been made on the cession of territory to any other existing state (internal secession is a different matter), undertakings which were respected

---

[53] Colin S. Gray, 'War-Fighting for Deterrence', *Journal of Strategic Studies*, 7 (1984), 5–28.

[54] Jeffrey Richelson, 'PD-59, NSDD-13 and the Reagan Strategic Modernization Program', *Journal of Strategic Studies*, 6 (1983), 125–45.

[55] R. Jeffrey Smith, 'Clinton Directive Changes Strategy on Nuclear Arms', *The Washington Post* (7 December 1997); Steven Lee Myers, 'U.S. "Updates" Nuclear War Guidelines', *New York Times* (8 December 1997). During the first presidency of Ronald Reagan, Vice-President George H. W. Bush was asked what President Reagan meant when he spoke about 'victory' in nuclear war. Bush replied: 'You have a survivability of command and control, survivability of industrial potential, protection of a percentage of your citizens, and you have a capability that inflicts more damage on the opposition tha[n] it can inflict upon you. That's the way you have a winner.' Quoted in Peter Pringle and William Arkin, *SIOP: The Secret U.S. Plan for Nuclear War* (New York, 1983), 40.

by all sides during the disintegration of the Soviet Empire in 1989–91. It could be argued that the relative freedom from any fear that NATO would exploit the situation was a central reason why the Warsaw Pact collapsed peacefully, since the embattled Communist regimes could not rally support for their own survival on the pretext that they confronted an external threat.

In both East and West, the CSCE process, which finally led to the creation of the OSCE at the end of the Cold War, was detached from military strategy. This dual track approach, in which the two tracks were practically uncoordinated on both sides, was largely to blame for the last peak of the Cold War, from the Soviet invasion of Afghanistan to the arrival of Gorbachev (1979–85).

The Clausewitzian concept of war as a contest of wills influenced a parallel strand of thinking in the West, and this concerned conflict management. Here the contest of wills was extended to include the manipulation of the adversary's imagination with regard to the further development of a conflict. Conflict managers argued that the enemy's imagination should be influenced to deter him from escalating a conflict and to coerce him to act in ways advantageous to one's own side. In *On War*, Clausewitz had written:

If the enemy is to be coerced you must put him in a situation that is even more unpleasant than the sacrifice you call on him to make. The hardships of that situation must not of course be merely transient—at least not in appearance. Otherwise the enemy would not give in but would wait for things to improve. Any change that might be brought about by continuing hostilities must then, at least in theory, be of a kind to bring the enemy still greater disadvantages.[56]

This idea of signalling and threatening impressed some of Clausewitz's American disciples, among them in particular Bernard Brodie and Thomas Schelling. They added to it the metaphor of the commercial transaction: Clausewitz had written towards the end of book I, chapter 2 that 'The decision by arms is for all minor and major operations in war what cash payment is in commerce [*Wechselhandel*].'[57] For Clausewitz and his contemporaries, the *Wechselhandel* took the form of presenting, but normally not cashing, a cheque for a high amount, in order to obtain credit. (Clausewitz's contemporary Heinrich Heine, for example, had angered his rich uncle by actually cashing such a *Wechsel* given to him by his uncle with the sole purpose of persuading a bank to give young Heinrich credit.) What Clausewitz was implying was that you could influence the adversary by merely threatening battle, or threatening to intensify hostilities, without *necessarily* carrying out the threat. But if the enemy called one's bluff, a bluff it had better not be: the readiness to fight must always underpin the threatening, deterrent, or coercive gesture.

[56] *On War*, I, 1, § 4, p. 77.   [57] Ibid. I, 2, p. 97.

Brodie, Schelling and the colleagues they influenced took this as an important key to a new way of thinking about a possible future war with the Warsaw Pact. They developed concepts of conflict management through deterrent and coercive threats. Under the presidency of John F. Kennedy, Robert McNamara introduced these ideas to the Pentagon, ideas which made some sense in the context of a war between NATO and the Warsaw Pact in Europe or Turkey. By the time McNamara was in office the only hope in any such war was to restore the *status quo ante*. In the 1960s, NATO no longer had a war aim of 'victory':[58] under the shadow of the nuclear bomb, the most one could realistically hope for was to dissuade an adversary from attacking, or if he attacked, to force him to agree to an armistice.

These concepts were unsuccessful, however, in the context of a conventional war, which Robert McNamara and his successive presidents tried to win in Vietnam. Here, the Americans found that trying to influence the adversary through complex political signalling wrapped in air attacks with intricate limitations and threats of steady escalation merely led the Communist North Vietnamese regime and the Communist fighters in South Vietnam to put up with slowly increased pain. Just as Clausewitz had seen in Russia in 1812 and then Prussia in 1813, North Vietnam continued to resist. The Vietnamese Communists had truly vital stakes in the conflict, and they had time on their side. The American commitment was limited, notwithstanding years of government rhetoric about the 'vital' importance of Vietnam to America, and the political bargaining with military tools finally led to the most spectacular defeat in America's history.

The lesson to be drawn from this is that in a military context, a political compromise is only of lasting quality if the military underpinning is there to stay for a very long time, or else if the political solution is such that the militarily weaker party is prepared for political reasons to espouse it, and permanently to give up its previous political aims. Otherwise, the armistice or peace will only be temporary, and the party defeated militarily will wait for the adversary to withdraw its armed forces to return to its previous aims. Such 'political–military' bargaining is based on calculations of costs and gains which can easily change if the military circumstances are altered. The determination of Ho Chi Minh to unite Vietnam under his rule survived all American attempts at coercion, and brought him lasting victory once the US forces were withdrawn.

In the years after Vietnam, Western political advisers such as Edward Luttwak, in good part inspired by Soviet insistence on victory in nuclear war,

---

[58] Beatrice Heuser, 'Victory in a Nuclear War? A Comparison of NATO and WTO War Aims and Strategies', *Contemporary European History*, 7 (1998), 311–28.

called for a new espousal of the aim of *military* victory in war, focused on a decisive battle at least in a purely *conventional* context.[59] The United States returned to this sort of thinking, reflected in Field Manual 100-5 of the 1982 (revised in 1986),[60] and the war aims of 'AirLand Battle'. The underlying concept was one of swift movements (manoeuvre) and deep strikes: the aim was to envelop the enemy's first echelon of attacking forces, cutting it off from vital supplies while destroying a second or even third echelon when they were still far away from the battle area by deep interdiction.

AirLand Battle was first enacted in reality against the Iraqi forces in 1991: air strikes 'shaped' the battlefield, knocked out enemy radar, and paralysed or destroyed Iraq's air force, and subsequently a swift enveloping movement by the ground forces accompanied by close air support annihilated the mass of the enemy's ground forces. *Desert Storm*, the Allied offensive against Iraq, was celebrated as a textbook example of a victory.[61] The act that had triggered war, the invasion of one sovereign state by another, had been reversed, and thus in narrow legal terms, as defined by the UN Security Council, the *casus belli* removed. On 27 February 1991, President George Bush Senior declared: 'Kuwait is liberated. Iraq's Army is defeated. Our military aims have been achieved.'

But what was celebrated as an overwhelming and decisive military victory failed to produce a lasting peace. In 1990 and 1991, the UN Security Council went further and demanded a series of other measures, which were initiated unenthusiastically and were finally largely met with non-compliance. Paraphrasing Maistre and Foch, we find ample evidence in European history that a war is ended decisively only if the defeated party accepts its defeat and does not seek a return match even in the long term. Just as after Napoleon's great victories, the Franco-Prussian War of 1870–1 or the First World War, the military victory was 'lost' due to the defeated party's determination to hold out, to show defiance, and sooner or later to reverse the military decision and the peace conditions imposed by the victorious side. After a dozen years, during which further American and British air strikes within an interdiction area had taken place for months on end, the United States and the United Kingdom felt obliged, as permanent members of the UN Security Council, to resume military action. In 2003, they again won a sweeping military victory, which this time included the occupation of the entire country and the removal of the Iraqi dictator, Saddam Hussein. But to this day, even occupation and 'regime change' have not transformed the military victory into an

---

[59] Edward Luttwak: 'On the Meaning of Victory', *The Washington Quarterly*, 5/4 (Autumn 1982), 17–24.
[60] Follow-on force attack (FOFA) was accepted by NATO 1985.
[61] David Eshel, 'Desert Storm: A Textbook Victory', *Military Technology*, 4 (1991), 28–34.

unchallenged political victory. Iraq is not pacified, and resistance movements are using guerrilla tactics, including terrorism in particular, to deny the Western powers and the Iraqi factions interested in a new democratic society lasting control of Iraq.

In 1944–5, Germany, too, tried to resort to guerrilla tactics in the form of a people's mobilization (*Volkssturm*) to prevent its final defeat. Boys and old men were mobilized, and units of 'grey wolves' (as they were called) attempted the in-depth defence of the homeland. Nevertheless, they were quickly defeated when the German government collapsed with the death of Hitler. Twelve years after the end of the Second World War, the Federal Republic of Germany was so thoroughly at peace with Germany's former enemies that it had joined them in the European Coal and Steel Community, the Western European Union, NATO, and the European Economic Community. At the very least this proves that a thorough political exploitation of a military victory within such a period of time is possible.

The mobilization of guerrilla resistance leads to another problem with the concept of victory, if defined merely in terms of military victory. It is all but impossible to apply in conflicts in which one side does not operate with large forces, acting together in large entities. When the adversary avoids a classical battle, a classical military victory cannot be achieved. Many civil wars (with crucial exceptions, such as the British and American Civil Wars) and most wars involving guerrilla movements are not decided by a decisive battle. In low-intensity conflicts, the militarily weaker side fights precisely by trading time for a decision. Using what is now called 'asymmetric conflict', it aims to erode the will of the militarily stronger side, reckoning that it will usually be weak as a function of a limited commitment to the cause. Terrorism especially can be kept going by even the smallest group of strong-willed individuals, bedevilling all efforts by more moderate leaders of (previous or actual) guerrilla (or terrorist) movements to conclude a lasting peace with their adversaries, as has been so amply documented both in Northern Ireland and in Israel and the occupied territories.

Imposing one's will upon the enemy[62] must therefore be something larger and more encompassing than a mere military victory (remembering full well that even that is very hard to achieve). There seem to be two prerequisites for a lasting change of the enemy's will to resist. One is to convince him that he is truly defeated and that the defeat is irreversible: this can necessitate the commitment of occupation forces over the long term (Allied forces stayed in Germany for almost fifty years after the end of the Second World War). The other seems to be a factor of a different nature. It is perhaps best alluded to the

---

[62] *On War*, I, 1, p. 75.

response made by the Spanish philosopher Miguel de Unamuno to the Fascists, 'vincereis, pero no convencereis' [you will win, but you will not convince]. This concept, incidentally, is also contained in embryo in Clausewitzian thinking, as he recognized the persuasive force of ideals in the popular mobilization both of the French and of Napoleon's adversaries.

After Germany's defeat in the Second World War, the rapid reconstruction of West Germany gave almost the entire population a stake in the new economy: through prosperity, victory was turned into political persuasion. This was backed by a far-reaching campaign of political re-education, which went beyond the elimination of a small group of war criminals, and revolved round the four 'Ds': de-Nazification, demilitarization, decartellization, and democratization. Beyond this, the occupying forces sought to win the Germans over to their own side. In the words of Marshal Zhukov, the Soviets wanted to 'conquer the souls of the Germans',[63] while the Western powers fought a 'battle for the souls of the Germans' (General Sir Brian Robertson, Commander-in-Chief UK Forces in Germany).[64] Through re-education, the occupants gave the Germans a vested interest in the success of the new orders in East and West Germany. The West Germans benefited from the Marshall Plan, while both sides were integrated into the two economic and defence blocs that were formed within a decade after the end of the war, and both became almost equal members within each bloc. The occupying powers restricted themselves to removing and punishing a very tiny National Socialist leadership; the large mass of party members and fellow-travellers got away unscathed. Particularly in the West, the civilian population was treated with the greatest generosity—there were no persecutions, no mass executions, no forced labour camps. Thus the occupants, particularly in the West, were indeed able to win the battle for the hearts and minds of the Germans. The same was true for Italy (where there had, however, been a sizeable internal resistance against the Fascists) and even for Japan, despite the devastating American attacks on the civilian populations of Tokyo, Hiroshima, and Nagasaki. After the imposition of their will, the Western powers in particular succeeded in winning the moral support of the defeated peoples. After *vincere*, there was *convincere*.

The same applied to successful campaigns elsewhere. In Malaya in the late 1940s, the British overcame the Communist insurrectionists through agrarian reforms which won the support of the majority of the population and gave them a stake in a non-revolutionary solution. In the Vietnam War, the Australians in particular tried to apply the British recipe from Malaya—with

---

[63] Quoted in S. Tulpanow, *Deutschland nach dem Kriege 1945–1949* (Berlin Ost, 1985), 15.
[64] The National Archives, FO 317/70587, Sir Brian Robertson to Ernest Bevin, Berlin, 29 April 1958.

considerable success in the small area where Australian forces operated.[65] Eventually, even the Americans in South Vietnam adopted a strategy of trying to win over the population's 'hearts and minds', but this proved too little, too late, and the Diêm government that was backed by the Americans was so obviously corrupt and tyrannical that the democratic rhetoric of the Americans was seen as hollow.

Since the end of the Cold War, the long-term commitment of forces has been needed in Bosnia-Hercegovina, Kosovo, Afghanistan, and Iraq. Equally, political persuasion is needed in each of them, and will be needed for some years yet.

Particularly in dealing with terrorists, the imposition of one's will can only lead to a lasting peace if the adversaries can be persuaded that they have a major stake in such a settlement. And here the structural problem is frequently found that terrorist leaders, once they start negotiations with the adversary, risk losing control of fanatical splinter groups who persist in carrying on the fight. The latter's actions are usually sufficient to undermine the peace effort and to bring down the delicate bridges of reconciliation. Clausewitz was right when, late in his life, he realized that the centre of the enemy's 'gravity' could be many different things—the enemy's army, his capital, and the opinion of his people. Indeed, it might be the leader of a resistance movement, whom Clausewitz thought one might have to strike down to win a lasting victory.[66]

CONCLUSION

From Clausewitz's writing one can deduce that 'strategy is the use of any available instruments, up to and including the threat of force or the use of force, for the ends of policy, in a dialectic of two opposing wills, with the aim of imposing our policy and our will upon the enemy'. Concomitantly, 'victory is the successful and lasting imposition of our will upon the enemy, resulting in lasting peace.'

What, according to our reading of Clausewitz and in the light of European history, are the conditions of a victory that leads to a lasting peace? A decisive battle may or may not be required. A decisive military defeat of the enemy certainly was a major precondition for breaking the enemy's will to resist, but on its own it was rarely a sufficient precondition for a lasting peace. A crushing defeat could prepare the ground for a thorough re-structuring of the

---

[65] Robert O'Neill, *Vietnam Task* (Melbourne, 1968).
[66] *On War*, VIII, 4, p. 596; see also. 'Über die sr. königl. . . . ', *Vom Kriege*, 1049 f.

enemy's culture and beliefs, as in Germany and Japan in 1945. But without the latter, the former did not necessarily guarantee a lasting effect from the shock of defeat, as the examples of Germany in 1918 and Iraq in 1991 amply demonstrate. It is not enough to aim to impose one's will upon the enemy in the short term. Crisis management with political signalling and threats of escalation, or air raids which avoid casualties to one's own side, can thwart an enemy's military campaigns for the time being, but will not eliminate the causes of the conflict. Conflict management is not enough, and it is not sufficient to impose one's will on the enemy merely temporarily, through a successful military campaign.

A long-term victory that leads to a robust peace must change the enemy's mind and not just his will. It must convince him, not just temporarily disable him. It must win over the heart of the enemy so that his population is no longer hostile. The peace must hold promises of a good life for all sides. To paraphrase Clausewitz, in order to be effective and lasting, a victory has to be built on military success, but has to contain a very large admixture of politics. Politics has to construct a peace settlement in which all sides have a vested interest. Only then is military victory the true end of war and the foundation of peace, not a prelude to the next war.

# 9

# On Defence as the Stronger Form of War

*Jon Sumida*

> I am not suggesting that Clausewitz must therefore remain an impenetrably obscure thinker, the reserve of a few learned and logically skilled specialists, who alone can separate out what is best in him from what is confused and fallacious. On the contrary, it would be truer to say that I want to rescue Clausewitz from the Clausewitzian specialists.
>
> W. B. Gallie (1978)[1]

Carl von Clausewitz wrote two notes in which he explained his intentions in relation to the revision of the unfinished manuscript that was to become *On War*. In the first, dated 10 July 1827, Clausewitz maintained that the study of war would be greatly facilitated by the concept 'war is nothing but the continuation of policy with other means'.[2] He then stated that he was going to use this proposition as the basis of a complete rewriting of his book. In a second undated note, purportedly written in 1830, Clausewitz confessed that he was dissatisfied with most of the manuscript, and conceded that he was going to have to 'rewrite it entirely and to try and find a solution along other lines'. Just the first chapter of book I, Clausewitz observed, was 'finished', and he suggested that it indicated 'the direction I meant to follow elsewhere'.[3] In this chapter, the argument 'war is not a mere act of policy but a true political instrument, a continuation of political activity by other means' was a major feature of Clausewitz's exposition.[4] In the autumn of 1830, Clausewitz stopped writing after being recalled to active duty. Before he could resume his work, Clausewitz died suddenly from cholera in November 1831.

The two notes have heavily influenced the consideration of Clausewitz's theoretical masterpiece. In the first place, they served as the basis for the view

---

[1] W. B. Gallie, *Philosophers of Peace and War: Kant, Clausewitz, Marx, Engels, and Tolstoy* (Cambridge, 1978), 49.
[2] Carl von Clausewitz, *On War*, trans. and ed. Michael Howard and Peter Paret (Princeton, NJ, 1976), 69.
[3] Ibid. 70.   [4] Ibid. I, 1, p. 87.

that the manuscript of *On War* was little more than a preliminary draft that had been all but repudiated by its author. In the second, they have promoted the use of the first chapter of book I as a conceptual template for the balance of the study. And third, they have caused many scholars to concentrate their formal analysis of *On War* as a whole on the one aphorism on the relationship of war and policy/politics, and in particular its significance with respect to the definitions of limited/real and unlimited/absolute war. These factors have promoted highly selective reading, the interpretation of fragments with little regard for textual or historical context, and the dismissal without engagement of most of the book. What has become customary practice, however, is problematical for two reasons.

In the first place, in the note of 10 July 1827, Clausewitz stated that a reading 'of the first six books as they were would enable "an unprejudiced reader in search of truth and understanding" to discover "basic ideas that might bring about a revolution in the theory of war" '. Two conclusions follow almost inescapably from this passage. First, Clausewitz believed arguments that challenged existing conceptions of war in a fundamental way could be discerned from a careful reading of the entirety of his unrevised text, and second, whatever these arguments were, they did not require exposition that was planned for the books on attack or war plans (what became books VII and VIII). In the second place, Azar Gat, in a book first published in 1989, made a strong case for the undated note supposed to have been written in 1830 having been written in 1827 or even earlier.[5] If Gat is correct, this would allow consideration of the possibility that Clausewitz revised his manuscript between 1827 and 1830. That this indeed occurred is supported by the fact that book VI, which Clausewitz characterized as in an unsatisfactory preliminary form ('sketch' in the standard English translation, perhaps more accurately translated as 'attempt') in the undated note, was in its published form twice the length of the next longest book (book V) and triple that of the others, and addressed the issue of the relationship of war and politics in no uncertain terms.

If *On War* provides an essentially sound representation of Clausewitz's considered views, or at least what he believed was most important, there is far less justification for either restricting careful reading to the first chapter of book I, or imposing its supposed perspective on the balance of the text. This chapter is based on the study of the entirety of *On War* as given in the standard English version edited by Michael Howard and Peter Paret. Whatever its shortcomings as an accurate rendering of the German text, this edition

---

[5] Azar Gat, *A History of Military Thought: From the Enlightenment to the Cold War* (Oxford: Oxford University Press, 2001), 257–65.

has been for a generation the point of departure for most academic discussion of *On War* in the English-speaking world, and virtually all professional military instruction. I contend that the unifying concept of *On War* is the proposition 'defense is the stronger form of war'. This was established clearly in book I, explained in detail in book VI, and supported and amplified in books II through to V, VII, and to a degree in VIII. Failure to recognize the significance of Clausewitz's ideas about the superiority of the defence over the offence is to misunderstand fundamentally his primary line of thought and, among other things, his particular treatments of the relationship between war and politics, strategies of attrition and annihilation, and limited and unlimited war.

I

Much of the first chapter of book I was devoted to definitions of unlimited/absolute and limited war. Unlimited/absolute war was conflict in which the behaviour of one or both combatants was driven by the need to maximize the use of force with no restriction.[6] Limited war was conflict in which the propensity to maximize the use of force was restrained.[7] Clausewitz characterized pure unlimited/absolute war as an abstraction, limited war as real,[8] but he made it clear that war that closely approximated the unrestrained use of violence—also designated unlimited/absolute war—could occur, and thus presumably was also real.[9] With respect to barely restrained or highly restrained war and everything in between, Clausewitz argued that political considerations had influence—more or less congruence with the maximization of force in the former case, shifting to incongruence in the latter.[10] In all forms of real war, therefore, war could be considered 'an act of policy'.[11]

The foregoing discussion was connected to Clausewitz's introduction of his views on defence, which were presented as a subject of the first importance. 'As we shall show,' he declared, 'defense is a stronger form of fighting than attack.' 'I am convinced', Clausewitz went on to say,

that the superiority of the defensive (if rightly understood) is very great, far greater than appears at first sight. It is this which explains without any inconsistency most periods of inaction that occur in war. The weaker the motives for action, the more will they be overlaid and neutralized by this disparity between attack and defense, and the more frequently will action be suspended—as indeed experience shows.[12]

[6] Clausewitz, *On War*, I, 1, p. 75; VIII, 3A, p. 582.  [7] Ibid. I, 1, pp. 78–80.
[8] Ibid. I, 1, p. 78.   [9] Ibid. I, 1, pp. 87–8.   [10] Ibid. I, 1, p. 88.
[11] Ibid. I, 1, p. 87.   [12] Ibid. I, 1, p. 84.

Clausewitz, in other words, maintained that the weaker the attacker's motive—which by definition had political origins—the greater the negative effect of the relative superiority of the defence over the attack would have on the attacker's willingness to seek decisive action, with the implication that inaction on the part of the attacker would promote commensurate behaviour in the defender.

In the event of conflict that approached the conditions of unlimited war, Clausewitz was still convinced that political considerations would ultimately come into play in ways that disfavoured the offence. In the real world, Clausewitz observed, the attacker could not achieve a decision with 'a single, short blow'. In the time that would elapse between the initiation of attack and the point of decisive battle, a defender could mobilize or deploy additional regular troops augmented by a supportive population; exploit through skilful retreat the effects of topography, distance, and fixed defences; and receive the support of allies.[13] 'Even when great strength has been expended on the first decision', Clausewitz maintained, 'and the balance has been badly upset, equilibrium can be restored.'[14] And a defender could concede defeat and wait for more propitious times to restore what had been lost. Thus, Clausewitz noted, 'the ultimate outcome of a war is not always to be regarded as final. The defeated state often considers the outcome merely as a transitory evil, for which a remedy may still be found in political conditions at some later date.'[15]

Clausewitz's discussion of the relationship of war and policy/politics, in short, was not independent, but linked to discussion of the superiority of the defence over the offence. This was also true of Clausewitz's description of war as a 'remarkable trinity' of emotion, contingency, and rational action, which were associated respectively with the people, commander-in-chief, and crown. Clausewitz's intent with regard to this formulation was quite specific. Its defining context was a situation in which resistance to invasion by a superior enemy by an aroused populace could prove decisive. This point was made clear in the opening of the next chapter. Here, Clausewitz explained that even the destruction of a nation's regular army and the occupation of its territory were not enough to constitute final defeat—that could occur only after the government and its allies formally abjured hostilities, which was the prerequisite to the cessation of further resistance by the population. As in the case of the connection between the famous aphorism and Clausewitz's views on defence, this matter would receive more extensive treatment in book VI.

Much of the balance of the second chapter of book I was devoted to an examination of defence in the case of resistance to attack by a much stronger

---

[13] *On War*, I, 1, p. 79.   [14] Ibid. I, 1, p. 79.   [15] Ibid. I, 1, p. 80.

enemy. Under such circumstances, Clausewitz observed, the proper objective of the defence could not be the disarming of the enemy, but rather 'wearing down' the invader, which meant 'using the duration of the war to bring about a gradual exhaustion of his physical and moral resistance'.[16] Adopting the perspective of the defence, Clausewitz then stated that

> if we intend to hold out longer than our opponent we must be content with the smallest possible objects, for obviously a major object requires more effort than a minor one. The minimum object is *pure self-defense*; in other words, fighting without a positive purpose. With such a policy our relative strength will be at its height, and thus the prospects for a favorable outcome will be the greatest.[17]

Clausewitz believed that the defence's acting to preserve its forces without combat was justifiable if a large imbalance in strength made such a course necessary. But he also emphasized the fundamental importance of the destruction of the enemy's forces through fighting. These were not necessarily mutually exclusive forms of behaviour. Clausewitz resolved the apparent contradiction by explaining that the preservation of one's own forces and the exhaustion of those of the enemy could also be the preliminary to acting with a positive purpose, that is the destruction of the enemy forces through fighting. In this case, the action to preserve one's own forces

> is transposed into waiting for the decisive moment. This usually means that *action is postponed* in time and space to the extent that space and circumstances permit. If the time arrives when further waiting would bring excessive disadvantages, then the benefit of the negative policy has been exhausted. The destruction of the enemy—an aim that has until then been postponed but not displaced by another consideration—now reemerges.[18]

Put succinctly, Clausewitz stated it thus: 'The policy with a positive purpose calls the act of destruction into being; the policy with a negative purpose waits for it.'[19] Hans Delbrück, among many others, seems to have regarded Clausewitz's discussion of attrition and annihilation as essentially taxonomic—that is, as an attempt to categorize forms of strategy in a manner analogous to the identification of the forms of war in terms of limited and unlimited conflict.[20] This Clausewitz may in effect have done, but his specific

---

[16] Ibid. I, 1, p. 93.    [17] Ibid. I, 2, p. 99.    [18] Ibid. I, 2, p. 99.
[19] Ibid. I, 2, p. 98.
[20] Gordon A. Craig, 'Delbrück: The Military Historian', in Edward Mead Earle (ed.), *Makers of Modern Strategy: Military Thought from Machiavelli to Hitler* (New York, 1966; first published 1941), 272–3; Raymond Aron, *Clausewitz Philosopher of War*, trans. Christine Booker and Norman Stone (London, 1983; first published in France in 1976), 70–81; and Arden Bucholz, *Hans Delbruck and the German Military Establishment: War Images in Conflict* (Iowa City, IA, 1985), 35–6.

intent was to provide a prolegomenon to his discussion of the defensive use of retreat and counterattack that was to be given in book VI.

In the third chapter of book I, Clausewitz described the salient characteristics of an effective commander-in-chief, on which the fortunes of either offensive or defensive action would depend. For Clausewitz, such 'military genius' was a matter of both intellect and temperament. High intelligence was necessary to perform complex problem-solving. But in addition, qualities such as courage and determination were no less essential because decisions often had to be made in the absence of certain knowledge and in the face of great danger. In war, Clausewitz warned, a commander-in-chief was faced by complex problems that would tax the cognitive capabilities of a brilliant mathematician, while setbacks, uncertainty, and prospects of disaster assaulted his moral equilibrium.[21] Although he did not say so at this time, these challenges were more pronounced for the leader of the attacking force, and likely to be attenuated for the general in charge of the defence, in the latter case especially so when action was avoided entirely in order to preserve his forces. There can, therefore, be little doubt that this chapter was meant to set up Clausewitz's explicit discussion of the favourable implications for the defence of the greater psychological difficulties that were inherent to the attack that he provided in books VI and VII.[22]

The next four chapters 'identified danger, physical exertion, intelligence, and friction as the elements that coalesce to form the atmosphere of war, and turn it into a medium that impedes activity'.[23] They thus constituted a coda to chapter 3, listing and briefly describing factors that affected positive action, and thus were likely to be more applicable to the attacker than the defender. The eighth and final chapter of book I continued this line of argument by prescribing war experience as the antidote to the negative effects of the factors given in the preceding four chapters, in the absence of which manoeuvres or foreign advisers with experience were not considered to be adequate compensation. An unstated though obvious implication was that, though Clausewitz's remedy would not be available to an attacker at the beginning of a conflict that started after many years of peace, it might be possessed by the defender in some measure at the time of counterattack after a period of armed resistance.

In book II of *On War*, Clausewitz advanced a novel concept of theory and its relationship to history. Conventional operational history, he argued, was incapable of providing an adequate basis for the study of action by the commander-in-chief because the historical record did not contain

---

[21] Clausewitz, *On War*, I, 3, pp. 108, 112.

[22] Note especially the anticipation of the discussion of political considerations and its effects on the attacker in book VI, for which see ibid. I, 3, p. 112, and II, 8, p. 387.

[23] Ibid. I, 7, p. 122.

enough information to evaluate the motives that underlay high-level military decision-making during crises. In response, Clausewitz formulated a theory that identified and considered the multiple vectors that influenced decision-making under difficult conditions, which in effect delineated the psychological as well as material conditions of directing an army on campaign. Proper case study of supreme operational command was to be based on a combination of verifiable information that was the property of conventional military history and intelligent surmise generated by theory. The primary object of such an exercise was not the evaluation of the rightness or wrongness of conduct in a particular instance, which was so often the objective of conventional analysis, but empathetic comprehension through the re-enactment of the dilemma of why the exercise of choice was difficult in emotional as well as rational terms.[24] In book II, Clausewitz thus prescribed a method of study that would facilitate understanding of the psychological factors that favoured the defence over the attack, which was a major concern of books VI and VII.

In books III, IV, and V, Clausewitz's concerns were broader, and observations that supported his views on defence made for the most part in passing while addressing other matters. In book III, which was entitled 'Strategy in General', Clausewitz dealt with three subjects that, for reasons that have been explained or should be obvious, favoured the proposition that defence was the stronger form of war. These were the critical importance of the moral element in strategy,[25] the enormous psychological difficulty of being able to use all forces simultaneously (which Clausewitz argued was important for the attacker),[26] and the suspension of action in war.[27] In book IV, which was entitled 'The Engagement', Clausewitz argued that the attacker needed a great battle to achieve decision in the event of resistance by the defender, but that mustering the will to accomplish this was extremely difficult.[28] Moreover, he contended that the pursuit and destruction of an enemy army after a great battle, which he considered to be essential for strategic success, posed especially difficult challenges of will for the victorious commander-in-chief.[29] In book V, which was entitled 'Military Forces', Clausewitz maintained that inferior forces could resist effectively,[30] that swift offensive action through rapid marching was exhausting and thus could seriously debilitate an attacking army,[31] and that, in the event of a delayed decision, inadequate billeting or logistics during

---

[24] Jon Tetsuro Sumida, 'The Relationship of History and Theory in *On War*: The Clausewitzian Ideal and Its Implications', *Journal of Military History*, 65 (2001), 333–54. See also Gallie, *Philosophers of Peace and War*, 46.
[25] Clausewitz, *On War*, III, 3, pp. 184–5.   [26] Ibid. III, 12, p. 209.
[27] Ibid. III, 16, pp. 216–19.   [28] Ibid. IV, 11, p. 259.   [29] Ibid. IV, 12, pp. 263–70.
[30] Ibid. V, 3, p. 283.   [31] Ibid. V, 12, p. 322.

the period of suspended hostilities were more likely to afflict the attacker than the defender.[32]

Clausewitz divided book VI into three main sections. In the first eight chapters, he 'surveyed as well as delimited the whole field of defense'.[33] In chapters 9 to 26, Clausewitz covered 'the most important methods of defense'.[34] In chapters 27 to 30, he examined 'the defense of a theater of war as a subject in itself' and looked 'for the thread that ties together all the subjects discussed'.[35] The first and last sections are each approximately thirty pages, and constitute the introduction and conclusions. The middle section is roughly 100 pages long—or twice the length of most of the other books. In book VI, Clausewitz used length and balanced structure to present carefully rendered arguments that followed from and made sense of what had come before. It cannot be dismissed out of hand as a sketch, defective trial run, or mere compendium of obsolete technical observations. Book VI is in fact the expository culmination of *On War*.

Clausewitz's basic definition of defence, given in the first chapter of book VI, had two elements: 'the parrying of a blow' and 'awaiting the blow'. Awaiting the blow was critical, because 'it is the only test by which defense can be distinguished from attack in war'.[36] Clausewitz argued the great advantage of defence over offence was

> the fact that time which is allowed to pass unused accumulates to the credit of the defender. He reaps where he did not sow. Any omission of attack—whether from bad judgment, fear, or indolence—accrues to the defenders' benefit.[37]

That being said, Clausewitz made it clear that parrying and awaiting did not rule out offensive action. 'If defense is the stronger form of war', he observed,

> yet has a negative object, it follows that it should be used only so long as weakness compels, and be abandoned as soon as we are strong enough to pursue a positive object. When one has used defensive measures successfully, a more favorable balance of strength is usually created; thus, the natural course in war is to begin defensively and end by attacking. It would therefore contradict the very idea of war to regard defense as its final purpose, just as it would to regard the passive nature of defense not only as inherent in the whole but also in all its parts. In other words, a war in which victories were used only defensively without the intention of counterattacking would be as absurd as a battle in which the principle of absolute defense—passivity, that is—were to dictate every action.[38]

---

[32] *On War*, V, 14, pp. 339–40.
[33] Ibid. VI, 8, p. 385.
[34] Ibid. VI, 27, p. 484.
[35] Ibid. VI, 27, p. 484.
[36] Ibid. VI, 1, p. 357.
[37] Ibid. VI, 1, p. 357.
[38] Ibid. VI, 1, p. 358.

In chapters 2 to 4, Clausewitz examined the relative merits of the offence and defence. In the second chapter, Clausewitz argued that the replacement of passive cordon defence by mobile defence in depth during the Wars of the French Revolution and of Napoleon had shifted the balance of defence and offence in favour of the former.[39] In the third chapter, he first examined the weaknesses of the offence by discounting the significance of offensive strategic surprise and initiative, ruling out the offensive use of strategic concentric attack, observing that offensive strategic action created vulnerabilities that could be exploited by defensive counterattack, and noting that moral forces that favoured the attacker would not come into play until after the decisive blow had been struck; Clausewitz then enumerated the strengths of the defence, which were the ability to gain strength in retreat because of the support of fortresses, the shortening of supply lines, and the action of militias and armed civilians.[40] In the fourth chapter, Clausewitz maintained that manoeuvre and operational depth would enable a defender to exploit the advantages of interior lines and greater concentration.[41]

In chapters 5 and 6 of book VI, Clausewitz focused his analysis on the specific characteristics of defence. 'War', he observed in chapter 5,

serves the purpose of the defense more than that of the aggressor. It is only aggression that calls forth defense, and war along with it. The aggressor is always peace-loving (as Bonaparte always claimed to be); he would prefer to take over our country unopposed. To prevent his doing so one must be willing to make war and be prepared for it. In other words it is the weak, those likely to need defense, who should always be armed in order not to be overwhelmed.[42]

In chapter 5, Clausewitz also declared his views on the crucial importance of counterattack. 'Once the defender has gained an important advantage', he observed,

defense as such has done its work. While he is enjoying this advantage, he must strike back, or he will court destruction. Prudence bids him strike while the iron is hot and use the advantage to prevent a second onslaught.... this transition to the counterattack must be accepted as a tendency inherent in defense—indeed, as one of its essential features. Wherever a victory achieved by the defensive form is not turned to military account, where, so to speak, it is allowed to wither away unused, a serious mistake is being made. A sudden powerful transition to the offensive—the flashing sword of vengeance—is the greatest moment for the defense.[43]

---

[39] Ibid. VI, 2, p. 362.   [40] Ibid. VI, 3, pp. 363–6.   [41] Ibid. VI, 4, p. 368.
[42] Ibid. VI, 5, p. 370.   [43] Ibid. VI, 5, p. 370.

Defence as it should be, Clausewitz concluded, meant that

> all means are prepared to the utmost; the army is fit for war and familiar with it; the general will let the enemy come on, not from confused indecision and fear, but by his own choice, coolly and deliberately; fortresses are undaunted by the prospect of a siege, and finally a stout-hearted populace is no more afraid of the enemy than he of it. Thus constituted, defense will no longer cut so sorry a figure when compared to attack, and the latter will no longer look so easy and infallible as it does in the gloomy imagination of those who see courage, determination, and movement in attack alone, and in defense only impotence and paralysis.[44]

In chapter 6, Clausewitz provided a systematic reprise of his examination of the character of the defence by enumerating its major resources, which he regarded to be militia, fortresses, the favourable disposition of a country's inhabitants to its government, armed civilians, and allies. With respect to the latter, Clausewitz stated that 'we believe...that as a rule the defender can count on outside assistance more than can the attacker; and the more his survival matters to the rest—that is, the sounder and more vigorous his political and military condition—the more certain he can be of their help'.[45]

In chapter 7, Clausewitz returned to the question of the interaction of the offence and defence and amplified views given in chapter 5. 'The idea of war', he maintained, 'originates with the defense, which does have fighting as its immediate object, since fighting and parrying obviously amount to the same thing.... It is the defender, who not only concentrates his forces but disposes them in readiness for action, who first commits an act that really fits the concept of war.'[46]

In chapter 8, which concluded his introduction to the subject of defence, Clausewitz restated his major arguments. No summary of this material is necessary except with respect to Clausewitz's clear rejection of preventive or preemptive action as legitimate properties of the defence. 'Since defense is tied to the idea of waiting,' he observed,

> the aim of defeating the enemy will be valid only on the condition that there is an attack. If no attack is forthcoming, it is understood that the defense will be content to hold its own.... The defense will be able to reap the benefits of the stronger form of war only if it is willing to be satisfied with this more modest goal.[47]

The most striking feature of chapter 8, however, is Clausewitz's examination of the effect of politics on defence and offence, which he held was greater and usually negative in the case of the latter, and which, it will be recalled, he had

---

[44] On War, VI, 5, p. 371.   [45] Ibid. VI, 6, p. 376.   [46] Ibid. VI, 7, p. 377.
[47] Ibid. VI, 8, p. 380.

introduced in the first chapter of book I. 'The reason for the ineffectiveness of most attacks', Clausewitz insisted,

lies in the general, the political conditions of war.... But these general conditions have transformed most wars into mongrel affairs, in which the original hostilities have to twist and turn among conflicting interests to such a degree that they emerge very much attenuated. This is bound to affect the offensive, the side of positive action, with particular strength. It is not surprising, therefore, that one can stop such a breathless, hectic attack by the mere flick of a finger. Where resolution is so faint and paralyzed by a multitude of considerations that it has almost ceased to exist, a mere show of resistance will often suffice.[48]

'The counterweights', Clausewitz wrote to conclude this line of argument,

that weaken the elemental force of war, and particularly the attack, are primarily located in the political relations and intentions of the government, which are concealed from the rest of the world, the people at home, the army, and in some cases even from the commander.... If military history is read with this kind of skepticism, a vast amount of verbiage concerning attack and defense will collapse, and the simple conceptualization we have offered will automatically emerge. We believe that it is valid for the whole field of defense, and that only if we cling to it firmly can the welter of events be clearly understood and mastered.[49]

In closing, Clausewitz indicated that he considered the material presented in chapter 8 to be of the first importance. 'We should like to add', he wrote in his final sentence, 'that this chapter, more than any other of our work, shows that our aim is not to provide new principles and methods of conducting war; rather, we are concerned with examining the essential contents of what has long existed, and to trace it back to its basic elements.'[50]

The main body of book VI was divided into three subsections. In chapters 9 to 23, Clausewitz examined the physical dimensions of defensive action, covering defensive battle, fortresses, various kinds of defensive positions, and defence with respect to the major forms of terrain. In these discussions, Clausewitz argued against dependence on fixed defences centred on fortresses and terrain features, and for action that maximized the effects of freedom of manoeuvre in general, and counterattack in particular. In chapters 22 to 24, Clausewitz criticized and dismissed certain standard concepts of defensive action that he regarded as weak. In chapters 25 and 26, he identified two courses of action—retreat into the interior of the country and armed resistance by the populace—as potentially capable of producing major effects. These were, from the spatial and socio-psychological points of view, the ultimate forms of defence in depth. Given the significance of this matter in

---

[48] Ibid. VI, 8, p. 387.   [49] Ibid. VI, 8, p. 388.   [50] Ibid. VI, 8, p. 389.

Clausewitz's conception of the superiority of the defence over the offence, his specific views on these subjects deserve separate consideration.

Clausewitz observed that 'voluntary withdrawal to the interior of the country...destroys the enemy not so much by the sword as by his own exertions'. 'Debilitation in the course of an advance is increased', he added, 'if the defender is undefeated and retreats voluntarily with his fighting forces intact and alert, while by means of a steady, calculated resistance he makes the attacker pay in blood for every foot of progress.'[51] If major military defeat of the defence was avoided, Clausewitz argued that the attacker would not only be weakened substantially in the course of his advance, but exposed to powerful counterattack whose effects would be magnified by his isolation deep in hostile territory.[52] Clausewitz discounted the significance of the forfeiture of human and material resources occasioned by retreat, observing that 'it cannot be the object of defense to protect the country from losses; the object must be a favorable peace'.[53] He had serious concerns, however, about the negative psychological effects of large-scale withdrawal, which could demoralize both the army and the general population, and thereby weaken the defensive effort or even cause it to collapse.[54]

Clausewitz ended his examination of methods of defence with the chapter on popular insurrection in support of the war effort of a national government fighting a defensive campaign, which he entitled 'The People in Arms'. 'Any nation that uses [people's war] intelligently', he asserted, 'will, as a rule, gain some superiority over those who disdain its use.' 'The effect of people's war', Clausewitz observed,

is like that of the process of evaporation: it depends on how much surface is exposed. The greater the surface and the area of contact between it and the enemy forces, the thinner the latter have to be spread, the greater the effect of a general uprising. Like smoldering embers, it consumes the basic foundations of the enemy forces.[55]

Because of the considerable potential effectiveness of people's war, Clausewitz believed that it had to be taken into strategic account, and that this was especially the case in the event of catastrophic military defeat. 'A government must never assume', he argued,

that its country's fate, its whole existence, hangs on the outcome of a single battle, no matter how decisive. Even after a defeat, there is always the possibility that a turn of fortune can be brought about by developing new sources of internal strength or through the natural decimation all offensives suffer in the long run or by means of help from abroad.[56]

[51] *On War*, VI, 25, p. 469.  [52] Ibid. VI, 25, p. 470.  [53] Ibid. VI, 25, p. 471.
[54] Ibid. VI, 25, p. 471.  [55] Ibid. VI, 26, p. 480.  [56] Ibid. VI, 26, p. 483.

In the last chapters of book VI, which were devoted to the defence of a theatre of operations, Clausewitz advanced four major propositions. In chapter 27, he argued that for the defender, in general, preservation of the army was more important than preservation of territory.[57] In chapter 28, he maintained that territory that had been abandoned as the prelude to counterattack was no less defended than if it had been contested.[58] In chapter 29, Clausewitz stated that continuous vigorous resistance by the defender's regular forces combined with the negative effects of other factors previously described would in most cases be sufficient to bring about a peace that offered the attacker no more than a 'modest advantage'.[59] And finally, in chapter 30, Clausewitz observed that when the political motivation of the attacker was weak, and his actions thus feeble, the reaction of the defender was likely to be similar, producing a situation in which no great battle would occur because neither side sought a decision.[60] That being said, he warned that either side could at any time choose to seek a decision through more vigorous action, a possibility that had to be taken into account at all times.[61]

In these final chapters, Clausewitz made it clear that he was not building a general theoretical system based on terms that were defined precisely and applied according to fixed conventions, but rather using approximate language to generate understanding and prompt insight about a particular phenomenon, the defence, whose dynamics were complicated and could vary widely. 'We want to reiterate emphatically', he declared in chapter 27, 'that here, as elsewhere, our definitions are aimed only at the centers of certain concepts; we neither wish nor can give them sharp outlines. The nature of the matter should make this obvious enough.'[62] Clausewitz's objective, in other words, was not comprehensive explanation, but, because of exposure to proper theory—as explained in book VI—and sound historical study—as explained in book II—more intelligent observation. 'We admit', he confided in chapter 30,

in short, that in this chapter we cannot formulate any principles, rules, or methods: history does not provide a basis for them. On the contrary, at almost every turn one finds peculiar features that are often incomprehensible, and sometimes astonishingly odd. Nevertheless it is useful to study history in connection with this subject, as with others. While there may be no system, and no mechanical way of recognizing the truth, truth does exist. To recognize it one generally needs seasoned judgment and an instinct born of long experience. While history may yield no formula, it does provide an exercise for judgment here as everywhere else.[63]

---

[57] Ibid. VI, 27, p. 485.  [58] Ibid. VI, 28, p. 488.  [59] Ibid. VI, 29, p. 500.
[60] Ibid. VI, 30, p. 513.  [61] Ibid. VI, 30, p. 517.  [62] Ibid. VI, 27, p. 486.
[63] Ibid. VI, 30, pp. 516–17, see also VIII, I, p. 578.

In book VII, Clausewitz amplified his major arguments on the superiority of the defence over the offence by devoting most of his attention to the weaknesses of the attack. His major arguments on this issue are as follows. First, although the strengths of the defence 'may not be insurmountable, the cost of surmounting them may be disproportionate'.[64] Second, an offensive that does not achieve the destruction of the defender's forces is vulnerable to counterattack, the danger of which increases over time.[65] Third, while decisive battle is essential to the attacker, it is extremely difficult to achieve if the defender is in a good defensive position or is unwilling to stand.[66] And fourth and above all, the psychological challenges of the attack are so great as to weaken the resolve of all but the most determined commanders.[67]

In book VIII, Clausewitz attempted to connect ideas concerned with 'the problem of war as a whole' and the planning of a particular campaign. This was not a summary of what had come before, but a consideration of operational military questions in the light of general concepts whose proper application required accurate comprehension of what Clausewitz had written in earlier books. Clausewitz was clearly afraid that his general concepts would be used in the absence of such understanding. He thus confessed that he approached the consideration of war in general terms with 'some diffidence'.[68] 'We are overcome with the fear', Clausewitz went on to say, 'that we shall be irresistibly dragged down to a state of dreary pedantry, and grub around in the underworld of ponderous concepts where no great commander, with his effortless *coup d'oeil*, was ever seen.'[69] Clausewitz explained his objective as improved perception of the particular, not general prescription. 'Theory cannot equip the mind with formulas for solving problems', he maintained,

> nor can it mark the narrow path on which the sole solution is supposed to lie by planting a hedge of principles on either side. But it can give the mind insight into the great mass of phenomena and of their relationships, then leave it free to rise into the higher realms of action.[70]

There is little text devoted to defence in book VIII, because the main work of re-orienting the reader's fundamental outlook on defence was supposed to have been accomplished in the earlier books. With his or her intuition thus remodelled, the reader was to be capable of examining properly particular cases in the light of certain general propositions. Consideration of Clausewitz's direct discussion of defence in book VIII would thus be pointless, while interpretation of general propositions in the light of his views on defence would

---

[64] *On War*, VII, 1, p. 523.   [65] Ibid. VII, 2, p. 524; 5, p. 528; 15, p. 547; 22, pp. 571–2.
[66] Ibid. VII, 6, p. 529; 8, pp. 533–4; 9, pp. 535, 536.   [67] Ibid. VII, 22, p. 573.
[68] Ibid. VIII, 1, p. 577.   [69] Ibid. VIII, 1, p. 578.   [70] Ibid. VIII, 1, p. 578.

require what would amount to a reprise of that which has already been given. To do either would in any case violate the spirit of Clausewitz's masterpiece.

II

Nineteenth-century readers of Clausewitz tended to ignore his arguments on the superiority of the defence over the offence.[71] The long-standard, abridged Penguin Books version of *On War* omitted book VI entirely.[72] Britain's leading military theorist of the twentieth century, Basil Liddell Hart, portrayed Clausewitz 'as a relentless advocate of mass and the offensive'.[73] The critical essays in the standard English language edition of *On War* fall in between: while Peter Paret says nothing on the subject, Michael Howard and Bernard Brodie acknowledge Clausewitz's views while not making much of them.[74] Raymond Aron examined the question of attack and defence in *On War* perceptively and at length in his classic study of Clausewitz, without, however, recognizing its full significance.[75] In contrast, Paret, in his long-standard monograph on Clausewitz and in a well-known critical essay, disregarded or discounted the importance of the issue.[76] The recent studies of Michael Handel, Azar Gat, Christopher Bassford, Colin Gray, Beatrice Heuser, and Hugh Smith have followed the approach of Howard and Brodie—Clausewitz's views on defence are identified but not connected to discussion of the relationship of war and politics, the latter issue also receiving greater—in some cases much greater—attention.[77] The underestimation—not to say marginalization—of Clausewitz's views on the relative merits of the offence

[71] Michael Howard, 'The Influence of Clausewitz', in ibid. 33.
[72] Carl von Clausewitz, *On War*, ed. Anatol Rapoport (Harmondsworth, UK, 1968).
[73] Christopher Bassford, *Clausewitz in English: The Reception of Clausewitz in Britain and America 1815–1945* (New York, 1994), 129.
[74] Peter Paret, 'The Genesis of *On War*'; Howard, 'Influence'; and Bernard Brodie, 'A Guide to the Reading of *On War*', in Clausewitz, *On War*, pp. 33, 678–80.
[75] Aron, *Clausewitz Philosopher of War*, 144–71.
[76] Peter Paret, *Clausewitz and the State* (Oxford, 1976), 356–81, and 'Clausewitz', in Peter Paret (ed.), *Makers of Modern Strategy from Machiavelli to the Nuclear Age* (Princeton, NJ, 1986), 205. Paret even expressed surprise when Clausewitz used the successful French offensive against Prussia in 1806 as an example of the potential strength of the defensive, for which see Paret, *Clausewitz and the State*, 359. The issues of attack and defence, he argued in his essay, were 'of more limited relevance than are the concepts of friction and genius', for which see Paret, *Makers of Modern Strategy*, 205.
[77] Michael I. Handel, *Masters of War: Classical Strategic Thought*, 3rd edn (London, 2001; first published 1992); Gat, *History of Military Thought*; Bassford, *Clausewitz in English*; Colin S. Gray, *Modern Strategy* (Oxford, 1999); Beatrice Heuser, *Reading Clausewitz* (London, 2002); Hugh Smith, *On Clausewitz: A Study of Military and Political Ideas* (Houndmills, UK, 2005).

and defence is epitomized by a recent collection of essays on these two related issues, in which *On War* for all intents and purposes does not exist.[78]

In the great work of theory for which he is known, however, Clausewitz not only declared that the defence was the stronger form of war, but made this proposition the central theme to which all others were connected and subordinate. Clausewitz did indeed contend that war was an extension of politics by other means, but in addition made it clear that politics would usually exert a greater negative effect on the attacker than the defender. This formulation was critical to Clausewitz's consideration of the reasons for suspension of action in war, which was a fundamental issue because he believed that the primary advantage of the defence relative to the attack was the fact that deferment of decision favoured the former and disfavoured the latter. Prior to inventing his famous aphorism, Clausewitz may well have explained inactivity in war in terms of the discouraging effect of the inherently greater strength of the defence alone. That is to say, the attacker broke off when the going became too difficult for essentially military operational reasons. But by making the strength or weakness of the political motive the critical variable on which the influence of the greater strength of the defence with respect to the offence depended, Clausewitz adopted a concept that offered a secure point of departure for inquiry that addressed the full range of factors that shaped the volition of the supreme commander.[79]

Other ideas regarded as characteristic of Clausewitz's thought must also be considered in terms of their relationship to his views on the greater strength of the defence with respect to the offence. The achievement of positive objectives, the chosen course of the attacker, was more susceptible to disruption by the fog of war and friction than the waiting or reacting of the defence. Similarly, successful positive action by the attacker required command genius—a quality that Clausewitz maintained was the basis of effective direction of military action in war—in greater measure, or at least of a different and perhaps rarer quality, than the defence. And even when this was the case, success was not sure to follow. Napoleon was a military genius without peer, yet the offensives that he initiated were ultimately contained and rolled back by defensive action followed by counterattack. Determining the culminating point of victory accurately was of critical importance to the offence in order

---

[78] Michael E. Brown, Owen R. Cote Jr., Sean M. Lynn-Jones, and Steven E. Miller, *Offense, Defense, and War* (Cambridge, MA, 2004). *On War* is not referenced in the bibliographical section entitled 'Early Discussions of Offense-Defense Theory and Related Issues', 439, and was mentioned only once in passing in the text, for which see 56.

[79] This discussion addresses issues raised in his undated note now thought to have been written before July 1827, in which Clausewitz made no reference to the relationship of war and politics and confessed that his sketch of book VI would have to be rewritten 'along other lines', for which see Clausewitz, *On War*, p. 70.

to avoid overextension—the fact that this was a difficult task meant that attackers tended to err on the side of caution; on the other hand, gauging the culminating point of victory of the attacker was of no less importance to the defence as an indicator of the moment for timely counterattack. Quick decisive victory was highly desirable if not essential for the attacker, but extremely difficult to achieve unless the defender made great mistakes, while a protracted war of attrition—waged if necessary after retreat and through recourse to irregular warfare—offered a defender the means to defeat an attacker that was greatly superior in strength. The 'remarkable trinity', that closed the first chapter of book I, was an evocative but no more than transitional device that set the stage for the discussion of the advantages of a defensive strategy of attrition.

Clausewitz discussed unlimited and limited war in terms that supported his conception of the defence as the stronger form of war. The central issue in both cases of war was the will of the combatants. Unlimited war occurred when the attacker was determined to destroy the political independence of the defender through battle if necessary, and the defender no less determined to preserve its political independence. Equivalence in the strength of will did not, however, mean the outcome would be determined by the balance of military forces and the fortunes of war. Even catastrophic military defeat at the hands of a militarily superior attacker, Clausewitz believed, would not produce a decision if the defender had the will to preserve what remained of his regular military forces by retreat even to the point of abandonment of all national territory, and to resort to armed popular support against the invader in spite of its potential to promote anarchy. Limited war meant a situation in which the attacker's objectives did not involve the destruction of the political independence of the defender, and the defender's stake in the outcome was thus not one of survival. With will attenuated on both sides, the inherent difficulties of taking strong positive action would delay or even prevent strong positive action by the attacker to the advantage of the defence.

The function of the foregoing in the real world of action was to prompt the asking of certain serious questions. For the attacker, these are: can decision be achieved quickly? If not, are the costs of a long war worth the potential gain? And finally will attack bring exposure to successful counterattack and even military disaster? For the defender, these are: is armed resistance of any kind viable and thus worthwhile? Must effective armed resistance involve the sacrifice of national territory and if so how much? And is popular support for the government such as to permit resort to irregular warfare in the event that large amounts of or even all national territory have been occupied? The answers to the attacker's questions depend on the answers to those of the defender. The character of the defence in short determines the character of the war. At the strategic level, this meant it was the defender, not the attacker, who possesses the initiative.

Clausewitz's belief that he had written a book that would 'bring about a revolution in the theory of war' was based on his confidence that his exposition of the superiority of the defence over the offence would counter the almost universal conviction that the opposite was the case.[80] Such an argument addressed the specific strategic conditions of Prussia, which was the smallest, militarily weakest, and geographically most exposed of the European great powers. Reflection on his own extensive war experience was the source of Clausewitz's revisionist impulse. As early as 1811, Clausewitz had explored the possibilities of irregular warfare as a valuable support to action by regular forces in the face of a militarily superior enemy, which addressed major Prussian concerns at this time.[81] Clausewitz wrote a book about the French invasion of Russia in 1812, which chronicled and analysed the retreat of the Russian army into the interior, and its subsequent successful counterattack.[82] Clausewitz's history of the campaign of 1814 in France, which Paret described as one of the 'most successful offensives in the history of war' was used 'to illustrate the potential strength of the defensive'.[83] In his account of the Waterloo campaign of 1815, Clausewitz argued that had Napoleon enjoyed the full support of the French people, he could have adopted a defensive strategy that would have been much more effective than the offensive approach that domestic division compelled him to adopt.[84]

The major implications of the foregoing are as follows. First, Clausewitz presented a coherent conception of armed conflict between nation-states in *On War* that demands careful reading of much more than the first chapter of book I to engage and comprehend. While mastering *On War* in its entirety is not essential, a minimally effective selection would probably involve coming to terms with the first three chapters of book I, all of book II, and the first nine and last five chapters of book VI. Second, Clausewitz's best-known concepts and terminology were formulated to facilitate explanation of his views on defence as the stronger form of war under the circumstances of his time, and not as universal truths. Piecemeal consideration of the Clausewitzian text without reference to his unifying concept and with no appreciation of the contemporary problems that animated his scholarship, therefore, is an

---

[80] Bernard Brodie, 'A Guide to the Reading of *On War*', in Clausewitz, *On War*, p. 678.
[81] Roger Parkinson, *Clausewitz: A Biography* (New York, 1971), 125–30.
[82] General Carl von Clausewitz, *The Campaign of 1812 in Russia* (New York, 1995).
[83] Paret, *Clausewitz and the State*, 359.
[84] Christopher Bassford and Gegory W. Pedlow, 'On Waterloo: The Exchange between Wellington and Clausewitz', chapter 7, unpublished manuscript courtesy of Christopher Bassford.

unsound basis for serious criticism of his thought, and likely to be problematical if used in support of the study of current affairs, history, or theory. And, third, Clausewitz believed that effective historical case study for military professionals should be based on the contemplation of the psychological factors that had made command decision difficult, not whether the action taken was either right or wrong with respect to the principles of war. Existing practice in war colleges more closely resembles the latter than the former. Doing as Clausewitz thought appropriate, therefore, will require fundamental changes in pedagogical materials and techniques.

The major substance of Clausewitz's thought in *On War* is not hard to understand provided one is not misled into believing it incomplete or misconceived, or provided one avoids making it something that he did not believe it to be, namely a taxonomy or phenomenology of war. In addition, readers must recognize that Clausewitz often used language to intimate and evoke rather than to define and explain. Or, as R. G. Collingwood put it, his approach possessed 'that expressiveness, that flexibility, that dependence upon context, which are the hall-marks of a literary use of words as opposed to technical use of symbols'.[85] Clausewitz wrote in this fashion because his primary concern was not the knowing of certain things, but the character of perception that preceded knowing. By correcting the faulty intuitive assumptions that underlay the strategic thinking of his day, and ours as well, Clausewitz hoped to clear the way for productive learning as the foundation of strategic choice. To follow Clausewitz's instruction, therefore, is to ask difficult questions that should have been asked by the current administration of the United States before it decided to launch a preventive war, but perhaps were not.[86]

---

[85] R. G. Collingwood, *An Essay on Philosophical Method* (Bristol, 1995; first published in 1933), 204–7.

[86] Postscript. Since writing this chapter, the author has subsequently revised his view that absolute/real and unlimited/limited war should be treated as equivalents. A more accurate consideration of this matter will be given in his monograph 'Engaging the Clausewitzian Mind'.

# 10

# Clausewitz and Small Wars

*Christopher Daase*

The fashion for negating the relevance of Clausewitz and his thinking for understanding today's wars has been particularly pronounced in relation to 'small wars'. Martin van Creveld argues that, given the fact that low-intensity conflict is the dominant form of war today, Clausewitz's thoughts are no longer valid or simply wrong.[1] Prominent strategists like Edward Luttwak and Steven Metz have supported this view.[2] Similarly, Mary Kaldor has used Clausewitz to define what she calls 'old wars' and to differentiate them from 'new wars' in which sub-state actors are the predominant force. A non-Clausewitzian understanding of war is needed, she argues, to comprehend recent changes in the use of political violence.[3] This creed is also the starting point of much of the literature on civil war economies. David Keen thus argues in a distinctly anti-Clausewitzian mode that war is no longer politics, but economics by other means.[4]

Many of these allegations can be attributed to intellectual ignorance. It is well known that Clausewitz is more often cited than read. He simply stands, especially in the English-speaking world, for a particular image of war which has consolidated through continued misinterpretations of his writings despite a number of attempts to correct such errors. But even authors who defend Clausewitz, most recently Klaus-Jürgen Gantzel and Stuart Kinross, do so by attacking the critics rather than by pointing out Clausewitz's analytical

---

[1] Martin van Creveld, *The Transformation of War* (New York, 1991), ix.
[2] Edward Luttwak, 'Towards Post-Heroic Warfare', *Foreign Affairs*, 74/3 (1995), 114; Steven Metz, 'A Wake for Clausewitz: Toward a Philosophy of 21st Century Warfare', *Parameters*, 24 (Winter 1994–5), 126–32.
[3] Mary Kaldor, *New and Old Wars: Organized Violence in a Global Era* (Cambridge, 1999), 13–30.
[4] David Keen, 'The Economic Function of Violence in Civil Wars', *Adelphi Papers* 320 (London, 1998), 11.

strengths.[5] A more compelling strategy would be to demonstrate that the new forms of warfare underscore Clausewitz's contemporary relevance and that his ideas about 'small wars' allow a more sophisticated approach to political violence than is provided by his critics. Doing so, however, demands that we go beyond his famous book *On War* and study the more arcane manuscripts—correspondences, lectures, and memoranda—most of which have not been translated into English.

My argument is that Carl von Clausewitz was one of the first theorists of wars of national liberation. In his 'Lectures on Small War', given at the Berliner Kriegsschule in 1811–12, he analysed guerrilla warfare by studying the rebellion in the Vendée 1793–6, the Tyrolean uprising of 1809 and, most prominently, the Spanish insurrection from 1808 onward. In his famous *Bekenntnisdenkschrift*, or memorandum of confession, of 1812, in which he insists on 'a Spanish civil war in Germany', Clausewitz outlined a comprehensive guerrilla strategy against Napoleonic France and supported his view with theoretical reflections about the nature of defence and offence.[6] In *On War*, Clausewitz included a concise chapter on 'The People in Arms' in book VI, that on defence, in which he deals with practical as well as theoretical aspects of popular uprising and guerrilla warfare. It is safe to say, then, that biographically and intellectually 'people's war' was at the heart of Clausewitz's career.

The eminent military historian, Werner Hahlweg, wrote in 1986: 'Clausewitz describes the nature of guerrilla war with words that are in some aspects still applicable today'.[7] As a political scientist, I am inclined to go beyond this cautious assessment and make the following three arguments. First, Clausewitz provides the means for a superior conceptualization of political violence that allows us to describe historical and recent changes of war, including the emergence of guerrilla warfare and terrorism. Second, he offers theoretical insights into the dynamics of defence and offence which help to explain why certain actors apply certain strategies and tactics. Third, Clausewitz allows us to reflect on the effects of war on both actors and structures and helps to explain why big states often lose small wars.

---

[5] Klaus Jürgen Gantzel, 'Der unerhörte Clausewitz. Eine notwendige Polemik wider die gefährliche Tendenz zur Mystifizierung der Krieges', in Astrid Sahm, Manfred Sapper, and Volker Weichsel (eds), *Die Zukunft des Friedens*. Band 1: *Eine Bilanz der Frieden- und Konfliktforschung*, 2nd edn (Wiesbaden, 2006), 25–50; Stuart Kinross, 'Clausewitz and Low-Intensity Conflict', *Journal of Strategic Studies*, 27 (2004), 35–58.

[6] Carl von Clausewitz, *Schriften—Aufsätze—Studien—Briefe*, ed. Werner Hahlweg, 2 vols, Göttingen, 1966–90), I, 729.

[7] Werner Hahlweg, 'Clausewitz and Guerrilla Warfare', in Michael Handel (ed.), *Clausewitz and Modern Strategy* (London, 1986), 131.

## CLAUSEWITZ AND THE CONCEPTUALIZATION OF POLITICAL VIOLENCE

Most concepts in political and military affairs are contested; some even say 'essentially contested'.[8] What exactly 'war' is, and what constitutes 'guerrilla', what defines 'militarized disputes', and what determines 'terrorism', have all remained difficult to decide. Positivist scholars of war in particular have become frustrated by the inability of the scientific community to agree on the meaning of key terms like 'war' and 'peace', 'violence' and 'conflict', rendering strategies for cumulative knowledge elusive.[9] Post-positivist scholars, on the other hand, are less astonished by this fact, pointing to normative and political disagreement out of which conceptual disputes arise.[10] Decision-makers and politicians, in turn, have used the conceptual discord as licence to apply political terms to fit their own interests, further undermining semantic precision and erasing institutional distinctions such as between 'war' and 'crime' or 'guerrilla' and 'terrorism'.[11] The notorious sentence that 'one man's terrorist is another man's freedom fighter' is indicative for the problems contested concepts pose politically.

Two principal strategies have been proposed to deal with the problem of contestability: deconstruction and reconstruction. Where meaning is essentially contestable and attempts to reach common ground remain doomed, deconstructivists like William Connolly argue for the analysis of social practices determining social meaning and political contexts in turn.[12] On the other hand, reconstructivists, such as Felix Oppenheim, insist on the need to reach working definitions by historical and logical concept analysis in order to create a basis for the scientific study of social and political reality that is independent from language and discourse.[13]

---

[8] Simon Dalby, 'Contesting an Essential Concept: Reading the Dilemmas of Contemporary Security Discourse', in Keith Krause and Michael C. Williams (eds), *Critical Security Studies* (Minneapolis, MN, 1997), 3–31.

[9] Harvey Starr and Randolph M. Siverson, 'Cumulation, Evaluation and the Research Process: Investigating the Diffusion of Conflict', *Journal of Peace Research*, 35 (1998), 231–7.

[10] Karin Fierke, 'Links Across the Abyss: Language and Logic in International Relations', *International Studies Quarterly*, 46 (2002), 331–54.

[11] The 'war on terror' is in itself a peculiar language game that allows certain strategies, but forestalls others. See Christopher Daase, 'Zum Wandel der Amerikanischen Terrorismusbekämpfung. Der 11 September und die Folgen', *Mittelweg 36. Zeitschrift des Hamburger Instituts für Sozialforschung*, 10/6 (2001–2), 35–48; Daase, 'Terrorismus—Der Wandel von einer reaktiven zu einer proaktiven Sicherheitspolitik der USA nach dem 11 September', in Christopher Daase, Susanne Feske, and Ingo Peters (eds), *Internationale Risikopolitik. Der Umgang mit neuen Gefahren in den internationalen Beziehungen* (Baden-Baden, 2002), 113–42.

[12] William E. Connolly, *The Terms of Political Discourse* (Oxford, 1981).

[13] Felix E. Oppenheim, *Political Concepts: a Reconstruction* (Oxford, 1981).

Clausewitz's definitions and conceptual strategies have much to offer to both approaches. First, his idea of war as an 'extended duel' and as 'a continuation of policy by other means' is in fact a distinction of social spheres and an allocation of political roles.[14] By reclaiming war as a political instrument belonging to the state, he reinvents the very concept of war which he saw disappearing in nationalist upheavals, but which was re-institutionalized by the Congress of Vienna. Deconstructing Clausewitz's concept of war and relating it to the concept of policy (or politics, depending on how the word *Politik* is translated from German) allows the identification of social practices of political change and stability as well as strategies of legitimation and delegitimation of collective violence.[15]

Second, Clausewitz's tripartite conceptualization of war provides an excellent basis for the reconstruction of 'war' and the creation of a comparative typology of political violence. It helps to understand concepts not as being defined by one, or some, essential descriptors, but rather as being constituted by similarities building a family resemblance. Different forms of political violence can thus be compared with respect to specific properties and can be grouped as 'war', 'guerrilla', or 'terrorism' even if no single defining feature of them exists.[16]

Clausewitz's definition of war, some scholars have pointed out,[17] has a certain similarity to what Max Weber later called 'ideal type'.[18] However, Weber has given little guidance on how to accentuate aspects of a phenomenon in order to create an ideal type. He also stressed that the ideal type is not 'true' in any sense and 'even less fitted to serve as a schema under which a real situation or action is to be subsumed as one instance'.[19] Clausewitz, on the other hand, was very precise about the defining features of the phenomenon he was interested in. In addition, he was willing to go beyond individualized comparison and generalize over cases. Thus, Clausewitz's concept of war is

---

[14] Clausewitz, *Vom Kriege*, ed. Werner Hahlweg, 19th edn (Bonn, 1980), I, 1, § 2, p. 191, and I, 1, § 24, p. 210.

[15] Vivienne Jabri, *Discourse on Violence: Conflict Analysis Reconsidered* (Manchester, UK, 1996). I leave the textual description and historical interpretation of Clausewitz's writings on small war to a later project (see note 57) and concentrate in what follows on their use for our understanding of current conflicts.

[16] James W. Davis, *Terms of Inquiry: On the Theory and Practice of Political Science* (Baltimore, MD, 2005).

[17] Raymond Aron, *Clausewitz. Den Krieg denken* (Frankfurt a.M., 1980); Herfried Münkler, *Clausewitz Theorie des Krieges* (Baden-Baden, 2003).

[18] Max Weber, 'Die "Objektivität" sozialwissenschaftlicher und sozialpolitischer Erkenntnis', 1904, in Max Weber, *Gesammelte Aufsätze zur Wissenschaftslehre*, ed. Johannes Winckelmann (Tübingen, 1988), 146–214.

[19] Max Weber, *The Methodology of the Social Sciences*, trans. and ed. Edward A. Shils and Henry A. Finch (Glencoe, IL, 1949), 93.

probably better understood as 'prototype' or 'radial concept',[20] since it implies a schema of political violence in the Kantian sense.[21]

A conceptual schema is a mediating representation that links a concept with an image. Clausewitz provides such a schema by defining war as an 'extended duel'.[22] Through this metaphor he reduces the social complexity of war to a violent contest between two collective actors. He further determines the purpose of this contest as 'to compel our enemy to do our will'.[23] In order to specify further this social function of war, Clausewitz goes beyond a simplistic means–ends relationship. By categorically distinguishing war and policy and subsuming the former under the latter, he offers a tripartite stipulation of war as the application of violent means (*Mittel*) to realize military aims (*Ziele*) to achieve political ends (*Zwecke*). If we add the two actors from the initial situation, we arrive at five elements that constitute the conceptual schema of war which Clausewitz had in mind: the attacker, the defender, violent means, military aims, and political ends. With this schema, diverse forms of political violence can be described and compared without the need to draw strict conceptual boundaries or to identify conceptual cores.

Reconstructed in such a way, Clausewitz's understanding of war is the application of armed forces (means) by a state (the attacker) to destroy the enemy army (aim) to compel another state (the defender) to follow the attacker's will (end). While this concept captures the traditional notion of interstate war as conceived in Clausewitz's time and even today, it also allows for the identification of less typical kinds of war. By changing one or more elements in the schema, new forms of political violence are envisaged and we move away from the concept of war as used in ordinary language. Clausewitz's notion of 'small war' in his 1811–12 lectures is a good example. He describes states applying small-scale organized violence against military targets in order to exhaust the enemy and to compel him to change his policy.[24] However, Clausewitz does not yet conceive of small wars as independent from big wars. He regards them as a specific form of military operation by small units to reconnoitre the enemy's positions and harass his lines of communication. Clausewitz talks at length about terrain (e.g. measures to be taken while crossing mountains, woods, rivers, or bogs) and the use of light weapons. While recognizing the defensive strength of small wars, he does not see them as decisive for victory.

---

[20] George Lakoff, *Women, Fire and Dangerous Things: What Categories Reveal about the Mind* (Chicago, IL, 1987).

[21] Immanuel Kant, *Kritik der reinen Vernunft* (Hamburg, 1956; first published 1787).

[22] *Vom Kriege*, I, 1, § 2, p. 191.   [23] Ibid.   [24] Clausewitz, *Schriften*, I, p. 240.

Thus, in his 'Lectures', Clausewitz remains faithful to the eighteenth-century tradition of the *petite guerre* which considered small wars to be an auxiliary resource of big wars.[25]

In the *Bekenntnisdenkschrift*, however, Clausewitz changes his view. Facing the overwhelming military power of the Napoleonic forces in Prussia, he sees small wars in a much more revolutionary way. The driving force of war is no longer the state, represented by a hesitant king and a reactionary bureaucracy, but the nation. Drawing on various narratives of popular uprisings in the Vendée, Tyrol, and most prominently in Spain, Clausewitz comes to regard the spontaneous mobilization of the masses as a crucial element in war. So, his second definition of small war would be the application of organized and unorganized violence by non-state actors against military forces to harass and exhaust the enemy's army in order to change his policy. Small war has now gained a rather distinct form in Clausewitz's thinking as 'people's war' or guerrilla.

It is evident that this conceptual tool can also be used to describe and compare more recent forms of political violence. Terrorism, for example, can be seen as a situation in which a non-state actor uses organized violence against civilian targets (means) in order to spread fear and terror among the public (aim) to compel a state government (actor B) to change its policy. This captures today's ordinary language notion of terrorism and adequately describes, for instance, the strategy of al-Qaeda. Again, by changing one or more elements of the schema, we arrive at new forms of terrorism that are different from 'pure terrorism' as currently perceived, but still 'terrorism enough' to allow concepts like 'religious terrorism', 'state terrorism', and other 'terrorisms' with adjectives.[26]

Although key concepts in the study of war defy definition in terms of essential characteristics whose meanings are independent of time and space, the claim of radical post-positivists that 'anything goes' cannot be sustained. Furthermore, political defeatism regarding the distinctiveness of particular forms of violence and their ethical levelling is unwarranted. Rather, a rediscovery of Clausewitz's means–aims–ends distinction provides a schema for mapping out the changing historical and geographical landscape of political violence and helps to maintain conceptual and normative differences.

---

[25] Beatrice Heuser, 'Clausewitz und der "kleine Krieg"', in Lennart Souchon (ed.), *Kleine Krieg* (Hamburg, 2005), 35–65.

[26] David Collier and Steven Levitsky, 'Democracy with Adjectives: Conceptual Innovation in Comparative Research', *World Politics*, 49 (1997), 430–51.

## DEFENCE, OFFENCE, AND THE STRENGTH OF SMALL WARS

Aside from conceptual clarity, Clausewitz provides critical insights into the dynamics of war. In particular, he offers a sophisticated conception of the dialectics of defence and offence that is crucial for understanding unconventional warfare then and now. Indeed, Clausewitz's discussion of defence and offence goes far beyond the current debate in international relations on the same topic, where neo-realist scholars like Robert Jervis and Steven van Evera discuss whether factors favouring the offence may be considered causes of war.[27] Like most realist accounts, offence–defence theory suffers from state-centrism and a lack of precision with regard to its explanatory variables. By opening up the debate to include non-state actors and by incorporating Clausewitz's ideas, this literature would gain in theoretical depth and policy relevance.

First, however, we need to correct the popular misconception that Clausewitz flatly favoured the offensive use of force. Through Basil Liddell Hart's interpretation in particular it has become common to regard Clausewitz as the 'Mahdi of the mass' who preferred a direct strategic approach and the concentration of force to crush the enemy's army in a decisive battle.[28] But in his early writings and book VI of *On War*, he takes the opposite view: there he favours an indirect approach and praises the strengths of the defence. Clausewitz even goes further, arguing that, philosophically speaking, 'war begins only with defence'.[29] While the invader would always prefer to conquer a territory without confrontation, it is the defender who starts the fighting when he resists the appropriation by force. The defence, Clausewitz argues, is the stronger form of war, because it concentrates on the negative end to *hold* a position. The offence, on the other hand, is the weaker form of war, because it requires additional means to realize its positive end: to conquer.[30] It thus depends on the relative strength of the opponents which form of war is more appropriate for them.

The defence is never absolute, however. Passive defence, as Clausewitz sees it, is contradictory to the very concept of war.[31] Rather, defence means awaiting and averting the enemy in order to realize the moment for retaliation.[32] Clausewitz takes the notion of 'active defence' from his friend and patron Scharnhorst and develops it into a coherent doctrine by identifying different layers of defence. For this, Clausewitz utilizes his innovative interpretation

---

[27] Michael E. Brown, Owen R. Coté, Sean M. Lynn-Jones, and Steven E. Miller (eds), *Offense, Defense, and War* (Cambridge, MA, 2004).
[28] Basil Liddell Hart, *The Ghost of Napoleon* (London, 1933).
[29] *Vom Kriege*, VI, 7, p. 644.   [30] Ibid. VI, 1, p. 615.   [31] Ibid.
[32] Ibid. VI, 8, p. 649.

of the tactics–strategy distinction. Traditionally, tactics had been defined as any troop action within the range of enemy fire, whereas strategy was understood as all military activity beyond this range.[33] Clausewitz goes beyond the empiricist definition by linking the tactics–strategy distinction to his schema of means, aims, and ends of war: 'Thus, tactics is the teaching of the use of the armed forces in combat, strategy the teaching of the use of combat for the aim of war'.[34] Politics, we might add, entails the teaching of the use of war for the ends of policy.

Consequently, Clausewitz determines three levels of defence: tactical, strategic, and political defence.[35] *Political defence* means that a nation struggles for its liberation or very existence, not for its extension or expansion. *Strategic defence* is the protection of national territory as opposed to the guarding of foreign land. *Tactical defence* finally is the awaiting of an enemy attack, as opposed to taking the initiative and striking first. Clausewitz stresses that strategic defence does not necessarily imply tactical defence. Quite the contrary: 'Within the theatre of war which we have decided to defend, we can attack the enemy where and how it pleases us. There we have all the means completely to destroy the enemy army, just as in any offence. Indeed, in our own theatre of war, this is much easier for us than for our enemy.'[36] The idea of 'active defence' is the classical calculus of guerrilla warfare and aims not at crushing the enemy's army, but at destroying it through exhaustion. To quote Clausewitz once more: 'Thus, the enemy corps will have to overcome a situation of the most difficult defence and will daily lose power in this most unhappy of all wars.'[37]

What Clausewitz helps us to understand is the political and military difference between big wars among states and small wars between states and (more or less) non-state actors. The strategic aim in big wars is the abolition of the enemy through the destruction of his army;[38] the tactical means are combat and ultimately the decisive battle. In symmetrical wars, Clausewitz argues, it is important not to get lost in tactical skirmishes, but to seek the strategic decision. Therefore, conventional big wars tend to be waged tactically in the defence, strategically in the offence. In unconventional small wars, this relationship is reversed. Since the non-state actor is militarily weak,

---

[33] Peter Paret, *Clausewitz and the State: the Man, His Theories and His Times* (Princeton, NJ, 1976), 78–97.

[34] Clausewitz, *Schriften*, I, p. 646; *Vom Kriege*, II, 1, p. 271. Clausewitz does not use the words *Zwecke* (ends) and *Ziele* (aims) in a terminologically strict way, but interchangeably. In *Vom Kriege*, e.g., he speaks of some ends being means of some 'higher ends' (III, 8, p. 373). I have tried to disentangle these ends by calling the military *Ziele* aims and political *Zwecke* ends. Strategy is thus the utilization of combat for the purpose, or aim, of war.

[35] Clausewitz, *Schriften*, I, p. 742.   [36] Ibid. 745.   [37] Ibid. 731.

[38] *Vom Kriege*, VIII, 2, p. 952.

he cannot directly assault the enemy forces, but must resort to small-scale attacks against detachments, logistical outposts, and lines of communication, as Clausewitz describes so meticulously in his 'Lectures'. In this sense, small wars are waged strategically in the defence, but tactically in the offence.

Clausewitz proposed such a small war for the national liberation of Prussia from Napoleonic forces in 1812. Prussia would be too weak to meet the French in open battle, he argues. The alternative, however, should be neither surrender nor an unholy alliance with France, but the strongest possible defence through a 'Spanish civil war in Germany'[39] in order to mobilize formerly unused resources. These ideas were clearly too revolutionary for the Prussian king, Friedrich Wilhelm III, who opted for the alliance with Napoleon instead. As a consequence, Clausewitz left Prussia and joined the Tsarist army to witness the strategic defence bearing fruit. Clausewitz later described the Russian campaign in detail and drew the theoretical conclusion that an attacking force loses momentum over time. At the 'point of culmination', when Napoleon took Moscow without resistance, the superiority of the offensive forces dwindled away and the defensive force gained the advantage.[40] Although Prussia lacked the strategic depth of Russia, Clausewitz was convinced that unconventional forces and civil unrest would have been just as effective to frustrate the imperial army, if not to destroy it completely.

The crucial element, it seems, is time, which works against the offensive force while it does not affect—or does so to a lesser extent—the defender. Small wars, waged by a population on its own territory, can be sustained for a long time. States, on the other hand, waging a counterinsurgency campaign are more restrained. Without tactical results, they lose strategic power. Thus, for offensive and defensive forces in small wars, different criteria for success apply. Henry Kissinger summarized this Clausewitzian insight, when he reflected on the US experience in Vietnam by declaring that 'the guerrilla wins if it does not lose. The conventional army loses if it does not win.'[41]

Given the three levels of offence and defence, Kissinger's dictum might even be radicalized. Guerrilla forces can lose small wars strategically and yet be successful politically. The Palestine Liberation Organization (PLO) army and leadership were encircled and defeated by Israeli forces in Beirut in 1983. But instead of being the end of the PLO, this defeat led to its resurrection through the first intifada. A similar pattern of 'successful failure' can be identified in the cases of the African National Congress (ANC) and the South-West Africa People's Organization (SWAPO). Both organizations were never strategically

---

[39] Clausewitz, *Schriften*, I, p. 729.  [40] *Vom Kriege*, VII, 5, p. 879; VIII, 4, p. 980.
[41] Henry Kissinger, 'The Viet Nan Negotiations', *Foreign Affairs*, 47, 2 (January 1969), 214.

successful, but emerged as political winners nevertheless.[42] To understand this paradox, small wars have to be understood not only as conflicts waged by the weaker, usually non-state, actor tactically in the offensive and strategically in the defensive. They are also waged politically in the offensive, since they are struggles for political legitimacy and recognition. A strategic defeat, therefore, might convince others—be they members of national societies or the international community—to recognize the legitimate demands of the defeated, thus turning the strategic defeat into a political victory.[43]

For a regular army waging a big war, General Douglas MacArthur's maxim might apply, that 'in war there is no substitute for victory'. For an irregular army or a rebel group waging a small war, the substitute for victory in war is success in politics.

## AGENT, STRUCTURE, AND THE THEORY OF SMALL WAR

Whether Clausewitz in fact intended to write a second volume of *On War* about guerrilla warfare, as Hahlweg once suggested, is an open question. However, in Clausewitz's writings we find many necessary ingredients for a theory of small war that can help to explain why big states often lose small wars. In recent decades, this question has troubled scholars and practitioners alike. Various explanations have been proposed focusing on different factors. Authors who apply a motivational approach have argued that the balance of will is decisive. Weak but highly motivated actors, Andrew Mack maintains, have the capacity to undermine the resolve of strong, but less motivated states to continue the fighting.[44] Authors, working within a realist paradigm, see the balance of power as key. Strong states, Ivan Arreguín-Toft argues, tend to misjudge the true power of weaker enemies and often apply unsuited strategies, causing them to lose asymmetric conflicts.[45] Liberal theorists finally point to the impact of domestic factors. Gil Merom holds that democracies in particular are restrained from escalating violence and brutality to a level necessary to crush guerrilla armies.[46] This is not the place to discuss these

---

[42] David Burns, 'Insurgency as a Struggle for Legitimation: the Case of Southern Africa', *Small Wars and Insurgencies*, 5 (1994), 29–62.
[43] Christopher Daase, *Kleine Krieg—Grosse Wirkung. Wie unkonventionelle Kriegführung die internationalen Beziehungen verändert* (Baden-Baden, 1999), 224–8.
[44] Andrew Mack, 'Why Big Nations Lose Small Wars: the Politics of Asymmetric Conflict', *World Politics*, 27 (1975), 175–200.
[45] Ivan Arreguin-Toft, 'How the Weak Win Wars: a Theory of Asymmetric Conflict', *International Security*, 26 (2001), 93–128.
[46] Gil Merom, *How Democracies Lose Small Wars* (Cambridge, 2003).

theories or to add my own account of the transformational power of small wars.[47] Rather, I would like to point out that Clausewitz, not restricted by paradigmatical thinking, has something to add to each approach. He thus offers a more complex, if less parsimonious theory of small war.

It is true that Clausewitz did not elaborate his ideas about small war to the same extent as his thoughts on major war. It is also true that his thinking changed over time in relation to changing political and personal circumstances. Thus, we can identify three phases in Clausewitz's thinking on small wars, with slightly different emphases on various aspects of guerrilla warfare: first, the traditional eighteenth-century understanding of small war as consisting of limited operations of small, light detachments, as described by Clausewitz in his 'Lectures on Small War'; second, his emphatic embrace of the idea of a national insurrection in the form of a Prussian guerrilla war against Napoleonic France, as put forward in his *Bekenntnisdenkschrift*; third, Clausewitz's more sober and cautious treatment of people's war in *On War*, in which he reintegrates guerrilla warfare into the general theory of the defence. While the 'Lectures' reflect the will of the young instructor to digest the conventional wisdom, the *Bekenntnisdenkschrift* shows the enthusiasm of the eager patriot to design a plan for national liberation. Years later, by the early 1830s, the world had been thoroughly restored through the Congress of Vienna and the state-centric concept of war had been re-institutionalized domestically and internationally. Not surprisingly then, Clausewitz takes a more cautious stance on people's war in *On War*, not for opportunistic reasons, but rather as a political thinker and statesman of a recently liberated nation who is interested in the consolidation of internal and external political structures.

With regard to motivation, Clausewitz concurs that breaking the will of the opponent is critical for military victory. In fact, he considers an actor's power to be the product of two factors which are distinct yet difficult to disentangle: the magnitude of means (number of soldiers, amount of weapons, etc.) and the strength of his will. Will power, he admits, is particularly difficult to judge and might be estimated by the 'intensity of the motive'.[48] In this respect, Clausewitz had witnessed the most radical change in modern warfare: the advent of nationalism in war through the French Revolution and the *levée en masse*. However, Clausewitz emphasizes that national enthusiasm cannot only be used offensively to conquer foreign countries but also defensively to protect the national homeland. For him, people's war is the defensive side of the offensive *levée en masse*. 'The war of today's time is a war of all against all. The king does not wage war against the king, the army not against another [army], but one people against another [people], and king and army are part of the

[47] Daase, *Kleine Krieg*.     [48] *Vom Kriege*, I, 1, § 5, p. 195.

people'.[49] National will—or, to use more current parlance, political identity—is particularly crucial in asymmetrical constellations, since it tends to help the underdog. Clausewitz understands that national sentiments arise more easily, and are more durable, for the purpose of national self-preservation and defence than for the purpose of conquest and offensive measures. Thus, nationalism—or other forms of ideology—adds to the existing advantage of the defence in favouring the weak.

This links the motivational approach to the balance-of-power argument already developed with regard to the offence–defence dialectic. Given the high costs of strategically offensive campaigns in comparison to the strategic defence, it is easy to see that over time the balance of power will change in favour of the weak. This is all the more the case, Clausewitz maintains, if the attacker is engaged on various fronts and forced to disperse his resources too widely. Clausewitz provides precise calculations as to how rebel groups bind large numbers of regular troops through tactical attacks, thus weakening the imperial army strategically.[50] The political economy of small war may thus explain the decline of French forces in Europe just as well as the decline of American forces in Vietnam.[51] However, why strong states are constrained in exploiting their initial advantages more effectively is another question.

Various reasons have been discussed, why states, democracies in particular, are hesitant to use the violence necessary to destroy rebel armies and win small wars. Institutional reasons and misperceptions, rational considerations, and moral constraints may all play a role.[52] But on the bottom line, it is the escalation dominance of the weak, which in small wars keeps the strong from fully exploiting his superiority. Traditionally, escalation dominance is the prerogative of the strong to control every level of conflict from conventional to nuclear war.[53] But in small wars a similar escalation exists which consists of various degrees of brutality and repression through the application of torture, terror, and similar tactics. Clausewitz was aware of this fact and elaborates the point lucidly in his *Bekenntnisschrift*. He expects, quite correctly, that a state, facing an unconventional war, will try to demoralize the rebels by applying inhumane treatment and executions. In such a situation, Clausewitz argues, the insurgents must 'repay atrocity with atrocity, outrage with outrage'. But the rebels might even go beyond retaliation and escalate the violence: 'It

---

[49] Clausewitz, *Schriften*, I, p. 750.   [50] Ibid. 722 f.
[51] James Lee Ray and Ayse Vural, 'Power Disparites and Paradoxical Conflict Outcomes', *International Interactions*, 12 (1986), 315–42.
[52] Eliot Cohen, 'Constraints on America's Conduct of Small Wars', *International Security*, 9 (1984), 151–81; Arreguin-Toft, 'How the Weak Win Wars'; Merom, *How Democracies Lose Small Wars*.
[53] Herman Kahn, *On Escalation: Metaphors and Scenarios* (New York, 1965), 290; Lawrence Freedman, *The Evolution of Nuclear Strategy*, 2nd edn (Houndsmills, UK, 1989), ch. 14.

will be a simple matter for us to outdo the enemy and lead him back into the boundaries of self-control and humanity.' In small wars, the escalation dominance lies with the insurgent since the state will be the first to quit the 'competition of outrage'.[54]

Although Clausewitz understands the spiral of brutality and terror, he insists out of *naïveté* or political calculus on the ability to control this dynamic. However, his own insights about the tendency of real war to approach absolute war could have led him to a more sceptical view. States, fighting small wars strategically in the offence, tactically in the defence, are forced to increase pressure constantly. In this process, they undermine their own state institutions and normative standards as well as the rules of the international system. Non-state actors in turn, fighting strategically in the defence, but tactically in the offence, have no incentive to wage war according to any rules. Thus, in small wars, there is nothing that keeps both, state and non-state actors, from escalating the violence, and international institutions from deteriorating; nothing except the self-restraint of the powerful.[55]

This analysis of the small war could also describe the current situation in the so-called 'global war on terror', which in fact is a small war writ large. Clausewitz has argued that 'war begins only with defence'. Where no resistance exists, military violence would be dispensable. Michael Howard has taken this further by stating: 'There is no war without resistance, but without resistance, and the possibility of resistance, there is no international order.'[56] Currently, there are two trends in international politics that tend to render resistance obsolete. First, terrorism, which holds every man and every women and every child hostage by randomly selecting civilian targets in order to demonstrate the impossibility of defence and resistance. Second, the drive towards supremacy, based on defensive invulnerability and offensive superiority, which signals to friends and foes alike that dissidence is unacceptable and resistance futile. These trends, I would argue, are inversely linked. One is the reaction to the other, based on the assumption that denying the enemy resistance would mean winning the war. This creates a situation in which considerations of justice, law, and human dignity no longer play a role. As long as resistance and the possibility of defence are not restored, unconventional warfare will undermine domestic and international institutions.

Clausewitz helps us to understand these issues. Not *despite* the emergence of small wars and terrorism, but *because of* the changing form of war, Clausewitz and his thinking are relevant today. He provides a superior conceptualization of political violence and theoretical insights into the dialectic of defence

---

[54] Clausewitz, *Schriften*, I, pp. 733–4.  [55] Daase, *Kleine Krieg*.
[56] Michael Howard, *The Lessons of History* (Oxford, 1991), p. 166.

and offence and offers elements for a theory of unconventional warfare that explains why states have such problems in fighting asymmetrical conflicts. Maybe it is time to translate the manuscripts, in which Clausewitz develops his ideas on small war, in order to convince more scholars and practitioners of his continuing relevance today.[57]

---

[57] Indeed, in Spring 2006 a consortium was founded to take on the task of translating Clausewitz's most important manuscripts on small war and publish them in English.

# 11

# Clausewitz and the Nature of the War on Terror

*Antulio J. Echevarria II*

Carl von Clausewitz devoted the entire first and much of the last book of *On War*, nearly a quarter of his masterwork altogether, to discussing the nature of armed conflict, that is, war's principal properties or characteristics and how they interact. The fact that so much of his treatise was given over to this discussion reveals the importance he placed on getting those properties and their interactions clear in his own mind. This emphasis is not surprising since Clausewitz's manuscript is essentially a search for what he called objective, or universally valid, knowledge (*Wissen*) of war; this search, he believed, had to begin with a 'glimpse of the nature of the whole', which was to be kept in mind while considering each of war's component parts.[1] As he explained, the task of a theory of armed conflict—and hence his purpose in writing *On War*—was 'to examine the main elements that comprise war, to make more distinct what at first glance seems merged, to describe in detail the unique characteristics of war's means, to demonstrate their probable effects, and to determine clearly the nature of war's purposes'.[2] In other words, Clausewitz sought to present an anatomy of war, an analysis and verification of all knowledge that pertained to armed conflict. If principles emerged in the process, theory would highlight them, as it must all truths; however, the work's primary goal was not to search for principles, but to set down verifiable knowledge. Had he lived to finish his manuscript, it would have presented this knowledge 'fully illuminated and in good order', so that others might use it as a basis for developing their own subjective knowledge or ability (*Können*).[3]

History's 'greatest generals', Clausewitz observed, possessed a well-developed, or innate, talent for reducing war's many complexities to simple,

---

[1] Carl von Clausewitz, *Vom Kriege*, ed. and intro. Werner Hahlweg (19th edn, Bonn, 1980), I, 1, p. 191; hereafter, *Vom Kriege*.
[2] *Vom Kriege*, II, 2, pp. 290–1, 299.   [3] Ibid. II, 2, p. 291.

yet accurate, expressions.[4] He saw this talent, or affinity, for reductionism not as a negative trait, as it is so regarded today, but as evidence of genuine skill, even genius; it went hand-in-hand with the commander's *coup d'oeil*, 'the rapid recognition of a truth', which he clearly prized.[5] Accordingly, *On War* complements the development of this affinity not by producing a facile set of rules or principles, but by explaining the vast and complex realities from which the simple concepts were derived. For that reason, *On War* proceeds, as its author explained, from the 'simple to the complex', that is, in the opposite direction to that in which skilled commanders think, and in this way it serves to enlighten the student. In the work's first chapter, for instance, Clausewitz introduced the simple concept of war typically employed by experienced soldiers, specifically, that war is 'nothing but personal combat (*Zweikampf*) on a larger scale', and then moved towards a more complex definition, namely, that war is 'an act of violence (*Gewalt*) to force an opponent to fulfil our will'.[6] He then discussed the individual components—violence, purpose, and effort—of this definition in some detail, eventually bringing them together in a synthetic expression, which he termed a 'wondrous trinity'.[7] He left it up to the reader to internalize the objective knowledge he captured in *On War*, 'to transfer it completely into the mind', and allow it to guide the subsequent development and exercising of their subjective abilities.[8]

Moreover, by approaching his treatise, indeed his theory of war overall, as an opportunity both to capture and to convey knowledge rather than as something that would prescribe action, Clausewitz could realize his ambition of writing a book 'that would not be forgotten in two or three years', and that might serve as a reference for others interested in the subject.[9] This approach, while admittedly ambitious, also allowed him to set the record straight, so to speak, regarding the many false theories of his day. Clausewitz was, therefore, not concerned with showing us how to think, as some have supposed, but rather with establishing the proper foundation for what we think.

This chapter examines the objective knowledge Clausewitz established nearly two centuries ago concerning the nature of war, and considers to what

---

[4] Ibid. VIII, 1, pp. 950–1.
[5] Ibid. I, 3, pp. 234, 237; the English translations of *On War* also render *Überblick*, which appears in VIII, 1, as *coup d'oeil*.
[6] Ibid. I, 1, p. 191. The simplified concept of war as the expression of the skilled commander is also mentioned in Ibid. VIII, 1, p. 950, and the two references appear to relate to each other.
[7] Ibid. I, 1, p. 213.   [8] Ibid. II, 2, p. 299.
[9] 'Author's Comment' (1818) in Carl von Clausewitz, *On War*, ed. and trans. Michael Howard and Peter Paret (Princeton, NJ, 1976), 63. The note actually refers to a lost collection of essays addressing theory; Peter Paret, *Clausewitz and the State: The Man, His Theories, and His Times* (Princeton, NJ, 1985), 360–1.

extent it remains valid today, especially with respect to the nature of the war on terror, or the 'struggle against extremism' as it is now called in some circles.[10] As *On War*'s author pointed out, no contradiction or gap should exist between sound theory and good practice.[11] Accordingly, if his theory of the nature of war is sound, it should offer something of value to good practice, though that value may not always be self-evident. The nature of war—or rather our understanding of its nature—does indeed influence how we use it. If we understand war principally as an act of violence with a tendency to spiral out of control, we may choose to use it sparingly, or not at all. If, on the other hand, we see war as little more than an instrument of policy, we might try to use it to achieve a great deal, perhaps too much. Hence, our understanding of war's nature may exert a profound influence—however indirectly—on the way we approach armed conflict in general, or any particular war, and how we develop grand strategy, military concepts, and forces in war as well as in peacetime. Appreciating Clausewitz's theory of the nature of war and whether it might help us understand the nature of the struggle against violent extremism is thus more than an academic exercise.

Before proceeding further, we must address Clausewitz's assumption, though not at all uncommon for his day, that an individual can attain objective knowledge. Today, scholars might challenge this assumption on grounds that objective knowledge, like objectivity itself, cannot be achieved because all perspectives, even those that lay claim to universality, inevitably devolve into subjective interpretation. Some of Clausewitz's critics in fact have charged, wrongly as we shall see, that his views are too subjective, too much a product of his own times, and that they pertain only to the Western model of the nation-state and, thus, overlook unconventional and so-called non-trinitarian wars.[12] However, the argument that all knowledge is inescapably subjective contradicts itself by making an objective claim that—by virtue of its own contention—cannot be valid. Leaving this conundrum aside, by objective knowledge, Clausewitz meant simply those truths he could prove or verify scientifically or philosophically, which in his case consisted of establishing the validity of a theorem or proposition by means of a combination of critical analysis (*Kritik*), personal experience, and the use of historical examples.

---

[10] Kim R. Holmes, 'What's in a name? "War on Terror" out, "Struggle against Extremism" in', Heritage Web Memo, 26 July 2005; http://www.heritage.org/Research/NationalSecurity/wm805.cfm. However, the White House prefers to retain the original label, 'war on terror'.

[11] *Vom Kriege*, II, 2, p. 292.

[12] Cf. Martin van Creveld, *The Transformation of War* (New York, 1991); John Keegan, *A History of Warfare* (New York, 1994); and Jeff Huber, 'Clausewitz Is Dead', *Proceedings*, 127/3 (March 2001), 119–21.

Clausewitz's notion of objective knowledge appears to stem from the definition provided in Johann Kiesewetter's *Grundriss einer Allgemeinen Logik*, a compilation of lectures delivered at the War College in Berlin on the Kantian system of logic.[13] In fact, many of Clausewitz's definitions resemble closely those found in this two-volume work. Kiesewetter defined knowledge as a realization derived either from a subjective or from an objective basis: a subjective basis is one that is valid only for an individual; the latter, in contrast, is one that has universal validity (*Allgemeingültigkeit*). As Kiesewetter explained, an example of the former would be an individual's realization that 'snow is white', which is valid for that individual, but not necessarily for everyone else; an instance of the latter would be the realization that the three angles of a triangle always equal two right angles, which one can prove to be universally valid.[14] However, Clausewitz used the subjective–objective dualism in more than one way. He mentioned it in the first chapter of *On War* when referring to the objective and subjective natures of war. He used it again in the next chapter, when describing war as a series of smaller clashes or engagements, each of which can be considered to have a certain unity based on the level and type of military units (their subjective aspects) involved and the purpose (objective aspect) of the particular engagement.[15] In both of these cases, therefore, he has identified purpose as objective, or universal, and means as subjective, or unique. Clausewitz also employed the dualism once again in book II, chapter 4, *Methodismus*, when defining objective and subjective principles; the former are valid for all, while the latter are valid only for an individual. Thus, these definitions parallel those regarding objective and subjective knowledge.[16]

The concept of critical analysis that Clausewitz employed consisted of three interrelated components: the historical unearthing and weighing of the facts, the tracing of effects to their causes, and the investigation and assessment of the combatants' available means.[17] To be sure, history—the interpretation of

---

[13] Johann G. K. Kiesewetter, *Grundriss einer Allgemeinen Logik nach Kantischen Grundsätzen zum Gebrauch für Vorlesungen*, 2 vols (Leipzig, 1824); volume I addresses pure logic, while volume II deals with applied logic. Paret, *Clausewitz*, 69, and Hans Rothfels, *Carl von Clausewitz: Politik und Krieg* (Berlin, 1920), 23–4, both refer to Kiesewetter's role in the education of Clausewitz.

[14] Kiesewetter, *Grundriss*, I (140), 463–4.

[15] *Vom Kriege*, I, 2, p. 223. Paret, *Clausewitz*, 154, notes that Clausewitz used the same objective–subjective dualism in an earlier essay entitled 'Strategie und Taktik' (1804); E. Kessel, 'Zur Genesis der modernen Kriegslehren', *Wehrwissenschaftliche Rundschau*, 3/9 (July 1953), 405–32, esp. 410–17, suggests Clausewitz also viewed *Politik* in terms of objective (universal) and subjective (particular) qualities.

[16] *Vom Kriege*, II, 4, p. 305. Cf. Kiesewetter, *Grundriss*, I, 463, and the Table of Categories in book I, chapter 1, of any edition of Kant's *Critique of Pure Practical Reason*.

[17] *Vom Kriege*, II, 5, pp. 312–13; this chapter actually lays out guidelines for conducting what soldiers today might recognize as campaign analyses. Also, it reminds critics that: every effect has more than one cause, no theory should be considered sacred, war involves a real rather

the past—is a subjective discipline, and Clausewitz was aware of only some of its limitations; however, a number of German historians of his day, including Leopold von Ranke, considered by some to be the founder of modern history, saw subjective interpretation as an essential, if complementary, path to historical truth.[18] History's shortcomings notwithstanding, the use of historical examples—which was Clausewitz's primary concern—can nonetheless facilitate critical thinking and evaluation and, therefore, critical analysis.[19] Moreover, his emphasis on personal experience as a safeguard against drifting into disembodied abstractions accords with the general importance ascribed to subjective interpretation in his day. Subjective interpretation, because it could capture the spirit or essence of things in ways that empirical research alone could not, was something to be embraced, rather than eschewed. The triad of personal experience, critical analysis, and historical examples thus became something of a system of 'checks and balances' in Clausewitz's thinking with each one serving as a counterweight to the others while also contributing to a greater understanding of the whole. More specifically, the objective knowledge reflected in *On War* consists of a series of individual propositions or postulates, the validity of which Clausewitz subjected to rigorous testing via his triad in order to demonstrate, or to refute, not unlike what one might endeavour to do with mathematical theorems. Our own test, therefore, should not be whether Clausewitz's theory reaches the impossible standard of a purely objective observation, but whether his proof, though in some respects ineluctably subjective, makes a meaningful contribution to our own (invariably subjective) knowledge of war.

## CLAUSEWITZ'S NATURE OF WAR

Clausewitz's particular theory of the nature of war hinges on three separate but interrelated dualisms, which, in turn, stem from his practice of regarding

---

than an abstract enemy, and one always had to conduct analysis rigorously. It also warns of the three principal errors that critics make: using one-sided analytical systems as laws; using jargon, technicalities, and metaphors; showing off their erudition, and misusing historical examples. *Vom Kriege*, II, 5, pp. 332–4.

[18] Leopold von Ranke, *The Secret of World History: Selected Writings on the Art and Science of History*, ed. Roger Wines (New York, 1981), 21; Leonard Krieger, *Ranke: The Meaning of History* (Chicago, IL, 1977), 10–11; and George G. Iggers, *The German Conception of History: The National Tradition of Historical Thought from Herder to the Present* (Middletown, CT, 1983), 63–89.

[19] Antulio J. Echevarria II, 'The Trouble with History', *Parameters*, 35/2 (summer 2005), 78–90.

the same phenomenon from different perspectives in order to understand it better: practical, historical, and philosophical or logical. The first dualism is that of purpose–means, *Zweck* and *Mittel*, which is established in the opening chapter of *On War*, 'What War Is', and is developed further in the second chapter, 'Purpose and Means in War'. This dualism, in fact, forms the organizing concept for most of the treatise. Books III through to VII, for instance, are arranged in a descending hierarchy of purpose and means: book III discusses strategy, the means policy employs to achieve its ends; book IV addresses combat or the engagement (*Gefecht*), the means strategy uses to accomplish the purposes set for it; book V deals with military forces, the means that do the fighting; book VI examines defence and book VII attack, the means military forces use when fighting. The prevalence of this purpose–means relationship throughout the various levels of war both reflects and reinforces Clausewitz's point in book VIII, 'The Plan of War', that political considerations exert a crucial influence on the overall plan of a war, of a campaign, and even of a battle.[20] Book VIII, moreover, was intended to present a practical framework that the strategist or war planner could use, a framework that would also tie the separate themes or elements discussed throughout *On War* into 'one single clear idea' that would enable the mind to grasp the 'true and the right'.[21] However, it is partially given over to reconciling war's nature with the fact that armed conflict can be of two completely different types: one aimed at the total defeat of an opponent and one intended merely to bring him to the negotiating table.[22] Clausewitz initially thought the existence of two types of armed conflict exposed a fundamental flaw in his concept of war's nature, for if war had a single nature, how then could it assume one form in certain, indeed most, historical situations and then a completely different one in others? The answer he arrived at was that war was not a thing-in-itself, but an extension of political activity, which itself establishes the purpose for war, and thus determines what kind it will be. That Clausewitz spent so much of book VIII addressing this apparent contradiction further underscores the importance that he placed on arriving at a valid theory of the nature of war.

The purpose–means dualism presents war in an eminently practical light, one that does not differ substantially from the views of his contemporaries. When we compare Clausewitz's conception with that advanced by August Rühle von Lilienstern, his colleague at the General War School in Berlin, we find little difference. Lilienstern had revised the Prussian officers' *Handbuch*, which explained that 'war as a whole always has an ultimate political purpose',

[20] *Vom Kriege*, VIII, 6B, p. 992.  [21] Ibid. VIII, 1, p. 951.
[22] The prefatory note of 10 July 1827.

and that it is undertaken 'to realize the political purpose upon which the State decided in view of the nation's internal and external conditions'.[23]

The second dualism, documented more than a century ago by the historian Hans Delbrück, arises from the first, and reflects Clausewitz's realization that war can be of two kinds.[24] Contrary to the claims of some, Clausewitz continued to think of and write about war throughout his masterwork in terms of this basic dualism. To be sure, he admitted that each type of war might have endless gradations; however, he also clearly saw that the basic nature of each was radically different from the other, due principally to the fundamental disparity in their respective purposes. These purposes, measured against the enemy's will and physical capabilities, would in turn influence the amount of violence and physical and psychological effort required to accomplish them. Hence, the purpose to be achieved is the first consideration in determining the nature of the war one is embarking on; harkening back to Clausewitz's purpose–means hierarchy, the war's purpose helps identify the proper strategy, the type of engagements required, the types and amount of forces needed, and whether the war should be offensive or defensive in nature. In book VIII, Clausewitz identified different planning considerations for wars where negotiated settlement is sought (chapters 7 and 8) and wars in which the goal is the complete defeat of the enemy (chapter 9). He clearly thought, therefore, that we ought not to fight a war of limited aims in the same manner as a war of conquest, and he expected to bring this point out in subsequent revisions of his manuscript. Similarly, we should not delude ourselves into believing that we face an enemy with a limited purpose, when in fact he is after much more.

The third dualism is the objective–subjective one discussed earlier. When referring to the objective nature of war, Clausewitz appears to have meant its universal elements, consisting of purpose, hostility, and chance; this last element includes the sundry factors—such as danger, physical exertion, chance, and uncertainty—that he categorized more broadly as friction.[25] As his discussion in chapters 4 to 7 of book I indicates, he considered all wars have these elements in common regardless of when or where they are fought, though naturally the prominence and influence of those elements would vary from one war to another, and indeed may do so perhaps many times in the same war. In contrast, by the subjective nature of conflict, Clausewitz seems to have

[23] R[ühle] von L[ilienstern], *Handbuch für den Offizier zur Belehrung im Frieden und zum Gebrauch im Felde*, 2 vols (Berlin, 1817–18), II, 8; cited in Paret, *Clausewitz*, 314–15, and Beatrice Heuser, *Reading Clausewitz* (London, 2002), 30.

[24] Hans Delbrück, 'Carl von Clausewitz', *Historische und Politische Aufsätze* (Berlin, 1887); see also Kessel, 'Zur Genesis der modernen Kriegslehren'.

[25] These factors appear in *Vom Kriege*, I, 3, and are addressed in more detail in chapters 4–7.

meant the specific means of war—the actual military forces, their doctrines, methods, and weapons—that the belligerents employ to do the fighting. Maritime conflicts involve means that are completely different in nature from wars on land; likewise, the Tartar bands to which Clausewitz referred several times in book VIII used weapons and techniques that differed in nature from those of Napoleon's armies. Interestingly, Clausewitz pointed out, albeit indirectly, that any variation in the subjective nature of war can alter the intensity and proportion of some of its objective characteristics. New weapons or methods can increase or diminish the degree of violence or uncertainty, though never eliminate them entirely. Likewise, variations in war's objective qualities can cause changes in its subjective characteristics; changes in political purpose, for instance, can cause belligerents to use, or refrain from using, certain types of weapons or tactics. We find an example of the latter in the Cold War where both the United States and the former Soviet Union established a number of treaties and other measures to prevent escalation to nuclear war (though the Soviet Union nonetheless had extensive biological and chemical weapons programmes to augment a nuclear holocaust, should it have occurred). Similarly, purposes can require respect for, or violation of, the borders of neutral states, which in turn can either further limit or expand war's means. In other words, the objective and subjective natures of war are not separate phenomena but rather aspects of the same phenomenon.

As Clausewitz explained, war's subjective and objective natures make it '*more* than a simple chameleon' that only changes its colour as its environment changes.[26] A chameleon can change its colour, but not its internal composition. War's internal or objective tendencies, in contrast, can vary in intensity and proportion, even as its means change. By implication, then, the nature of war can vary so much in degree that, for all practical purposes, we might as well consider that variance the same as a change in kind: we may be involved in a war of minimal violence in one moment, and a war of rapidly escalating violence in the next; in some cases, the value of the original political motives for the war may be superseded by the cost. *Politik* must, therefore, understand that its instrument—a dubious choice of terms in some respects—is a dynamic one. Because war involves living forces rather than static elements, it can change quickly and significantly in ways the logic of policy may not expect; in effect, Clausewitz's use of the objective–subjective dualism enabled him to explain why all wars are, at once, the same and yet different. It also contradicts the widely held belief that he saw the nature of war as

---

[26] *Vom Kriege*, I, 1, p. 213. Emphasis added. See also the discussion by Christopher Bassford in this book.

essentially unchanging, that only its character—its external features—changed over time.

Clausewitz's wondrous trinity captures the principal tendencies or forces at work in war by bringing them together in the form of a brilliant synthetic metaphor. As the Prussian theorist stated in *On War*'s introductory paragraph, after duly considering the 'individual *elements*' of war he intended to examine its '*parts or sections*', and then finally to discuss '*the whole* in terms of its internal relationships'.[27] This approach parallels the modern definition of a synthetic dialectic, which is an examination of 'the ways in which a whole depends on, because it interdepends with, its parts and how a new whole emerges from a synthesis of opposing parts'.[28] The key difference is, however, that Clausewitz's synthesis does not produce a new whole, but rather indicates how the separate parts interrelate in a whole that he revealed to the reader only in stages. Whether the trinity is a true synthesis or simply a conclusion is thus a matter of judgement.[29] In any case, Clausewitz's choice of the word trinity (*Dreifahltigkeit*) appears to be quite deliberate, for it conveys the sense that the parts of war are distinct in their own right, yet at the same time belong to an indivisible whole; the resemblance to the Christian mystery of three-spirits-in-one, a metaphor that Clausewitz's Protestant and Catholic contemporaries would have recognized instantly, is self-evident. Moreover, the trinity reinforces the point that war is not an 'independent thing', and thus can be regarded as a whole only when it is considered within its political (or sociopolitical) context, that is, as an instrument of *Politik*.[30]

In formulating the wondrous trinity, Clausewitz also seems to have employed the same objective–subjective dualism described earlier. The trinity is made up of three objective forces: a subordinating or guiding influence, the play of chance and probability, and the force of basic hostility.[31] These tendencies are represented, more or less, by the three subjective institutions, which Clausewitz introduced in book VIII in his historical survey of warfare over the ages: the government, which attempts to use war for the accomplishment of some purpose; military institutions, which must address the violence, chance, and unpredictability of combat; and the populace, which more or less embodies basic hostility. These three institutions are subjective because, unlike the objective tendencies, they might be valid only for a particular

---

[27] *Vom Kriege*, I, 1, p. 191; emphasis original.
[28] Archie J. Bahm, *Polarity, Dialectic and Organicity* (Albuquerque, 1988), 228.
[29] Michael Howard, *Clausewitz* (Oxford, 1983), 73, considers it the latter.
[30] *Vom Kriege*, I, 1, pp. 212.
[31] Cf. van Creveld, *Transformation of War*, 35–40, 125–6, for the trinity misconstrued. For the correction, see Christopher Bassford and Edward J. Villacres, 'Reclaiming the Clausewitzian Trinity', http://www.clausewitz.com/cwzhome/keegan/keegwhol.htm

time and place.[32] The term 'government', as he used it, included any ruling body, any 'agglomeration of loosely associated forces', or any 'personified intelligence'. Similarly, the term 'military' referred not only to the trained, semi-professional armies of the Napoleonic era, but a warring body from any period. Likewise, his references to the 'populace' were meant to include the populations of any society or culture from any period of history.[33] These three forces, as he indicates, come into play in every war, though one might be more pronounced or influential than the others. Of course, making distinctions between government, military, and people can be somewhat artificial at times; yet this is also the case with the Christian concept of the trinity. Governments can display hostility as much as militaries or peoples; chance can influence the development of policy as much as the course of military events.

The trinity also indicates that none of the tendencies of the nature of war is a priori more influential in determining the shape and course of actual conflict than any other. Thus, to single out policy or politics as *the* central element of war's nature is to distort the intrinsic balance implied by the mere concept of the trinity itself, and ultimately to compromise its dynamism. Put differently, while *Politik* exerts a subordinating influence over war for the purpose of realizing its aims, its influence runs up against, and is in turn reduced or elevated by, the play of chance and the force of basic hostility. These latter forces affect the kinds of ends that war can achieve as well as the extent to which it can attain them. Consequently, policy's influence over war is never absolute; not only should it not act as a 'despotic lawgiver', it is actually impossible for it to do so, unless chance and hostility are somehow removed.[34] In a very real sense, as we shall see, the influence of policy is also limited by the conditions and processes from which it emerged, in a word, by politics.

Before proceeding further, it is important to underscore the difference between policy and politics. As a number of scholars have pointed out, the German word *Politik* can mean either, and Clausewitz repeatedly shifted from one to the other.[35] Policy is generally understood to be the decision to do something and often to do it in a certain way; the term politics, in contrast, is usually taken to mean those activities and relationships, both internal and external, which influence the formulation of policy. Clausewitz defined policy as the 'trustee' or 'representative of the separate interests of the whole community', and essentially regarded it as an outcome of political activity.[36] He considered the formulation of policy to be an art rather than a science, a product of human 'judgement' and other qualities of 'mind and character'.[37]

---

[32] *Vom Kriege*, I, 1, pp. 212–13.   [33] Ibid. VIII, 3B, pp. 962, 964–5.
[34] Ibid. I, 1, p. 210.
[35] Jehuda Wallach, 'Misperceptions of Clausewitz's *On War* by the German Military', in Michael Handel (ed.), *Clausewitz and Modern Strategy* (London, 1986), 213–39.
[36] *Vom Kriege*, VIII, 6B, p. 993.   [37] Ibid. VIII, 3B, pp. 961–2.

He also believed that states as well as non-states arrived at policy decisions in similar ways, even if those ways varied significantly in terms of details; his example of the Tartar tribes, which we have already mentioned, illustrates the case for non-states, and puts paid to the view that Clausewitz thought only in terms of the nation-state model.[38] Tartar warfare, for instance, was shaped by the resources or means available to wage it, while its purpose was influenced by the tribes' geopolitical position as a composite of Turkish and Mongol peoples in Central Asia, their nomadic culture and traditions, and the religious influence of Islam.[39]

However, in Clausewitz's usage, the term *Politik* assumes still other meanings, not all of which are necessarily tenable. One such use lends credence to those who argue that he had been influenced in important ways by several of the ideas of the German philosopher Georg Hegel, whose theories, albeit in diluted and diffused form, had gained considerable currency by the 1820s.[40] In book VIII, chapter 3B, 'On the Magnitude of the Military Purpose and its Corresponding Efforts', Clausewitz presents a brief survey that shows how the historical 'period and its circumstances' have determined conduct of war over the ages:

The half-civilized Tartars, the republics of antiquity, the feudal lords and commercial cities of the Middle Ages, kings of the eighteenth century, and finally, princes and peoples of the nineteenth century all waged war in their own way, conducted it differently, with different means, and for different aims.[41]

It is in this survey that the importance of three institutions—government, military, and populace—emerged. In the Middle Ages, for example, the political, military, and socio-economic institutions of feudalism restricted military operations in both scope and duration, and thus made medieval wars quite distinctive in type. Conflicts mainly involved the military in the form of vassals and servants, and the people in terms of feudal levies, since no central government existed. The aims or purposes of such wars, Clausewitz stated, were more to punish than to subdue, and they tended to last no longer than was necessary to burn the enemy's castles and drive off his cattle.

However, throughout this historical survey and in the ensuing discussion, the meaning of *Politik* expands to encompass not only the political conditions of the era, but also its dominant ideas and conventions, its military institutions

---

[38] *Vom Kriege*, VIII, 3B, p. 974. Cf. van Creveld, *Transformation of War*, and Keegan, *A History of Warfare*.

[39] Douglas S. Benson, *The Tartar War* (Chicago, IL, 1981).

[40] Azar Gat, *Military Thought from the Enlightenment to Clausewitz* (Oxford, 1989).

[41] *Vom Kriege*, VIII, 3B, p. 962.

and their capacities, as well as the general 'spirit of the age' (*Zeitgeist*).[42] In book VIII, chapter 6B, 'War is an Instrument of *Politik*', for instance, Clausewitz characterized the three principal institutions—government, military, and populace—that 'make up war and determine its main tendencies' as fundamentally political in nature, and in fact remarked that they were inseparable from 'political activity' itself.[43] In his mind, *Politik* was a deterministic force that shaped history, determined the character of peace as well as war, and used the latter as an instrument to achieve those ends that diplomacy alone cannot. By way of illustration, Clausewitz referred to the 'three new Alexanders'— Gustavus Adolphus, Charles XII, and Frederick the Great—who aimed to use their 'small but highly disciplined armies to raise little states to the rank of great monarchies', but had to 'content themselves with moderate results' due to the countervailing influence of a 'very refined system of political interests, attractions, and repulsions'; this system, in turn, was brought about by the collective interests of the states of Europe, which desired to prevent any one state from gaining 'sudden supremacy' over the others.[44] Furthermore, it is only when political conditions themselves change, as they did as a result of the French Revolution, that 'real changes in the art of war' can take place.[45] Thus, the wars of history owe their forms more to the prevailing political conditions, or politics, than to policy. Such political determinism severely restricts policy choices, however. In other words, Clausewitz's argument often has less to do with the primacy of policy, as some scholars have maintained, than with the deterministic influence of politics, broadly defined.[46] This concept vaguely resembles Hegel's notion that international politics and war function as instruments that advance the dialectic of history.[47] Clausewitz, however, avoided, indeed eschewed, the teleology inherent in Hegel's philosophy.[48]

Clausewitz thus concluded that the nature of war was diverse and changeable, and that theory must, therefore, account for war's major tendencies, each of which functions in a unique way, without being unduly influenced by any of them.[49] In a sense, the wondrous trinity is his attempt to capture war from

---

[42] Ibid. VIII, 3B, p. 974. The last three books ('Defence', 'Attack', and 'The Plan of War') reflect Clausewitz's increasingly historicist perspective.

[43] Ibid. VIII, 6B, p. 991.    [44] Ibid. VIII, 3B, pp. 966–8.    [45] Ibid. VIII, 6B, p. 997.

[46] See, e.g. Bernard Brodie, 'A Guide to the Reading of *On War*', in Clausewitz, *On War*, ed. and trans. Howard and Paret, esp. p. 645; see also Brodie's *War and Politics* (New York, 1973), 8–11, and *Strategy in the Missile Age* (Princeton, NJ, 1965), 67–8, 97.

[47] G. W. F. Hegel, *Philosophy of History*, trans. J. Sibree (New York, 1952). A similar teleology with regard to the role of war is evident in Kant's works; see Yirmiyahu Yovel, *Kant and the Philosophy of History* (Princeton, NJ, 1989), esp. 8, 151–3.

[48] Paret, *Clausewitz*, 438.

[49] Colonel James K. Greer, 'Operational Art for the Objective Force', *Military Review* (September–October 2002), 22–9, is representative of this view.

three different perspectives: social, military, and political. The trinity does, however, negate the notion that Clausewitz's theory was principally about the primacy of policy. While establishing the purpose for which the war is to be waged is clearly our first consideration, purpose will not necessarily be the dominant influence on the actual conduct of war. Rather, the trinity conveys the sense that, from the standpoint of objective knowledge, the subordinating influence of purpose is as significant in war as the play of chance and the force of hostility. Only when we view a particular war after the fact, from a subjective standpoint, can we determine which tendency, if any, exerted the predominant influence on the way that war was waged.

## THE NATURE OF THE WAR ON TERROR

If Clausewitz's wondrous trinity, which captures in a single synthetic statement war's principal tendencies, represents objective knowledge of the nature of war, it should also prove useful in analysing the nature of a specific conflict such as the war on terror. Indeed, this multifaceted war is perhaps the first conflict in which the changes wrought by globalization—the dispersion and democratization of technology, information, and finance—have been evident in any significant way.[50] While the debate over the pros and cons of globalization continues, few dispute that the phenomenon itself is causing change.[51] Its effects have, among other things, increased the real and virtual mobility of people, things, and ideas, thereby altering war's subjective nature—its means.[52] By extension, war's objective nature—its principal tendencies—is also changing. For instance, globalization is accelerating the ability of political leaders to communicate their purposes to the forces under their command, whether irregular or conventional, to their constituencies as well as their opponents' constituencies, and to neutral audiences. Conversely, adverse images and commentary can now appear at any time and from any number of sources to compete with or undermine the messages of those leaders.

[50] See Thomas Friedman, *The Lexus and the Olive Tree* (New York, 2000), 9, which offered perhaps the first definition of globalization; and *The World Is Flat: A Brief History of the 21st Century* (New York, 2005).

[51] Peter Marber, 'Globalization and Its Contents', *World Policy Journal* (Winter 2004–5), 29–37.

[52] 'Measuring Globalization', *Foreign Policy* (May–June 2005), 52–62, quantifies globalization based on four criteria: economic integration, technological connectivity, personal contact, and political engagement. Globalization is, of course, not the only force shaping the future; the US National Intelligence Council, *Mapping the Global Future* (Washington, DC, December 2004) identifies the growing demand for energy, the proliferation of weapons of mass destruction, and population growth, as other factors likely to influence change.

Images of prisoner abuses at Abu Ghraib and accusations of acts desecrating the Koran, all of which spread almost overnight among the international media and the Internet, created strategic effects that ran completely counter to American goals in Iraq and in the broader struggle against terror. In other words, first-, second-, and third-order effects caused by the interaction of war's objective tendencies can now be felt in far less time. Globalization is thus bringing the tendencies of purpose, hostility, and chance closer together, and making the effects of their interaction more immediate, less predictable, and potentially more influential. That may not change the basic concept of one group seeking to impose its will on another, but it certainly affects the tactics and the means one might decide to use. Thus, understanding the relationship of subjective to the objective nature of war may be more important than in Clausewitz's day, since the room for error appears to be less.

The purposes at odds in the war on terror are, not unlike the Thirty Years War in which religious and secular aims were inextricably intertwined, as numerous as the many belligerents involved. While many identify with the jihadist vision of al-Qaeda, or at least are inspired by it, others pursue purposes that appear quite secular, such as political self-determination, or are only regional or local in nature. For its part, al-Qaeda's leadership has portrayed itself as an advance guard in a worldwide jihadist movement, an *intifada* on a global scale reflective of a general Islamist awakening; the group's stated goal is to 'move, incite, and mobilize the [Islamic] nation' to rise up to end US interference in Islamic affairs and to recast Islamic society according to Salafist interpretations of Islamic law.[53] As bombings and other attacks in Tunisia (April 2002), Bali (October 2002), Casablanca (May 2003), Madrid (March 2004), Manila (February 2005), and London (July 2005) indicate, that movement is in full swing; in 2004 alone, some 200 attacks—not counting those directly related to operations in Iraq—were carried out worldwide by extremist groups or networks linked to, or in sympathy with, al-Qaeda.[54]

---

[53] 'Usama Bin Laden's Message to Iraq', *Al-Jazirah Television*, 11 February 2003; 'Bin Laden Interviewed on Jihad against U.S.', *Al Quds Al Arabi* (London), 27 November 1996; cited from 'Al Qaeda: Statements and Evolving Ideology', Congressional Research Service, 20 June 2005, 13. Kenneth Katzman, 'Al Qaeda: Profile and Threat Assessment', Congressional Research Service, 10 February 2005. Rohan Gunaratna, *Inside Al Qaeda* (Cambridge, 2002).

[54] US Department of State, Office of Coordinator for Counterterrorism, *Country Reports on Terrorism 2004*, Washington, DC, April 2005, pp. 7–8. These attacks killed about 1,500 and wounded about 4,000 people, not including the many victims of operations in Iraq. One-third of all attacks involved non-Western targets, but the bulk of the victims overall were Muslims. National Counterterrorism Center, *A Chronology of Significant International Terrorism for 2004*, Washington, DC, 27 April 2005, pp. 81–2. International terrorists were responsible for 190 attacks during 2003, down from 198 in 2002, and 355 in 2001; the casualty total was 1,888 in 2003, down from 2,742 in 2002, and 3,875 in 2001. For 2006 data, see: US Department of State, *Country Reports on Terrorism*, Washington, DC, 2007 http://www.state.gov/s/ct/r/s/crt/2006/82727.htm.

In July 2006, British authorities reported that, according to polls, 'around 400,000 people in the UK are sympathetic to violent jihad around the world'; moreover, the flow of new cases involving terrorist-related incidents in the UK is not abating—'if anything it is accelerating'.[55]

Such aims and the many networks that pursue them clearly threaten US interests which, despite the purportedly profound impact of 9/11 on US grand strategy, have changed remarkably little over the last decade.[56] Those interests are the protection of the lives of American citizens at home and abroad, and the maintenance of US national sovereignty, political freedoms, and independence, while also safeguarding its values, institutions, and territory.[57] The stated aims of the United States in the war on terror are to reduce terrorism to an 'unorganized, localized, nonsponsored' phenomenon, and to persuade all responsible nations and international bodies to adopt a policy of 'zero tolerance' for terrorism, and to agree to delegitimize it, much like 'piracy, slave trading, and genocide' have been in the past.[58] However, the *U.S. National Strategy for Combating Terrorism* also includes an essential, but rather ambitious, goal of diminishing the conditions that terrorists typically exploit, such as poverty, social and political disenfranchisement, and long-standing political, religious, and ethnic grievances; reducing these conditions requires, among other things, fostering political, social, and economic development, good governance, the rule of law, and consistent participation in the 'war of ideas'.[59]

While the purposes at stake in the war on terror are as diverse as the belligerents involved, the motives of the principal antagonists—the United States and al-Qaeda—have been relatively consistent and remain, at root, ideological in nature; in other words, they are based on a system of ideas and assumptions about the world and one's place in it.[60] The ideology that guides the former may or may not be more secular in character than that which

---

[55] http://news.bbc.co.uk/go/pr/fr/-/2/hi/uk_news/5142908.stm; 3 July 2006.

[56] Steven E. Miller, 'Terrifying Thoughts: Power, Order, and Terror after 9/11', *Global Governance*, 11 (2005), 247–71, reviews a number of books, all of which claim that US strategy underwent a profound change after 9/11.

[57] The White House, *A National Security Strategy of Engagement and Enlargement*, Washington, DC: February 1996; and *The National Security Strategy of the United States*, Washington, DC: 2002; The US Department of Defense, *The National Defense Strategy of the United States of America*, Washington, DC: March 2005.

[58] US Government, *National Strategy for Combating Terrorism*, Washington, DC: February 2003, p. 13; The Honorable Paul Wolfowitz, 'The Greatest Deeds Are Yet to Be Done', *Naval War College Review*, 47/1 (Winter 2004), 13–19, esp. 15.

[59] *Combating Terrorism*, 22–3.

[60] On the US ideology driving the war, see David Frum and Richard Perle, *An End to Evil: How to Win the War on Terror* (New York, 2004); Anatol Lieven, *America Right or Wrong: An Anatomy of American Nationalism* (Oxford, 2004). On al-Qaeda's ideology, see Gunaratna, *Inside Al Qaeda*.

inspires the latter, but neither can be considered temporal. Both antagonists seek the political destruction of the other, and at this point neither appears open to the possibility of a negotiated settlement. However, as the histories of the Thirty Years War and other protracted conflicts show, psychological and physical exhaustion can turn what seemed at the outset inconceivable into something that appears acceptable, perhaps even desirable. Indeed, as one scholar has pointed out, too little thought is generally given to how terrorist campaigns typically end, or rather wind down; that denouement can take several forms, ranging from a stalemate entailing mutual concessions, a transition from terrorism to criminal activities such as kidnapping and drug trafficking, and to retraining and eventual rehabilitation of the fighters themselves.[61] A key element in ending the campaign is the realization that terrorism is a 'highly problematic means of bringing about change', a realization that requires, among other things, inflicting demoralizing losses on the terrorists through military action and law enforcement activities; it also requires convincing the terrorists themselves that they have been defeated politically, or at least that they cannot succeed, and actively deterring sponsors who support terrorist groups, and eliminating the conditions that gave the terrorists legitimacy in the first place.[62]

Interestingly, the purposes pursued by each of the major belligerents have run up against, and to a certain extent been undermined by, what Clausewitz often referred to as the nature of circumstances: the 'first and most comprehensive of strategic tasks', he pointed out, 'is to recognize correctly the kind of war one is about to undertake' or to be drawn into, and 'not to mistake it for, or desire to turn it into, something that, according to the nature of the circumstances, it cannot be'.[63] Thus, in his view, existing domestic and international circumstances tend to create a constellation of possibilities and, by extension, impossibilities which influence what policy can and cannot achieve, especially through the use of military force. The period following the Cold War saw the gradual unfolding of a political realignment in which some states came to view the United States, the world's remaining superpower, much more warily than hitherto. Concern that the United States was on a unilateralist course was already widespread in Europe by the summer of 2001, that is, prior to 9/11.[64] The lively debates that appeared in US policy and defence journals over whether America had become a de facto empire as a result of the collapse of the Soviet Union, and what that meant for its strategy, were as much about

---

[61] Adam Roberts, 'The "War on Terror" in Historical Perspective', *Survival*, 47/2 (Summer 2005), 101–30, here 123.
[62] Roberts, 'War on Terror', 127–30.   [63] *Vom Kriege*, I, 1, p. 212.
[64] 'Bush and U.S. seen as Unilateralist', Survey Report, Pew Research Center for the People and the Press, 15 August 2001.

reflexive hubris as they were about the need for reflective thinking.[65] However, few of those debates seriously considered that the so-called new world order might include a political realignment, albeit passive, against the unilateralism of the United States.[66] Even some of America's staunchest allies and strategic partners now regard her actions with greater scepticism.[67] In important ways, therefore, US foreign policy aims have run up against the nature of circumstances, to return to Clausewitz's term. Of course, this situation does not mean that the United States will not be able to accomplish many, or even most, of its strategic aims, but it may now cost more in time and other resources, in some cases possibly a lot more.

Along similar lines, while Osama bin Laden has enjoyed considerable popularity, even tangible support, among Muslims worldwide, his global jihadist movement has not yet been able to move the broader Islamic community to a revolutionary critical mass. To be sure, as the London bombings of 7 and 21 July 2005 and those in Sharm al-Sheikh on 23 July 2005 indicate, terrorist groups either affiliated with or simply inspired by al-Qaeda, such as those rings rounded up in Canada and the United States in 2006, will probably attempt to launch such attacks for some time to come. Moreover, until now, the ranks of violent extremist groups do not seem to want for recruits, though hard data confirming this is elusive.[68] Nonetheless, certain cleavages within the Muslim community—Sunni and Shia branches of Islam, the Arab and non-Arab polities, national and subnational divisions, tribal and clan loyalties, and generational gaps—have been significant enough to work against the instigation of a widespread uprising.[69] Also, major Muslim organizations, such as the Organization of the Islamic Conference, have repeatedly expressed 'strong condemnation and denunciation' of terrorist bombings, which it points out 'have brought nothing but harm to the Muslim world and its standing' by 'demonizing the image and reputation of Muslims in the eyes of the world'.[70]

---

[65] Eliot A. Cohen, 'History and the Hyperpower', *Foreign Affairs*, 83/4 (July–August 2004), 49–63; and Jack Snyder, 'Empire: A Blunt Tool for Democratization', *Daedalus* (Spring 2005), 58–71, capture the critical contours of those debates.

[66] For an exception that proves the rule, see G. John Ikenberry, 'America and the Ambivalence of Power', *Current History* (November 2003), 377–82.

[67] 'A Year after Iraq War: Mistrust of America in Europe Ever Higher, Muslim Anger Persists', The Pew Global Attitudes Project, Washington, DC, 16 March 2004; a year later, evidence suggested the image of the United States had recovered somewhat: 'American Character Gets Mixed Reviews: U.S. Image Up Slightly, but still Negative', The Pew Global Attitudes Project, Washington, DC, 23 June 2005.

[68] Rohan Gunaratna, 'New Threshold Terrorism', in Gunaratna (ed.), *The Changing Face of Terrorism* (Singapore, 2004), 30–1.

[69] The major divisions are examined in Angel M. Rabasa et al., *The Muslim World after 9/11* (Santa Monica, CA, 2004).

[70] Press release, 23 July 2005; http://www.oic-oci.org/press/english; see also *Khaleej Times Online*, 20 July 2005; http://www.khaleejtimes.com. The OIC, however, faces some challenges in

The Free Muslims Coalition, the Muslim American Society, the Muslim Council of Britain, and the Islamic Conference of Spain have made similar statements, the last condemning bin Laden as an 'apostate'.[71]

Whether those denouncements, and others like them, are enough and in time to prevent the demonization of Muslims remains to be seen. Indeed, suicide-murder bombings, and other terrorist tactics, not only seem to be counterproductive to al-Qaeda's stated purpose and of those who share its aims, they also hurt the efforts of the many Muslims who wish to integrate into Western societies. While terrorists may want to undermine those efforts, the violent tactics they employ are also creating deeper divisions among Muslim communities worldwide, which in turn undermine the creation of a unified *umma*.

Moreover, in Clausewitz's trinitarian construct purposes may well be inchoate or personal rather than political in nature; the general desire to see the purpose for which a war is fought as political in nature (rather than cultural, for instance) stems as much from the peculiarities of English translations of *On War* as from the interpretive influence which political science and international relations theories have had on the book itself. Clausewitz's aim in this regard is to capture the influence exerted by those who attempt to use war for some purpose. That purpose may well be to exact revenge, achieve material gain, enhance prestige, or express personal rage against the world. Acts of terrorism, as with other forms of war, may emerge from existing political conditions, and thus may be a continuation of political activity, but the motives themselves need not be wholly political. In a real sense, however, globalization is helping to convert personal acts of violence, such as the massacre at Virginia Tech. University in the United States in 2007, into political statements, because the media coverage of such incidents amplifies, if not generates, political effects, however local.

For the principal belligerents in the war on terror, ideology and purpose remain inextricably linked. Both the United States and al-Qaeda are clearly using, or attempting to use, armed force to achieve ends that are as political as they are religious or secular in nature. Cultural norms and expectations surely influence how each side chooses to wage the conflict, and how it prefers to define the ends it seeks. However, that important fact provides little basis

---

purporting to speak for a Muslim community marked by significant divisions and increasingly 'frustrated by the organization's failure to move beyond rhetoric', Shahram Akbarzadeh, Kylie Connor, 'The Organization of the Islamic Conference: Sharing an Illusion', *Middle East Policy*, 12/3 (Summer 2005), 79–92.

[71] http://www.freemuslims.org; http://www.masnet.org; http://www.mcb.org.uk; similar comments dating back to 12 September 2001 can be accessed at: http://www.unc.edu/~kurzman/terror.htm.

for maintaining, as some scholars have done, that culture therefore supplants policy or politics, and that this somehow negates Clausewitz's theory.[72]

Hostility clearly runs high in this war, on all sides. There is, in fact, a long history of enmity underpinning this conflict. However, catch-phrases such as 'War of Ideas' or 'Clash of Civilizations' or 'World War IV' tend to exploit more than they explain.[73] This hostility, the result of years of real and perceived injustices and repression, informs the policy choices, strategies, and tactics of the parties involved, and has subverted peace talks and negotiations—most especially regarding the Palestinian issue—on numerous occasions. As a consequence, the views of hardliners and extremists appear validated by each new instance of violence. Indeed, in this context, enmity often appears to be a cause in search of a purpose, whether that purpose stems from atrocities perpetrated in Bosnia, Chechnya, Somalia, Afghanistan, Iraq, or elsewhere. History is both essential to understanding the conflict and an inevitable barrier to its resolution.

In this conflict, as in most throughout history, the populace is both a weapon and a target, physically and psychologically. Al-Qaeda and those terrorist groups lacking a global vision, such as Hamas and Hezbollah, have turned their constituencies into effective weapons by creating strong social, political, and religious ties with them. These groups have become an integral part of the social and political fabric of Muslim societies by addressing everyday problems: establishing day cares, kindergartens, schools, medical clinics, youth and women's centres, sports clubs, social welfare, and programmes for free meals and health care; in contrast, most government bodies in the Middle East, generally perceived as corrupt and ineffective by Muslim communities, have failed to provide such basics.[74] Hamas and Hezbollah have also achieved substantial political representation in their respective state governments. Put differently, many of these extremist groups, whether their purpose is local or global, have become communal and political activists for their constituencies. Those constituencies have, in turn, become an important weapon in the arsenal of such groups by providing the means to facilitate the construction and maintenance of considerable financial and logistical networks and safe houses, all of which aid in the regeneration of the groups, as well as providing other

---

[72] Keegan, *History of Warfare*.

[73] *Combating Terrorism*, 23; Samuel P. Huntington, 'A Clash of Civilizations', *Foreign Affairs*, 72/3 (Summer 1993), 22–68; Norman Podhretz, 'The War against World War IV', *Commentary*, February 2005; James Woolsey, 'World War IV', an address delivered at the National War College, 16 November 2002.

[74] Shaul Mishal and Avraham Sela, *The Palestinian Hamas: Vision, Violence, and Coexistence* (New York, 2000), 18–26; Sami G. Hajjar, *Hizballah: Terrorism, National Liberation or Menace?* Strategic Studies Institute, US Army War College, August 2002. Gunaratna, *Inside Al Qaeda*, 55, 227, 230.

support.[75] The role of communal activist does not, of course, preclude using tactics of disinformation, fear, and intimidation to keep one's constituencies loyal; hence, one's populace also serves as a target, especially for purposes of recruiting and other kinds of assistance.

Of course, terrorism also targets an adversary's population, in both a physical and a psychological sense, though this is not entirely new. The roadside bombs and insurgent tactics employed in Iraq, and the suicide bombings carried out elsewhere, appear aimed more at the respective publics of the United States and its coalition partners than their militaries. In some cases, as in Madrid 2004, these tactics have achieved desired political results, but—as the London bombings of 2005 indicate—not in others. In fact, each successive attack, as with any act of violence, creates unintended consequences, such as the distancing of the extremists from their respective constituencies, however incrementally. The old adage that armed force alone cannot win wars, particularly this kind of war, holds true for both sides. Evidence suggests that, despite the rhetoric that appears on jihadist websites and in television and radio messages, at least some extremists can be rehabilitated: the debate between Islamic scholars and al-Qaeda prisoners in Yemen over whether extremist beliefs are justified by the Koran, which resulted in the prisoners' renunciation of violence, offers one instance; the many stories, or confessions, of other terrorists who have been converted provide yet other examples.[76]

As in most wars, the outcome of this conflict ultimately becomes a question of the will or commitment of the belligerents, and will is most effectively addressed through that tendency Clausewitz described as basic hostility. Any number of methods, ranging from infiltration to propaganda (or information warfare in contemporary military parlance) to offering alternatives to the jihadist lifestyle, can be used to undermine commitment to a cause. Such alternatives might begin with offering amnesty, financial assistance, job training, and relocation to all but those deemed to be hardcore terrorists. This approach would help counter, or at least provide a counterweight to, the communal activism, or social dependency, that extremist groups have fostered for decades among their constituencies. It would also accord with the United States' strategic goal of 'diminishing the conditions that terrorist groups exploit', and it does not differ substantially from the ways in which Americans have treated enemy combatants, or criminals who have given state

---

[75] Ed Blanche, 'Al-Qaeda Recruitment', *Janes Intelligence Review*, 14 (January 2002), 27–8; Paul J. Smith, 'Transnational Terrorism and the al Qaeda Model: Confronting New Realities', *Parameters*, 32/2 (Summer 2002), 33–46.
[76] Brian Michael Jenkins, 'Strategy: Political Warfare Neglected', *San Diego Union-Tribune*, 26 June 2005; http://www.rand.org/commentary.

evidence, in the past; while official US policy has always been not to negotiate with terrorists, Washington has sometimes done so in the past, depending on the circumstances.[77] The risk of this approach, of course, is that rehabilitated terrorists will revert back to extremism once they have reaped the material benefits of efforts to convert them. Undoubtedly, recidivism will occur. Yet the purpose of such an 'offensive of alternatives' is less to convert extremists than to sow doubt, discord, and distrust among organizations that already need to employ a fair amount of fear and intimidation to maintain loyalty. The growth of discord also would likely have an adverse effect on recruitment.

Paradoxically, the increase in information and the spread of information technology brought about by globalization have amplified rather than reduced chance and uncertainty. Chance, as Clausewitz used the term, meant not only random occurrence, but also the fact that we can be certain about very little in war: armed conflict is a matter of assessing probabilities and making judgements. The certainty that Saddam was stockpiling weapons of mass destruction, for instance, proved to be unfounded. The whereabouts of bin Laden, assuming he is still alive and that the video and audio recordings are not simply attempts to keep his spirit alive, are at present unknown, though a number of other leading members of his organization have been captured or killed; we cannot say for certain, therefore, when or if he will be captured or killed.

The vast array of information technology with which US and coalition forces are now equipped has done little to help locate improvised explosive devices before they kill, to locate and avoid ambushes, and—perhaps most important of all—to distinguish non-combatant friend from irregular foe. To be sure, the key to accomplishing one's objectives in counterinsurgency operations, as in any kind of military operation, is timely and reliable intelligence. However, the entire process of intelligence gathering and assessment is clearly more art than science.[78] In short, the greater access to information and the larger number of expert opinions available to the public have amplified rather than reduced uncertainty.

Further compounding the problem of uncertainty is the fact that experts do not agree on the root causes of extremism, or that any necessarily exist, because they fear that identifying such causes can be construed as justifying or affording legitimacy to terrorism. Nor, therefore, do experts agree on the nature of, or even the need for, enduring solutions to the problem. Poverty, demographic trends, globalization, religious extremism, failed or failing states, repressive regimes, unresolved conflicts, US and Western foreign policies, lack

---

[77] *Combating Terrorism*, 22–3; Timothy Naftali, 'US Counterterrorism before bin Laden', *International Journal* (Winter 2004–5), 25–34.

[78] Scott Shane, 'Eavesdropping Isn't Easy, the Master at It Says', *New York Times*, 17 August 2005.

of education, and alienation and rage have all been offered, individually or in combination, as principal causes of terrorism.[79] All are eminently plausible, and an examination of local conditions might lead to identifying which particular combination of causes may be responsible for the rise of a specific terrorist group, yet consensus has not materialized. Instead, the theories of experts such as Jessica Stern, Bernard Lewis, Bruce Hoffman, Rohan Gunaratna, and Michael Scheurer remain at odds, perhaps not so much in the broad strokes, but in the details, where it matters.[80] Uncertainty regarding fundamental causes of terrorism hampers development of a comprehensive, integrated strategy capable of going beyond military action. However, a comprehensive strategy does run the risk of exposing the 'politically awkward situations and policy choices' of numerous states to the broader public.[81] In other words, political concern over the possibility of a public backlash of sorts may also be working against the development of long-term strategies for countering terrorism. Uncertainty—or the 'fog of war' as some theorists refer to it—is, thus, still very much a factor not only in tactics and operations, but also in the realms of policy and strategy as well.[82]

The preceding discussion has shown that each of the tendencies in Clausewitz's wondrous trinity remains alive and well. Each is at play in the war on terror, despite the proliferation of information and information technologies. The war on terror is precisely the kind of conflict that scholars, such as van Creveld, wrongly refer to as 'non-trinitarian' on the grounds that it does not fit within Clausewitz's concept of the trinity.[83] Yet, as we have seen, the trinity is not the people, government, and military—as some have argued, but rather the principal tendencies: hostility, purpose, and chance. Clausewitz held that the institutions themselves to be little more than the subjective representations of those tendencies. Thus, the fundamental problem with so-called non-trinitarian war is that it does not understand the concept it purports to negate.

Clausewitz's theory, though inevitably subjective, nonetheless appears to have captured the nature of war from the standpoint of objective knowledge.

---

[79] Margaret Purdy, 'Countering Terrorism: The Missing Pillar', *International Journal* (Winter 2004–5), 3–24.

[80] Jessica Stern, *Terror in the Name of God: Why Religious Militants Kill* (New York, 2003); Bernard Lewis, *Crisis of Islam: Holy War and Unholy Terror* (New York, 2003; Bruce Hoffman, *Al Qaeda, Trends in Terrorism, and Future Potentialities: an Assessment* (Santa Monica, CA, 2003); Gunaratna, *Inside Al Qaeda*; Anonymous [Michael Scheuer], *Imperial Hubris: Why the West Is Losing the War on Terror* (Washington, DC, 2004).

[81] Karin von Hippel, 'The Root Causes of Terrorism: Probing the Myths', *Political Quarterly* (September 2002), 35.

[82] [Adm.] Bill Owens, *Lifting the Fog of War* (New York, 2000).

[83] Creveld, *Transformation of War*, 192–233.

However, while the importance of objective knowledge is to serve as a basis for subjective knowledge, that does not mean we should develop prescriptive theories from either. In fact, there is little in Clausewitz's concept of the nature of war that would justify the development of such a theory, though some will no doubt try. We might, however, want to emulate Clausewitz's approach in developing objective or verifiable knowledge of war, and thus fill in the gaps he left, which are many, and so add to the sum of what we know about armed conflict. The key will be to develop and adhere to a solid methodology that blends practical experience, rigorous logic, and historical examples. We also need to have the courage to attack our own assumptions and predilections, though, even if doing so leaves us ungrounded or adrift for a time. And that may be the hardest test of all.

# 12

# Clausewitz and the Privatization of War

*Herfried Münkler*

The classical inter-state war, which has shaped European history for centuries, seems to be a model on the way out. Not wars between states but wars in which sub-state and even private actors are seizing the initiative have dominated armed conflict throughout the world over the last one-and-a-half decades. Of course, states are of importance in these conflicts but—in contrast to classical wars—they no longer occupy the position of a monopolist of war. Certain branches of the political sciences, in international relations and peace and conflict studies, have recognized and adopted individual aspects of this development, but for a long time they remained so narrowly focused on the East–West conflict, despite its termination at the end of the 1980s, that these individual observations were not assembled into an overall picture.[1] Here, as elsewhere, the growing decline of historical perspectives from the political sciences over the last two decades has once again taken its toll. Individual aspects have been, continually and with growing ingenuity, compared with each other but the process has stopped short of the large-scale historical comparisons by which an overall picture of the situation could be obtained. Had the political history of ideas still been as central to the profession as it once was, this could have been prevented. The political history of ideas creates an obligation to reflect comprehensively on the present situation and to grasp it conceptually. The fundamental changes in warfare, which can be summarized by the term 'new wars'[2], have escaped the attention of German political scientists at least for too long.

---

[1] One of the few who relatively early on pointed out the fundamental changes in war and its consequences for the Western state system was Martin van Creveld, *The Transformation of War* (New York, 1991).

[2] Mary Kaldor, *New and Old Wars. Organized Violence in a Global Era* (London, 1999); Herfried Münkler, *The New Wars* (Cambridge, 2005, Polity Press; originally published in German, Reinbek b. Hamburg 2002). Following the appearance of Münkler's book, an animated discussion has developed in Germany focusing on the question of what analytical quality the term 'new wars' possesses and whether there really are fundamental changes in war at all. Sceptical are Martin Kahl and Ulrich Teusch, 'Sind die "neuen Kriege" wirklich neu?', *Leviathan*, 32 ( 2004), 382–401; supportive are Monika Heupel and Bernhard Zangl, 'Von "alten" und "neuen" Kriegen.—Zum Gestaltwandel kriegerischer Gewalt.' *Politische Vierteljahresschrift*, 45 (2004), 346–69.

By now, some states even seem to have grown to like the loss of their monopoly of war. These states, as could recently be observed in the case of the United States in Iraq, have no scruples about privatizing areas of military responsibility, not only in logistics but also in areas that extend into fighting itself. Whereas the ratio of members of private military companies (PMCs) to regular soldiers in the 1991 Gulf War was 1:50, it changed to 1:10 in the recent Iraq War, a fivefold increase. In view of these facts, the privatization of logistics and combatants alike can no longer be treated as a scientifically interesting but politically marginal observation. Quite a few observers assume that the US Army could not retain its ability to act without taking up the services of PMCs. The services offered by private actors under market conditions have thus become indispensable, even for a superpower like the United States, in its aspiration to possess the military ability to act globally. The state has not withdrawn from war, but it increasingly shares warfare with private actors.

This could be viewed as yet another example of the triumphant progress of neo-liberal strategies of privatization; one could refer to the common procedure of outsourcing, or speak of new forms of job-sharing between states and private security companies. In this case, the privatization wave within military affairs is described as being part of a general development which has gained momentum since the 1990s: as the reversal of a secular trend, in the course of which the state has seized more and more responsibilities without simultaneously generating demonstrably better and more cost-effective results. But one could also view it as the beginning of the end of an order of politics that is determined by states, an order characterized above all by the loss of order. Absolute control of military affairs and the monopolization of warfare marked the beginning of the rise of states; the loss of this monopoly and the increasing privatization of war could toll the knell for not just their decline, but possibly even their end.[3]

At any rate—the control of military affairs and warfare was not just any responsibility of the state but became the core element of the state order in Europe after the end of the Thirty Years War. Granting the state status depended on military control, and the *de jure* recognition of a state under international law still rests on that principle today. The monopoly of legitimate

---

[3] The observation concerning the declining regulative and integrative ability of the state refers not only to the wide belt of precarious statehoods along the fringes of prosperity zones that run from Columbia via sub-Saharan Africa to Central- and South-East Asia, but also to the OECD countries themselves. Various observers have reached the conclusion that the power of the state, which had reached its summit in the 1970s, is now on the wane in these states too—though admittedly much more slowly, in different forms and in different spheres, than in the case of failing states. See Martin van Creveld, *The Rise and Fall of the State* (Cambridge, 1999), and Wolfgang Reinhard, *Geschichte der Staatsgewalt. Eine vergleichende Verfassungsgeschichte Europas von den Anfängen bis zur Gegenwart* (München, 1999), 480 ff., 509 ff.

physical violence was, and still is, the legal core of the state order, and the enforcement of the monopoly of actual violence became the proof that a state was really equal to its responsibilities.[4] The privatization of war marks the end of an order in which states were the sole masters of war. The gradual retreat of the state and the increasing privatization of areas of military responsibility, as can be observed in the United States and Europe, are seemingly harmless manifestations of state disintegration. Here, it occurs as a *process*, not as *collapse*. However, the latter is the case in wide areas of what was formerly called the Third World. The term 'failed states', which the former US Secretary of State Madeleine Albright coined, has established itself in political vocabulary. It denotes a condition in which the institutional framework of statehood has been smashed. The police and the armed forces have dissolved into gangs, robbing and tyrannizing the population. In certain parts of Latin America, in most parts of sub-Saharan Africa, in Central Asia, and also in South-East Asia this condition has become a political day-to-day reality. There, clan chiefs, militia leaders, and warlords are waging war off their own bat and on their own account.

The privatization of war, therefore, takes place in two very different forms, so very different that it is not always easy to regard them as expressions of the very same phenomenon. Where privatization occurs as *process*, the gradual withdrawal of the state represents for the most part a rationalization and an increase in effectiveness under economic constraints. Here, the state monopoly of violence within foreign affairs remains untouched, even though it slowly frays on the fringes. When it occurs as *collapse*, the picture is a very different one as the state loses the instruments for the enforcement of its will to a number of individual actors, who take its place. As far as the OECD-states are concerned, the privatization of the ability to wage war is a process which needs to be politically directed and which equally can be stopped by

---

[4] This is not to deny that the state monopoly of domestic violence has been enforced in various ways: a simple comparison between the United States and Europe reveals clear differences. In Latin America the influence of big landowners (*hacendados*) and large companies remained so strong that they could successfully pit themselves against the interest of the state whenever it opposed their own; see Peter Waldmann, *Der anomische Staat. Über Recht, öffentliche Sicherheit und Alltag in Lateinamerika* (Opladen, 2002); in Africa and parts of Asia, where the collapse of the European colonial empires and later of the Soviet Union resulted in large post-imperial regions, state-building processes were late to start and came under the pressure of globalization early on in the process; see Klaus Schlichte, *Der Staat in der Weltgesellschaft. Politische Herrschaft in Asien, Afrika und Lateinamerika* (Frankfurt/New York, 2005). That, of course, does not change anything about the model of statehood as it developed in Europe still being both the *form* and the *norm* of the world order. Should its further erosion question the formative as well as the normative side of the world order, then this will not be just another small quantitative step towards the destruction of statehood, but the world order as a whole will be collapsing. Also, international law will be affected.

political means if need be. In the case of failed states, the manner by which it occurs destroys the very possibility of the formulation of political demands and objectives, and this is a pattern which can only be forestalled—at best—by outside intervention.

The two central characteristics of the new wars, privatization and asymmetries in military ability, in principle take two distinct shapes. Where asymmetry is concerned, it is possible to differentiate between asymmetries of power and asymmetries due to weakness, the asymmetrically superior power endeavouring to sustain its superiority through constant technological development or at least upgrading. Through the further development of its military technological capabilities, the United States brings to bear the asset which is more at its disposal than at that of any other actor, and which is a constant companion of its socio-economic development. One of the aims of its technological innovation is to minimize human losses in armed conflicts. Advanced societies have to rely on such minimization of losses if they wish to retain their ability to act. Essentially, these are post-heroic societies which are unable to cope with heavy losses in the course of war. The answers to the problem are technological superiority and/or the deployment of mercenaries, who include all those who do not belong to the electorate of the warring government. The former belongs to the 'asymmetricalization' of war, the latter is part of privatization.[5] The former is represented by strategies of air war carried out by an air force inaccessible to the enemy or by satellite guided missiles; the latter by a growing number of PMCs, but also by a high percentage of immigrant recruits, so-called green-card soldiers, within the ranks of the US military.

The problem posed by asymmetries, however, is a very different one for technologically backward societies. They are not capable of compensating for the superiority of the enemy by efforts of appropriate 'resymmetricalization' within a reasonably short period, as can be observed in European military history between the sixteenth and twentieth centuries. Rather, if they want to bring their political will to bear by force of arms, they have to develop forms of asymmetry of their own in order to transform the enemy's strength into weakness and their own weakness into strength. This means too an increased readiness to make sacrifices, that is the mobilization of a heroism not only which has disappeared in advanced societies but also whose appearance spreads fear and terror within those societies. For some considerable time, the symbol of such increased heroism has been the suicide bomber. In Western societies terrorist attacks using suicide bombers have not only an instrumental, but above all a symbolic component. Crucial, of course, is the fact that terrorist

---

[5] Problems of asymmetry and the question of post-heroic society are treated in detail in Herfried Münkler, *Der Wandel des Krieges* (Weilerswist, 2006).

suicide squads undercut the system of deterrence by being organized like non-governmental organizations, specifically as sub-state networks displaying increased political aspirations. That too is a form of privatization.[6]

Not only when looking at asymmetries but also in the case of 'de-statization' or privatization, it is possible to determine precisely whether either takes place from a position of (relative) strength or one of weakness. In the latter case the state gives corporate actors, run as a private enterprise, a share of its domain of action; in the former those actors take its place. It is not surprising, then, that privatized military actors have rather diverse appearances. In one case, they are private military companies, which frequently are listed on the stock exchange, and generally and completely follow the rules of the market.[7] In the other, they are warlords, sharing out the territory of a state among each other and plundering the resources of the area controlled by them. As a rule, the civilian population is robbed first.[8]

Before making a great fuss about all this and jumping to the conclusion that decline is looming large, it must be recalled that in Europe the state monopolization of war certainly did not lead to a condition of peace. The monopolist 'state' gathered and amalgamated the violence that had before been scattered in space and time in order then to turn its concentrated forces against those outside. The state did not put an end to war but set up a different order of war and violence that could be described in the terms 'disciplining' and 'professionalization'. The troops of mercenaries that before had been organized by independent war entrepreneurs[9] were placed under state supervision: from then on, they were soldiers of the king, no longer travelling around looking to be hired but concentrated in garrisons and subjected to generally brutal disciplinary measures. In return, the state provided for their living and issued pay, regardless of whether they were dwelling in barracks or going into battle. The population, as a result, was no longer regularly looted but instead had to finance the military through periodic taxation. The change in the regime of violence did not result in the material burden of war on the population being dissolved or even dramatically reduced. Those regions, which had been largely spared in the past from the depredations of

---

[6] In the case of terrorist networks, de-statization is synonymous with de-territorialization.

[7] Peter Warren Singer, *Corporate Warriors: The Rise of the Privatized Military Industry* (Ithaca and London, 2003), 73 ff.

[8] Jakkie Cilliers and Peggy Mason (eds), *Peace, Profit or Plunder? The Privatisation of Security in War-torn African Societies* (Pretoria, 1999); Dario Azzellini and Boris Kanzleiter (eds), *Das Unternehmen Krieg. Paramilitärs, Warlords und Privatarmeen als Akteure der Neuen Kriegsordnung* (Berlin, 2003).

[9] Michael E. Mallett, *Mercenaries and their Masters: Warfare in Renaissance Italy* (London, 1974); John R. Hale, *War and Society in Renaissance Europe 1450–1620* (Stroud, 1998), 75 ff.

mercenaries as they marched through, must have suffered from an increase in the costs of war as a consequence of the state's periodic taxation. But the costs became calculable: one knew in advance what was to be spent on the military and so was able to prepare for it. Even if a region became a war zone, the civilian population might be largely spared, because, at least formally speaking, eighteenth-century armies were supplied by magazines and did not need to plunder for food.[10] Security expenditures and the costs of war became a calculable part of an economic practice oriented towards the future. This constitutes a significant difference from the savage economies of war during the time of the mercenary, when there would be no certainty of not losing one's entire possessions to a passing army.

In the course of the sixteenth and seventeenth centuries the state thus placed a trade, the mercenary profession of arms, that had originally followed the rule of the market, under state control. With it, the conditions for planning and acting on market economy lines improved noticeably in all areas of economic life. How the state succeeded in doing so requires explanation, particularly in retrospect. According to some commentators on the most recent developments in warfare, the new wars are not a matter of state disintegration or privatized wars, but rather are analogous to those wars of the fifteenth to seventeenth centuries, and to be understood as state-building wars in which the state slowly and gradually asserts itself and becomes the sole master of military violence.[11]

The establishment of the state as the monopolist of policy had consequences for the political order that went far beyond the adaptation of war to a purpose that was exclusively political (and not even commercial). The latter was, of course, the proposition to which Clausewitz gave a general validity in his famous definition of war. With the rise of the bureaucratic state, as opposed to states governed by personal networks, as had been the case in the ancient world and in the Middle Ages, those who practised political and military skills acquired similar characteristics across Europe. They developed a body politic in which all the actors had the same qualities and features. It existed in one defined territorial space, in which the population lived, and which had one sovereign, who was responsible for the political and military business conducted by the country and the representatives of its people. This was the core of what would later be called the Westphalian order: a political system

[10] Jürgen Luh, *Kriegskunst in Europa. 1650–1800* (Köln u.a, 2004), 18–80. Martin van Creveld, *Supplying War: Logistics from Wallenstein to Patton* (Cambridge, 1977), presents a somewhat less rosy picture.

[11] This view is taken in Johannes Burckhardt, 'Die Friedlosigkeit der Frühen Neuzeit. Grundlegung einer Theorie der Bellizität Europas', *Zeitschrift für Historische Forschung*, 24 (1997), 509–74.

marked by symmetry and reciprocity, which earned universal respect, and which until very recently was believed to have global acceptance and would continue to have it.

In this way, the fact that every political actor engaged in military matters possessed a body politic was tied to his capacity to act and to a specific form of vulnerability: all the violence which could be used by such a political actor could also be used against him. The symmetry of rationality, standards, and choices enjoyed by political actors was based on this reciprocity of potential violence. What this meant for the political order cannot be easily overestimated. From this foundation developed something akin to a system of military deterrence, long before it acquired nuclear connotations. Everyone had to give proper consideration as to whether he should deal out blows, because the same could possibly be done to him. In contrast to states, non-state actors have no such body politic and for that very reason they are able to detach themselves from such a system of reciprocal deterrence. Because they have a less defined territorial identity, they do not acknowledge a clear and identifiable corporate nature, and therefore they are not vulnerable in the same ways as states. That applies particularly to the networks, which have acquired a capacity for supporting violence, which they did not otherwise possess. They act as though under a cloak of invisibility and are therefore difficult to identify for those they have attacked and hard to come to grips with. That was the decisive precondition for the development of those factors that have since come to be described as asymmetric warfare.

The analogy between this situation and early modern warfare is tempting since it presents the prospect of violence subsiding in areas shattered by persistent wars. The problem such an analogy faces is that it is most probably false—and that becomes quite clear when we look at the reasons which in the early modern era allowed states to bring military affairs and warfare under control. The crucial factors for the state monopolization of war were growing revenue from taxes and its corollary, a substantial increase in the costs of warfare. The increase in costs, brought about among other things by developments in artillery and drilled infantry, made warfare unprofitable for private war entrepreneurs. Due to the multiplication of internal revenue, states were soon the only actors that were able to afford such costly forms of warfare.[12]

---

[12] On the causes of the cost explosion in the military affairs of the early modern era, see Geoffrey Parker, *The Military Revolution. Military Innovation and the Rise of the West, 1500–1800* (Cambridge, 1988); on the state's growing need for money as a result of military innovations, see I. A. A. Thompson, ' "Money, Money, and Yet More Money!" Finance, the Fiscal-State, and the Military Revolution: Spain 1500–1650', in Clifford J. Rogers (ed.), *The Military Revolution Debate. Readings on the Military Transformation of Early Modern Europe* (Boulder, San Francisco and Oxford, 1995), 299–333.

With the current privatization of war, exactly the opposite developments can be observed: the new wars are waged by means of cheap weaponry and cheap equipment such as anti-personnel mines, semi-automatic and automatic weapons, small rocket launchers, and pick-up trucks in their double function as troop carrier and agile combat vehicle. The warlords make sure that they and their armed following can live on war. They loot the population, sell drilling and mining rights to international companies, or traffic in drugs and trade in human beings in association with organized crime. For them, war is turned into a business and, hence, they have no interest in letting it end. This is one of the reasons why the new wars go on endlessly.[13]

The process of state disintegration is accompanied simultaneously by a slump in internal revenue. Police and military can no longer be paid; the units become independent and take taxation into their own hands—by corruption, at roadblocks where bribes have to be paid in order to pass, or through openly robbing the population of the area under their control. The warlords gradually misappropriate the state, but they do not thereby become the moving force of a new state-building process. Pinning one's hopes on the assumption that the new wars are state-building wars is completely unjustified. The globalization of the economy, in the shadow of which the warlords generate their resources from shady transactions, gives no reason to expect them, like some *condottieri* of the early modern era, to hit on the idea of investing in their country in order to secure their reign for the future. As long as natural resources are available and can be exploited by dealings with international consortiums or organized crime, there is no reason to get involved in the laborious and lengthy process of reconstructing statehood.

Above all, the state-building wars in Europe led to those involved in them being more and more dragged into a cycle of innovation and modernization. The core elements were an increase in taxable capacity, the extension of the state machine, and finally greater obedience and conformity on the part of the population as a result of state protection. Their corollary was the population's heightened influence on and participation in the affairs of the state. Whatever the decisive factor within this cycle, innovations within military affairs were always of crucial importance, logistically as well as technologically. War and military affairs became the pacemaker for change. Where the new wars are concerned, this is not the case. They do not produce stimuli that work towards a strengthening of the state. They are not innovative with regard to technology because they are fought with cheap weaponry obtained from abroad. Above all, they do not strengthen the relations between the government and its people. They merely block development opportunities and destroy what has

---

[13] Münkler, *The New Wars*, 16 ff.

already been achieved in the past without producing any prospects at all. The wars in early modern Europe and even those of the twentieth century, in spite of all the destruction they caused and all the suffering they brought on people, started processes of political and technological progress as well. They were part of an upward spiral. By comparison, the new wars are part of a downward spiral, 'asymmetricalization' due to weakness as well as the privatization of the regimes of violence in disintegrating states accelerating the downward trend.

The states of the Third World are crushed between tribalism and globalization. The warlords take advantage of it on both sides: the social fabric of clan and tribe secures the recruitment of a reliable following and the channels of the 'shadow globalization' facilitate a cross-border trade in illegal goods: diamonds, drugs, and human beings. And if, in addition, warlords are supported politically from the outside, then the fragile order of the state stands no chance. That the warlords have little interest in becoming the force to build states goes without saying, since then they would have to hand over to the community control of the sources of power and income which had previously been theirs. They would run the risk that assets which they currently control would fall into the hands of their political adversaries. Above all, they would be forced to invest in a country they had previously only exploited.

But is it the case that war which instantly becomes permanent necessarily has to be what replaces the state? Are there no other substitutes that could bring about a relatively non-violent and stable condition? Evidently, this is not the case. The old loyalties ingrained in tribal and clan structures can secure an affluent warlord a following but socio-economic change means that they have grown too weak to provide the basis for a stable order. And the warlords themselves are unable to create such an order because they extract far more resources from the area under their control than they invest in it. Because they rule to loot, violence is and stays their constant companion: violence against the civilian population, violence against internal adversaries, and violence against outside rivals. That is how the privatized wars of the warlords smoulder away. Major battles are unknown; instead, there are brutal massacres time and again.[14]

The outsourcing of faculties and competences that has accompanied the modernization process of modern armed forces over the last decade and a half must be clearly distinguished from the warlord's privatizing of war. The state remains the monitoring body of the process and private military companies are paid from its internal revenue. The drivers are the need to get good value for money while ensuring the availability of military capacity. But what is the

---

[14] On the dynamics of massacre and its social function, Wolfgang Sofsky, *Zeiten des Schreckens. Amok, Terror, Krieg* (Frankfurt/Main, 2002), 147–83.

point beyond which private enterprises gain influence over political decisions or at least over their implementation? The problem is that this limit cannot be identified clearly and conclusively. The picture is altered as particular challenges present themselves. The United States, in deploying private military companies to Iraq, has gone furthest. As a result, clear responsibilities and accountability have been blurred—military as well as political. Logistically, the US forces in Iraq depend greatly on Halliburton, the main company responsible for supplying the forces.[15] In this way, it became possible to reverse developments which had been perceived as dangerous during the Vietnam War, in the course of which the number of soldiers engaged in battle steadily decreased while that of the soldiers required to guarantee stable supplies increased. In the end, the ratio in Vietnam was 1:10. The modernization of the US armed forces over the past decade has aimed, among other things, to reverse this ratio and, as the Iraq figures show, it has been successful. The price that has had to be paid is the outsourcing of the logistic tasks by entrusting them to private companies. They carry out highly dangerous tasks transporting goods, using drivers recruited on concessional terms in neighbouring countries. Hence, it is hardly surprising that these transports have become a primary target of the Iraqi underground resistance.

This development results in the state losing control of its armed forces. Other actors have rapidly become involved in areas aside from logistics. For example in Afghanistan (and probably also in Iraq), bounty hunters started searching for wanted persons to secure the rewards offered for capturing or killing them. The prospect of success improves at the same rate as persons already detained are 'questioned' by the use of forceful methods. The incompetent administration of the Abu Ghraib Detention Facility resulted from, among other factors, semi-official, that is semi-private, interrogation specialists having been allowed access to the detainees. At the same time, the privatization of areas of military responsibility leads to a loss of the control which a democratic society exercises over its political leadership. This could well be deliberate. Modern industrial societies and service economies are post-heroic societies. Sacrifice and honour are not of central importance to them. Such societies are not particularly ready to go to war; they are fired with enthusiasm for wars only by constant mass media excitement, and even that only for a short time. Soon the ploys and deception of the government become public knowledge; then the short-lived enthusiasm collapses and the government must worry about its re-election. The use of private military companies reduces these problems. Although the political risks may remain,

---

[15] Dario Azzellini, 'Der Krieg im Irak und die Armeen der Privaten', *Blätter für deutsche und internationale Politik*, 3 (2005), 334–9.

the pressure on the government in case of heavy losses is eased, if those killed or wounded in action come from all over the world and not just from its own ranks of voters. That pressure should promote the privatization of war.

New regimes to regulate the violence of private purveyors of military services are now being actively considered. Essentially, this regulation aims to differentiate between the two forms of privatization, as they have been sketched here.[16] The 'good' suppliers, offering their services to the rich states or the United Nations, are to be separated from the freebooters of the new wars who follow their malignant business on the fringes of prosperity zones. What cannot be abolished, so the idea runs, must be regulated. Nonetheless, the worst-case scenario of future wars could look like this: on one side warlords who have turned war into a lucrative business and on the other PMCs who carry out humanitarian interventions on behalf of national governments (or the UN). That would be, to all intents and purposes, a return to the conditions which existed in Europe between the fourteenth and seventeenth centuries, the era of the *condottieri* and the military entrepreneurs. Hence, a look back becomes—at least partly—a look forward.

At the beginning of the twenty-first century, we have to ask whether Clausewitz's theory of war is still able to provide insights into, or even answers to, the fundamentally changed wars of recent years. Wars no longer follow the rules of symmetric confrontations between states; increasingly sub-state and private actors fight not in order to achieve a political objective but to secure an income. What of Clausewitz's thinking remains relevant for the analysis of wars today, when only very rarely are they inter-state wars in the classical sense? Instead they mutate from wars within societies to trans-national wars, that is a hybrid of inter-state and civil war, where the political will of the participating parties is hard to make out. It seems as though Clausewitz's much quoted phrase, that war is the continuation of politics by other different means, has become obsolete.

However, Clausewitz's *original* theory of war as an act of violence so as to force the adversary to fulfil our will seems still to be valid, even if the *battle* as a symmetric confrontation of equally equipped adversaries has been replaced by the *massacre* and asymmetric use of violence of totally different actors. The people behind the 9/11 terrorist attacks used violence to force their adversary, the United States, to fulfil their will. Their intentions included forcing the United States to withdraw not only its military but also its economic and cultural presence from the Arab-Islamic countries. The strategic

---

[16] Stefan Mair, 'Die Rolle der Private Military Companies in Gewaltkonflikten', in Sabine Kurtenbach and Peter Lock (eds), *Kriege als (Über)Lebenswelten. Schattenglobalisierung, Kriegsökonomien und Inseln der Zivilität* (Bonn, 2004), 260–73, esp. 270 ff.

planners of al-Qaeda could not achieve their goal with military means, since the superiority of the United States is so incomparable that every attempt at a symmetric confrontation would be in vain, and so they fell back on the means of asymmetric warfare.[17] Such an analysis of the recent forms of international terrorism derived from Clausewitz's theory seems to be much more useful for the purposes of prediction, and more rational, than the culturally impregnated speculations which have flourished, not least since the publication of Samuel Huntington's *The Clash of Civilizations and the Remaking of the World Order* in 1996. With the help of Clausewitz's analysis, terrorism could be defined as a strategy, which from a position of weakness tries to pursue the stronger object in a weaker form, achieving its effects through radical disintegration and subsequent redefinition. Al-Qaeda only lighted on this offensive capability because the new forms of international terrorism tore down the boundaries between war and peace, as well as between combatants and non-combatants, and because it was able to redefine the civil infrastructure of the attacked country—in this case passenger aircraft—as weapons. One will be a better match for them, if the fighting is based more than ever on Clausewitz, rather than on Huntington and all the others.

[17] For a first attempt to analyse the 9/11 attacks with Clausewitz's categories, see Herfried Münkler, 'Sind wir im Krieg? Über Terrorismus, Partisanen und die neuen Formen des Krieges', *Politische Vierteljahresschrift*, 42 (2001), 581 9; as well as Herfried Münkler, 'Grammatik der Gewalt. Über den Strategiewandel des Terrorismus', *Schriftenreihe der Johann Joachim Becher-Gesellschaft zu Speyer*, 17 (2003), 5–16.

# 13

# Clausewitz and Information Warfare

*David Lonsdale*

According to the influential Revolution in Military Affairs (RMA)/Military Transformation hypothesis, the information age appears to promise a number of changes to the character of war. In particular, increased access to information brings with it the promise of being able to do substantially more with significantly less. The information age allegedly will be characterized by more efficient operations. Indeed, information operations may become the arbiter of success and failure in war. At first glance, this presents no major challenges to strategic theory, or to Clausewitz in particular, since the character of war is recognized as being mutable. Each period, indeed each war, has its own particular character, depending on factors such as the belligerents involved, technology available, and geography. However, much of the RMA literature[1] goes a step further and, either explicitly or implicitly, concludes that these changes will also bring about changes to the nature of war.[2] This is significant since the nature of war, which is given theoretical form by Clausewitz, should in theory be unchanging and guides preparation for the conduct of operations. What one perceives as the nature of war greatly influences the development of doctrine, force composition, and training. Clausewitz himself noted that the nature of war affects which forces will be used.[3] This thought is echoed in the United States Marine Corps' (USMC) doctrine manual *Fleet Marine Force Manual 1 'Warfighting'* (FMFM-1): '...our understanding of the nature and the theory of war...must be the guiding

---

[1] In the context of this chapter, the term 'RMA literature' is used to refer collectively to those works that generally subscribe to the notion that revolutionary change, fuelled by the information age, is occurring. Knox and Murray offer an alternative term to describe the RMA enthusiasts by referring to them as 'technological utopians': MacGregor Knox and Williamson Murray, 'Conclusion: The Future Behind Us', in MacGregor Knox and Williamson Murray (eds), *The Dynamics of Military Revolution, 1300–2050* (Cambridge, 2001), 179.

[2] See John Arquilla and David Ronfeldt, 'Cyberwar Is Coming', in Arquilla and Ronfeldt (eds), *In Athena's Camp: Preparing for Conflict in the Information Age* (Santa Monica, CA, 1996), 25, and Robert R. Leonhard, *The Principles of War for the Information Age* (Novato, CA, 1998), 6.

[3] Carl von Clausewitz, *On War*, trans. Michael Howard and Peter Paret (Princeton, NJ, 1976), V, 4, p. 288.

force behind our preparation for war'.[4] It follows that, if the nature of war should be altered by the information age, then the whole panoply of war preparation will require amendment in order to prepare for a very different kind of conflict than has occurred historically. As a result, we may have to look towards other works of strategic theory to inform our doctrine. At present, *On War* and to a lesser extent Sun Tzu's *The Art of War* and Jomini's *The Art of War* are regarded as the founders of modern military thought, and as performing the role of enabling students of war to understand the central elements of the activity.[5] The language and ideas expressed in these works permeate a great deal of modern military doctrine and academic work on war. Indeed, *Warfighting* stipulates that Clausewitz's *On War* is 'the definitive treatment of the nature and theory of war'.[6]

This chapter seeks to put the various claims of the RMA literature to the test. By this, we can determine whether the work of Clausewitz still constitutes the key text when attempting to define and understand the nature of war. In order to achieve this, a number of steps must be undertaken. In the first instance, the Clausewitzian nature of war must be defined. From here, the changes envisaged by the RMA literature can be presented. It will thus become obvious that if the said changes indeed come to pass, then the Clausewitzian paradigm will come under serious pressure. However, when they are examined in detail, it becomes apparent that many of the promised changes are unlikely to be realized. Ultimately, the five core elements of strategy, identified below, will ensure that any changes are limited, and that the nature of war remains unaffected.

The RMA literature, which developed into its current form after the experiences of the 1991 Gulf War, continues to exert significant influence among various defence communities. Alvin and Heidi Toffler, early exponents of the information age RMA, became particularly important in defence circles with their book, *War and Anti-War: Survival at the Dawn of the 21st Century*.[7] Christopher Coker describes how the Tofflers' *War and Anti-War* 'has become a revered text in the US military since its publication in 1991'.[8] Even in the aftermath of 9/11, which forced back onto the agenda a form of war ignored by most of the RMA enthusiasts, the zeal for 'military transformation' is largely

---

[4] H. T. Hayden (ed.), *Warfighting: Manoeuvre Warfare in the U.S. Marine Corps* (London, 1995), 66.

[5] See Crane Brinton, Gordon A. Craig, and Felix Gilbert, 'Jomini', in Edward Mead Earle (ed.), *Makers of Modern Strategy: Military Thought from Machiavelli to Hitler* (Princeton, NJ, 1943), 80–3, and Michael I. Handel, *Masters of War: Classical Strategic Thought* (2nd edn, London, 1996), 16.

[6] Hayden, *Warfighting*, 43.

[7] Alvin and Heidi Toffler, *War and Anti-war: Survival at the Dawn of the 21st Century* (London, 1994).

[8] Christopher Coker, *Humane Warfare* (London, 2001), 15.

unabated. For some, including the US Secretary of Defense Donald Rumsfeld, the 2003 invasion of Iraq represented an early test for a partially transformed US military.[9] It is reported that Rumsfeld had hoped that a smaller 'transformed' force would be able to achieve the same results as an older, much larger force.[10] Furthermore, in April 2004 Jason Sherman said that Rumsfeld had ordered new 'speed goals' for future military operations, 'challenging the military services to structure themselves to deploy to a distant theatre in 10 days, defeat an enemy within 30 days, and be ready for an additional fight within another 30 days'.[11] However, as the insurgency in Iraq continues to occupy US forces, these speed goals seem naively optimistic. In fact, Rumsfeld's proclivity for military transformation has come under increasing pressure: 'The continued fighting in Iraq, however, shows the limits of what he [Rumsfeld] has accomplished.... To be sure, many of the current problems in Iraq result from Rumsfeld's failure to send enough troops there.'[12]

## THE CLAUSEWITZIAN NATURE OF WAR

For Clausewitz, the nature of war is composed of elements that are always present, but fluctuate in their relationships with each other. Christopher Bassford describes in his chapter in this book how the relative strength and influence of each of the forces within Clausewitz's 'fascinating trinity' varies with context. Thus, the nature of each particular war is unique, and can be discovered floating somewhere between these forces. Alan Beyerchen in his chapter also focuses on the complexity of war as described by Clausewitz, seeing it a non-linear activity, where small fluctuations can have significant consequences.

Prominent among other aspects which are always present in the nature of war are uncertainty and violence.[13] In addition, war is of course characterized by human participation, and *On War* presents us with a vision of war that is

---

[9] Julian Border and Richard Norton-Taylor, 'US Generals Embrace New Kind of Warfare', *The Guardian*, 22 March 2003, 4.
[10] Bernard Weinraub and Thom Shanker, 'War on the Cheap?', *International Herald Tribune*, 2 April 2003, 1–2.
[11] Loren B. Thompson, 'Military Transformation Falters in Mesopotamia' (16 April 2004), http://www.lexingtoninstitute.org/defense/040416.asp
[12] Max Boot, 'The Struggle to Transform the Military', *Foreign Affairs* (March–April 2005), http://www.foreignaffairs.org/20050301faessay84210/max-boot/the-struggle-to-transform-the-military.html
[13] For a discussion of the difference between narrow and general friction, see Barry D. Watts, *Clausewitzian Friction and Future War*, McNair Paper 52 (Washington, DC, National Defense University, October 1996), especially ch. 4.

dominated by the human element. Human psychology plays a crucial role in war as it has to master what Clausewitz calls the 'climate of war', composed of danger, exertion, uncertainty, and chance.[14]

Finally, the Clausewitzian concept of friction illuminates additional elements in the nature of war. Friction itself is perhaps best expressed through the 'unified concept of general friction', as developed by Barry D. Watts in *Clausewitzian Friction and Future War*, which embraces eight broad factors. These are danger, physical exertion, uncertainties and imperfections in information, resistance within one's own forces, chance events, physical and political limits on the use of force, unpredictability emanating from interaction with the enemy, and disconnections between ends and means.[15] Thus, we are left with a vision of war's true nature that is characterized by a complex series of relationships and interactions, which take place between rational and non-rational forces, and in an environment in which uncertainty, violence, and friction are prominent.

Now that we have defined what Clausewitz sees to be the nature of war, we can focus on those elements that are challenged by the RMA hypothesis. These are uncertainty, violence, chance, friction, and human participation. Many of the causes of uncertainty centre on information. These include the fact that information is rarely in real time; is often incomplete; contains contradictions; and is subjected to human perceptions and interpretations. Uncertainty also emanates from the ever-present play of friction and chance. Finally, uncertainty springs from the fact that war is an activity characterized by human interaction. War is fought against an intelligent foe whose intentions can never really be known with absolute certainty.

Alongside uncertainty, violence is another ever-present feature of war, and is central to Clausewitz's belief in the significance of battle.[16] On the very first page of book I, chapter 1, Clausewitz states: 'War is thus an act of force to compel our enemy to do our will.' He develops this thought, 'Force—that is, physical force...is thus the means of war.'[17] Later on he proclaims, 'Essentially war is fighting, for fighting is the only effective principle in the manifold activities generally designated as war.'[18] Finally, to distinguish war from other activities, he notes: 'War is a clash between major interests, which is resolved by bloodshed—that is the only way in which it differs from other conflicts.'[19] Clausewitz emphasizes the 'dominance of the destructive principle' and the

---

[14] *On War*, I, 3, p. 104. In the Clausewitzian taxonomy 'human factors' can be best thought of in terms of the danger and exertion elements of the climate of war.
[15] Watts, *Clausewitzian Friction*, 32.
[16] Colin S. Gray, *Modern Strategy* (Oxford, 1999), 104.   [17] *On War*, I, 1, p. 75.
[18] Ibid. II, 1, p. 127.   [19] Ibid. II, 3, p. 149.

direct annihilation of enemy forces.[20] Even if fighting does not actually occur in a conflict, the result still relates back to its central position in warfare.

In the Clausewitzian paradigm, 'friction is the only concept that more or less corresponds to the factors that distinguish real war from war on paper'.[21] As Clausewitz himself notes when defining friction: 'Countless minor incidents—the kind you can never really foresee—combine to lower the general level of performance, so that one always falls short of the intended goal.'[22] An element which itself is prominent within the broader concept of friction is the role of chance. In Clausewitz's view, the element of chance is never absent from war. Consequently, guesswork and luck also play a significant role in warfare.[23] Taken together, friction and chance propel warfare further from being an activity that can be controlled with any degree of certainty. This is in contrast to much of the RMA literature, which perceives war as an increasingly malleable phenomenon. Indeed, John Arquilla and David Ronfeldt, two of the most prominent writers in the RMA literature, suggest that the Clausewitzian emphasis on friction should be replaced by a vision of war in which the manipulation of entropy is the key.[24]

The bottom line in this discussion is that war, above all else, is a human activity. This is true both in terms of the units that actually do the fighting and in reference to the fact that it is an activity best thought of in terms of human interaction. This fact endows war with many of the elements that have been discussed thus far. In the battle-space, the existence of danger and exertion has an impact on operational performance and unleashes powerful moral forces. However they choose to organize themselves politically or socially, and whatever terms they employ to describe the motivations behind their decision to wage war, humans fight each other for human reasons. As a result of this, the trinity, climate of war, and the unified concept of general friction, and therefore the work of Clausewitz, come closest to defining the true nature of war.

## THE RMA CHALLENGES THE CLAUSEWITZIAN PARADIGM

Despite Rumsfeld's plans for Iraq, based as they were on military transformation, the insurgency and terrorist campaigns have painfully revealed that the current battle-space is the realm of infinite possibilities and complex interactions. That is not what some of the RMA literature had envisaged. In

---

[20] Ibid. IV, 3, pp. 227–8.   [21] Ibid. I, 7, p. 119.   [22] Ibid. I, 7, p. 119.
[23] Ibid. I, 1, p. 85.   [24] Arquilla and Ronfeldt, 'Cyber Is Coming', 156.

their different ways, many of the RMA enthusiasts each portray a vision of the future that is narrow, sterile, and often ignorant of strategic considerations.

The contemporary RMA hypothesis is fuelled by the increased application of information technology (IT) to the battle-space and the consequent digitization of forces. From this, the prime commodity and engine of change is information. As Robert R. Leonhard has noted: 'If twenty-first century warfare has any theme, it is information.'[25] Another important component of some of the literature is an emphasis on the relationship between the increased availability of real-time information and precision-guided munitions (PGMs). Taken together, these developments allegedly establish assured destruction in the battle-space.

The claims that emanate from the above themes offer a radical vision of the future, one that goes a significant way towards rendering the Clausewitzian paradigm seemingly anachronistic. The promise of an increasing abundance of information has led some writers to proclaim the significant decline of uncertainty in war. They postulate that operational concepts such as 'situational awareness' and 'dominant battle-space knowledge' will lift the fog of war for friendly forces.[26] Also evident is a proclivity to view war merely as an act of bombardment, in which victory is assured through the destruction of a limited number of key enemy targets with stand-off PGMs. These visions reflect both emerging capabilities and an alleged sensitivity to casualties in Western societies and polities.[27] Extreme manifestations of these trends are 'post-heroic warfare' and 'virtual war'.[28] Indeed, a leading writer on the future battle-space, Martin Libicki, argues that due to sensitivity to casualties, the United States must adopt and perfect stand-off warfare.[29]

A related consequence of the reconnaissance-strike complex (the linking of reconnaissance assets and PGMs) is the demise of the manned platform, either to be replaced by unmanned vehicles or mini-projectiles, or indeed rendered partially obsolete by the concepts of 'virtual presence' and 'air occupation'.[30]

[25] Leonhard, *Principles of War*, 219.
[26] See, e.g. Admiral William Owens with Ed Offley, *Lifting the Fog of War* (New York, 2000).
[27] Michael O'Hanlon describes how 'The RMA Movement' includes an emphasis on technology and sensitivity to casualties: see O'Hanlon, *Technological Change and the Future of Warfare* (Washington, DC, 2000), 7.
[28] Luttwak, 'A Post-Heroic Military Policy', and Michael Ignatieff, *Virtual War: Kosovo and Beyond* (New York, 2001).
[29] Martin C. Libicki, 'Information and Nuclear RMAs Compared', *Strategic Forum 82*, July 1996, www.ndu.edu/inss/strforum/forum82.html
[30] This concept originated in the USAF, and though it accepts that at times physical presence will be required, it does postulate: 'There is an informational form of presence—a virtual presence'. See Glenn W. Goodman Jr., 'The Power of Information: Air Force Clarifies its Misunderstood Virtual Presence Concept', *Armed Forces Journal International*, July 1995, 24. For a critical assessment of 'virtual presence', see Squadron Leader Peter Emmett, 'Information

The latter exhibits striking similarities to control from the air, and in this sense it suffers from similar limitations to those expressed by General Norman Schwarzkopf: 'There is not a military commander in the entire world who would claim he had taken an objective by flying over it.'[31] In our efforts to understand this removal of man from the battlefield we can look towards a combination of technological determinism and socio-political considerations. J. F. C. Fuller may have identified this trend as far back as 1946, when he described a hidden impulse in technological development, which has as its objective 'the elimination of the human element both physically and morally, intellect alone remaining'.[32]

Potentially the biggest change to the existing character of warfare, and therefore also the most substantial challenge to the Clausewitzian nature of war, is provided by strategic information warfare (SIW). The ability to conclude wars by attacking the national information infrastructure (NII) of an enemy through cyberspace would seem to question significant aspects of the nature of war. Like strategic bombing, SIW seeks to bypass enemy surface forces to strike directly at the perceived centre of gravity. However, whereas air power still works through the application of destructive firepower and physical force, SIW primarily operates through such non-violent means, such as 'malicious software', and electromagnetic pulses.[33] In this sense, SIW does not constitute an act of physical violence, nor does it involve any real degree of physical exertion. The instrumental aim of SIW is more often than not to create strategic effect via disruption rather than destruction.[34]

---

Mania—A New Manifestation of Gulf War Syndrome?', *RUSI Journal*, 141/1 (1996), 19–26. For a discussion of 'air occupation', see Major Marc K. Dippold, 'Air Occupation: Asking the Right Questions', *Aerospace Power Journal*, Winter 1997, www.airpower.maxwell.af.mil/airchronicles/apj/apj97/win97/dippold.html

[31] Michael R. Gordon and General Bernard E. Trainor, *The Generals' War: The Inside Story of the Conflict in the Gulf* (Boston, MA, 1995), 442.

[32] J. F. C. Fuller, *Armament and History: A Study of the Influence of Armament on History from the Dawn of Classical Warfare to the Second World War* (London, 1946), v.

[33] There is an ongoing debate about what actually constitutes 'information warfare'. It is certainly true that NIIs can be attacked by physical acts of destruction. However, Schwartau has defined (pure) information warfare as 'the total absence of bombs, bullets, or other conventional tools of physical destruction'; see Schwartau, *Information Warfare: Cyberterrorism: Protecting Your Personal Security in the Electronic Age* (2nd edn, New York, 1996), 464. Although it is accepted that SIW can be waged with conventional tools of physical destruction, this chapter will test the strategic efficacy of SIW in its 'pure' form. Schwartau's information warfare poses the greatest challenge to the nature of warfare. Also, even if SIW contained some limited instances of conventional physical attacks, the change in the character of warfare would still prove substantial if malicious software and its like comprised the majority of the attacks.

[34] Greg Rattray notes, 'Strategic Information Warfare can be conducted in either a physically violent or nonviolent way', in Rattray, *Strategic Warfare in Cyberspace* (Cambridge, 2001), 19.

The conclusion to be drawn from the above predictions is that an increased ability to gather and disseminate information, allied to the assumed reliability of PGMs, creates a battle-space in which the conflict over information is perceived to be the key to success. In this vein, Libicki foresees a battle-space that is characterized by 'hide and seek' warfare rather than a 'force-on-force' experience.[35] Alvin Toffler has joined this fray by stating explicitly: 'The wars of the future will increasingly be prevented, won or lost based on information superiority and dominance.'[36] Aside from this emphasis on information, Lawrence Freedman has identified in the RMA literature a desire for victimless war, typified by the achievement of victory through disruption rather than destruction.[37] This feature would be at its most extreme form in SIW. Christopher Coker proclaims that the ultimate manifestation of post-modern war is 'humane warfare', in which the mission is to neutralize rather than kill.[38]

Evidently, these visions of future war do not fit well with the emphasis placed on violence and uncertainty in the Clausewitzian nature of war. The notion of victory through information dominance reads like the theory of war by algebra, which Clausewitz largely dismissed.[39] Finally, although rarely explicitly rejected in the RMA literature, there does appear to be a reduced emphasis on friction in much of the enthusiasts' work.[40] By significantly removing humans from the battlefield, by reducing or eliminating violence and destruction, and by lifting the fog of war, the RMA visionaries are going a considerable way towards removing significant causes of friction.

Should the future battle-space resemble the visions outlined above—in which war is a significantly less uncertain activity; is concluded with little or no violence; is to a large extent devoid of human involvement at the sharp end; and is much less vulnerable to friction—then warfare would almost be unrecognizable to Clausewitz. In many respects, certainly in relation to the climate of war, the nature of war would have been transformed. Such a change would have a number of important implications, and therefore these claims are worthy of study. Bearing in mind the role of theory in the education of

---

[35] See Martin C. Libicki, 'Technology and Warfare', and Lawrence E. Casper, Irving L. Halter, Earl W. Powers, Paul J. Selva, Thomas W. Steffens, and T. LaMar Willis, 'Knowledge-Based Warfare: A Security Strategy for the Next Century', *Joint Force Quarterly*, 13 (1996), 83.

[36] Alvin Toffler, 'Looking at the Future with Alvin Toffler', www.usatoday.com/news/comment/columnists/toffler/toff05.htm

[37] Lawrence Freedman, *Information Warfare: Will Battle Ever Be Joined?*, International Centre for Security Analysis (Launch), 14 October 1996, 6.

[38] Coker, *Humane Warfare*, 14.     [39] *On War*, I, 1, p. 76.

[40] Murray and Knox note the perspective of the technological utopians that war could become a frictionless engineering exercise: see 'Conclusion: The Future Behind Us', in Murray and Knox (eds), *The Dynamics of Military Revolution*, 178.

officers, changes as radical as those proffered in the RMA literature would make Clausewitz's work much less meaningful. In this respect, Mackubin Thomas Owens reports that a US Army general has declared that technological advances will soon result in the end of Clausewitz.[41]

## THE CORE ELEMENTS OF STRATEGY

Perceptions of the future nature of war can have significant implications for future strategic performance. Therefore, it is important to test these claims against the core elements of strategy. Strategy, which can be defined as *the art of using military force against an intelligent foe(s) towards the attainment of policy objectives*, can be broken down in a number of ways. Clausewitz identified five types of elements: moral, physical, mathematical, geographical, and statistical.[42] Another approach developed by Michael Howard and Colin Gray is to identify the various dimensions of strategy.[43] While the seventeen dimensions identified by Gray are all valid, five are offered here as having the most significant impact on the character, and therefore the nature, of war. They are policy, the existence of an intelligent enemy, the fact that war can take many forms (the character of war is polymorphous and therefore the belligerents have a number of options available to them with regards to the style of conflict they adopt), geography, and finally that war is a human activity. Taken together, and considered alongside the trinity, these factors produce complex interactions in war and prevent it from attaining any degree of uniformity and predictability.

If, as Gray notes, strategy is the bridge between policy and war, then the requirements of policy must influence the conduct of war in fundamental ways.[44] Unfortunately, the RMA literature often portrays a perspective on war that is focused at the technical, tactical, and operational levels, and therefore appears ignorant of policy considerations. The nature of war could in theory be affected by significant technological and operational innovation, but only

---

[41] Mackubin Thomas Owens, 'Vietnam as Military History', *Joint Force Quarterly*, 3 (1993–4), 64.

[42] *On War*, III, 2, p. 183.

[43] Howard identifies four of these dimensions, while Gray's taxonomy constitutes seventeen. See Michael Howard, 'The Forgotten Dimensions of Strategy', *Foreign Affairs*, 57 (1979), 976–86 and Colin S. Gray, *Modern Strategy* (Oxford, 1999).

[44] Colin S. Gray, *War, Peace, and Victory: Strategy and Statecraft For the Next Century* (New York, 1990). Indeed, Eliot Cohen describes the relationship between policy objectives and the military as the 'unequal dialogue', in which the world of policy dominates: Cohen, *Supreme Command: Soldiers, Statesmen, and Leadership in Wartime* (New York, 2002), 207.

if it could be translated into assured success at the strategic level. Victory in war must be assessed at this higher level, as tactical success is not sufficient. That being the case, an RMA-based force (whether it be a force based around stand-off munitions or information operations) that performs flawlessly at the tactical level does not guarantee victory.

Policy objectives often require the physical presence of troops, and/or the destruction of enemy forces and resources. An example of the former is counter-insurgency warfare. In such campaigns control of the population is often the key to success or failure.[45] Stand-off weapons simply cannot do this mission. The objective of war, to use Admiral J. C. Wylie's terminology, is to exert some measure of *control* over the enemy and/or the situation.[46] Wylie describes the method by which control is enforced: 'The ultimate determinant in war is the man on the scene with the gun. This man is the final power in war. He is control.' [47] The concept of 'control' is defined as being concerned with 'influence' and/or 'unchallenged presence'.[48] The destruction of enemy forces may also be an expressed objective. This was certainly the case in the post-D-Day campaign against the Wehrmacht. In a more extreme example, sections within the Roman Republic viewed the destruction of the Carthaginian civilization as the final goal of the protracted Punic Wars.[49]

The RMA literature should also take account of the fact that political concerns frequently place limitations on the use of force; in which case, RMA-based forces will often be unable to reach, or indeed approach, maximum operational efficiency. The use of air power in both the 1991 Gulf War and the 1999 conflict over Kosovo presents examples of the kind of limitations that can be placed on the military instrument. In both cases, air power, to some degree, represented the RMA vision of war by stand-off bombardment cued in by situational awareness assets. In the Gulf War, the al-Firdos bunker incident (a well-publicized incident in which a number of civilians were killed by a coalition air strike) reveals how political sensitivities 'routinely preclude the unconstrained employment of military means', with the result that 'the mere possession of advanced technology is no guarantee of its practical utility'.[50] Kosovo is just as revealing. Concerns over allied casualties obliged ground

---

[45] Leroy Thompson, *Ragged War: The Story of Unconventional and Counter-Revolutionary Warfare* (London, 1996), 135.

[46] J. C. Wylie, *Military Strategy: A General Theory of Power Control* (Annapolis, MD, 1967), 66. Clausewitz expressed a similar concept when he described the objective of war as 'an act of force to compel our enemy to do our will'. See *On War*, I, 1, p. 75.

[47] Wylie, *Military Strategy*, 72.      [48] Ibid. 88.

[49] See Dwight D. Eisenhower, *Crusade in Europe* (London, 1948), 247, and Nigel Bagnall, *The Punic Wars: Rome, Carthage and the Struggle for the Mediterranean* (London, 1999).

[50] Paul Van Riper and Robert H. Scales, Jr., 'Preparing for War in the 21st Century', *Parameters*, 27/3 (1997), 9.

attack bombers to fly above 15,000 feet. Although the significance of this should not be overplayed, it did diminish the operational efficacy of some attacks, particularly as it made them more vulnerable to acts of Serbian deception. Other political restrictions emanated from the fact that the war was a coalition effort and was therefore hostage to the unanimity principle within NATO.[51] Such limitations on the use of force will in all likelihood preclude the sufficient operational performance necessary to fulfil the hopes of RMA advocates. Ironically, the impulses that drive the desire for stand-off, post-heroic forms of war, also place restrictions on operations, and in turn these may diminish the chances of success.

Aside from the demands of policy, the RMA will be shaped by the existence of intelligent foes. With its focus on the technological dimension, the RMA literature often overlooks the existence and influence of an intelligent enemy. When asked why the Confederates lost at Gettysburg in 1863, General George Pickett famously replied, 'I think the Union Army had something to do with it'.[52] It is all too easy to focus on the performance of one's own side without taking sufficient account of the dialectical nature of strategy. Libicki is guilty of overestimating the omnipotence and invulnerability of any future 'mesh' of sensors. He acknowledges that deception and stealth will be utilized by those in the battle-space hunted by the mesh, but then declares that the plethora of multispectral sensors will ensure that the hunter triumphs in the final analysis.[53] Such overconfidence is based primarily on assessments at the tactical and technical levels, and therefore fails to consider the application of paradoxical logic at the higher levels of strategy. This failure to address the issue of countermeasures at the higher levels shows yet again how many of the most strident advocates of the RMA restrict their analysis to the lower levels of strategy. An enemy wishing to counter an RMA-competent enemy can do so at all levels: technical, tactical, operational, strategic, and grand strategic.

Aside from attacking the information systems that underpin the current RMA,[54] those faced with an RMA-equipped foe can opt for other, less technical, countermeasures. The Serbian use of UN hostages as human shields in

---

[51] Benjamin S. Lambeth, *NATO's Air War For Kosovo: A Strategic and Operational Assessment* (Santa Monica, CA, 2001), 185.

[52] R. L. DiNardo and Daniel J. Hughes, 'Some Cautionary Thoughts on Information Warfare', *Airpower Journal*, 9/4 (1995), 76.

[53] Martin Libicki, *The Mesh and the Net: Speculation on Armed Conflict in an Age of Free Silicon*, McNair paper 28 (Washington DC, 1996).

[54] Nick Cook, 'War of Extremes', *Jane's Defence Weekly*, 7 July 1999. See Toffler, *War and Anti-war*, 144; Emmett, 'Information Mania', 23; Carlo Kopp, 'The E-Bomb—A Weapon of Electrical Mass Destruction', in Schwartau, *Information Warfare*, 296–333; O'Hanlon, *Technological Change*, 194; Colonel M. D. Starry and Lt Colonel C. W. Arneson Jr., 'FM 100-6: Information Operations', *Military Review*, 76/6 (1996), 3–15.

Bosnia illustrates how a simple act can negate the advantages conferred by millions of dollars' worth of technologically advanced equipment. Ground forces threatened by an enemy composed primarily of stand-off capabilities have various simple options available, including dispersal, utilization of the terrain and weather, and blending into local populations.[55] At another level, a conventionally superior force can be denied victory if the enemy refuses to take the field.

Operational and organizational innovations that confer advantage are usually offset and/or copied, and therefore attritional forms of warfare often re-emerge. In both world wars of the twentieth century, once Germany had failed to achieve quick and decisive victories, attritional forms of warfare ensued. Although Andrew Krepenevich is correct to note that exploiting an RMA first usually confers advantages, these advantages are fleeting and sometimes do not translate into strategic success.[56] In this respect, the examples of Napoleon and Nazi Germany suggest that operational efficiency is no guarantee of strategic victory. With these examples in mind, it is reasonable to assume that any monopoly in RMA capabilities could be negated, and therefore any revolutionary operational breakthroughs would cease to offer the same returns.

Much of the RMA literature fails to take sufficient account of the fact that warfare can assume various forms. Instead, the focus tends to be on high-intensity, regular conflict.[57] Faced with a conventionally superior enemy, a foe may well adopt an asymmetric form of warfare.[58] In this respect, the options include irregular warfare, SIW, or escalation by the use of weapons of massive destruction (WMD). Lawrence Freedman points out just how insignificant the RMA was on 9/11: 'The attack was instigated using the most ancient of military technologies—the knife—in order to turn the most modern civilian aviation technology against the West.'[59] While advanced conventional forces have a role to play in the war against terrorism, whether in a reconnaissance role

---

[55] Colonel Volney J. Warner, 'Technology Favours Future Land Forces', *Strategic Review*, 26/3 (1998), 52.

[56] A. F. Krepinevich, 'Why No Transformation?', *Joint Force Quarterly*, 23 (1999–2000), 37.

[57] Jeffrey Cooper, 'Another View of the Revolution in Military Affairs', in Arquilla and Ronfeldt, *In Athena's Camp*, 107; Christopher Jon Lamb, 'The Impact of Information Age Technologies on Operations Other Than War', in Robert L. Pfaltzgraff, Jr. and Richard H. Shultz, Jr. (eds), *War in the Information Age: New Challenges for U.S. Security Policy* (Washington, DC, 1997), 247.

[58] On this issue Ralph Peters observes: 'We confront, today, creatively organised enemies employing behaviours and technologies ranging from those of the stone-age to those at the imagination's edge'; Peters, 'After the Revolution', *Parameters*, 25/2 (1995), 8.

[59] Lawrence Freedman, 'The Future of Strategic Studies', in John Baylis, James Wirtz, Eliot Cohen, and Colin S. Gray (eds), *Strategy in the Contemporary World: An Introduction to Strategic Studies* (Oxford, 2002), 341.

or in operations against terrorist bases or sponsors, intelligence operatives, light infantry, and special forces undertake the main effort. Commentating on WMD, Gray persuasively argues: 'the absolute quality to nuclear weapons about which Bernard Brodie and his collaborators wrote so eloquently in 1946 means that an information-led RMA might be trumped by the "old reliable" equalizer of a nuclear arsenal'.[60]

Indeed, too much emphasis on the RMA could leave a military both physically and culturally incapable of operating at lower or higher levels of intensity. To take irregular warfare as an example, the theoretical and historical literature suggests that forces optimized for regular operations often fail to cope effectively with the different challenges posed by this form of conflict. Murray and Knox note how in Vietnam, 'technological sophistication [was] irrelevant to the war actually being fought'.[61] In contrast to the RMA literature's emphasis on quick and decisive operations with stand-off munitions, irregular conflicts are usually protracted, attritional, and people intensive.[62] T. R. Moreman notes that after the First World War British battalions trained for conventional war were often unprepared for tribal conflict in the colonies.[63]

The fourth core element that will affect prospects for full realization of the RMA is the inescapable reality of geography and the ubiquitous nature of the elements.[64] In this context, geography is taken to mean the physical environment in which strategy is conducted. Clausewitz himself notes: 'geography and the character of the ground bear a close and ever-present relation to warfare'.[65] Terrain often shapes operations significantly. For example, G. J. Ashworth suggests that the most fundamental characteristics of urban warfare emanate from the physical environment.[66] From his study of the Russian campaign to capture Grozny in the First Chechen War, Anatol Lieven notes that urban warfare is mainly conducted at the section level and

[60] Colin S. Gray, *The Second Nuclear Age* (Boulder, 1999), 157. Similarly, Richard Betts suggests that a large conventional foe who stands at a disadvantage in the face of a digitized enemy, could escalate up to WMD as an asymmetric form of warfare: Betts, 'The Downside of the Cutting Edge', *The National Interest*, 45 (1996), 82–3. See also James R. Fitzsimonds, 'The Coming Military Revolution: Opportunities and Risks', *Parameters*, 25/2 (1995), 34.

[61] Murray and Knox, 'Conclusion: The Future Behind Us', 185.

[62] Gray, *Modern Strategy*, 179.

[63] T. R. Moreman, 'Small Wars and Imperial Policing: The British Army and the Theory and Practice of Colonial Warfare in the British Empire, 1919–1939', in Brian Holden Reid (ed.), *Military Power: Land Warfare in Theory and Practice* (London, 1997), 118.

[64] For an excellent assessment of just how inescapable geography is, see Colin S. Gray, 'Inescapable Geography', in Colin S. Gray and Geoffrey Sloan (eds), *Geopolitics: Geography and Strategy* (London, 1999), 161–77.

[65] *On War*, V, 17, p. 348. Of course, weather also can have a significant effect on operations, see N. A. M. Rodger, 'Weather, Geography and Naval Power in the Age of Sail', in Gray and Sloan, *Geopolitics*, 178–200.

[66] G. J. Ashworth, *War and the City* (London, 1991), 116–22.

highlights the significance of infantry in such an environment: 'It cannot be emphasised too strongly, therefore, that the key to success in urban warfare is good infantry'.[67] Wilson concludes that an increased emphasis on urban operations 'will likely call for a more infantry intensive force structure. Preparing for urban combat runs counter to the current planning imperative, which calls for military operations that minimise US casualties.'[68] Many of these thoughts do not fit well with the proposed RMA and indicate that the RMA is not omnipotent and cannot be applied regardless of geography. Geography can also neutralize the operational efficacy of certain war-forms. In 1941, the German army failed to replicate the success of 1940, partly due to the sheer geographic depth and width of the Soviet Union. Similarly, weather has proven to be an important influence on the conduct of operations. It played a debilitating role both in 1812 and in 1941, and a weather front exerted enough friction on Burnside's famous 'mud march' in 1862 to block his plans completely.[69] The elements have proven to be an ongoing influence on war, as NATO air operations over Kosovo and dust storms during the invasion of Iraq indicate.[70]

Certain technological, tactical, and operational innovations can offset the influence of terrain and the elements. The current RMA, in particular the exploitation of global positioning systems, has already reduced the significance of cloud cover and the featureless nature of desert terrain.[71] Yet, physical geography is so pervasive, and so varied a dimension in warfare, that its influence can never be reduced significantly. This is only intensified by the fact that the enemy can make use of geography. Indeed, this thought can be extended further to illustrate how four of the major influences on war can interact. Policy may require operations to be conducted in an environment that is less favourable to an RMA force. The same policy rationale that dictates the location for operations may also call for the utilization of infantry forces in close proximity with the enemy. This foe, taking note of both the environment and the conventional superiority of the enemy, may exploit the paradoxical nature of strategy and opt to wage asymmetrical and/or violent forms of warfare, perhaps concentrating on irregular operations (thereby utilizing the

---

[67] Anatol Lieven, 'The World Turned Upside Down', *Armed Forces Journal International*, August 1998, 40.

[68] *Preparing for Early 21st Century War: Beyond the Bottom-Up Review*, CGSC Monograph, 'Toward 2000' Series/5 (The Centre for Global Security Cooperation), 28.

[69] Harold A. Winters, with Gerald E. Galloway Jr., William J. Reynolds, and David W. Rhyne, *Battling the Elements: Weather and Terrain in the Conduct of War* (Baltimore, MD, 1998), 34–9.

[70] Williamson Murray, 'Some Thoughts on War and Geography', in Gray and Sloan, *Geopolitics*, 206, and James Meek, 'US Advance Grinds to Halt in Teeth of Storm', *The Guardian*, 26 March 2003, 1.

[71] Winters et al., *Battling the Elements*, 270, and Gray, *Modern Strategy*, 251–2.

terrain to maximize small unit actions) and/or the employment of WMD. And, of course, underlying all of the above is the fifth element of strategy. The participation and interaction of human belligerents is the foundation on which the other elements are based.

The above discussion reveals why the RMA vision will not come to pass in its entirety. An enemy, or indeed policy requirements, can impose a form of warfare that is less suited to the currently dominant vision of the RMA or 'military transformation'. Each conflict has its own complex character, and consequently the nature of war as espoused, directly or indirectly, by the RMA literature will not come to pass in its entirety. In 1998, Colonel Dick Applegate concluded that what was required was investment, not in the RMA, but in a broad range of capabilities, in order to avoid disappearing up a strategic cul-de-sac.[72] Similarly, to reject the classical works of theory too readily could have deleterious results on military culture and war preparation more generally.

## THE UNCHANGING CLIMATE OF WAR

Having explored the core elements of strategy, we can now conclude that the climate of war (a significant element of the nature of war) will not be altered by the information age. Physical violence is one of the primary characteristics that distinguishes war from other activities in grand strategy. It is, therefore, significant that this basic aspect of the nature of war has been challenged within the RMA literature. The challenge takes various forms with differing degrees of severity. At the more reasonable end of the spectrum is a greater emphasis on disruption, as opposed to destruction, as a means to victory. Such claims do not necessarily dictate an absolute end to violence, though they do seek to diminish its occurrence and severity. The more extreme comments in this argument can be found in Libicki's notion of information dominance and information-provided transparency rendering physical expressions of force redundant. Of equal significance is the potential professed for SIW. Within the RMA literature, there exists a tendency to reduce the complex activity of war to a point at which information becomes the decisive element. This proclivity is exemplified by Leonhard's *The Principles of War for the Information Age*, and

---

[72] Colonel Dick Applegate, 'Towards the Future Army', in Brian Bond and Mungo Melvin (eds), *The Nature of Future Conflict: Implications for Force Development*, The Occasional, 36 (Camberley, Strategic and Combat Studies Institute, 1998), 79.

similarly can be found at the heart of the works of Libicki and Arquilla and Ronfeldt.[73]

There are four main reasons why violence cannot be removed from the act of war. First, as noted above, strategy may require the physical destruction of enemy forces and assets. This is not to suggest that such objectives will always be appropriate. On this point, Wylie is generally correct when he notes that control should usually be achieved somewhere between extermination and not solving the problem.[74] The key to strategic judgement is identifying where that point lies and if it has been reached. Second, in some instances violent destruction of enemy forces will prove much simpler and therefore easier to execute than a finely tuned disruption campaign. Third, control will often require the physical presence of ground forces in which case the enemy will probably need to be physically removed from the territory in question. Although at times an enemy on the wrong side of information dominance will cede control, there will surely be many occasions in which the enemy will have to be physically and violently removed. An example of such a situation is the 1991 Gulf War, in which it took the coalition offensive to compel Iraqi forces to withdraw from Kuwait. Finally, because war is an interaction between at least two intelligent actors, an enemy can always reintroduce violence into a non-violent conflict. Reflecting his emphasis on the pre-eminence of battle, Clausewitz persuasively argues, 'the enemy can *frustrate everything through a successful battle*... Thus it is evident that destruction of the enemy forces is always the superior, more effective means, with which others cannot compete.' [emphasis in the original][75] In the modern world, violence can be reintroduced in the extreme form of WMD. We should also keep in mind Charles Dunlap's idea that an enemy may perceive that strategic advantage can be obtained by pursuing especially violent forms of conflict.[76] This mindset may partially explain the public display of beheadings carried out by certain groups operating within the Iraqi insurgency.

The limits of its strategic potential indicate that the challenge posed by SIW to the nature of war is less apparent than first seems to be the case. Indeed, SIW suffers from many of the problems also faced by strategic bombing.[77] In particular, the inability to convert SIW into a strategic theory of victory

---

[73] In the case of the latter, particularly guilty of this sin is Arquilla and David Ronfeldt, 'Cyberwar Is Coming'.

[74] Wylie, *Military Strategy*, 70.   [75] *On War*, I, 2, p. 97.

[76] Charles J. Dunlap, 'Sometimes the Dragon Wins: A Perspective on Information Age Warfare', in Schwartau, *Information Warfare*.

[77] David J. Lonsdale, *The Nature of War in the Information Age: Clausewitzian Future* (London, 2004), 135–78.

indicates that, though SIW does represent a new form of warfare, in most circumstances it will merely act as a supporting element to traditional forces.

The dominant factors in the above deliberations are the requirements of strategy and its dialectic nature. It is strategy that largely dictates whether and how much violence is required. War is usually violent, but strategy requires more than just the application of violence and destructive force. Indeed, a large part of the art of strategy involves making a judgement on when to apply violent and destructive force, how much, in what form, and against which targets. At times, such as in the context of a nuclear deterrence strategy, the mere threat of the use of force may suffice. Nonetheless, even in these circumstances the possibility of battle is the key. This latter point works on two levels. First, it is the potential destructive power of nuclear forces (or conventional forces in conventional deterrence) that acts as the prime mover for a deterrence strategy. Second, being prepared to fight a nuclear 'battle' (having a war-fighting doctrine), as opposed to existential deterrence, enhances the credibility of a deterrence posture.[78] In certain contingencies, such as counter-insurgency, counterterrorism, or colonial policing, a more minimal use of force may be judicious.[79] By contrast, in the face of an enemy as regular and substantial as the Third Reich, the strategy of unconditional surrender was translated into the direct application of large levels of destructive and violent force.

The optimism apparent in the RMA literature's claim to be able to reduce significantly or eliminate violence from war is matched by its visions concerning the reduction of uncertainty in conflict. Again, the significance of this issue relates to both the preparation and the conduct of war. The inherent dangers in all too readily accepting the conclusions of those who profess the coming dominance of concepts such as dominant battle-space knowledge are persuasively expressed in Wylie's assertion that 'planning for certitude is the greatest of all military mistakes'.[80]

While accepting the potential for increased transparency, it is important to correct the error in the RMA literature that too readily links success in the information environment (infosphere) to a theory of victory. Aside from the fact that strategy requires competence across a whole range of dimensions,[81] it is also important to note that certainty will in all likelihood never be achieved. This is due to at least seven main reasons. First, because war is an interaction with an intelligent enemy, certainty is reduced by the non-linear results of

---

[78] For a discussion of these issues, see Colin S. Gray, 'War-Fighting for Deterrence', *The Journal of Strategic Studies*, 7 (1984).
[79] See David E. Omissi, *Air Power and Colonial Control: The Royal Air Force 1919–1939* (Manchester, UK, 1990).
[80] Wylie, *Military Strategy*, 72.   [81] Gray, *Modern Strategy*.

the interaction itself, and also by the deliberate actions of the enemy. This latter category includes acts of deception and attacks to degrade information systems. Second, war is infused by intangible elements, many of them relating to humans and therefore of an unquantifiable nature. The third element of uncertainty is intent. Seeing the disposition of enemy forces is not the same as understanding what he will do with them, though dispositions can give an idea of intent. Fourth, information overload will complicate the task of identifying certainty. In this respect, there is an important distinction between having information and knowing the true state of affairs. We can extrapolate from the case of Pearl Harbor that the increase in information in the twenty-first century will not only see an increased production of useful information, but will also witness a growth in noise.[82] The fifth factor that maintains uncertainty relates to the geography of any particular battle-space. Uncertainty in urban warfare is not just a product of the physical structure of an urban area, but can also be produced by an enemy mingling with the civilian population. The so-called 'system-of-systems' will not solve the age-old problem of distinguishing a guerrilla from a civilian. In the many forms war can take, some do not include regular identifiable forces. The sixth problem is that of human error or bias. Ultimately, information has to be handled and used by humans. Certain commanders (a point which reflects directly on Clausewitz's concept of military genius) may not have the cognitive abilities to make effective use of the information they receive. Judgement in war is still very much an art, not a science. Finally, the level of certainty attainable will be affected by the play of chance. Warfare in the information age will not run like clockwork. In which case, a plan based on perfect and complete information can still fail because of some unforeseeable incident. In conclusion, these seven main factors that reduce certainty mean that warfare still lies in the realms of the unpredictable. Therefore, war is still an environment in which the judgement of the commander (the military genius) is paramount.

In many respects, the current RMA reflects the strategic culture of elements within the United States. This translates into a tendency to seek technological fixes to strategic problems, and the increasing removal of humans from the sharp end of war. The former of these traits could result in poor strategic performance, whereas there is some, albeit limited, rationale for the latter. There is a certain operational logic in the increased utilization of unmanned combat aircraft, stand-off munitions, and artificial intelligence. These developments offer the potential for higher operational tempo. As with many of the proposals and visions of the RMA, problems with these concepts arise if they are not considered within a strategic framework.

[82] Roberta Wohlstetter, *Pearl Harbor: Warning and Decision* (Stanford, CA, 1962).

To understand why humans must remain directly involved in the prosecution of war, we need look no further than the requirements of strategy, war's varied forms, and strategy's dialectic nature. Wylie's concept of control once again serves as the most useful frame of reference in relation to strategic needs. Wylie helpfully concludes that control is about people.[83] From this perspective, we can begin to recognize the value of infantry and ground forces more generally. To reiterate, it is only these forms of military power that can provide a prolonged, durable presence and exert control over the key issue, whether that be a population or some other resource. This is of particular importance in irregular conflicts, in which the direct protection of the population is often paramount, and when the political dimension is more pronounced. The flexibility of the man on the scene with a gun is also of merit when we consider the geography of certain battle-spaces. In this respect, urban, heavily forested, and mountainous regions are obvious candidates. In conclusion, certain strategic requirements, allied to specific geographical environments, make it almost imperative that ground forces, and infantry especially, be the leading edge in a campaign.

A fundamental point that much of the RMA literature, with its emphasis on technology and/or information operations, misses or undervalues is that strategy is about, and is done by, people.[84] Since war will continue to be characterized by violence, human involvement, uncertainty, strategic needs, and interaction with an intelligent enemy, friction and chance will invariably continue to operate as well. It can, therefore, be concluded that the information age has not de-legitimized the Clausewitzian climate and nature of war.

The current RMA will instigate many changes to the character of warfare, and many of these, such as digitization, hybrid command structures, and SIW, should be exploited. However, we should not expect these changes to alter the nature of war. In this respect, it appears that much of the theory which has been produced during the information age does not reflect the true nature of war; rather, it represents a philosophical fad which reflects political and social desires for post-heroic warfare, and which has an undue emphasis on information as the decisive dimension of strategy. Consequently, military culture, doctrine, and innovation should be based on the Clausewitzian paradigm that still represents the closest description of the true nature of war. It is, therefore, fitting to end with a quotation from *On War* that provides a superior understanding of the need to balance the requirements of the day with the universal nature of war. How this fine balance is achieved lies at the heart of strategy.

---

[83] Wylie, *Military Strategy*, 89.   [84] Gray, *Modern Strategy*, 26.

We can thus only say that the aims a belligerent adopts, and the resources he employs, must be governed by the particular characteristics of his own position, but they will also conform to the spirit of the age and to its general character. Finally, they must always be governed by the general conclusions to be drawn from the nature of war itself.[85]

[85] *On War*, VIII, 3, p. 594.

# 14

## Clausewitz and the Two Temptations of Modern Strategic Thinking

*Benoît Durieux*

One of the most striking features of the Clausewitzian bibliography is the contrast between the perennial fame of the Prussian general and the recurrent judgement that his ideas are outdated, useless, incomprehensible, or dangerous. In France, a few years before the Great War, Lieutenant-Colonel Grouard, a clever military writer, whom Raymond Aron thought to be one of the brightest of his generation, wrote: 'As for me, I must admit I have never understood the general craze for Clausewitz. I think that a military which has the *Commentaries* of Napoleon, the works of Jomini and the Archduke Charles and the *Memoirs* of Gouvion Saint-Cyr and Marmont does not need to read the works of this Prussian general to learn the art of war.'[1] To explain this discrepancy between the diffusion of Clausewitz and the opposition he regularly seems to arouse, one should pay attention to another characteristic of the Clausewitzian bibliography. The themes that have awoken the interest of the thinkers have been very different since the first edition of *Vom Kriege*. Quite naturally, the first readers devoted much attention to the recipes they found in the book that would enable them to achieve operational success. The French school that emerged after the Franco-Prussian conflict emphasized the importance of moral forces in war; they found in Clausewitz's work strong arguments to support their stress on energy and on the total destruction of the enemy. Marxists used Clausewitz's ideas about the people in arms to elaborate their theory of revolutionary war. America's thinkers of the 1970s and 1980s, led by Colonel Harry Summers, were the first to underline the importance of the paradoxical trinity and the fog of war.[2]

Indeed, there is not one single Clausewitzian theory, but several, elaborated at different periods in close conjunction with the prevalent political, strategic,

---

[1] A. Grouard, *Stratégie–Objet–Enseignement–Eléments* (Paris, 1895), 5.
[2] For a development of these readings of Clausewitz, see Hew Strachan's chapter in this book.

and military context. This is completely consonant with Clausewitz's original conception of his own work:

> Theory should be study, not doctrine [...] It is an analytical investigation leading to a close acquaintance with the subject; applied to experience—in our case, to military history—it leads to thorough familiarity with it. The closer it comes to that goal, the more it proceeds from the objective form of a science to a subjective form of a skill, the more effective it will prove in areas where the nature of the case admits no arbiter but talent.[3]

Indeed, Clausewitz does not wish to propose solutions for the military commander, because such solutions, supposing that they were possible, would limit his freedom of action. On the contrary, he wants to enable him to exercise his freedom of action: 'Theory is meant to educate the mind of the future commander, or, more accurately, to guide him in his self-education, not to accompany him to the battlefield.'[4] But this self-education is not only for the military commander. If 'the absurd difference between theory and practice'[5] is to be ended, then the correspondence between theory and practice implies the correspondence between the military commander and the military thinker. Therefore, self-education is useful to the thinker too; he should not be provided with a single theory of war, but with the means to develop his own ideas. The objective knowledge of war will give him a subjective capacity for reflection thanks to his own talent.

In other words, the differences and even the contradictions between the various conclusions the readers of Clausewitz have drawn from *On War* are but a reflection of the variety of military conflicts and the diversity of the points of view from which these conflicts have been observed. These points of view depend on time, culture, and political context; this phenomenon has been analysed through the concept of strategic culture, that is 'a distinctive and lasting set of beliefs, values and habits regarding the threat and the use of force, which have their roots in such fundamental influences as the geographical setting, history and political culture'.[6] But most of these opinions about war remain consistent with the Clausewitzian theory of the formation of military doctrine.

Conversely, these differences and contradictions of analysis regarding a strategic situation may be better understood if they are related to an overarching theory of war, so as to take into account the influence of this interaction between the thinker and his object. This is the reason why Clausewitz is

---

[3] Carl von Clausewitz, *On War*, trans. and ed. Michael Howard and Peter Paret (Princeton, NJ, 1976), II, 2, p. 141.
[4] Ibid. II, 2, p. 141.      [5] Ibid. II, 2, p. 142.
[6] Ken Booth and R. Trood, *Strategic Cultures in the Asia-Pacific Region* (London, 1999), 8.

particularly relevant in analysing the current strategic debate. The phenomenon of war is more diverse than ever: from terrorism to inter-state war, from information war to riots in rural areas, from air strikes to intifada, a loose network of limited wars has replaced the expectation of a nuclear apocalypse that characterized the Cold War. In addition, this extremely heterogeneous situation is analysed from very different perspectives. Thus, it has become obvious that Europeans and Americans tend to have different views on strategic problems, and the reason for these divergences probably goes beyond the defence of short-term interests. These differences of strategic cultures combined with the variety of conflicts on which the debate has focused make it difficult to criticize the theories of war produced by different Western countries. Moreover, it is difficult to validate the doctrines that reflect these different theories by the use of examples of operational success or failure. The needs for a theory of the theory of war therefore remain valid.

This chapter argues that Clausewitz provides the framework required to analyse the strategic debate, because he developed a theory about the theory of war. From this perspective, the different strategic doctrines and theories prevalent today illustrate two temptations, two possible readings of Clausewitz regarding the most effective way to use military force. First, the temptation of ideal war consists of using extreme, instantaneous violence in relative autonomy from the political context. Second, the temptation of non-violent war considers using limited violence for a longer time in complete continuity with the political environment. But these two temptations may be misleading. Clausewitzian theory provides interesting insights about how to understand their limits and to avoid their pitfalls.

## CLAUSEWITZ AND THE TEMPTATIONS OF MODERN STRATEGY

There is no doubt that Clausewitz wanted to achieve an overarching theory of war. To obtain this result, he had to solve the dilemma between the necessity for a philosophical approach to war and his personal experience that war is a very concrete phenomenon. In book I of *On War*, Clausewitz explains the fundamental difference between ideal war and real war. Three features differentiate the latter from the former. First, ideal war consists of using extreme violence, because of the the reciprocal action between both opponents. 'War is an act of force and there is no limit to the application of that force. Each side, therefore, compels its opponent to follow suit; a reciprocal action is started which must lead, in theory, to extremes.' In addition, war being the collision of two living forces, 'so long as I have not overthrown my opponent I am bound to fear he may overthrow me'.[7] Moreover, each adversary tends to make his efforts as great as possible, so as to ensure that he overwhelms the enemy's power of resistance. Ideal war possesses two additional features, as the following paragraphs about real war show. It is quite instantaneous and it is independent of its environment. Finally, ideal war consists of an autonomous and instantaneous discharge of extreme violence.

Conversely, real war can be considered as a limited but protracted use of violence, which is closely dependent on the political context. As Clausewitz explains it, 'war is never an isolated act', 'war does not consist of a single short blow', and 'in war the result is never final', as 'the defeated state often considers the outcome merely as a transitory evil, for which a remedy may still be found in political conditions at some later date'.[8] These three moderating factors explain in turn why belligerents do not use extreme violence.

The current strategic debate is framed by these concepts of ideal and real war. It seems to be structured around two opposing temptations. The first is the temptation of ideal war. While ideal war remains unattainable, the temptation exists to get close to this paradigm: it consists of using extreme violence so as to win as quickly as possible while limiting any external interference once war is decided. On the other side, the temptation of non-violent war aims at limiting as much as possible the level of violence to be used, but it envisages longer operations in close connection with the political and cultural environment. These two opposing trends in the strategic debate differ in three ways.

The first difference between the temptations of ideal war and of non-violent war concerns the level of violence to be used. To a certain extent, any war can be understood as a means to reach a political goal by overpowering enemy forces using the least possible number of one's own forces, but each paradigm of war attempts to reach this goal in a specific way. In the first case, the aim is to use extreme violence during a very short time, while in the second case, the limitation of violence is obtained by limiting its level.

To be sure, many quotations from Clausewitz can be used in support of the ideal war approach:

What do we mean by the defeat of the enemy? Simply the destruction of his forces, whether by death, injury or any other means—either completely or enough to make him stop fighting. Leaving aside all specific puposes of any particular engagement, the complete or partial destruction of the enemy must be regarded as the sole object of all engagements.[9]

[7] *On War*, I, 1, § 4, p. 77.     [8] Ibid. I, 1, § 9, p. 80.     [9] Ibid. IV, 3, p. 227.

Indeed, as Clausewitz puts it in the first lines of his book, 'war is thus an act of force to compel our enemy to do our will'.[10] The act of force has frequently been understood as destruction, at least of the enemy forces, and often of the enemy nation. More recently, the temptation to solve military problems by resorting to the use of extreme violence has been fuelled by several factors, among which the development of technology is central.

Not only has the power of weapons increased, but also their precision has significantly raised the probability of hitting any target at the exact time that has been chosen. Mini-nukes, stand-off weapons and unmanned combat air vehicles (UCAVs) exemplify this phenomenon. Indeed, in the concept of ideal war, the focus on extreme violence does not mean that violence will be used indiscriminately throughout the theatre of operations. It will not even be used over a wide area as it was in the Second World War, for example in the bombing of Dresden or Hiroshima. Only some very specific targets will be chosen, but those targets will be struck with an overwhelming violence that will ensure their total destruction.

In addition to technology, the influence of air power theorists has been a key factor in the development of this tendency. The concepts of 'parallel warfare' and 'shock and awe' exemplify its temptations, where destruction is the dominant principle of war. Following the same trend, John Warden's theory proposes to strike the centres of gravity of different rings he has identified in the enemy system, so as to paralyse it.[11]

While this temptation of ideal war influences any military doctrine, the stress on destruction is especially consonant with certain strategic cultures. The perception of the enemy is an important element to be taken into account. Only if the enemy is assimilated with evil can he be destroyed with extreme violence. History suggests that this pattern occurs when there is a significant difference in culture between the belligerents. Obviously, American strategic culture is especially prone to consider the adversary as the 'bad guy' to be annihilated. By contrast, the non-violent war temptation appears to be more specific to Europe. While war has always been part and parcel of Europe's culture, the slaughter the 'old' continent suffered during the first half of the twentieth century has rendered Europeans very suspicious of the use of military force. The European collective unconscious has integrated the imperative to avoid any repetition of the mechanisms that led to the First World War in 1914, just as it has absorbed the necessity never again to yield to military pressure as the Western democracies did in Munich in 1938. Beyond the perceived need to

---

[10] Ibid. I, 1, § 2, p. 75.
[11] John Warden, 'The Enemy as System', *Air Power Journal*, available HTTP<http://www.airpower.maxwell.af.iml/airchronicles/apj/warden.html> accessed 25 June 2005.

avoid major conflict as a good in itself, European strategic culture has always been shaped by the certainty that the belligerents will have to live together after the conflict. Therefore, the control of violence has become the mantra of the strategists who have conceptualized the use of military force. Obviously, this reluctance has been reinforced by the situation in which the European powers now find themselves: as Robert Kagan argues, they are no longer dominant on the international stage.[12] This concern has been progressively rationalized by the introduction of the rule of law to the battlefield. The lawful use of force is very often limited to the case of legitimate self-defence. In many respects, some Western militaries have substituted the constabulary ethic for the warrior ethic, as described by Morris Janowitz: 'The military establishment becomes a constabulary force when it is continuously prepared to act, committed to the minimum use of force.'[13] This reluctance to use violence reveals the widespread assumption that violence is unable to provide enduring solutions to problems that require political solutions. While the ideal war temptation relies on the certainty that violence is the right means to coerce the enemy, the non-violent war temptation considers that the military presence alone in the face of a sometimes violent enemy is likely to produce the same result, provided it is given sufficient time to do so.

Both temptations have a very different relation to time, and this is the second distinction between them. The temptation of ideal war envisages a very short war. Ideally, war should be an instantaneous blow against the enemy. For example, airpower theory, which is very close to the ideal war paradigm, aims at 'dominating the fourth dimension—time...[through] its ability to telescope events'.[14] Similarly, General D. A. Deptula asserts, 'Simultaneous application of force (time) across each level of war uninhibited by geography (space) describes the conduct of parallel warfare.'[15] The concept of 'first in, first out' is another example of this tendency, and is particularly representative of American society, where the volatility of public opinion has often led leaders to look for a short but decisive war. As a consequence, when the decision to wage war has been made, the war should be ended as soon as possible. The growth of media involvement has only reinforced this phenomenon. Public opinion needs quick and spectacular action. Terrorist movements have understood this principle, and the 9/11 destruction of the twin towers is a vivid example of a terrorist attack fulfilling the criteria for an ideal war: it was

[12] Robert Kagan, *La puissance et la faiblesse* (Paris, 2003), 20.
[13] Morris Janowitz, *The Professional Soldier* (New York, 1960), 430.
[14] Philip Meilinger, *The Paths to Heaven: The Evolution of Airpower Theory* (Maxwell, 1977), 8.
[15] D. A. Deptula, *Effect-based Operations: Change in the Nature of Warfare* (Arlington, VA, 2001), 5.

extremely violent, it was instantaneous, and no 'political' authority on the part of the terrorist organization was able to interfere once the decision had been made to launch the attack.

By contrast, the non-violent war temptation accepts the perspective of an enduring military action. Many peacekeeping operations exemplify this phenomenon, with military forces remaining deployed for decades, as is the case in Lebanon or Cyprus.

The Clausewitzian theory of attack and defence provides useful insights into this temporal dimension of the problem. The ideal war temptation relates back to an image of decisive offensive war, whereas the non-violent war temptation is much closer to the rationale of defence. The passage of *On War* in which Clausewitz develops his ideas about defence is probably one of the most brilliant and significant of the book. He explains what the function of time is in war:

The essence of defence lies in parrying the attack. This in turn implies waiting, which for us is the main feature of defence and also its chief advantage. [...] The nature of the matter demands that so much importance should be attached to waiting. [...] Waiting is such a fundamental feature of all warfare that war is hardly conceivable without it.[16]

In fact, the feature of Clausewitzian theory which the proponent of non-violent war implicitly emphasizes is the exploitation of the cyclical variations of the enemy's morale. Addressing the problem of coercion, Clausewitz stresses that 'the most important method, judging from the frequency of its use is to wear down the enemy. [...] Wearing down the enemy in a conflict means using the duration of the war to bring about a gradual exhaustion of his physical and moral resistance.'[17]

Thus both temptations refer to different ideas about how to achieve coercion. According to the ideal war temptation, coercion is obtained through strategies of punishment, annihilation, or paralysis. Violence is supposed to have a direct impact on the will of the enemy. On the contrary, the non-violent war proponents hold time as the main factor in coercion. As defence consists of waiting for the most favourable moment to strike a blow, war will consist of waiting until the adversary is morally weak enough to use only a small amount of violence and have him sign the peace.

Third and finally, these two concepts of war rely on a very distinctive set of beliefs about the role of politics. This problem is hardly new; the question of the relationship between the prince and the general is one of the oldest issues of military theory. However, while in Western democracies no one contests the primacy of the civilian authority, the way this primacy

---

[16] *On War*, VI, 8, p. 380.   [17] Ibid. I, 2, p. 93.

should be exercised has never been clearly defined. Two different approaches can be observed, which correspond to the two temptations of ideal and non-violent war.

In the ideal war temptation, war is conceived in a very Jominian way. Once war is decided, there should be no further political interference in the conduct of operations. Thus, the sharing of power between the government and the military commander is sequential: the former makes the decision to wage war and to sign the peace treaty, but between those two events the military commander bears the whole responsibility for the campaign. Therefore, military considerations take precedence over political considerations during this period.

The non-violent war temptation relies on the illusion of a seamless continuity between the policy and the military action. Each single military action will be planned in accordance with political guidance, while the result of each military action will influence policy. The principle on which the non-violent war temptation relies consists of alternating diplomatic negotiations and military gestures, so as to coerce the opponent while limiting as much as possible the amount of violence to be used.

The different ways these two temptations of ideal and non-violent war relate to politics may illustrate one of the trickiest problems in the translation of *Vom Kriege*. Is war the continuation of 'politics' by other means or the continuation of 'policy'? Michael Howard and Peter Paret chose the word 'policy', especially because of the pejorative connotation of 'politics'. In fact, 'policy' seems to be more appropriate to the concept of conflict that stems from the ideal war temptation. In this case, war is merely an instrument designed to reach a political aim, that has been decided before the military action. This political aim is to be attained by the military, whatever the means. Conversely, 'politics' echoes the non-violent war temptation, in which the military action is considered as a particular mode in a relationship. Rather than 'politics', the best term could be 'political bargaining' or 'political negotiation': the famous sentence could in this case be translated as: 'war is the continuation of political negotiation by other means'.

Clausewitz explains at great length that the difference between ideal war and real war is due to the existence of friction: 'We have identified danger, physical exertion, intelligence, and friction as the elements that coalesce to form the atmosphere of war, and turn into a medium that impedes activity. In their restrictive effects, they can be grouped into a single concept of general friction'.[18] It is therefore quite natural that both schools of

---

[18] *On War*, I, 8, p. 122.

thought have different appreciations of the reality and the importance of this phenomenon.

Very coherently, the advocates of the ideal war temptation have argued that friction is not a perennial feature of war. More specifically, they have drawn attention to the promises of technology to suppress the fog of war. At the tactical level, network-centric warfare and the notion of a 'common operational picture' exemplify the focus of modern military doctrine on the means to eliminate any source of uncertainty in war. At higher levels, technology is supposed to provides the means no longer to be entangled with the enemy in close combat. Stand-off strikes are said to allow not only quick and decisive victories, but also to avoid any hazardous and uncontrollable combat with the enemy. Ideal war doctrines rely on immaterial rather than material superiority through advanced technology and sophisticated doctrine. Information dominance is supposed to provide the means to be able to strike certain and precise blows.[19]

The philosophy of the non-violent war temptation is at odds with that of the ideal war proponents. Not only does it not underestimate the importance of friction, but also it considers it to be the main factor that can procure success in war. This school emphasizes the importance of moral virtues. In an environment characterized by danger, uncertainty, hazard and physical fatigue, human resistance, courage, and *coup d'oeil* are the dominant qualities. In a relationship with the enemy that excludes any rational calculation, the non-violent trend underlines the importance of interaction and morale, as well as the decisive superiority of political intercourse to persuade the adversary to yield. The opposition between these two temptations has been clearly illustrated during recent conflicts. In his book dealing with the Kosovo crisis of 1999, General Wesley Clark explains the debates he had with the Europeans and his arguments precisely correspond to the various criteria we have identified to differentiate ideal war and non-violent war, that is time, decisive force, political influence, and chance:

Was this the European way of war, then, to begin without assurance of decisive force, hoping to break the enemy's will, and then pick your way toward success at a cost of increased time and casualties? Armies had fought in the manner before and won. But I would have to resist. The ground campaign would have to be swift and decisive—for reason of timing, maximizing our chances for operational success, and minimizing the political risks.[20]

---

[19] On these points, see David Lonsdale's chapter in this book.
[20] Wesley Clark, *Waging Modern War* (New York, 2001), 318–19.

## USING CLAUSEWITZ TO RESIST THE TEMPTATIONS OF MODERN STRATEGY

One of the most important characteristics of Clausewitz's thinking is his permament concern for the realism of theory, and therefore the remarkably balanced position he adopts on most of the important theoretical debates about war. More specifically, his theory provides many arguments to point out the flaws in both the temptations which structure the current strategic debate.

For Clausewitz, ideal war was not a real concept. Book I contains all the relevant arguments. 'War does not consist of a single short blow.'[21] 'At this stage, it is enough to show that the very nature of war impedes the simultaneous concentration of all forces.'[22] In addition, his theory provides the elements that expose the real loopholes in the ideal war temptation and its practical consequences.

First, the ideal war model relies on destruction. But the concept of destruction in *On War* is much more subtle than some caricatured images of Clausewitz have generally suggested. Many important aspects of Clausewitz's theory deserve to be underlined in this regard. First, destruction is always a means designed to reach an end, which is the purpose of an engagement. And the goal of that engagement remains the means to reach the political end, not the annihilation of the enemy. It can get close to this extremity of violence, but only in the historical circumstances of total war. 'The more powerful and inspiring the motives for war, the more they affect the belligerent nations and the fiercer the tensions that precede the outbreak, the closer will war approach its abstract concept, the more important will be the destruction of the enemy.'[23]

Second, when Clausewitz advocates actual destruction, he means something very specific: 'The fighting forces must be destroyed: that is, they must be put in such a condition that they can no longer carry on the fight. Whenever we use the phrase "destruction of the enemy's forces" this alone is what we mean.'[24] Besides, to put the enemy forces in such a condition that they can no longer carry on the fight, Clausewitz stresses the importance of attacking the enemy's will as much as his physical capabilities.

Third, the ideal war temptation relies on the dream that the bloody reality of a protracted conflict can be avoided by achieving an instantaneous success. But this goal contradicts one of Clausewitz's main points. The aim of military action is to have the enemy admit his defeat; this enemy concession is supposed to be based on a prospective cost–benefit analysis. The aim of the ideal

---

[21] *On War*, I, 1, § 8, p. 79.  [22] Ibid. I, 1, § 8, p. 80.  [23] Ibid. I, 1, § 25, p. 87.
[24] Ibid. I, 2, p. 90.

war approach is to have the enemy concede defeat, without his taking account of the political risks associated with a protracted campaign. Obviously, these two ends are contradictory. As Thomas Schelling argued, bargaining is the art of commitment.[25] The instantaneous character of ideal war makes it extremely difficult to demonstrate a political commitment. Indeed, it preserves complete freedom of action for the future; it removes most risks of being entangled in a protracted conflict. However, there is an obvious contradiction between this tactical advantage and the resulting political drawback. If the political authority can suspend military action at any time, the adversary can hope that is exactly what will happen. Therefore, this flexibility increases the difficulty of communicating one's commitment.

In addition, the ideal war approach can be counterproductive. By inflicting immediate destruction, it denies the enemy any flexibility and deprives him of a political escape route. This implicit contradiction figures strongly in John Warden's theory. He argues, 'unless the stakes in the war are very high, most states will make desired concessions when their power-generation system is put under sufficient pressure or actually destroyed'.[26] In fact, it is arguably the very act of striking at vital centres such as power-generation systems that raises the stakes in the conflict. In other words, there is a basic contradiction between attempting to influence the rational cost–benefit analysis of the enemy government and simultaneously giving to the conflict the characteristics of a nearly total war that precisely excludes any cost–benefit calculus. Indeed, the ideal war model relies on the use of extreme violence against a very limited number of important targets; the theory of strategic paralysis is significant in this regard. Clausewitz answered that argument with considerable foresight, when he protested against

the highly sophisticated theory that supposes it is possible for a particularly ingenious method of inflicting minor direct damage on the enemy's forces to lead to major indirect destruction; or that claim to produce, by means of limited but skillfully applied blows, such paralysis of the enemy's forces and control of his will power as to constitute a significant shortcut to victory.[27]

It is therefore likely that a campaign conducted in accordance with the ideal war approach will lead to major destruction. As a consequence, this approach brings about the risk of accelerating escalation to the extremes of violence, and that is part and parcel of its philosophy.

This unintended result is nothing but one of the manifestations of the phenomenon of friction that the ideal war temptation tends to deny. Indeed,

---

[25] Thomas Schelling, *Arms and Influence* (New Haven, CT, 1966), 43.
[26] John Warden, 'The Enemy as System', 7.     [27] *On War*, IV, 3, p. 228.

the ambition to eliminate friction seems doomed to failure, as Barry Watts has brilliantly demonstrated. By taking historical examples and relying on arguments drawn from the theories of chaos and non-linearity, he made a strong argument to 'build a case for the conclusion that general friction will continue to be central to future warfare regardless of technological changes in the means of combat'.[28]

Thus, the ideal war temptation has adverse consequences on the doctrines it influences. Its focus on instantaneous action makes it ineffective in bringing about the enemy's submission. This is directly linked with its disconnection from the political rationale. Indeed, to a certain extent, time is the dimension of politics, as politics consists of persuading one's interlocutor to change his mind through negotiation. In addition, the use of extreme destruction increases the risk of fuelling the escalation to the extremes of violence; indeed, short of total destruction of the enemy, no action can guarantee political success.

If Clausewitz is a persuasive critic of the ideal war temptation, he has as trenchant observations to make about the temptation of non-violent war, and its attendant risks. One of the primary aims of Clausewitz's writing was to react against the form of war that had prevailed during the eighteenth century, which consisted of manoeuvring so as to obtain sucess without fighting a battle. The words he pronounced two centuries ago seem to characterize some modern theories of military action:

> Governments and commanders have always tried to find ways of avoiding a decisive battle and of reaching their goals by other means or of quietly abandoning it. Historians and theorists have taken great pains, when describing such campaigns and conflicts, to point out that other means not only served the purpose as well as a battle that was never fought, but were indeed evidence of higher skill. This line of thought had brought us almost to the point of regarding, in the economy of war, battle as a kind of evil brought about by mistake—a morbid manifestation to which an othodox, correctly managed war should never have to resort. [...] Recent history has scattered such nonsense to the winds. Still, one cannot be certain that it will not recur here or there for shorter or longer periods, betray those responsible into mistakes which, because they cater to weakness, cater to human nature.[29]

Clausewitz suggests two kinds of arguments to support his opinion. First, the general who is reluctant to commit his troops in a violent decisive battle will most probably be defeated by a more determined enemy:

---

[28] Barry Watts, *Clausewitzian Friction and Future War*, McNair Paper 52 (Washington, 1996), 131.

[29] *On War*, IV, 12, p. 269.

We are not interested in generals who win victories without bloodshed. The fact that slaughter is a horrifying spectacle must make us take war more seriously, but not provide an excuse for gradually blunting our swords in the name of humanity. Sooner or later someone will come along with a sharp sword and hack off our arms.[30]

The second loophole in the non-violent war temptation lies in its inability to show the political commitment of the belligerent who has made the decision to launch a military action. His commitment is arguably stronger than the commitment of the side that relies on the ideal war model, as it implicitly accepts a protracted military campaign. But the reluctance to accept casualties is opposed to the necessity to show a strong resolve. The determination of Serb President Milošević to resist NATO pressure during the Kosovo conflict in 1999 was certainly fuelled by the reluctance of the Western countries to resort to ground attack. The failure of several peacekeeping missions mandated by the United Nations can be attributed to the limitations placed on military options by restrictive rules of engagement.

In addition, the non-violent war approach, if it is to work, needs both appropriate resources, and enough of them, in order to have some capacity for what is termed 'escalation dominance'. The recurrent difficulty of obtaining sufficient resources from the different nations that take part in multinational operations makes it equally difficult to ensure the credibility of such forces.

This self-limitation in the use of violence has often induced the adversary to raise his own level of violence so as to take the advantage. The wars in the former Yugoslavia exemplified this phenomenon. The inability of the United Nations forces to use military force not only resulted in the failure to impose a peace settlement, but also permitted the belligerents to use violence against civilians.

Therefore, both ideal war and non-violent war temptations appear to be at odds with the ideas of Clausewitz. In fact, these two temptations have one common feature. They are the temptation to avoid violence in war, and finally war itself, either by limiting the time violence is to be used, or by limiting the level of violence. Not only are they both rarely effective in bringing about the desired political outcome, but they often result in the use of a higher overall amount of violence in the conflict. Today, as it did two centuries ago, Clausewitzian theory is a useful conceptual base for discarding theories that conceive of war as a rapid or cheap remedy for a political problem.

---

[30] Ibid. IV, 11, p. 260.

## CLAUSEWITZ AND BALANCING THE TWO TEMPTATIONS

Most current strategic theories and military doctrines can be associated with one of the two temptations of ideal and non-violent war. This highlights the importance of violence in the theory of war. Clausewitz has often been described as an advocate of total war. This is partly because of the inability of many readers to understand the difference between ideal and real war. But the place of violence in the theory of the Prussian general probably goes beyond this distinction. He had participated in most of the campaigns of the Napoleonic era. He knew how ugly war could be: 'The fact that slaughter is a horrifying spectacle must make us take war more seriously.'[31] His theory suggests a balanced conclusion. On the one hand, the decision to wage war is always a very serious one because it is impossible to know how the conflict is to evolve. The escalation to extremes is bound to be the dominant trend in conflicts. Therefore, raising the level of violence too much may have tragic consequences. On the other hand, it is sometimes necessary to take the difficult decision to wage war; in this case, Clausewitz warned of the dangers of underestimating the level of violence that will be necessary. It could lead to a dramatic military failure and, in turn, to a human tragedy.

The question remains: how do we calibrate the level of violence to the political goal pursued? The answer cannot be only a compromise between the temptation of ideal war and the temptation of non-violent war, as those two temptations are not two opposite hypotheses but two versions of the natural trend to avoid a long and violent war.

The solution arguably lies in the role of politics in war. The paradoxical trinity is one of the most original points of Clausewitz's theory. The supremacy of the political pole over the military pole has been rightly underlined as a major argument in Clausewitz. But this supremacy is meaningless unless it is associated with a certain separation between the political and military institutions. This separation entails in turn a certain autonomy, which is consistent with the fact that each pole of the trinity is characterized by a different quality: chance and courage for the military, rationality for the government, and passion for the people. The relation between the three poles of the trinity is a mix of control and independence.

This separation is a central element in the management of violence in war. The military commander must be, to a certain extent, free to decide which level of violence he needs to use, depending on the tactical situation in the field. As that freedom of action will inevitably be circumscribed by rules of engagement, the key task of the commander is therefore to make it clear to the

---

[31] *On War*, IV, 11, p. 260.

political leader which rules of engagement are appropriate for the conditions in which he must deploy. Military action in the field resorts more easily to the model of attack, as attack implies using violence against the adversary. In fact, the paradigm of ideal war—i.e. an autonomous, instantaneous, and extremely violent action—is arguably more consistent with the fighting at the lowest echelon than with the conduct of war at the political or even operational level. But the military commander should be permanently concerned not to come too close to the ideal war model, though that will be his natural temptation, so as to limit the escalation to the extremes of violence.

Conversely, the political side of the conduct of war is probably more easily comparable with defence, as it consists of wearing down the enemy, that is of 'using the duration of the war to bring about a gradual exhaustion of his physical and moral resistance',[32] so as to have the enemy accept the desired political outcome. The political leader has the possibility of limiting the level of violence that will be used, because he is protected from the sentiments of fear, desire for revenge and anger that reigns over the battlefield. But the political leader should also be permanently concerned not to come too close to the non-violent war model, once he has decided to wage war. Although a natural temptation, this model is ineffective and risky. The military operation in eastern Slavonia in 1997 is a good example of a successful mission. The force had a strong mandate, sufficient forces and of the right type. It was able therefore to dislodge Serb militias from an oil field, a particularly important operational and economic target, without a shot being fired.

As a conclusion, the two temptations that threaten the efficiency of modern military action—the ideal war paradigm and the non-violent war paradigm—arise from the difficulty of recognizing the necessity for a certain separation of the military and the political authorities. The reason for this difficulty may certainly be ascribed to developments in the technologies of communication and the media. On the one hand, this phenomenon explains why some theories of war give too much of a military role to the political authority, which results in the ideal war paradigm. On the other hand, it explains why some other theories give too much of a political role to the military commander, which results in the non-violent war paradigm. In any case, Clausewitz will not provide a solution for winning the war. But he remains a sure guide in avoiding most major failures in the use of military force. He reminds us that war is never desirable but sometimes necessary.

---

[32] Ibid., I, 2, p. 93.

# 15

# Civil–Military Relations and Democracies

*Wilfried von Bredow*

Modern societies, especially democracies, seem to have difficulties with their armed forces, and the armed forces seem to have difficulties finding a suitable place in the network of organizations in modern democracies. On the one hand, the military functions as an agent of modernization. In this process, however, the meaning of violence in social and political conflict, and the roles of the armed forces and of warfare are losing some of their former political relevance. Even if we do not subscribe to the idea of 'democratic peace',[1] we have to admit that at the beginning of the twenty-first century modern (mostly Western) democracies, with one notable exception, are less inclined to use their armed forces for purposes of conflict management and conflict solution. This trend, if it is a trend, invites us to reconsider both the interplay between politics and war, and the current state of civil–military relations in Western societies in particular.

Carl von Clausewitz was a thorough observer of the interplay between politics and war. Although his famous remarks about the primacy of politics refer to the pre-democratic societies of the eighteenth century, they implicitly form the nucleus of a theory of civil–military relations in democratic societies. Taking Clausewitz's observations as a point of departure, this chapter sketches the outline of that theory in the light of recent developments both within modern societies and on the international and transnational levels.

## VIOLENCE, ORGANIZED VIOLENCE, AND ORDER

Violence in its virtual and real forms indicates the fragility of any web of order between human beings. In social and political relations, violence does not mark the breakdown of order, but functions as an important part of it. Only

---

[1] Spencer R. Weart, *Never at War: Why Democracies Will Not Fight One Another* (New Haven, CT, 1998).

eruptive and spontaneous violence endangers the emerging or existing order and, if it is not contained, may cause fatal damage to it.

Containing and controlling violence is one of the permanent challenges for social organizations that are responsible for the collective survival of people (families, clans, communities, and states). The modern territorial state is unthinkable without its successful claim on the monopoly of legitimized violence. It is only with this concentration and organization of violence that the latent violence between individuals and groups within a state can be controlled, channelled, and defused. In a functioning state, violence is concentrated in public organizations like the police, the gendarmerie, and the armed forces. The emergence of organized violence outside the public sphere is an indicator of problems of legitimation that the state has to face. A state whose political system is unable to contain and control violence between its citizens and which has to concede the existence of organizations which promote violence beyond its reach is doomed to fail.

Violence between states is deeply embedded in the structure of international systems. An international system is not viable without a minimum of order, accepted by its member-states. Ideally, the acceptance of an international system permanently increases and thus expands the quantity and quality of codes, norms, rules, and regulations for the international behaviour of the member-states. One of the aims of this process is to minimize interstate violence.

In a state-centred international system, organized violence is a phenomenon between states only. International systems have *never* been exclusively state-centred, and especially today a growing number of non-state actors characterize the current international system. Some observers see the future of the modern state in rather bleak terms. They predict the decline or even the fall of the state—both as the dominant actor in international relations and as the pillar of the order of violence. For Susan Strange the 'perceived need for the state as an institution necessary to defend society against violence within or beyond its territory still exists, but in many societies at a much lower level'.[2] Martin van Creveld's study of the rise and fall of the state is conceived as a kind of dirge for the modern state.[3] In his view, the retreat of the state from the position of monopolist of organized violence creates growing security problems at both the centres and the peripheries of the planet.

Other observers predict a brighter future for the peaceful development of international relations with or without strong states. In their eyes, democratic societies neither want nor need organized violence to flourish. Because of

---

[2] Susan Strange, *The Retreat of the State: the Diffusion of Power in the World Economy* (Cambridge, 1996), 73.
[3] Martin van Creveld, *The Rise and Fall of the State* (Cambridge, 1999).

the democratization of the international system, traditional inter-state wars at least will occur less and less. Democratic structures within a state encourage the strengthening of peaceful and non-violent means of communication with other states. Trading states are non-military states.[4] These two perspectives contradict each other to a certain degree, but their proponents can find sufficient data to support their respective views.

A third perspective on the future of organized violence tries to combine the other two and to emphasize the considerable difficulties emerging from the pressure of globalization on the current international system. The rearrangement of the international system, not only on the state-centred but also on the non-state level, encourages all kinds of violent moves. It is therefore necessary to expand and to strengthen the international acceptance of an order of violence that concentrates on two aims. First, it should minimize the amount of organized violence in the international system by an array of measures ranging from arms control and partial disarmament to the peaceful settlement of conflicts and incentives for non-violent behaviour. Second, it should be prepared to punish the deviant behaviour of outsiders and rogue actors, if necessary with military means that are both effective and based on a multinational consent. The international order of violence is, more than ever before, a political concern of the global community.

## ORGANIZED VIOLENCE AND POLITICAL GOALS

Any group that strives for longevity must earmark some of its resources in order to sustain its collective interest. The group has to develop a policy. Policies are actions (and frameworks for actions) designed to guarantee the well-being and the survival of the group. Internal and external dimensions of policy are often studied separately, but in fact they overlap and complement each other.

Not always, but very often, the collective interest of a group is challenged by other groups and their respective collective interests. In many cases, the competition between different groups is characterized by the use of organized violence (at least it was in the past). Organized violence functions as a means to help achieve the group's collective goals. Evidently, this relationship of means and goals does not depend on the size and the shape of the group. Nor does it depend on the sophistication of the group's division of labour—violence is organized in very different ways.

[4] Richard Rosecrance, *The Rise of the Trading State* (New York, 1986).

The relationship between organized violence and political authority is part of the general relationship between war and politics. According to Clausewitz, 'war is not merely an act of policy but a true political instrument'.[5] War occurs as the violent clash of interests between two or more collective actors. Each of them acts or reacts after a moment in which it is necessary to make a *political* decision. One main factor in the decision to risk war is the perceived strength of the organization for waging war, the armed forces. The armed forces are an instrument in the hands of the political decision-makers.

Some critics of Clausewitz point to the socio-political environment in which he lived and conclude that his observations about the nature of war and the relationship between the political and the military spheres of society are of limited value for the present. In their view, his arguments are confined to a late-absolutist state system. Although we have to acknowledge that certain of his opinions and perspectives have lost parts of their relevance over time, it would be wrong to reduce Clausewitz to the dimension of a defunct *Zeitgeist*. Nobody would seriously discount Kant's ideas about eternal peace because he lacked experience of modern-style democracy.

The concept of war being a consequence of conflicting political interests is not a concept only for the late eighteenth century, but for any political actor with some internal stability. The core of Clausewitz's concept of war is not unbound violence but the idea of politics as the source of war and its guiding principle.[6] This insight transcends the peculiarities of a specific historic era and proves its explanatory power about different forms of war in different cultural contexts and at different times.

Violence can also be a spontaneous expression of anger or the result of a destructive urge for superiority. However, when it is organized in forms of trained collectives, it is usually designed for use as an instrument to achieve certain goals. The definition of these goals and the decision to use organized violence or other instruments to realize them is a political decision. Whoever is in charge, and is responsible for this decision, decides in political terms. However, violence does not lose its character when used as a political instrument. The danger that violence will get out of the hands of its organizers is always lurking behind the attempts to contain, to channel, and to control violence.[7]

---

[5] Carl von Clausewitz, *On War*, trans. and ed. Michael Howard and Peter Paret (Princeton, NJ, 1989), I, 1, § 24, p. 87.

[6] Raymond Aron, *Clausewitz. Den Krieg denken* (Frankfurt am M., 1980; first published in 1976), 159.

[7] Wolfgang Sofsky, *Traktat über die Gewalt* (Frankfurt am M., 1996). Sofsky reminds us that war is very often not a fight between warriors but a massacre of unarmed people. This is unfortunately true. In some cases, these actions are based on political decisions; in others, they are just the expression of violence running amok. The canon of the *ius in bello* stigmatizes such actions as criminal behaviour.

The differences between controlled and uncontrolled violence were clearly visible in the seventeenth and eighteenth centuries, the era which saw the emergence of the modern state in Europe. The Thirty Years War (1618–48) was experienced by contemporaries as a war during which the use of violence was emancipated from political guidance and fostered lawlessness— with disastrous consequences for individuals and societies in central Europe. Therefore, in the absolutist era following the peace of Westphalia in 1648, with its inauguration of the so-called 'Westphalian system', the armed forces were put into the firm hands of the monarch, so that he could use them as a tool to pursue the interests of the state.

It is important to note that even in 'militaristic' societies like Prussia, the armed forces, although expensive and in a way dominant in civil society, did not really influence the definition of the interests pursued by the king. Instead, they were the instrument he used to develop the country and to enhance its political influence in the region.

After 1789 and the decline of aristocratic influence in Europe's political landscapes, some political philosophers, like Auguste Comte, expected the role of organized interstate violence to decrease in the same way as the level of internal violence had decreased as a result of the rise of the modern state. This was, of course, much too optimistic. On the contrary, the nineteenth century and the first half of the twentieth century saw an enormous expansion in the armed forces and, in some places, a militarization of civil society. However, even under the auspices of extreme nationalism and totalitarian rule or in cases of anarchist action[8] against the social order, the use of organized violence rarely lost its instrumental character.

Panajotis Kondylis reminds us that this juxtaposition of war and politics must not be translated into the pseudo-liberal credo that the political or civil agents are necessarily less belligerent than the military leadership. The assumption that strong civilian control over the military automatically implies a more cooperative and less militant policy has been too often proved wrong.[9] Clausewitz himself cautioned such expectations by pointing to the fact that policy 'can err, subserve the ambitions, private interests, and vanity of those in power'.[10]

In the twentieth century, a whole range of authors has contested Clausewitz's reflections on the political character of war and the primacy of the

---

[8] In most anarchist action, the political goal of the terrorists is the demonstration of the vulnerability of law and order. Sometimes anarchists followed a strategy of symbolic politics. This is impressively described in Joseph Conrad's novel *The Secret Agent* (first published in 1907).

[9] Panajotis Kondylis, *Theorie des Krieges. Clausewitz–Marx–Engels–Lenin* (Stuttgart, 1988), 103–15.

[10] *On War*, VIII, 6B, pp. 606–7.

political authority over the military commander. They emphasize the autonomy of violence—out of opposite perspectives. In 1935, the German general, Erich Ludendorff, published his study on total war.[11] In his view, total war is just the opposite of what Clausewitz thought about the nature of war. He restricts Clausewitz's term 'policy' to 'foreign policy' and argues that in times of total war the most important aspect of any policy is domestic policy, that is a policy which mobilizes every single person and all of society's resources for the purpose of war. Thus, policy becomes an instrument of the preparation for war. Politicians and the government have to follow the guidelines of the supreme commander who is therefore the genuine leader of the country and the people.[12] Ludendorff's argument was self-serving, for he wanted to remodel his role in the First World War in the collective memory of the Germans by presenting the history of a virtual German victory in that war. His diatribe against Clausewitz reveals a rather gruesome *political* perspective, for the supreme commander as the genuine leader of the country is, of course, a political leader.

Other opponents of Clausewitz point to the nuclear arms race in the Cold War and argue that through mutual assured destruction an East–West war would have destroyed the whole planet. Under such conditions, war can no longer be regarded as a rational option. Therefore, they conclude, Clausewitz's famous formula is no longer valuable.[13] This conclusion is wrong, for the era of East–West nuclear bipolarity was characterized by a strong primacy of the political over the military. President Harry S. Truman's decision to reject General Douglas MacArthur's request to introduce nuclear weapons into the Korean War and the management of the Cuban missile crisis, to name just the most dramatic events, each demonstrates the validity of Clausewitz's concept of war as a political instrument. This concept is not invalidated if political decision-makers decide to avoid war, to start arms control negotiations, and to accept negotiated agreements to reduce the level of armaments.

A third group of critics emphasizes the seemingly non-political aspects of warfare, the attraction of cruelty and torture for some warriors, the existential hatred between fighting soldiers, or the sudden bouts of solidarity between enemies in the trenches—all this, they contend, cannot be explained in political terms. Clausewitz himself pointed to this dimension of war at the end of book I, chapter 1: 'As a total phenomenon its dominant tendencies always make war a paradoxical trinity—composed of primordial violence, hatred,

[11] Erich Ludendorff, *Der totale Krieg* (München, 1935).   [12] Ibid. 115–19.
[13] This phrase was a kind of mantra among critics of nuclear strategy from the 1960s to the end of the East–West conflict. See, among others, Anatol Rapoport, 'Tolstoi und Clausewitz. Zwei Konfliktmodelle und ihre Abwandlungen', *Atomzeitalter*, 9 (1966), 257–66.

and enmity, which are to be regarded as blind natural force; of the play of chance and probability within which the creative spirit is free to roam; and of its element of subordination, as an instrument of policy, which makes it subject to reason alone.'[14]

These three aspects, related by Clausewitz to the people, the military commander and the armed forces, and the government, are present in every war. The history of warfare teaches us the melancholy lesson that the balance between them is often endangered. In the course of history, we also meet certain military cultures, which nurture primordial violence as an individual and collective virtue. Even in the most violence-prone groups and societies, however, political imperatives (sometimes in the guise of economic ambitions) are present and of decisive importance.[15]

## NATIONALIZATION AND PROFESSIONALIZATION

Charles Tilly proposes dividing Europe's history over the last ten centuries into four types of warfare, each reflecting state organization and the basis for the allegiance of the armed forces:

- patrimonialism (up to the fifteenth century)
- brokerage (roughly from the fifteenth to the seventeenth centuries)
- nationalization (from the eighteenth to the nineteenth centuries)
- specialization (from approximately the mid-nineteenth century to the recent past)[16]

The last two of these types are of special interest here. 'Nationalization' describes a period when states created mass armed forces, which were drawn increasingly from their own national populations. The organization of the armed forces became part of the state's administrative structure. There are (with ongoing arguments about the different types and models) at least two clearly distinguishable ways of nationalizing the armed forces, depending on the militarist or civic orientation of the dominant political culture. A strange, backward looking, but equally modernist militarism characterizes the Prussian and German development of civil–military relations in the

---

[14] *On War*, I, 1, § 28, p. 89. For a fuller discussion of the 'trinity', see Christopher Bassford's chapter in this book.
[15] See Andreas Herberg-Rothe, 'Primacy of "Politics" or "Culture" over War in a Modern World: Clausewitz Needs a Sophisticated Interpretation', *Defense Analysis*, 17 (2001), 175–86.
[16] Charles Tilly, *Coercion, Capital, and European States, AD 990–1990* (Oxford, 1990), 29.

nineteenth century and up to the end of the Second World War.[17] In many other Western states of that period, notably in the United States, armed forces with effective military discipline and technologically advanced weapons coexisted with emerging democratic political institutions. Morris Janowitz even contends that 'particular forms of military service can serve and have served as a form of effective civic education'.[18] The American model of the 'citizen soldier' earned its mythical aura in the American Revolution and survived for a long period in the form of militia duty. It re-emerged in the first half of the twentieth century in concepts like a citizen army based on universal military training, proclaimed by General John McAuley Palmer, or the 'Plattsburg movement', inaugurated by General Leonard Wood, or the Reserve Officer Training Corps (ROTC) programmes established since 1916.[19]

The German model of *Staatsbürger in Uniform*[20] was introduced for the newly founded Bundeswehr in 1955. It builds on the ideas of the Prussian reform movement (Scharnhorst, Gneisenau and others, including Clausewitz) during and after the wars against Napoleon. Its main feature is the granting of an unusually high number of democratic rights to the soldiers. They should perceive themselves as citizens and as an integrated part of democratic society: 'citizen soldier' and *Staatsbürger in Uniform* are models for a military man with strong allegiance both to the nation and to the various and developing forms of democracy. The most important task of the armed forces is the defence of the country and the protection of its peaceful society. This task should not be left to a group of experts in violence, for it is the most distinguished obligation of every (male) citizen to participate in the protection of the nation and its determination to be independent. The idea of military service as a national duty was established by the American Revolution and the French *levée en masse*. The myth of the more or less peaceful mass army had its dark side from its birth, and it was put in jeopardy by Napoleon. Nonetheless, from the French Revolution until after the Second World War, mass armed forces were regarded as the most efficient form of the military. Professional standards and political norms and values were amalgamated in the name of nationalism.

---

[17] Volker Berghahn, *Militarism: The History of an International Debate 1861–1979* (New York, 1982); Wilfried von Bredow, *Moderner Militarismus: Analyse und Kritik* (Stuttgart, 1983), 23–45.

[18] Morris Janowitz, *The Reconstruction of Patriotism: Education for Civic Consciousness* (Chicago, IL, 1983), 14.

[19] Meyer Kestnbaum, 'Citizenship and Compulsory Military Service: The Revolutionary Origins of Conscription in the United States', *Armed Forces and Society*, 27 (2000), 7–36.

[20] The civil executive and Parliament introduced the concept of the *Staatsbürger in Uniform* into the armed forces of the Federal Republic of Germany in order to express the tight democratic control of the military.

The anti-colonial wars of liberation in the twentieth century could rely on the mobilizing force of this nationalism, if the political and military leaders were able to paint themselves as national leaders.[21] Many of these wars started with the combined politico-military activities of a small group of partisans, guerrillas, or freedom fighters. In nearly all of them, the number of combatants involved (often disguised) expanded over time, and some of these wars eventually became wars of the people.

The armed forces and military service played an important role in the process of building or re-building the nation, integrating different social groups and immigrants. Nationalization did not necessarily incorporate the democratic control of the armed forces. In fact, this occurred only with certain reluctance on the part of the armed forces and their leaders. Even in the most advanced Western democracies, there was always an element of uncertainty about possible undemocratic or anti-democratic movements within the armed forces.[22] In most cases, the armed forces remained hostile to any organizational reform, which threatened to do away with traditional forms of hierarchy, rank, and chains of command. The protagonists of a liberal and democratic society, however, which on its ideological margins is even decidedly pacifist, were always trying to subordinate the armed forces to a strong civil control.

The term 'specialization' comprises several aspects. The Industrial Revolution also generated the 'industrialization of war'[23] and of the military profession. The never-ending process of innovation and the refinement of new weapons and weapons systems literally opened new dimensions for military action. This in turn demanded new skills of the soldiers and new forms of organization and management for the armed forces. The military thus became a driving force, but also an ambiguous element within the general process of modernization. The professionalism of the armed forces developed as a response to several developments that threatened the unity of the military profession. First, the pace of technological invention in weapons and military infrastructure created the need for more specialist military branches and more 'civilian' skills within the armed forces. This process of industrialization

---

[21] Nationalism was the most successful integrative ideology of the past two centuries. Sometimes, the nation invented itself through the fight against colonial forces or dominant ethnic groups. This is a widespread pattern, according to the comparative studies by Nikolaus Buschmann and Dieter Langewiesche (eds), *Der Krieg in den Gründungsmythen europäischer Nationen und der USA* (Frankfurt am M., 2003).

[22] To mention just two (quite different) examples: first, the notorious Dreyfus affair in France, and second the erosion of democratic structures in Western countries through the influence of nuclear deterrence and a powerful 'military–industrial complex' as anticipated by some peace groups and peace researchers in those countries.

[23] Anthony Giddens, *The Nation-State and Violence* (Cambridge, 1987), 5.

threatened the social homogeneity of the officer corps. Like other expanding professions which became more 'scientific' in the second half of the nineteenth century, the profession of arms developed the usual features of professionalism (common norms and values, common language, common behavioural patterns, and clear distinctions between members and non-members of the group) in order to control the process of growth in numbers. Specialization meant professional specialization, and also the division of the political sphere from the military in the organization of the state. Nevertheless, both developments were balanced, and powerful attempts were made to keep the unity of the military profession and to fine-tune the interaction between the political executive and the military leadership, in times not only of war but also in peace.[24]

## SOLDIER/DIPLOMAT

Raymond Aron introduced the fundamental distinction between the diplomat and the soldier as the authentic representation of a state in its foreign relations.[25] The civil ambassador and the soldier in uniform live out and symbolize the relationship between states. This distinction is still valuable. It has lost, however, some of its previously sharp contours:

- A steadily growing number of cross-border relations is no longer confined to states and governments but is of a transnational character. This weakens the position both of the diplomat[26] and of the soldier. It would be premature, however, to believe that the relative decline of the number of inter-state wars in the recent past will develop into a sound trend to eliminate war as an instrument of international politics.

- A special form of convergence or synthesis seemed necessary in the context of mutual nuclear deterrence in the East–West conflict after 1945. Political control of the possible escalation from a 'Cold' War into a direct military confrontation on the part of the nuclear powers was extremely important. This occupied not only the minds of the responsible politicians and military commanders but also the public imagination.[27]

---

[24] Under the shadows of a nuclear war in the East–West conflict, this fine-tuning became extremely important in order to avoid any escalation into forms of conflict that threatened to invalidate conflict management.

[25] Raymond Aron, *Frieden und Krieg: Eine Theorie der Staatenwelt* (Frankfurt am M., 1963).

[26] Paul Sharp, 'Who Needs Diplomats? The Problem of Diplomatic Representation', *International Journal*, 52 (1997), 609–34.

[27] A serious and amusing testimony to this is Stanley Kubrick's movie *Dr. Strangelove* (1963).

- Many anti-colonial wars in the 1940s, 1950s, and 1960s were characterized by a strictly organized convergence of political and military operations. Leaders like Tito, Mao Tse Tung, Fidel Castro, Ché Guevara, and other guerrillas were more or less successful in combining the roles of the soldier and the diplomat. Their concept of guerrilla warfare was based on the unity of the political and the military spheres. The myth of the violent birth of a new nation often did not survive the first generation.
- After the era of anti-colonial wars, which were legitimized and fought on the part of the indigenous peoples in order to liberate themselves, a new wave of wars between and within recently founded states emerged. It has often proved hard to identify the political contours of these violent conflicts. However, it would be wrong to think of these wars only or principally in terms of apolitical eruptions and as implosions of the social order.
- Violent intra-state conflicts and wars on the territory of failed states, of which there is an increasing number, often create (through the sheer intensity of physical violence) a new and brutal military culture. Warrior-soldiers in these wars often do not care to act in the name of a political interest and do not consider themselves actors in a nation-building process. They perform in a turbulent environment made up of cruelty, terror, and annihilation. The high number of child soldiers in such wars is a gruesome reminder of this kind of alienated violence beyond any political goal. A deeper analysis of the distribution of power and interest in these conflicts always reveals, however, their political context.
- A different kind of cooperation between the military and civilian agents is necessary in the cases of multilateral peace missions and the protection of humanitarian relief operations in the trouble spots of the globe.

The last two phenomena are particularly interesting in the context of this chapter. The second is mostly a reaction to the first. At the same time, however, they form the two extremes on a scale, which visualizes the different combination of the military and the diplomat. In the case of 'new wars'[28] or wars of the third kind,[29] violence appears to be motivated by emotions beyond political control.

In multilateral peace missions, which are designed to contain the violence of local wars, it is primarily the diplomats who decide on the scope and intensity of the action. The soldiers executing these decisions are not only obliged to stay

---

[28] Herfried Münkler, *Der Wandel des Krieges. Von der Symmetrie zur Asymmetrie* (Weilerswist, 2006), chs. 5 and 15.
[29] Kalevi J. Holsti, *The State, War, and the State of War* (Cambridge, 1996), ch. 2.

in close contact with the local political authorities and with the agencies of the international community (like the United Nations), they are also expected to display a diplomat's sensitivity.

## ASPECTS OF CIVIL–MILITARY RELATIONS

From an *organizational* perspective, civil–military relations reflect the relationship between the political leadership of a country and the commanders of the armed forces. From a *social* perspective, this relationship comprises all contacts between the realm of the military and civil society. There is a third, a genuine *political* perspective. Here, civil–military relations reflect the relationship between organized violence and political goals and interests. In modern times, political goals and interests, in so far as they concern the community or group as a whole, stem from the civil sector of society. Depending on the format and the legitimizing structures of the polity, the group members or some representatives or some circles, who claim to express the will of the people, are in charge of this process. The military is usually seen as a multifunctional organization with social, economic, and other roles. However, these are only secondary functions. Its primary function, as the professionally trained defender of society and its territory, is to provide security against any other state which threatens national interests. Clausewitz clearly emphasized this third perspective.

Clausewitz's famous contention that war is simply a continuation of political intercourse with the addition of other means follows from his general concept of war as 'an act of force to compel our enemy to do our will'.[30] An enemy in this sense is constituted by a clash of interests or values between collective actors. Planning and beginning a war is therefore a political process: 'It can be taken as agreed that the aim of policy is to unify and reconcile all aspects of internal administration as well as of spiritual values, and whatever else the moral philosopher may care to add. Policy, of course is nothing in itself; it is simply the trustee for all these interests against other states.'[31]

The armed forces and organized violence are instruments in the hands of the political leadership: 'In no sense can the art of war ever be regarded as the preceptor of policy, and here we can only treat policy as representative of all interests in the community.'[32]

Whenever a modern state is concerned, as an actor in war or as the prey in civil or guerrilla war, the guiding rationale for warfare is always the political

[30] *On War*, I, 1, § 2, p. 75.　　[31] Ibid. VIII, 6B, p. 606.　　[32] Ibid. VIII, 6B, p. 607.

interest of the parties involved. A major military development, or the plan for one, cannot be judged adequately if the judgement concentrates on its purely military aspects. When war is a continuation of political intercourse, of politics, it is only logical to contend that civil–military relations in times of peace are also characterized by the domination of the political leadership over the armed forces. In short, modernity always implies civilian primacy.

The shaping of civil–military relations differs from state to state and is part of each state's political culture. In some nations, the armed forces as an organization and the soldiers as members of this organization enjoy high social prestige. This does not imply that they rise beyond their status as precious instruments in the hands of the political leadership. Even in militarized states (e.g. after a military *coup d'état*), the formulation of national interests remains a non-military task. After a military *coup d'état* the masters of the country cannot but act as its political leaders. Sometimes, colonels and generals think they are more efficient in running a country and fulfilling non-military tasks. Usually, they are wrong.

Civil–military relations become a delicate affair in times of regime change or after a regime change has taken place. Germany's history in the twentieth century is a case in point. After the end of the First World War, the armed forces did not accept their defeat and refused to transfer their loyalty from the old monarchy to the new democracy. The failure to establish new kinds of civil–military relations deeply influenced the history of the Weimar Republic. Thus, not all, but many officers of the Reichswehr sympathized with the Nazi government that came to power in January 1933. Paradoxically, Hitler and the National Socialist Party were very successful in introducing a different kind of political primacy over the armed forces (renamed the Wehrmacht in 1934). After the Second World War, the Allied powers divided Germany into several parts. When the East–West conflict turned into the Cold War, the Western powers (principally the United States) put pressure on the West German government to contribute actively to the defence of the West against the perceived military threat from the Soviet Union. The new military, the Bundeswehr, founded in 1956 remained under the political control of Germany's NATO allies. The new and more stable democracy was therefore also able to establish a stable democratic control of the armed forces.

## DEMOCRATIC CONTROL

In the second half of the twentieth century, professionalism, bureaucratization, and the acceptance of a legitimate framework, namely the nation-state and democratic values, became the major conditions for a military career in most Western countries. The so-called equilibrium model of civil–military relations in its ideal form 'presumes that the military profession is composed of an educated elite whose role in society is the organization, control, and application of force in pursuit of democratic values as determined by the state. Complementing this is the concept that the profession not only controls and supervises the military instrument in accordance with established policy, but that professional morals and ethics require a commitment to democratic ideals which in turn presuppose a role in the political process.'[33]

Armed forces are *not* democratic institutions. Because of their internal structures and the imperatives of their missions, they are, in fact, non-democratic institutions. It would be futile to change this and all attempts to go in this direction have failed. However, what is feasible and reasonable is the attempt to make the armed forces compatible with their democratic environment.

Military sociologists use the concept of civilian control in order to describe the norms, attitudes, and rules that should guarantee the primacy of the political and civil leadership over the military leadership of the armed forces. The armed forces are obviously a dangerous organization—they are supposed to be well-equipped with instruments for violence, they are well-trained, easily mobilized, and placed in a position to threaten potential or actual enemies. Every society and every political system therefore need efficient devices to keep this organization under control. As David Segal has put it: 'The central issue in theories of civil–military relations is that of civilian control of the military.'[34] When the military successfully overrules civilian control, the danger of a military coup or military dictatorship is imminent. The attempt to integrate a society by means of military norms and values (often accompanied by virtual or openly demonstrated terror) can be called militarism.

The concept of civilian control is useful when we analyse civil–military relations on a relatively general level. However, it does not provide suitable distinctions between societies according to the degree of their democratization. Totalitarian dictators in the twentieth century were very successful in domesticating the armed forces. They used instruments such as ideological infiltration, propaganda, and positive sanctions, but also terror and purges in order to keep the armed forces under tight control. In the 1930s, both Stalin and Hitler were comparatively successful in subordinating the armed forces of their countries.

---

[33] Sam C. Sarkesian, 'Military Professionalism and Civil–Military Relations in the West', *International Political Science Review*, 2 (1981), 290–1.

[34] David R. Segal, 'Civil–Military Relations in Democratic Societies', in J. Kuhlmann and D. R. Segal (eds), *Armed Forces at the Dawn of the Third Millennium* (Strausberg, 1994), 40.

Civilian control refers only to the formal relations between a society, its political system and the armed forces. If we want to find out whether a given model of civil–military relations is compatible with the fabric of democratic society, we need a more normative concept which could be called democratic control.

Democratic control comprises all formal norms and rules, laws and regulations which are designed to integrate the organization of the armed forces into the democratic political system, and the soldiers, especially the officer corps, into the democratic political culture. This normative concept can be implemented in different ways. The mechanisms of democratic control of the armed forces depend on the political culture and the traditions of the country. In some cases (and not just a few), democratic control of the armed forces encounters special difficulties because of the salient role the armed forces have played in the process of nation-building. Sometimes, the military leadership enjoys a sort of institutional charisma because the armed forces have liberated the country or because they have overthrown an anachronistic regime and thus have prepared the conditions for a new national start.

The democratization of a political regime and of a society as a whole remains dangerously incomplete without the establishment of democratic control of the armed forces. A typical feature of any process of democratization is that it is actively pursued by the elites *and* is actively accepted by the majority of the population. These are the most important prerequisites for its success. Prescriptions and implantations do not suffice. This is true for both the civilian and the military sectors of a society: one cannot *order* democratization.

In the case of West Germany after the Second World War, the newly constructed democratic state lived for half a decade without armed forces of its own. When the Bundeswehr was eventually founded, the political framework for the new organization had been carefully designed so that democratic control could find enough institutional hooks. Evidently, democratic control of the armed forces has to develop on several levels:

- the political system must provide legal opportunities to exercise democratic control in an effective manner. It is primarily parliament which has to play an important role;
- the media and the public must show more than just a superficial interest in the armed forces and their internal functioning. They must be able and willing to operate as watchdogs;
- the armed forces as an organization must accept that they act under the auspices of democratic control; and

- the soldiers, especially the officer corps, must have internalized the norms and values of democracy and be willing to comply with the rules of democratic control.

These are not easy tasks.

## RELUCTANT CIVIL–MILITARY PARALLELISM

In most Western societies, civil–military relations have developed in a contradictory way over recent decades. It is evident that many of the changes in values and attitudes that have taken place in civil society have also influenced the armed forces. The role of women is a case in point. Women first gained access to positions in civil life which had been formally or tacitly reserved for men. After some time, and despite a considerable reluctance on the part of soldiers, the armed forces had to open their gates to women. Equally, the policy of the armed forces towards homosexuality is changing along with changes in civil society. These examples demonstrate a kind of 'reluctant parallelism' between civil society and the armed forces—an illustration of the contention that the gap between them cannot be too wide.

This parallelism, however, seems to be interrupted by other developments which are about to widen that gap.[35] Interestingly enough, the most important impulse in these developments stems not from the military, but from civil society:

- The abolition of universal conscription in many societies means that a traditional link between civilian society and the armed forces vanishes. In the past a considerable number of young males encountered military life, and the armed forces were obliged to cope with new generations of youngsters. When this kind of mutual adaptation does not take place, all sorts of mutual prejudices and misperceptions can establish themselves.

- In modern nation-states territorial defence is a generally accepted task. It is also a task common to society and to the armed forces. The new missions of the armed forces, although usually regarded with great sympathy by society, are the jobs of specialists often far away from home. Genocides and humanitarian catastrophes demand intervention, but whether this intervention is in the hands of 'our' soldiers or some other troops, or perhaps even of a private security firm, is of secondary importance.

[35] Peter D. Feaver and Richard H. Kohn (eds), *Soldiers and Civilians: The Civil–Military Gap and American National Security* (Cambridge, MA, 2001).

- As Bernard Boëne has observed, the future will see a return to radical professionalism, due mostly to the restoration of prestige, more frequent opportunities for military action, drastically reduced military establishments, and societal contexts for which the 'post-modern' label provides a convenient shorthand description. In terms of civil–military relations, the consequences will include—on the military side—stronger identities, more forcefully expressed interests, and less flexibility, while politicians, as is already the case in a number of countries, will exhibit a degree of diffidence, or at least less assurance, in dealing with military matters.[36] This vision may stretch the argument a little too far, but the tendency exists.

If the distance between society and the armed forces is growing, it remains a friendly distance. Societies do not become pacifist, but they are only sporadically interested in the armed forces. They do not want to spend too much money for their maintenance (in this respect, the United States is a remarkable exception). The public is proud of the armed forces when they intervene successfully and help to make peace, but it turns away from their activities when there is no quick and visible success.

Behind all the different forms of civil–military relations and of civilian and/or democratic control of the armed forces, we find the same structural pattern of political guidance. This structural pattern influences the decision to use the armed forces in a conflict that may consequently grow into a war. What is at stake in a war depends on the context. However, this context is always a political one, and the definition of what the stake is, is a political decision. Political actors, state and non-state alike, should be aware of this *fait social*, to use a term by Emile Durkheim.[37] The discovery of this *fait social* is Clausewitz's legacy.

---

[36] Bernard Boëne, 'Les rapports armée–Etat–société dans les démocraties liberals', *La Revue Tocqueville/The Tocqueville Review*, 17/1 (1996), 69.

[37] Emile Durkheim, *Regeln der soziologischen Methode*, trans. René König (Neuwied, 1961), 114. (*Les règles de la méthode sociologique* were first published in 1894.)

# 16

## Clausewitz and a New Containment: the Limitation of War and Violence

*Andreas Herberg-Rothe*

> Indeed, the great problem is the limitation of war, And (...) this is a cynical game... If it is not connected on either side With enmity becoming relative.
>
> Carl Schmitt (1963)[1]

With the end of the Cold War, the 'end of history' was also proclaimed. Accordingly, there was expected to be an end to war and violence.[2] With the return of war and violence throughout the world, history is also back on the agenda.[3] This chapter argues that we are witnessing a worldwide expansion of war and violence, which should be countered by a new containment. As George Kennan emphasized as early as 1987: 'We are going to have to develop a wider concept of what containment means...—a concept, in other words, more responsive to the problems of our own time—than the one I so lightheartedly brought to expression, hacking away at my typewriter there in the northwest corner of the War College building in December of 1946.' Sixty years have already passed, since George Kennan formulated his original vision of containment. Although altered in its application by various administrations in the United States, it has in practice been incorporated within the concept and politics of common security, which in turn has itself been the essential

---

[1] Carl Schmitt, *Theorie des Partisanen. Zwischenbemerkung zum Begriff des Politischen* (Berlin, 1963), 19, trans. Gerard Holden. See also Andreas Herberg-Rothe, 'Hannah Arendt und Carl Schmitt—"Vermittlung" von Freund und Feind', *Der Staat*, 1 (Berlin, 2004), 35–55.

[2] Francis Fukuyama, *The End of History and the Last Man* (New York, 2006). I am grateful for assistance and comments on the first draft of this chapter to David Held, Hew Strachan, Karl Cordell, and Antulio Echevarria II. Gerard Holden translated a first version of the German text, and Daniel Moran liberally and unselfishly edited the English and helped express my ideas with much greater clarity. Parts of it were the subject of a lecture delivered at the ECPR Conference in Budapest in September 2005.

[3] Joschka Fischer, *Die Rückkehr der Geschichte* (Cologne, 2005).

complement to purely military containment.[4] These ideas are still valid—and, as Kennan himself pointed out, more than ever they are in need of explication and implementation.[5]

## THE REMOVAL OF THE INHIBITIONS ON WAR, AND A NEW CONTAINMENT

In the wake of the Soviet collapse, the triumphant advance of democracy and free markets seemed to be unstoppable, to the point where it appeared for a time as if the twenty-first century would be an age defined by economics and thus, to a great extent, by peace. However, these expectations were quickly disappointed, not only because of the massacres and genocides in Africa, which are ongoing, but also because of the return of war to Europe (primarily in the former Yugoslavia), the attacks of 11 September 2001 in the United States, and then the Iraq war with its continuing, violent consequences. A struggle against a new totalitarianism of an Islamic type appears to have started, in which war and violence are commonly perceived as having an unavoidable role. Both are also perceived as having become more 'unbounded' than ever before—both in a spatial sense, for terrorist attacks are potentially ever present, and temporally, since no end to these attacks is in sight. One can also speak of a new dimension to the extent and brutality of violence—as exemplified by the horrors of the civil wars in Africa. We are facing completely new types of threats, for example the possession of weapons of mass destruction by terrorist organizations or the development of atomic bombs by 'problematic' states like Iran and North Korea. The potential emergence of a new superpower, China, and perhaps of new 'great' powers, like India, may lead to a fresh arms race, which presumably will have a nuclear dimension. In the consciousness of many, violence appears to be slipping the leash of rational control, an image the media has not hesitated to foster, especially with respect to Africa.[6] Will there be 'another bloody century', as Colin Gray has proposed?[7]

Although the current situation and the foreseeable future are not as immediately ominous as was the Cold War, the position may be worse in the

[4] Charles W. Kegley, Jr., 'The New Containment Myth: Realism and the Anomaly of European Integration', *Ethics & International Affairs*, 5 (1991), 99–115.

[5] George F. Kennan, 'Containment: 40 Years Later', in Terry L. Deibel and John Lewis Gaddis (eds), *Containment: Concept and Policy* (Washington, DC, 1986), 23–31.

[6] One important question is whether there really has been an overall increase in the number of wars since the end of the Cold War, or whether there has in fact been a decline after a short period of increased violence in the early 1990s: see Sven Chojnacki, 'Wandel der Kriegsformen?—Ein kritischer Literaturbericht', *Leviathan*, 32/3 (2004), 402–24.

[7] Colin Gray, *Another Bloody Century: Future Warfare* (London, 2005).

long run. On one side, the prospect of planetary self-destruction via nuclear overkill, which loomed over the Cold War, has been successfully averted. On the other hand, after having been granted a brief respite in the 1990s, mankind now feels itself to be confronting a 'coming anarchy' of unknown dimensions.[8] If the horrific destructive potential threat of the Cold War has been reduced in scale, less cataclysmic possibilities have also become more imminent. Hence my conclusion is that we need a new strategy of containment, which must be different from that of the Cold War, although based on some similar principles.

There is no longer one exclusive actor to be contained, as the Soviet Union was in the Cold War. Even if one were to anticipate China's emergence as a new superpower in the next twenty years, it would not be reasonable in advance of this actually happening to develop a strategy for the military containment of China similar to that used against the Soviet Union in the 1950s and 1960s, since doing so might well provoke the kinds of crisis and even conflict which such a strategy would be intended to avoid.[9] The attempt to build up India as a counterweight to China by facilitating its nuclear ambitions, for instance, might risk undermining the international campaign to limit the proliferation of nuclear weapons in the world. Therefore we need a quite different concept of containment, and one which could not be perceived as a threat by China.

The second difference is that current developments in the strategic environment display fundamentally conflicting tendencies: between globalization on the one hand, and local struggles for identity and regional advantages and interests on the other;[10] between high-tech wars and combat with 'knives and machetes' or attacks by suicide bombers; between symmetrical and asymmetrical warfare; between wars over the 'world order', with their re-politicization and re-ideologization,[11] and the privatization of war and violence;[12] between the imperial-hegemonic dominance of the only superpower and the formation

---

[8] Robert Kaplan, 'The Coming Anarchy', *Atlantic Monthly*, 273 (1994), 44–76; Martin van Creveld, *The Transformation of War* (New York, 1991).

[9] See, e.g. 'US denies new containment policy against China', in: http://english.people.com.cn/200511/24/eng20051124_223692.html, 15.3.06.

[10] Zygmunt Bauman has labelled these contrasting tendencies 'Glocalisation', a combination of 'globalisation' and 'localisation': see Bauman, 'Glokalisierung oder: Was für die einen Globalisierung ist für die anderen Lokalisierung', *Das Argument*, 217 (1996), 653–64; Bauman, *Globalization* (London, 1998).

[11] I have put forward the thesis that, after the breakdown of an empire or a system of world order, there has nearly always been a tendency for the privatization of war and violence, to a level beneath that which has broken apart, just as happened after the fall of the Soviet Union and the breakdown of the bipolar order of the Cold War. But I estimate that in the long run the importance of politics and ideology are even increasing. See Andreas Herberg-Rothe, 'Privatized Wars and World Order Conflicts', *Theoria*, 110 (August 2006), 1–22.

[12] Herfried Münkler, *The New Wars* (London, 2004); Mary Kaldor, *New and Old Wars: Organized Violence in a Global Era* (London, 1999).

of new regional power centres; between international organized crime and the institutionalization of regional and global communities; and between increasing violations of international law and human rights on one side and their expansion on the other. A strategy designed to counter only one of these conflicting tendencies may be problematic with respect to the others. I therefore stress the necessity of striking a balance among competing possibilities.

The third difference is that the traditional containment was perceived mainly as military deterrence of the Soviet Union, although in its original formulation by George Kennan it was quite different from such a reductionism. Our main and decisive assumption is that a new containment must combine traditional, military containment on one side and a range of opportunities for cooperation on the other. That is necessary with respect not only to China, but even to political Islam, in order to reduce the appeal of militant Islamic movements to millions of Muslim youths.

In response to the removal of inhibitions on war and violence, this chapter develops a conception of their containment, in the sense of a sustained and ongoing limitation through the fencing in and encircling of the same forces (Carl Schmitt used the word *Einhegung*).[13] The guiding perspective of the chapter is that of a peaceful, or rather a pacified, global society. But this perspective cannot be equated with 'peace' since, in order to reach this goal, non-peaceful, violent, and even military means must in some cases be employed. The limitation of war and violence in world society implies the expansion of non-violent zones, to which the Kantian conception of democratic peace or, for example, Dieter Senghaas's notion of the 'civilizational hexagon' refers, but it also implies the active containment and limitation of the expansion of war and violence.[14]

---

[13] There is a small, but decisive difference between my approach and the traditional limitation of war and violence as laid down in the law of nations, the UN Charter and The Hague Conventions on the conduct of war. As important as they are, they mainly set limits to the conduct of war, whereas my conception, while of course including such an approach, mainly concentrated on a political–military strategy, the limitation and containment of war and violence within world society.

[14] Dieter Senghaas, *Zum irdischen Frieden. Erkenntnisse und Vermutungen* (Frankfurt, 2004). Senghaas developed the 'civilizational hexagon', which consists of six 'cornerstones'. The first is a legitimate monopoly of force in the hands of the state, i.e. safeguarding the community based on the rule of law, which is of paramount importance for any peaceful modern order. 'Disarming' citizens is the only way to force them to conduct their conflicts over identity and interests through argument rather than violence. However, such a monopoly of force also creates a need for the kind of control via the rule of law that can only be guaranteed by, and indeed epitomizes, the modern constitutional state. The third major condition for internal peace is 'affect control', which arises from the range and richness of the many interdependences characterizing modern societies (for definitions of 'affect control', see http://indiana.edu/~socpsy/ACT/). Fourth, democratic participation is essential, precisely because of the indispensability of affect control. Fifth, in politicized societies, this approach to conflict management will only have permanence if there are continual efforts to ensure social justice. If there are fair opportunities

Such an overarching perspective has to be self-evident, little more than common sense, because it has to be accepted by quite different political leaders and peoples. The self-evidence of this concept could go so far that one could ask why we are discussing it. On the other hand, such a concept must be able to be distinguished by competing concepts. Not least, it should be regarded as an appropriate concept to counter contemporary developments. Finally, we need to take into account the fact that Kennan's concept would not have succeeded, if it had been directed against the actions of the international community or the United States. Therefore, the new concept should in some ways do no more than express what the international community is already doing anyway. As one American commentator has observed: 'Other states are instrumental in interrupting the flow of finances from one institution to another, in restricting the movements of terrorists, in eliminating their safe havens, in tracking down and arresting their principal leaders and in driving a wedge between the terrorist groups and the various populations they purport to champion.'[15] Such states are already pursuing a strategy of containment.

A concept that realized the demand for a political concept which met contemporary needs was that of 'common security', developed in the 1970s. In the special situation of the Cold War and of mutual deterrence this concept did not imply a common security shared among states with similar values and policies. On the contrary, this concept, perhaps developed for the first time by Klaus

---

in the public arena to articulate identities *and* to achieve a balance between diverse interests, it may be assumed that this approach to conflict management has been reliably internalized and that conflict management based on compromise—including the necessary tolerance—has thus become an integral element of political action. In my opinion, Senghaas differentiates Weber's concept of the 'legitimate monopoly on violence', which consists of two different aspects, the legitimacy and the effectiveness of the monopoly of force. He also differentiates the various conditions under which the monopoly of force is considered and accepted as legitimate. The importance of this part of the legitimate monopoly on violence was demonstrated in the collapse of the USSR, since the Communist Party and the Red Army had an effective monopoly of force, but it ceased to be regarded as legitimate.

It is probably unnecessary to point out that my perspective differs from that of Huntington's 'clash of civilizations' as well as from Kagan's reduction of political action to 'power politics'. As Kagan reminds us, despite the complaints heard today from Europe that Americans are 'from Mars' while Europeans are 'from Venus', it was the Europeans who originally reduced statecraft to power politics, which resulted in the First World War: Robert Kagan, *Of Paradise and Power* (Washington, DC, 2004). For his part, Huntington's basic assumption is that you only know who you are if you know whom you are against. Huntington's position is identical to Carl Schmitt's reduction of politics to a differentiation between friend and foe. Samuel P. Huntington, *The Clash of Civilizations and the Remaking of World Order* (New York, 1996). Hence, just as in Schmitt, the problem becomes that one's own value system is lost if one follows only this principle. It has to be said, however, that the concept of limitation of war and violence is in no way a new form of appeasement, but the overarching principle for deciding in which cases and for which purposes military and warlike measures must be taken, and in which cases non-military action is required.

[15] Antulio Echevarria, *Fourth-Generation Warfare and Other Myths* (Carlisle, PA, 2005), 5–6.

von Schubert, emphasized a quite different meaning. Traditionally, opponents have understood security as security *from each other*. The new approach laid down by Klaus von Schubert derived from the assumption that, in a world possessed of multiple capacities for destroying the planet, security could only be defined as common security. This small difference between security from each other and common security—shared security against a universal threat—was nothing less than a paradigm change effected during the Cold War.[16]

The question of course remains, how to deter the true believers, members of terrorist networks or people like the current President of Iran, for whom even self-destruction may be a means of hastening millenarian goals. Of course, 'true-believers' or 'hard-core terrorists' can hardly be deterred. But this is exactly the reason why containment cannot be reduced to a strategy of deterrence. The real task even in these cases, therefore, is to act politically and militarily in a manner which enables the separation of the 'true believers' from the 'believers' and both groups from the simple followers. This strategy can include military actions and credible threats, but at the same time it should offer a choice between alternatives. The reduction of the strategy to military means alone would only intensify violent resistance. Even the true believers could be confronted with a choice: either to be an accepted part of their social and religious environment (or to be excluded from it) or to reduce their millenarian aspirations. Of course, there is no guarantee that, by following this strategy, every terrorist attack will be averted. But that is not the real question. Assuming that the goal of the terrorists and millenarian Islamists is to provoke an overreaction on the part of the West in order to ignite an all-out war between the West and the Islamic world, we have no choice but to try to separate them from their political, social, and religious environment.

The perspective developed here is determined by two basic assumptions. First, I proceed from the assumption that the current proliferation of war and violence is so manifold and differentiated a phenomenon that it cannot be opposed through a single counter-strategy. Rather, an overarching perspective is required to determine which measures are appropriate in individual cases—although the possibility of gross errors and miscalculations is not thereby excluded. Second, in present-day world society—as well as in examples throughout history—one finds numerous processes that run counter to each other, and therefore the consideration of only a single counter-strategy can lead to paradoxical and unintended consequences. In contrast to this, the conception of containment as an overarching perspective could serve to limit

---

[16] Klaus von Schubert, *Von der Abschreckung zur gemeinsamen Sicherheit* (Baden-Baden, 1972).

the unintended consequences of our own counter-actions, thus moderating the inherent self-destructiveness that large-scale organized violence always includes.[17]

## CLAUSEWITZ'S CONCEPT OF POLITICS

Although he was an admirer of Napoleon's strategy for most of his life, Clausewitz recognized at the end of his writing of *On War* that just the same principles of unleashing violence, which served as one basis for the overwhelming success of Napoleon, contributed to his final defeat at Waterloo. From then on, Clausewitz faced the problem of how to treat strategies of limited war within the same conceptual framework as those designed to lead to the total defeat of the enemy (on which see the last parts of book VIII of *On War*). This was the turning point of his theory. Realizing that there are quite different and even contrasting kinds of war and strategy, he emphasized that war could no longer be regarded as having an identity of its own, but that it made sense only as a continuation of politics by other means. Of course Clausewitz had already analysed the important influence of politics in his early writings, especially with respect to the French Revolution and its impact on the success of the French army. But the conflicting tendencies in war and especially between limited and 'unlimited' warfare compelled him to search for a general principle that could unify these conflicting tendencies in war. That principle, he believed, was politics.[18] What Clausewitz recognized only implicitly was emphasized by Carl Schmitt and Hannah Arendt. For Carl Schmitt, war and violence must be limited, because unlimited war and violence would wipe out the possibility of the conduct of war and, by doing so, the possibility of politics. In Hannah Arendt's view too, unlimited war and violence (she says 'terror') destroy the possibility of politics.[19] Bearing in mind that politics, especially

---

[17] Ironically, this approach was also the guiding perspective of Basil Liddell Hart, despite his extensive criticism of Clausewitz after the First World War. My own approach is based on the writings of the very late Clausewitz. A good introduction to Liddell Hart's concept of containment is Azar Gat, *Fascist and Liberal Visions of War: Fuller, Liddell Hart, Douhet and other Modernists* (Oxford, 1998), Part II.

[18] I have elaborated this interpretation in Andreas Herberg-Rothe, *Das Rätsel Clausewitz. Politische Theorie des Krieges im Widerstreit* (Munich, 2001), 79–145, and in the English edition of the same book, *Clausewitz's Puzzle* (Oxford, 2007). We can find this conclusion in the trinity; within the note of 1827, in which Clausewitz mentioned both aspects as guiding principles for reworking the whole text; in book I, chapter 2 (which tends to be underestimated); and, of course, in most parts of book VIII of *On War*.

[19] Although Hannah Arendt and Carl Schmitt are articulating very different positions with respect to the concept of politics, they shared some important convictions; for details, see

in the ideological twentieth century, contributed to the unleashing of war and violence on an industrial scale, we must ask, which kind of politics could serve to contain war and violence in the twenty-first century?

Clausewitz's description of the relation of politics and war is unsurpassable; this is not to say that all kinds of war or warlike actions in history have been only political in essence. Nevertheless, if there is a connection between warfare and politics, then we have to take into account Clausewitz's description of this relationship. It must be stressed that his description of this relationship is based on an unavoidable tension between them, which cannot be avoided. Clausewitz describes war on the one hand as a continuation of politics, but on the other side as waged with *other* than political means. This implicit tension is the basis of the explicit contrast between the first and the third tendency of Clausewitz's trinity.[20] Furthermore, one could argue that recent developments, like globalization and the revolutionary consequences of information technologies, have created a worldwide political space from which no one can escape, however much his actions might be derived, in their immediate motivation, from private interests or from the cultural practices of ethnic or tribal communities.[21]

Clausewitz's descriptions of the relations between the various elements and tendencies of war are right in general, even if his concrete illustrations of these concepts are only those of his own times. His understanding of these concepts can still be valid for today, because Clausewitz's concepts are sometimes based on very general ideas about human action. Human nature and human communities are not fundamentally changed by the passage of a few centuries. The self-preservation of a community, for instance, still represents a higher goal or purpose than the pursuit of the private interests of its members.[22]

Andreas Herberg-Rothe, 'Hannah Arendt und Carl Schmitt, "Vermittlung" von Freund und Feind', *Der Staat*, 1 (2004), 35–55. It is especially notable that, although drawing different conclusions, they reacted similarly to the arms race in the 1960s. Hannah Arendt's book, *On Violence*, was first published in 1970, Carl Schmitt's *Theorie des Partisanen. Zwischenbemerkung zum Begriff des Partisanen* was published for the first time in 1963. Both reacted to the 'deprivation' of the concept of politics by overkill-capacities, which seemed no longer to have any political purpose. Arendt's position was additionally related to her criticism of totalitarianism; see Hannah Arendt, *The Origins of Totalitarianism* (New York, 1951).

[20] It can be demonstrated that, due to systematic reasons but also with respect to historical experience, trying to suspend this tension for the sake of the primacy of one of the two sides always leads to a primacy of the military means, of warfare and violence; see Beatrice Heuser, *Reading Clausewitz* (London, 2002).

[21] Antulio Echevarria II, 'Globalization and the Clausewitzian Nature of War', *The European Legacy*, 8/3 (2003), 317–32.

[22] Colin Gray, *Another Bloody Century* (London, 2005), 50. Although I agree with Jon Sumida's argument in his chapter in this book, on the importance of Clausewitz's proposition that 'defense is the stronger form of war', here I am taking a contrary tack, emphasizing Clausewitz's dialectical point. Clausewitz saw defence as 'the stronger form of fighting with the negative purpose' and attack as 'the weaker form with the positive purpose'. See, unfortunately without

Nevertheless, the perennial question with Clausewitz is whether his concept of politics can still be applied meaningfully today. This is most especially true for democratic societies, in which war must be waged by governments which are answerable to individual citizens and responsible in some degree for their welfare.

Although Clausewitz did not treat the concept of politics independently of its military instrument, he presupposed indirectly a special concept of politics which influenced his description of the relationship between war and politics. Clausewitz's concept of politics can be opened up through an examination of the international states system, as it has developed since the Thirty Years War. After the Treaty of Westphalia, war became the special province of states. Acts of violence not legitimized by the state were, as a result, criminal acts and as such were prosecuted and resulted in punishment. The European state has accomplished something very rare. As the state achieved its monopoly on the use of force, domestic peace was achieved, at least, in the sense that legalized social hostility could be excluded.[23] In the international sphere, the system was based on the following assumptions:

(1) Independent, sovereign states did not recognize any kind of supra-state instance or authority.

(2) Conflicts between individual states were eventually decided by means of power politics, if necessary by military means.

(3) Both the use of military means and war between states were legitimate.[24] Wars were avoided not for moral reasons, but because of cost–benefit calculations.[25]

Clausewitz's definition of war at the beginning of his book, in his famous first chapter, is derived from this implicit concept of politics, when he states, 'War is thus an act of force to compel our enemy to do our will.'[26] Although the legitimization of war in the Westphalian system contributed to a limitation of war between European opponents over long periods, it cannot be separated from outbreaks of war in the twentieth century. Their effect was, in contrast

treating Clausewitz separately, Michael Brown, Owen R. Coté, Sean M. Lynn-Jones, and Steven E. Miller (eds), *Offense, Defense, and War* (Cambridge, MA, 2004).

[23] Herfried Münkler, 'Die Kriege der Zukunft und die Zukunft der Staaten', *Berliner Debatte Initial*, issue 6/3–12 (1995), esp. 3–6.

[24] We find this same distinction between the 'use of military force' and war in our own times in the difference between 'military operations other than war' (MOOTW) and war itself.

[25] Wilfried von Bredow, 'Das Westfälische System internationaler Beziehungen. Vorgezogener Rückblick auf eine weltgeschichtliche Sequenz', in Heinz Schilling, Michael Behnen, Wilfried von Bredow, and Marie-Janine Calic (eds), *Die Kunst des Friedensschlusses in Vergangenheit und Gegenwart* (Hannover, 1998), 55–79, esp 61–2; translation by Gerard Holden.

[26] Carl von Clausewitz, *On War*, trans. and ed. Michael Howard and Peter Paret (Princeton, NJ, 1976), I, 1, § 2, p. 75.

to the Westphalian system's recognition of the right to wage war, to proscribe wars of aggression for the first time.[27]

After the war in Vietnam there was a similar debate—the just and limited war discourse which tried to combine the just war tradition with that of limited warfare. Although this was an important debate,[28] I would emphasize that we have to connect the just war tradition even more closely with the aim of limiting warfare, by stressing that war can be justified if it itself limits war and violence significantly. Clausewitz obviously thought in the categories of the Westphalian system. Especially in his early writings, he argued passionately against French hegemony. But at the same time he acknowledged the right in principle of the French state to try to expand its power across the whole of Europe. The later Clausewitz focuses more on the balance of power in an international system. Here too (as in his trinity), there is a threefold division. According to Clausewitz, the main requirement of a state's policy is the preservation of its own existence with regard to other states. The right to expand one's own power by military means supplements this principle. This attempt to expand one's own power, legitimate in itself, must in Clausewitz's view, however, consider the interests of the state's population as well as the interests of the international system of states.[29]

Which aspects of Clausewitz's concept of politics can still claim validity today? Both the self-preservation of the state[30] and the recognition of other states as equals within the international system remain the basis of every state's policy. But one of today's problems is the extent to which a state can be regarded as a state. Most of the states in black Africa are not really states in a modern sense. What do we do with states that exploit their international recognition by abusing and assaulting their own people?

To expand one's own power by military means is no longer regarded as legitimate—although, of course, such wars are being waged. Such wars have

---

[27] There is a debate about whether the 'World War of 1792–1815' fundamentally challenged the Westphalian system, or whether its eventual re-establishment at the Congress of Vienna in 1815 strengthened it. Wilfried von Bredow, for example, argues that the French Revolution caused a break; John Keegan sees in the Revolution the beginning of a development towards 'total war'; Martin van Creveld argues that the changes caused by the Revolution should not be exaggerated.

[28] W. O'Brien, *The Conduct of Just and Limited War* (New York, 1981); Michael Walzer, *Just and Unjust Wars: A Moral Argument with Historical Illustrations*, 2nd edn ( New York, 1992; first published 1977).

[29] Peter Paret, *Understanding War: Essays on Clausewitz and the History of Military Power* (Princeton, NJ, 1993), 169.

[30] With respect to the thesis of David Rodin, that the right of self-defence is sometimes based on a problematic distinction between the 'innocent victim' and the 'guilty aggressor', I use the broader and more general concept of self-preservation of states: David Rodin, *War and Self-Defense* (Oxford, 2002), 189–90.

nowadays to be fought under the banner of defensive war, though in reality they do not really belong to this concept. But this very problem exemplifies the need to develop a concept of politics for our times, if war is to remain a continuation of politics by other means.

## COMPETING CONCEPTIONS

The function of this conception can be clarified through the example of democratization. The limitation of war and violence lays the foundations of democracy. If the single counter-strategy to the proliferation of violence were a general, worldwide democratization (in the meaning of implementing democratic elections, a necessary, but not sufficient, precondition of establishing real democratic societies) effected (as would be necessary) through force, its results would almost certainly be counterproductive. This is particularly clear in those states and societies where fully developed constitutional democracies are not yet present, but which are undergoing the initial process of transformation. In the latter cases, speaking of the antinomies of democratic peace is more justified than when referring to developed democracies. Thus it is possible that a one-sided demand for democratic processes without regard to local conditions in individual cases might even contribute to the creation of totalitarian movements. The historical experience that corresponds to the change from democratic to totalitarian processes is embodied in developments during and after the First World War. In nearly all of the defeated states, there was at the beginning a process of democratization, including, in some cases, democratic revolutions. Yet almost all ended in dictatorships. In Eastern Europe and the Balkans, the 'right to national self-determination', proclaimed by the US President Woodrow Wilson, was interpreted in a nationalist rather than in a democratic way. It embraced the exclusion of entire ethnic groups, their displacement and, in some cases, their elimination. The most dramatic example, the massacre of the Armenians, began in the First World War itself.[31]

From the overarching perspective of the containment of war and violence, however, it can be reasonable in particular cases to renounce democratization in favour of disarmament. Thus in the case of Libya (a former 'rogue state') the United States has abandoned a policy of enforced democratization by military means in favour of Libyan nuclear disarmament, providing an almost watertight guarantee that Gaddafi can continue to rule and will be succeeded by his son. Clearly, this example does not exclude the possibility that in other

---

[31] Dan Diner, *Das Jahrhundert verstehen* (Frankfurt, 2000).

cases the processes of democratization promoted from the outside might involve the use of violence. Historically speaking, one must remember that after the Second World War there were a number of democratization processes following militarily disastrous defeats, for instance in Germany and Japan, and then in Serbia after the Kosovo war.

The central approach developed here, in contrast to other theoretical conceptions of peace, can be described as follows. Conceptions of democratic peace following Kant, those of the 'civilizational hexagon', those belonging to theories of equilibrium, and conceptions of hegemony and empire, have all been used to bring about a limitation of war and violence in world society. But these means have often become ends in themselves. In my approach, the containment of war and violence itself becomes the overarching aim of political and communal action. Proceeding from this *political aim*, one can then judge *which* goal and *which* action are the most appropriate.

This determination reflects the historical experience of the two most effective European traditions in the limitation of war. They are the notion of the just war, the right to go to war (*jus ad bellum*), and the notion of just conduct in war (*jus in bello*), which acknowledged the foe as an equal with the same rights—a principle which has unfortunately been recently overturned. Both conceptions succeeded in banishing irregular forms of violence to the margins of the European world. During the crusades of the Middle Ages and in the course of colonial conquests between the sixteenth and eighteenth centuries, non-European opponents were not merely fought but often exterminated. In both cases, the normalized, intra-European forms of violence ended in disaster. The idea of a just war, which contributed to a limitation of war and violence for long periods of the Middle Ages, dissolved in the religious conflicts of the sixteenth century and the Thirty Years War. The inter-state wars of the Westphalian era, which was based on a right to wage war between equal opponents, resulted in the catastrophes of the First and Second World Wars.

The beginning and end of any historical development cannot be separated from each other in so far as they rest on the same principles. One cannot idealize the model of a limited war in the seventeenth and eighteenth centuries, because this same model, when combined with the industrialization of war and new nationalist and totalitarian ideologies, ultimately resulted in the two world wars. Equally, there are no grounds for dismissing the idea of the just war simply in view of the religious wars and the Thirty Years War. Rather, the limiting and 'protecting' effects of war during long periods of the Middle Ages should be borne in mind.[32] 'In accordance with the Christian tradition of the major denominations, [the concept of just war] should not

---

[32] Cora Stephan, *Das Handwerk des Krieges* (Berlin, 1998).

promote military violence, but rather hinder it or at least help to limit it. It is appropriately understood only against the background of fundamental reservations about war for the purpose of peace. This means that the threat and employment of military force can only be justified conditionally—as instruments for preventing, limiting, and moderating violence'.[33] Despite this ideal definition of just war, three fundamental problems in this conception have appeared in the course of history: the encouragement of violence on the grounds that any measure is acceptable in a just cause; the consequent stigmatization of the opponent as a criminal; and a pronounced tendency, at least in Europe, for polities to choose violence when they feel themselves to be acting under profound moral compulsion (and not merely in the pursuit of 'interests'). In order to avoid these difficulties, it is necessary to conceive of the limitation of war and violence itself as an overarching political aim of national and international communities.[34]

## HUMANITARIAN INTERVENTION AND CIVIL CONFLICT MANAGEMENT

Humanitarian intervention and civil conflict management are fundamentally contrasting forms of action, even though it is certainly the case that, ideally, their goals are very similar: the prevention of large-scale violence. There have been very heated debates between people who favour these different approaches (especially in connection with the war over Kosovo), and this has a good deal to do with the fact that the two sides in this dispute are using strongly moral arguments to make the case for almost identical goals. In many cases, 'policy alternatives based on different moral principles are put forward in such a way that political judgements can only have a modest role to play.'[35] It seems that one of the central problems here is that the two sides are using

[33] Albert Fuchs, 'Gerechter Krieg? Anmerkungen zur bellum-iustum Lehre', *Wissenschaft und Frieden*, 19/3 (2001), 12–15.
[34] The concept of a containment of war and violence in world society could additionally be perceived as something like a third way between national and human security, combining aspects of both at the same time, avoiding developments which might lead to 'securitisation': David Held, *Global Covenant: the Social Democratic Alternative to the Washington Consensus* (London, 2004); Barry Buzan, 'Societal Security, State Security and Internationalisation', in Ole Wæver, Barry Buzan, Morten Kelstrup, and Pierre Lemaitre (eds), *Identity, Migration and the New Security Agenda in Europe* (London, 1993), 41–58; Barry Buzan, Ole Wæver, and Japp de Wilde, *Security: A New Framework for Analysis* (London, 1998).
[35] Herfried Münkler, 'Menschenrechte und Staatsräson', in Gustav Gustenau (ed.), *Humanitäre militärische Intervention zwischen Legalität und Legitimität* (Baden-Baden, 2000), 141–65, here 144.

primarily moral arguments to make the case for the form of action each of them considers morally appropriate, and not much effort is spent on working out which form of action is likely to be more effective.[36]

One objection to humanitarian interventions is that in this case the method employed (i.e. using force oneself) contradicts the express purpose—that is bringing about peace. It is argued that violence does not solve conflicts, but rather makes them worse by giving rise to further violence. In extreme cases, those who argue in favour of humanitarian intervention are accused of using this argument as a pretext to disguise their pursuit of their own power-political interests. This argument can be turned around, and one could make the case that in emergency situations where excessive violence is being used, the insistence that only non-military options be considered amounts to a more or less conscious acceptance that there will be a large number of victims, even though at least some of them could be saved by such modest measures as setting up protected zones. Michael Walzer describes this perspective as a 'policy of salvation'.[37] It would be especially unconvincing if we were to condemn a limited military intervention designed to prevent genocide as an act of aggression simply by virtue of its military character. It is not meaningful to reject murder on a massive scale without permitting the international community to intervene to stop it.[38]

A violent humanitarian intervention can be evaluated immediately, either as a positive or a negative action, or at least it can be more unambiguously evaluated than a civil conflict management plan, which usually needs more time. 'Peace work requires patience, it needs time..., and it must be allowed to grow from below. Unlike military action, peace work cannot claim to offer immediate solutions, bring these solutions about, pretend that they have been achieved, or enforce them. And experience teaches us that immediate, victorious solutions themselves create new injustices and fail to bring about peace.'[39] There are arguments for and against both approaches—military action and peace work. An act of 'emergency assistance' by a superior military power may make societal tensions and conflicts worse, and risk escalation. Civil

---

[36] This dilemma is clearly emphasized in most of the contributions in J. L. Holzgrefe and Robert Keohane (eds), *Humanitarian Intervention: Ethical, Legal and Political Dilemmas* (Cambridge, 2003).

[37] Walzer, *Just and Unjust Wars*; Michael Walzer, 'Die Politik der Rettung', *Berliner Debatte Initial*, 6 (1995), 47–54.

[38] Egbert Jahn, 'Intervention und Recht. Zum Widerspruch zwischen dem allgemeinen Interventionsverbot und einem Interventionsgebot bei Völkermord', in Matthias Albert, Bernhard Moltmann, and Bruno Schoch (eds), *Die Entgrenzung der Politik. Internationale Beziehungen und Friedensforschung. Festschrift für Lothar Brock* (Frankfurt, 2004), 65–94.

[39] Reinhard Voß, 'Leitbilder eines christlichen Pazifismus', Vortrag auf dem 8. Friedenspolitischen Ratschlag in Kassel, 1–2 December 2001.

conflict management may collapse when large-scale violence can no longer be prevented by the methods used up until then. However, the decisive way of looking at the problem should always be the question of what is appropriate in this particular case; in other words, what can be done and what is likely to be effective? This should take precedence over moral debates about the causes of the conflict.

In many cases, the differences between advocates of humanitarian intervention and those of civil conflict management are nowhere near as great as the debate conducted at the moral level would lead one to suspect. The main reason for this is that concepts of civil conflict management cannot fully exclude the use of enforcement measures, of a police or military type, taken by third parties. In the *Agenda for Peace*, which was initiated in 1995 by the then General Secretary of the United Nations Boutros Boutros-Ghali, a conflict management system which included both civil and military components was developed. It consisted of four categories: (*a*) prevention; (*b*) mediation, designed to lead to a written agreement of some sort, such as a ceasefire or a comprehensive accord; (*c*) peacekeeping in the form of military monitoring of ceasefires; and (*d*) peace-building, which includes the creation of the social and political conditions required for lasting peace.[40] In spite of the fact that concepts of humanitarian intervention and those of civil conflict management are not so very far apart, or perhaps for this very reason, we repeatedly see instances of borderline situations which, because they present considerable political–military difficulties, take on the character of fundamental moral debates that merely conceal the similarities between the two positions.

The great variety of wars and conflicts makes it impossible to come to a generally valid decision in favour of one approach or the other. Any insistence on either a general right or necessity to intervene would have paradoxical consequences. In effect, intervention in the affairs of the great powers is already prohibited to the extent that they possess weapons of mass destruction and, in particular, nuclear weapons mounted on long-range delivery vehicles. A general *obligation* to intervene would lead numerous states to develop their own nuclear weapons and the appropriate delivery systems, as a way of countering the threat of intervention.[41]

At this point, we can see clearly how the clash of moral principles I have already mentioned comes into play: 'Two crucial norms of international law,

---

[40] Oliver Wolleh, 'Zivile Konfliktbearbeitung in ethnopolitischen Konflikten', *Aus Politik und Zeitgeschichte*, 20, 26–36; Boutros Boutros-Ghali, *Agenda for Peace* (New York, 1995).

[41] Harald Müller, 'Frieden zwischen den Nationen. Der Beitrag der Theorien von den Internationalen Beziehungen zum Wissen über den Frieden', in Matthias Albert, Bernhard Moltmann, and Bruno Schoch (eds), *Die Entgrenzung der Politik. Internationale Beziehungen und Friedensforschung. Festschrift für Lothar Brock* (Frankfurt, 2004), 40–64, here 43.

and also of political morality, seem to contradict each other: the obligation to act peacefully in inter-state relations, and the community of states' obligation to protect human rights, if need be by employing violent, warlike methods.'[42] The conclusion we are forced to reach as a result of the variety of conflicts is that there can be no binary counter-strategy that comes down exclusively on one side or the other as it seeks to hinder the escalation of violence and the broadening of zones of war. Rather, what we need is an ethically informed but in the last instance *political* consideration, which weighs up the costs and benefits, the risks and prospects of success, of both humanitarian intervention and civil conflict management.

One must stress that the possibility of humanitarian intervention is foreseen in the idea of limiting war and violence, but this does not mean that this possibility takes priority over the ideas of prevention or civil conflict management, or that it is accorded a lower priority as a matter of principle. Leaving open the possibility of a humanitarian intervention corresponds to the traditional idea of using military force as a last resort. With this single exception, it does not seem to make any sense to accord primacy to any one of these different levels of action, since the levels are distinguished by different time dimensions. If acute, large-scale, and excessive violence is already being employed, it is too late for preventive measures. If humanitarian intervention or civil conflict management were generally treated as the primary form of action, this would make it too easy for one of the parties involved in the conflict to instrumentalize the forces intervening from outside (whether these were states or non-governmental organizations). It is only the combination of uncertainty with the realistic expectation that third parties may take action that opens up political space for conflicts to be dealt with in non-violent ways.

This combination of certainty and uncertainty was a decisive factor in the ending of the Cold War and the nuclear arms race. Similarly, in spite of all the rhetoric and the launching of medium-range missiles against Israel in 1991, Iraq did not attack Israel with weapons of mass destruction. This too is likely to have been based on a combination of certainty and uncertainty. It was reported that Israeli planes armed with nuclear bombs were on the way to Baghdad, but were ordered back just before they reached their targets. Regardless of whether this report was accurate, it is precisely this combination of assumed certainty and uncertainty about how one's opponent will react that can have a self-deterring effect and prevent escalation. As Clausewitz puts it, this is why we must admit that 'imperfect knowledge of the case must, in

---

[42] Jahn, *Intervention und Recht*, 92.

general, do much to stop military action and to moderate the principle of such action'.[43]

The idea of limiting war and violence has another advantage over the idea of pure humanitarian intervention. In different public debates, the interventions supported by the UN in Somalia, Rwanda, Haiti, Bosnia, and Kosovo were frequently perceived to have been unsuccessful overall. However, this assessment only follows if these interventions are associated with unrealistically high expectations. In the case of the intervention in Somalia, for example, it fails to take account of the fact that the intervention made possible the delivery of assistance which, in the short term, saved the lives of hundreds of thousands of people. In the case of Rwanda, the setting up of protection zones had the same result. In order to counter such negative evaluations of humanitarian interventions, there is a need not only for the UN and trans-national non-governmental organizations to put in place a 'post-intervention policy', but also for a clear awareness of what can and cannot be achieved by military interventions.[44]

## THE CONCEPT OF CONTAINMENT AND CONTEMPORARY WARFARE

The advantage of my concept could be additionally demonstrated by considering the nature of the end state for which the war on terror should be fought. Is the purpose to try to find terrorists and root them all out, as Donald Rumsfeld stated?[45] If so, the next question is, how do you fight organizations, which are not hierarchically structured, but function as networks? Here the conception of limitation could provide some thoughts.

Aharon Ze'evi Farkash, a former head of military intelligence in the Israeli Defence Forces, emphasized in an interview that the IDF is able *to contain* Hamas.[46] The goal of the war on terror should not be to try to gain victory, because there is no clear idea of what victory would mean with regard to such a war. In any case, trying to gain a decisive victory over terrorists will

[43] Clausewitz, *Vom Kriege*, ed. Werner Hahlweg, 19th edn (Bonn, 1980), I, 1, § 18, p. 206.
[44] Bernhard Zangl and Michael Zürn, *Frieden und Krieg* (Frankfurt, 2003), 273–4.
[45] 'You can only defend by finding terrorists and rooting them out', interview with Donald Rumsfeld, *The Daily Telegraph*, 25 February 2002.
[46] Aaron Ze'evi-Farkash, 'Israel is paying a heavy price', Ynetnews (http://www.ynetnews.com/Ext/Comp/ArticleLayout/CdaArticlePrintPreview/1,2506,L-3058202, 21.3.2005). Although the situation has changed since the victory of Hamas in the elections in early 2006, the Israeli government is still pursuing a politic of containing Hamas in the sense of isolating it, curbing its movements and denying it access to finance.

only produce more of them. The first problem is therefore how we ourselves conceive the concept of victory, but the second and more important issue is the ways in which low-tech enemies define victory and defeat. That is an exercise that requires cultural and historical knowledge much more than it does gee-whiz technology.[47]

Instead, one could argue that the goal is 'to contain terror', which is of course something quite different from appeasement. An essential limitation of the dangers posed by terrorist organizations could be based on three aspects: first, a struggle of political ideas for the hearts and minds of millions of young people; second, an attempt to curb the exchanges of knowledge, financial support, communication between the various networks with the aim of isolating them on a local level; and finally, but only as one of these three tasks, the destruction of what the Israelis call the terrorist infrastructure. Such an approach could additionally prevent the conglomeration of states, where, despite the differences between them, terrorists are free to move and communicate, and where there are no real borders to prevent this floating. Whether accidental or not, one of the most important successes of the interventions in Afghanistan and Iraq is the check on movements between Syria and Pakistan, and between some of the states of the former USSR and Iran. Trying to achieve victory over terrorism in a traditional military manner would not only fail, but could in addition lead to much more terrorism in the foreseeable future.

The concept of the 'centre of gravity' in warfare can provide another illustration of the way in which my conception makes a difference. Clausewitz defines war as an act of violence to compel our enemy to do our will. This definition suits our understanding of war between equal opponents, between opponents in which one side does not want to annihilate the other or his political, ethnic, or tribal body. But in conflicts between opponents with a different culture or ethnic background, the imposition of one's will on the other is often perceived as an attempt to annihilate the other's community and identity. Hence, for democratic societies, the only alternative is to perceive war as an act of violence where, rather than imposing our will on our opponent, we rendered our opponent unable to pursue his own will violently or to use his full power to impose his will on us or others. Consequently, the abilities of his power must be limited, so that he is no more able to threaten or fight us in order to compel us to do his will.

The purpose of containing war and violence, therefore, is to remove from the belligerent adversary his physical and moral freedom of action, but without attacking the sources of his power and the order of his society. The key to 'mastering violence' is to control not only certain operational domains,

---

[47] Robert D. Kaplan, 'The Story of a War', *Atlantic Monthly*, November 2003.

territory, mass movement, and armaments but also information and humanitarian operations. But this task of 'mastering violence' should no longer be perceived as being directed against the centre of gravity, but against the 'lines' of the field of gravitation. Instead of imposing one's own will on the adversary up to the point of controlling his mind, as the protagonists of strategic information warfare have proposed,[48] the only way to end conflict in the globalized twenty-first century is to set limits to action, but at the same time to give room for action (in the sense in which Hannah Arendt used this term) and even for resistance, which of course has the effect of legitimizing action within those limits.[49] The concept of *ius in bello* is helpful here: the enemy will fight to the bitter end if he is not given grounds to expect human and honourable treatment. The expectation of a just peace after the war, *ius post bellum*, has a more pacifying function than any attempt to shape an enemy's warlike spirit. The latter must necessarily be circumscribed and will therefore have an uncertain outcome, if it is not totally effective.

## THE POSITIVE SIGNIFICANCE OF DRAWING BOUNDARIES

In a civilization in which overcoming borders has become a symbol of progress and indeed has been celebrated as a veritable moral imperative, it is not easy to see the marking of boundaries in a positive light. In addition, of course, there is the specific experience of post-war Europe, in which the step-by-step relativization of borders and the symbolic tearing down of barriers has been a symbol of European unification and an expression of the way in which centuries of animosity can be overcome. Furthermore, in the course of debates about the significance of the drawing of spatial and social boundaries for the development of modernity, a discourse has emerged which either plays down the significance of borders or understands the exclusion of strangers as a precondition of their destruction.[50]

---

[48] David Lonsdale, *The Nature of War in the Information Age: Clausewitzian Future* (London, 2004), 208. See also his chapter in this book.

[49] Although there are some similarities between the military part of the concept of a new containment and 'coercive military strategy', the main distinction may be that, in my concept, one's own will is not directly imposed on the foe. Instead of that, there are 'only' boundaries, limits drawn to his actions, within which he is free to roam at his own will; see Stephen J. Cimbala, *Coercive Military Strategy* (College Station, TX, 1998). The possibility of giving room for legitimate action within these boundaries seems to be the only way to end conflicts between 'eternal' foes as well as between actors with a different cultural background.

[50] Zygmunt Bauman, *Modernity and the Holocaust* (Cambridge, 1989); Zygmunt Bauman, *Modernity and Ambivalence* (Cambridge, 1991).

Although one cannot fault Zygmunt Bauman's argument in its application to Nazism, it cannot be easily generalized. From the point of view of a systematic approach to concepts, one must point out that there is no reason why differences of identity must always coincide with a friend–enemy dichotomy. Other kinds of relations are possible, and these do not draw boundaries so sharply in the sense that the 'other' is automatically the enemy. The negative charge attached to the other side of a political border can become less important, and the main emphasis can be placed on positive rather than negative identifications. In this respect identification based on spatial relations always means singling out something or someone, but not necessarily segregation. A neighbourhood model would also be possible, in which, when assessing the boundary category, one must ask whether the boundary serves to include a neighbour or to exclude something or someone.[51]

Where the limitation of war and violence in world society is concerned, one must bear in mind that this term cannot be understood to mean an immanent drawing of spatial boundaries, something like the creation of geographically bounded, pacified islands where there is significantly less violence, in a sea of violence and war economies. Boundaries in the use of war and violence are determined and drawn in the context of political and social processes. Clausewitz emphasizes that there can be no inherent limits to the use of force; Wolfgang Sofsky insists that the fundamental feature of violence is the way it becomes autonomous, and Dirk Schuhmann treats violence as a constant transgressing of borders.[52]

The drawing of boundaries has positive consequences: this is how norms are given a foundation in law, and authority a foundation in politics. It can also have the effect of creating meaning by establishing clear boundaries of meaning and expectation.[53] The sociologist Georg Simmel stresses that a border is not 'a spatial fact with sociological effects', but rather 'a sociological fact which forms itself spatially'.[54] The drawing of boundaries has always played a fundamental, central role in human societies. The ten commandments of the Old Testament provide a good indication of this: almost all of them take the form 'Thou shalt not...'. Thus the main statement being made is not about how people should behave 'positively', but about the limits of individual behaviour. In this respect, the main function of law is to mark limits to

---

[51] Norbert Wokart, 'Differenzierungen im Begriff "Grenze". Zur Vielfalt eines scheinbar einfachen Begriffs', in Richard Faber and Barbara Naumann (eds), *Literatur der Grenze—Theorie der Grenze* (Würzburg, 1997), 275–89.

[52] *Vom Kriege*, I, 1, § 3, p. 194; Wolfgang Sofsky, *Violence: Terrorism, Genocide, War* (London, 2004); Dirk Schuhmann, 'Gewalt als Grenzüberschreitung. Überlegungen zur Sozialgeschichte der Gewalt im 19. und 20. Jahrhundert', *Archiv für Sozialgeschichte*, 37 (1997), 366–86.

[53] Claus Leggewie, *Die Globalisierung und ihre Kritiker* (Frankfurt, 2003), 22 f.

[54] Georg Simmel, *Soziologie* (Frankfurt, 1992), 695–7.

human behaviour,[55] just as law can be seen from the opposite perspective as the expression of boundaries that have been set by human decisions. In a globalized world the significance of boundaries drawn by symbols, norms, the law, and discourses is, unlike that of state borders, increasing.[56] Debordering processes of expansion, universalization, and globalization have in recent history repeatedly led to the drawing of new boundaries both within societies and within civilizations.[57] Both civil societies and civilizations have always required boundaries drawn in terms of society, culture, or community, especially against war and violence.[58]

## CONTAINING WAR AND VIOLENCE IN WORLD SOCIETY

The concept of containing war and violence in world society I am developing here is the common element shared by humanitarian intervention and the development of a culture of civil conflict management. One needs to add to this measures to counter the causes of war and violence, such as poverty, oppression, and ignorance, and the search for solutions to regional conflicts, in order to construct the 'task of the century' facing both the community of states and civil society.[59] As Antulio Echevarria writes in his chapter in this book, 'the *U.S. National Strategy for Combating Terrorism* also includes an essential, but rather ambitious goal of diminishing the conditions that terrorists typically exploit, such as poverty, social and political disenfranchisement, and long-standing political, religious, and ethnic grievances; reducing these conditions requires, among other things, fostering political, social, and economic development, good governance, the rule of law, and consistent participation in the "war of ideas".' Further important tasks include preventing

---

[55] Ernst-Wolfgang Böckenförde, 'Recht setzt Grenzen', in Ernst Ulrich von Weizsäcker (ed.), *Grenzen-los? Jedes System braucht Grenzen—aber wie durchlässig müssen diese sein?* (Berlin, 1997), 272–9, here 278.

[56] Thorsten Bonacker, 'Die Idee der (Un)Entscheidbarkeit—Zum Paradigmenwechsel in der Konflikttheorie nach dem Ende des Ost–West-Konflikts', in Wolfgang R. Vogt (ed.), *Gewalt und Konfliktbearbeitung* (Baden-Baden, 1997), 94–107.

[57] Jürgen Osterhammel, 'Kulturelle Grenzen in historischer Perspektive', in Weizsäcker (ed.), *Grenzen-los?*, 213–19, here 219.

[58] This does not exclude the fact that social, economic, and cultural boundaries have to be removed in the process of fostering economic, social, and political progress. But I want to emphasize that this is a dialectical process, in which the transgression of boundaries must be complemented by the drawing of new ones, within which one is free to roam, though at the same time enclosed by them. This is what enables the generation of order; Held, *Global Covenant*.

[59] Heinz Kluss, 'Jenseits von Clausewitz? Konfliktprävention und Kriegsführung im 21. Jahrhundert', in Gerhard Kümmel and Sabine Collmer (eds), *Asymmetrische Konflikte und Terrorismusbekämpfung. Prototypen zukünftiger Kriege* (Baden-Baden, 2003), 107–21, here 107.

the proliferation of weapons of mass destruction and of small arms. The concept of containment is associated with the insight that we cannot expect in the foreseeable future to see fully non-violent societies or a non-violent world society. In addition, the aspiration to a world without conflicts as such fails to recognize that in the course of history conflicts and conflict solutions have frequently been necessary for human development. The main task confronting politics and social forces in the twenty-first century is the radical limitation, even diminishing of violence and war, so that non-violent structures can be sustained and the mechanisms of the 'world of societies'[60] can come to fruition.

The overall political perspective on which the concept of the containing of war and violence in world society rests therefore consists of the following elements, the '*pentagon of containing war and violence*':

- the ability to deter and discourage any opponent from fighting a large-scale war and to conduct precise military action as a last resort;
- the possibility of using military force in order to limit and contain particularly excessive, large-scale violence which has the potential to destroy societies;
- the willingness to counter phenomena which help to cause violence, such as poverty and oppression, especially in the economic sphere, and also the recognition of a pluralism of cultures and styles of life in world society;
- the motivation to develop a culture of civil conflict management (concepts which can be summed up in the 'civilizational hexagon', global governance, and democratic peace), based on the observation that the reduction of our action to military means has proved counterproductive and in the end will exceed our military capabilities; and
- restricting the possession and proliferation of weapons of mass destruction, their delivery systems, as well as of small arms, because the proliferation of both is inherently destructive to social order.

The containment of war and violence in world society requires its own normative criteria, even though it does not itself provide direct moral instructions on how to act. Instead, it combines political–moral considerations with aspects relevant to every state's interest in self-preservation. It requires political actors to recognize the advantages of self-limitation as part of their own enlightened self-interest. In anthropological terms, we can see the roots of the political in the openness and indeterminacy of the human power to act. In historical

---

[60] Ernst Otto Czempiel, *Weltpolitik im Umbruch. Die Pax Americana, der Terrorismus und die Zukunft der internationalen Beziehungen* (München, 2002).

terms, we can follow Aristotle in seeing these roots in the way we are forced to limit ourselves once we become aware of the contingency of human actions.[61] It follows from this that one of the decisive questions for future developments is that of the possible self-interest of the United States, or regional powers, in making conflict subject to legal norms, in civil conflict management, and in binding military power into alliance systems.

In current circumstances, this raises the question of whether the United States in particular is interested in self-limitation. The United States has pursued a unilateral policy since the 11 September 2001 terrorist attacks and the 2003 Iraq war, and will perhaps continue to do so. However, one cannot exclude the possibility that the United States might, in the medium term, come to see a policy of self-restraint as being in its enlightened self-interest. One reason why it might do this is the fact that purely military attempts to 'solve' conflicts will give rise to more armed resistance than even the greatest military power can deal with. Intervention itself can lead to the disintegration of a state, which in turn offers opportunities for violent ideologies to flourish. In any event, given the globalization of the technologies needed for weapons of mass destruction, such ideologies and the movements they inspire will not remain restricted to the 'underdeveloped' areas of the world indefinitely. The readiness of the United States to bind itself within NATO during the Cold War showed that self-limitation 'adds political value'.[62] It also minimized the direct military costs of 'pacifying' alliance partners and so gave the United States an advantage over the USSR. This created a space for military–technological innovations, which proved to be one of the main reasons for the eventual victory of the West in the systemic competition with the USSR.

Although the beginning of this chapter referred to Carl Schmitt's argument about the need to limit war and violence in world society, there is a difference between my position and Schmitt's. Schmitt thought limitation was a necessary precondition of the further waging of war, and he continued to treat the possibility of enmity as a constitutive condition of the political. The position I have put forward is oriented towards a basically peaceful global policy, and treats the progressive limitation of war and violence as both an indefinite, ongoing process and as an end in itself. The lasting and progressive containment of war and violence in world society is therefore necessary for the self-preservation of states, even their survival, and for the civility of individual societies and world society.

---

[61] Hans-Georg Soeffner and Dirk Tänzler (eds), *Figurative Politik. Zur Performanz der Macht in der modernen Gesellschaft* (Opladen, 2002), 27.
[62] A point I owe to Herfried Münkler.

Such a perspective can only be based on Clausewitz's very late writings, after he had recognized that the unconditional and unquestioned adherence of Napoleon to his strategy of unleashing violence contributed to his disaster at Waterloo and his final defeat. Clausewitz's notions of limited warfare have their foundations in the last parts of book VIII. They find some reflection in book I, chapter 2: 'Be that as it may, we must always consider that with the conclusion of peace the purpose of the war has been achieved'; and further on: 'Since war is not an act of senseless passion but is controlled by its political object, the value of this object must determine the sacrifices to be made for it in magnitude and also in duration.'[63] In book VIII, he stated: 'In this way the belligerent is again driven to adopt a middle course. He would act on the principle of using no greater force, and setting himself no greater military aim, than would be sufficient for the achievement of his political purpose. To turn this principle into practice, he must renounce the need for absolute success in each given case.'[64] There is no great step needed, and no gap to be bridged, to move forward from a strategy of limited warfare to one of the limitations of war and violence as the overarching purpose of political action in our own times. Such a perspective is still based on Clausewitz's statement that war is a continuation of politics by other means, but at the same time it is trying to actualize his concept of politics.

Contrary to Raymond Aron, I do not believe that emphasizing the late Clausewitz implies that only his writings from this period are applicable to the twenty-first century. But we have to differentiate between the importance of Clausewitz's writings for the analytical study of the warfare of our own times and his normative assessments, which are sometimes deeply rooted within the thoughts which he shared only with his contemporaries.[65] Clausewitz did not always distinguish sufficiently clearly between the analytical and normative dimensions of his thoughts, especially in his early writings and even up until 1827. For example, the distinction is not at all clear in his discussion at the beginning of book I, chapter 1, of the three interactions which push war to the extreme, despite the fact that these sections were presumably written after the note of 1827, in which he recognized the need to rework the whole of *On War* according to his new insight, the distinction between limited war and war whose aim is to overthrow the enemy and render him powerless. An adequate treatment of Clausewitz and his thinking has to be based on the assumption that, for the purpose of analysing and studying war and warfare, the early as well as the late Clausewitz is of the greatest importance, whereas with respect

---

[63] *On War*, I, 2, pp. 91–2. [64] Ibid. VIII, 3B, p. 585.
[65] Raymond Aron, *Clausewitz: Philosopher of War* (London, 1983; first published 1976); Peter Paret, *Clausewitz and the State: the Man, His Theories and His Times* (Princeton, NJ, 1976).

to our political and military action perhaps only the late Clausewitz needs serve as an important basis. As Clausewitz himself emphasized at the end of his discussion of the trinity (his true legacy, in Aron's view), 'at any rate, the preliminary concept of war casts a first ray of light on the basic structure of theory, and enables us to make an initial differentiation and identification of its major components'.[66] Thinking about contemporary and future warfare with, and sometimes beyond, Clausewitz can still be the best way to begin.[67]

---

[66] *On War*, I, 1, § 28, p. 89.

[67] The importance of the search for an adequate 'beginning' for any theory should not be underestimated. Hannah Arendt put this concept at the centre of her thinking more often than all other political thinkers. Additionally one should remember the concept of the beginning in Hegel's 'Logic'. See for both issues, Andreas Herberg-Rothe, *Lyotard und Hegel. Dialektik von Philosophie und Politik* (Vienna, 2005).

# Index

absolute war 20–1, 26, 30, 32–5, 41, 64–7, 164, 165, 194
Abu Ghraib Detention Facility, Iraq 209, 228
action 12, 42, 51–3, 55–6, 63, 68–9, 108, 111, 117, 129, 141, 173
  suspension of 169, 178, 261
adversary *see* enemy
aesthetics 45, 122, 125, 128, 131
Afghanistan 4, 105, 156, 161, 214, 228
Africa 34, 190, 221, 284, 292, 299
aggression, acts of 171, 292, 296
aims and objectives, military 32, 47, 91–106, 158, 186, 189, 196, 212, 240
aims and objectives, political 11, 67, 71, 84, 90, 92, 100, 101, 102–3, 142, 149, 157, 201–2, 203, 268–72, 294, 306
air power 122–3, 152, 158, 222, 236, 237, 240–1, 244, 255, 256
Albright, Madeleine 221
*Allgemeine Deutsche Biographie* (dictionary of national biography) 19
allies 172, 174
Alsace and Lorraine 97
American Civil War (1861–65) 241, 244
American War of Independence (American Revolutionary War) (1775–83) 139, 273
ANC (African National Congress) 190
annihilation 23, 26, 32, 41, 144, 149, 150–4, 167, 235, 255, 260
anti-colonial wars 243, 276
anti-Semitism 152
antithesis 41, 75
Apel, Hans 5–6
Applegate, Colonel Dick 245
Arendt, Hannah 12, 125–6, 127, 134, 136, 289, 301, 307 n.
Aristotle 29, 129, 132, 305
armed conflict, theory of 196, 201
armed forces 80, 186, 189, 201, 202–3, 240, 249
  civil-military relations 266–82
  concentrated 149–50
  democratic control of 60–1, 278–81
  destruction of 61–4, 66

maintenance and supply of 39, 169, 220, 228
minimization of losses 222, 236, 244
nationalization of 146, 192, 272–4
numerical superiority 149
organization of 272
policy and 277
political instrument 269, 270
preservation of 167, 175
professionalization of 223–4
reluctant civil-military parallelism 281–2
specialization of 274–5
value of 243–4, 249
women in 281, *see also* commanders
Armenian genocide (1915) 293
armistice 153, 157, *see also* peace
arms control 271, *see also* deterrence
Aron, Raymond 11, 18, 37, 41, 43, 69, 177, 251, 275, 306, 307
Arquilla, John 235, 246
Arreguin-Toft, Ivan 191
Ashworth, G. J. 243
asymmetric warfare 159, 191, 193, 195, 222, 225, 230, 242, 244, 285
atrocities 193–4, 271, 276, 293, *see also* genocide
attack:
  and defence relation 24–5, 31, 42, 95, 165, 166, 168, 169, 171–81, 183, 188–91, 193–4, 257
  enemy's 'centre of gravity' 149–50, 155, 161, *see also* terrorism
attrition, strategy of 24, 26, 165, 167, 179, 242
Austerlitz, battle of (1805) 5, 15
Austria 94, 97
Austro-Prussian war (1866) 150
autonomous violence 254, 270, 302
autonomy, political and military 264

balance of power 69, 134, 191, 193, 272, 292
Bali bombings (October 2002) 209
Bassford, Christopher 3, 4, 10, 177, 233
battle 27
  contest of wills 147, 156
  decisive 148, 149, 150, 158, 166, 246, 262
  future 'virtual' 236

battle (cont.)
  psychological effect of 145–6
  use of 22–3
  victory in 143–4
battle-space 235–6, 238, 241, 247, 248
battlefields 256
Bauman, Zygmunt 302
Beaufre, General André 148
Beck, General Ludwig 32, 33, 71
Berenhorst, Georg Heinrich von 141
Berlin, Isaiah 130
Bernhardi, Friedrich von 25
Beyerchen, Alan 233
bin Laden, Osama 212, 213, 216
biology 55
Bismarck, Otto von 27, 97
Boëne, Bernard 282
boldness 115, 120
Bonapartism 126
Bonnal, Henri 22
Bosnia-Hercegovina 9, 161, 214, 241–2, 299
boundaries 155, 301–3
bravery 12, 23, 77, 114–17, 168, 264
Bredow, Wilfried von 12, 121 n.
Britain:
  air power strategy 152
  colonial conflicts 243
  invasion of Iraq 158
  Malaya 160
  terrorist attacks in 209–10
  *On War* 31, 33
Brodie, Bernard vi, 143, 153, 156–7, 177, 243
brokerage warfare 272
Brühl, Count Friedrich Wilhelm von 18, 57, 59
Brühl, Marie von (later von Clausewitz) 15, 17, 18, 35, 57, 129
Brzezinski, Zbigniew 136 n.
Bülow, Heinrich Dietrich von 40, 141
bureaucracy 50, 187
Burnside, Major General Ambrose 244
Bush, President George H. W. 155 n., 158
Bush, President George W. 43

Caemmerer Lieutenant-General Rudolf von 21, 22–3, 25
Camon, Colonel Hubert 20, 22, 36
Canada 212
Cardot, Lucien 147
Casablanca terrorist attack (May 2003) 209
Castex, Admiral Raoul 153
Castro, Fidel 276
centuries of warfare:

pre-sixteenth 103, 104, 206, 224, 227, 272, 294
sixteenth 222, 224, 294
seventeenth 51, 224, 229, 270, 272, 294
eighteenth 94, 97, 138, 139, 192, 272, 294
nineteenth 7, 21, 23, 45, 61, 103, 119, 124, 127, 138, 144, 149, 150, 206, 270, 272–3, 275
twentieth 97–8, 149, 150, 227, 270–1, 273, 291–2
twenty-first 2, 4, 35, 43, 45, 92, 229, 236, 248, 266, 290, 301, *see also* under specific wars
chance 52–3, 77, 79, 81, 88–90, 202, 204, 209, 216, 217, 234, 235, 249, 272, *see also* probability
Charles, archduke of Austria 23
Charles XII of Sweden 207
Chechnya 214
chemistry 55, 56
child soldiers 276
China 124, 284, 285, 286
chivalry 39
Churchill, Sir Winston 85
civil conflict management 295, 296–7, 303, 304
civil-military relations 277–82
civil society 270, 277, 281, 303
civil wars 87, 122, 137, 159
civilian population *see* people
civilizational hexagon 286–7 n., 294, 304
Clark, General Wesley 259
Clausewitz, Carl von 22, 305–6
  career 14–16
  comparison with Kant 132–3
  conception of own work 252
  correspondence wtih Karl von Roeder 99–100
  disobedience of 120
  instructions to crown prince 149
  modernity of 60
  schools of interpretation 75–6
  statements of belief (1812) 28–9, 37, 183
  study of logic and mathematics 124
  sudden death of 14, 163, see also *On War*
Clausewitz-Gesellschaft 5, 6
Cochenhausen, Friedrich von 29
coercion 84, 157, 257, 301 n.
Coker, Christopher 232, 238
Cold War 5, 6, 11, 35, 41, 43, 134, 142, 153–5, 203, 271, 278, 284–5, 288, 298, 305
Colin, Jean 22
Collingwood, R. G. 181

# Index

Columbine high school massacre (1999) 213
commanders 77, 81, 86, 166, 172, 178, 204–7
  ambition 115–16
  characteristics of best 95
  civil-military relations 277–8
  *coup d'oeil* 54, 113–14, 116, 119, 120, 129, 141, 176, 197, 259
  decisive battles 262
  defence 168
  errors of judgement 248
  freedom of action 252, 258, 264–5
  intelligence and temperament 168
  nation-building 280
  part in cabinet's decisions 18, 25–6
  personality 21
  reductionism 196–7
  total war 271
common security 287–8
computers 50, 109, *see also* information technology
Comte, Auguste 270
conflict management 156–7, 162, 295, 296–9, 303, 304
Connolly, William 184
conscription 14, 146, 281
containment of violence 12, 263, 282–307
  drawing of boundaries 301–3
  humanitarian intervention 295–9
  terrorism 287, 288, 299–300, 303
  in world society 303–7
cost-benefit analysis 260, 261, 291
counter-insurgency warfare 216, 240
counterattacks 168, 170, 171, 174, 175, 176, 178, 180
*coup d'état* 278
*coup d'oeil* 54, 113–14, 116, 119, 120, 129, 141, 176, 197, 259
courage 12, 23, 114–17, 168, 264
*courage d'esprit* 116–17, 120
Creveld, Martin van 7–8, 9, 37, 41, 43, 80, 82, 182, 267
crime 9, 226, 286
crisis management 149, 162
CSCE (Conference on Security and Cooperation in Europe) 155, 156
Cuban missile crisis (1962) 71, 271
culture 8, 10, 213–14, 300, 304

Daase, Christopher 11
danger 115, 131, 168
Daudet, Léon 65 n., 151
decolonization 221 n.

deconstruction 184–6
defeat 99, 142, 145, 179
  armed resistance after 174
  conceding 260–1
  irreversible 159
  just conduct in 294, 301
  overthrow of enemy 8, 61–4, 66, 67, 68, 73, 93, 96, 143–5, 147, 149
  strategic 190–1
  transitory 61, 166, 254
defence 12, 26, 39, 165–81, 290 n.
  attack and 24–5, 31, 42, 95, 165, 166, 168, 169–81, 183, 188–91, 193–5, 257
  citizen soldiers 273
  definition of 170
  function of time in 257
  guerrilla warfare 192
  homeland 105
  territorial 281
Delbrück, Hans 18, 22, 23, 24, 25, 27, 167, 202
democracy 72, 191, 193, 267–8, 293–4
democratic control of armed forces 60–1, 278–81
Deptula, General D. A. 256
destruction *see* annihilation
detainees 209, 228
deterrence:
  conflict management and 157
  nuclear 32, 153, 154
  reciprocal 225
  true believers 288
  'war-fighting' 154
dialectics 37, 41–3, 44, 45, 59, 75, 188, 245–6, 249
dictatorship 126, 279, 293
diplomat/soldier 275–7
disarmament 62–4, 145, 149, 293
disobedience 120–1
disorganized complexity 46–7, 48, 52, 53
Dreifaltigkeit, wunderliche, *see* trinity
drug trafficking 226, 227
Dunlap, Charles 246
Durieux, Benoît 12
Durkheim, Emile 282

eastern Slavonia, military operations in (1997) 265
Echevarria, Antulio 6–7, 12, 303
economics 84–5, 137, 143, 151, 160, 182, 224, 225
Edmonds, J. E. 78–9
Egypt 98, 212

# Index

emotions 99, 108, 112–13, 114
  human fear 109
  resolution and 117
  self-control of 118–19
  soldiers 271
  violent 77, 79, 82
enemy:
  annihilation of 150, 169, 240, 246, 254–5, 260, 262
  centre of gravity 149–50, 155, 161, 300, 301
  concession 260–1
  ideal war 253–4
  imposing one's will on 29, 144–5, 147, 148, 149, 154, 159, 192, 197, 229, 234, 255, 277, 291, 300
  intelligent 239, 241, 249
  just conduct in defeat 294, 301
  overthrow of 8, 61–4, 66, 67, 68, 73, 93, 96, 143–5, 147, 149
  public 146
  revenge over 118
  Sun Tzu on 135
  use of geography 244
  willpower 202
  winning 'hearts and minds' 160–1, 300
Engels, Friedrich 30
Enlightenment 40, 45, 51, 124, 131
escalation dominance 193–4, 263, 264
escalation of war 59–60, 61, 64, 92, 94–5, 98, 191, 298
  ideal war approach 261, 262
  political conditions 71–2
  treaties to prevent 203
  WMDs 242, *see also* deterrence
Evera, Steven van 188
existential war 28, 29, 37, 41, 42, 43
experience 38, 41, 132, 168, 175, 198, 200, 218

failed states 221, 222, 276
Farkash, Aharon Ze'evi 299
feudalism 39
First Chechen War 243
First World War (1914–18) 26–9, 158, 255
  attritional warfare 242
  democratization after 293
  mutual war of annihilation 150
  total war 151
Foch, Ferdinand 147, 148, 158
foe, *see* enemy
fog of war 2, 52, 144, 178, 217, 236, 238, 251, 259, *see also* uncertainty of war
force, *see* armed forces; violence

fortifications 140, 171, 172, 173
fractal 86 n.
France 16, 292
  first use of term 'total war' 65, 151
  *levée en masse* 146, 192, 273
  moral forces 251
  revolution 9, 14, 43, 101, 134, 135, 146
  *On War* 22, 26, *see also* Napoleonic Wars
Franco-Prussian war (1870–1) 19, 21, 22, 150, 158
Frederick the Great 15, 23, 39, 97, 100–1, 207
Frederick William III, king of Prussia 15, 16, 190
Free Muslims Coalition 213
Freedman, Sir Lawrence 143, 238, 242
French Revolution 9, 14, 43, 101, 134, 135, 146
French Revolution, Wars of the 171
Freytag-Loringhoven, Major-General Hugo von 20, 21, 22, 23, 25
friction of war v, vi, 2, 11, 20, 45, 53, 69, 95, 107, 131, 168, 202, 249
  disorganized complexity 52
  factors of 234–5
  future wars and removal of 238
  ideal war 258–9, 261–2
  main causes of 108–9
  military leadership and 30, 89
  mission command and 117
  moral forces and 119
Fuller, J. F. C. 31, 33, 78, 142, 237

Gallie, W. B. 59
Gantzel, Klaus-Jürgen 182
Gat, Azar 36, 38, 59, 74 n., 164, 177
*Geist* 40, 117
genius 126–7, 128, 132, *see also* military genius
genocide 149, 210, 281, 284, 293, 296
geography 239, 243–4, 248, 249, 256, 301–3, *see also* terrain
German nationalism 11, 15–16
Germany 294
  citizen soldiers 273
  civil-military relations 278
  European Union 159
  general staff system 116, 121
  Nazism 26, 29, 32–3, 72, 152, 160, 278
  occupation of 159
  people's mobilization (1944–5) 159
  post-war reconstruction 160, 162
  principle of mission command 117
  Second World War 72, 152

Germany (*cont.*)
  Versailles peace treaty 150–1, 162
  *On War* 27–30, 36–7
Gettysburg, battle of (1863) 241
Giap Vo Nguyen, General 139
globalization 12, 208, 213, 268, 285, 290, 303
Gneisenau, August von 15–16, 28
Goebbels, Joseph 30
government 77, 80, 86, 166, 204–7, 258, 264, 265, *see also* state
Graham, J. J. 19, 58, 60
grammar of war 25, 105
Gray, Colin 10, 86, 142, 148, 154–5, 177, 239, 243, 284
Grimsley, Mark 143
Grouard, Lieutenant-Colonel 251
guerrilla warfare 10, 119–20, 138–9, 159, 183, 185, 187, 190–2, 276
Gulf War (1991) 8, 158, 162, 220, 232, 240, 246, 298
Gunaratna, Rohan 217
Gustavus Adolphus of Sweden 39, 207

Hague Conventions (1922–3) 151
Hahlweg, Werner v, 35, 57, 59, 183, 191
Haiti 299
Halliburton 228
Hamas 214, 299
Handel, Michael 37, 142, 177
Hart, Basil Liddell 26, 31, 33, 142, 177, 188
Hegel, Georg Wilhelm Friedrich 40, 41, 59, 108, 124, 206, 207
hegemony 12, 14, 285, 292, 294
Heine, Heinrich 156
Helsinki Final Act 155
Herberg-Rothe, Andreas 12, 36, 38, 121 n.
heroism 222–3, *see also* bravery
Heuser, Beatrice 11, 177
Hezbollah 214
high-tech warfare 236, 240, 241, 242, 243, 248, 255, 259, 285
history 38–40, 125, 129, 133, 168–9, 173, 175, 198–200, 206, 214, 218, 219, 282
Hitler, Adolf 26, 72, 85, 120, 126, 278, 279
  anti-semitism 152
  Clausewitz quoted in *Mein Kampf* 29
  death of 159
  Versailles peace treaty 151
Ho Chi Minh 157
Hobbes, Thomas 108
Hoffman, Bruce 217
Holmes, Terence 118 n.
honour 118–19
hostility 202, 209, 214, 215, 217

Howard, Sir Michael 36, 65, 90, 177, 194, 239
  *Politik* translation 70–3, 76, 83–6
Howard, Sir Michael and Paret, Peter 3, 11, 18, 33–4, 40, 58, 59, 60–4, 139, 164, 258
human error 248
human nature 69, 290, *see also* emotions
human rights 154, 155, 286
human trafficking 226, 227
humanitarian intervention 229, 276, 281, 295–9, 303
Humboldt, Alexander von 55
Hume, David 108
Huntington, Samuel 230, 287 n.

ideal war 146, 253–9, 260, 264–5
idealism 28, 108, 124
imagination 126–8, 136, 156–7
India 284, 285
industrialization of war 274, 294, *see also* technological innovation
information technology 12, 50, 109, 216, 236, 259, 290
information theory 46
information warfare 109, 231–50
instrumental war 37, 41, 42, 61 n., 87
insurgency 246
intelligence 117, 118, 141, 168
intelligence gathering 216
intelligence services 109
interaction 48, 53, 209
international law 43, 110, 133, 151, 220, 286, 297–8
international relations 123, 142
interstate war 6, 186, 219, 229, 253, 267, 268, 270, 275, 294
intuition 113–14, 129
Iran 97–8, 284, 288
Iraq 97–8, 119, 161, 214, 216
  Gulf War 8, 158, 162, 220, 232, 240, 246, 298
  PMCs used in 220, 228
  terrorism in 159, 209
  US invasion of 4, 34, 105, 137, 158–9, 220, 233, 284, 305
  weather 244
Islamic Conference of Spain 213
Islamists 209, 286, *see also* jihadists; terrorism
Israel 159, 190, 299, 300
Italy 160

Jähns, Max 19
Janowitz, Morris 256, 273
Japan 153, 160, 162, 294
Jena, battle of (1806) 5, 15, 17, 35, 36, 66

Jervis, Robert  188
jihadist movements  209–10, 212, 214
Johnson, President Lyndon  71
Jolles, O. J. Matthijs  3, 58, 60
Jomini, Antoine-Henri  2, 20, 40, 83, 141, 232
judgement:
    errors of  248
    faculty of  113–14
    Kantian  122, 124–5, 126, 128, 130–6
    military  136–7
just war  294–5, 301

Kagan, Robert  256, 287 n.
Kaldor, Mary  9, 37, 43, 182
Kant, Immanuel  12, 20, 40, 55, 108, 199
    judgement  122, 124–36
    perpetual peace  133–4, 269, 286, 294
Keegan, John  vi, 8, 26, 37, 41, 80, 82
Keen, David  182
Kennan, George  282–3, 286, 287
Kennedy, J. F.  4, 71
Kennedy, Paul  vi
Khruschev, Nikita  32
Kiesewetter, Johann Gottfried  20, 40, 124, 129, 199
Kinross, Stuart  182
Kissinger, Henry  190
Kleemeier, Ulrike  11–12
Knorr, Klaus  v
Kondylis, Panajotis  270
Königgrätz, battle of (1866)  150
Korean War  271
Kosovo war (1999)  161, 240–1, 244, 259, 263, 294, 295, 299
Krepenevich, Andrew  242
*Kritik* (critical analysis)  128–9, 137, 198, 200
Kuwait  158

Latin America  221 n.
law  38, 43, 110, 133, 151, 220, 256, 297–8, 302–3
leadership:
    decapitation strategy  155, 161
    global communications  208
    messianic  27
    military  108, 117, 141
    political  130, 277
    qualities  vi
    'three new Alexanders'  207, *see also* commanders; military genius
League of Nations  134
Leinveber, Adolf, General (out of duty)  27
Leipzig, battle of (1813)  15
Lenin, Vladimir  30, 31

Leonhard, Robert R.  236, 245
Lewis, Bernard  217
Libicki, Martin  236, 238, 241, 245, 246
Libya  293
Lieven, Anatol  243
Lilienstern August Rühle von  201
limited war  64, 65, 67, 87, 92, 167, 179, 202, 240–1, 254, 289, 292, 306
    definition of  164, 165
    just war  294–5
    territorial gain  97–8
    and unlimited war  96, *see also* containment of violence
linearity  45, 48–50
Linnebach, Karl  29
logic of war  124, 127, 148, 199, 218
logistics  39, 169, 220, 228
London bombings (July 2005)  209, 212, 215
Ludendorff, General Erich  32, 65, 151–2, 271
Luttwak, Edward  157–8, 182

MacArthur, General Douglas  191, 271
Machiavelli, Niccolò  40
Mack, Andrew  191
McNamara, Robert  157
Madrid bombings (March 2004)  209, 215
Maistre, Joseph de  147, 158
Maizière, Ulrich de  5, 6
Malaya  160
Malcolm, Angus  vi
Manila terrorist attack (February 2005)  209
Mao Tse Tung  139, 276
maritime conflicts  203
Marks, Sally  151
Marshall Plan  160
Marx, Karl  30
Marxism  251
Marxist-Leninism, definition of strategy  142
mathematics  46, 49, 50, 52, 124, 131, 168, 200, 239
Maude, Colonel F. N.  58
means, war as a  8, 12, 30, 34, 54, 82, 91–3, 95, 99, 101, 114, 134, 136, 143, 186, 187, 189, 201–2, 208, 209, 213, 217, 234
mechanics  45, 46–7, 49, 51, 108, 124–5, 149–50
media  208–9, 213, 215, 256, 265, 280
medieval warfare  103, 104, 206, 224, 227, 272, 294
melancholy  112–13
mercenaries  222, 223–4
Merom, Gil  191
Metz, Steven  182
*Militär-Wochenblatt* (journal)  19

militarism 18, 25, 36, 60, 136–7, 279
military genius 2, 23, 40, 52, 95, 110–13, 128–9, 168, 178, 248
  as an artist 130–2
  character 95, 112
  flawed 102
  four qualities of 111
  reductionism 196–7
military history, *see* history
military leadership 108, 117, 141, *see also* commanders; leadership
military service 146, 192, 273–4
military training 38, 132, 140
millenarianism 288
Milošević, Slobodan (President of Serbia) 263
mission command 117
mobilization, civilian population 146–7, 151, 159, 187, 192
modernity 60, 124, 278
Moltke, Helmuth von 19–20, 23, 25, 26, 114, 147
monarchism 27, 146–7
Montesquieu, baron de 40, 108
moral forces v, vi, 23, 107–21, 131, 140, 171, 251, 259, 295–6, 297–8
morale 147–8, 150, 152, 257
Moran, Daniel 12
Moreman, T. R. 243
Mori, Massimo 111 n.
multilateralism 84–5, 87
Münkler, Herfried 11, 36
Murray, Major Stewart 21
Murray, Williamson 143
Murray, Williamson and Knox, MacGregor 243
Muslim American Society 213
Muslim Council of Britain 213
mysticism 78–9

Napoleon I, emperor of France 8, 11, 17, 44, 137, 180, 273, 289
  Clausewitz's political interpretation of 135–6
  execution of envelopment 22
  failure in Russia 101–2
  fall of 14, 16
  and Frederick the Great 100–1
  genius of 95, 131, 178
  personal psychology of 102–3
  political aims 149
  probability theory 52
Napoleonic Wars (1804–15) 4–5, 21, 30, 36, 38, 40, 42, 94, 101–2, 144, 146, 150, 190

nationalism 21, 28–9, 45, 146, 192–3, 270, 273–4
nationalization warfare 272–4
NATO 153, 154, 155, 156, 157, 159, 241, 244, 262, 278, 305
Nazism 26, 29, 32–3, 72, 152, 160, 278
new wars 219, 224, 226–7, 276, *see also* asymmetrical warfare: privatization of war
Newtonian mechanics 45, 47, 51, 79, 124
*Niederwerfung*, translation of 61–3, 67, 68, 73
NII (national information infrastructure) 237
non-linear nature of war 48–56, 74, 233, 247, 262
North Korea 284
Northern Ireland 159
nuclear weapons 11, 32, 243, 297
  arms race 271
  Cold War 153–4
  deterrent 5, 247, 275
  'problematic' states and 284
  proliferation 61, 96, 203, 285, 304
  Second World War 152–3

obedience 120–1
objective knowledge 197–200, 208, 217–18, 252
objective-subjective dualism 199–200, 202–3, 209
objectives in war 91–106, 196, 240
'Observations on the Wars of the Austrian Succession' (Clausewitz) 94
O'Etzel, Major Franz August 57
offence and defence, *see* attack and defence
*On War*:
  ambiguity 40–1, 65
  appeal to officers of 19–20
  Clausewitz's dated note to (10 July 1827) 35, 36, 41, 93, 99, 163–4, 306
  Clausewitz's undated notes to 35, 56, 123, 163–4
  commercial transaction metaphor (*Wechselhandel*) 156
  copy found in al-Qaeda safe house 1
  criticism of 7–9, 22
  differences and contradictions of analysis of 251–3
  *Hinterlassene Werke* 18, 39
  military history 38–40
  problems of text and translation 59–73
  prose style of 17
  publication of 17
  publishing history after 1871 19

*On War (cont.)*
  relevance of 2, 10, 12, 32, 92, 122, 182, 183, 188, 194–5, 269, 292, 306–7
  studies of 18–44
  superiority of the defence over the offence 165–77, 188–91
  textual changes to 18
  translations of 58, 74–90
Oppenheim, Felix 184
Organization of the Islamic Conference 212
organized complexity 47, 53–6
organized crime 226, 286
OSCE (Organization for Security and Cooperation in Europe) 156
outsourcing 220, 227, 228
Owens, Mackubin Thomas 239

pacifism 133–4, 151
Palat, General (Pierre Lehautcourt) 26
Palestine 214
Palmer, General John McAuley 273
Paret, Peter v, 3, 11, 35, 60, 65, 177, *see also* Howard, Sir Michael
passion 43–4, 77, 90, 95, 112–13, 118–19, 264
patrimonialism warfare 272
patriotism 115–16, 146–7
peace 133, 148, 153, 157, 286, 305, 306
  democratic 293–4, 304
  dictated 41
  domestic 291
  enduring 149, 160–2
  Gulf War 158
  just 294, 301
  Kantian peace 133–4, 269, 286, 294
  negotiated 25, 41, 92, 202, 214, 271
  treaties 29, 150–1
peacekeeping missions 257, 263, 276, 297
Peninsular War 138
people 77, 80–2, 86, 151, 152, 153, 166, 204–7, 223
  armed resistance 173, 179
  counter-insurgency warfare and 240
  defence 166, 172
  exploitation by warlords 223, 226, 227
  mobilization of the 146–7, 151, 159, 187, 192
  re-education of 160–1
  state disintegration 226
  terrorist groups 215–16
  Westphalian order 226
people's war *(Volkskrieg)* 103–4, 146–7, 174, 183, 187, 192
Peters, Ralph 242 n.
PGMs (precision-guided munitions) 236

phenomenon 3, 5, 48, 51, 71, 85, 90, 113, 114, 117, 125–6, 151, 175, 201, 203, 210, 255, 257, 271, 288
philosophy 14, 38, 40, 44, 56, 108, 122–4, 126, 128–9, 134, 136, *see also* Kant; Hegel
Pickett, General George 241
play of chance and probability 7, 43, 77, 79, 204, 205, 208, 248, 272, *see also* chance; probability
PLO (Palestine Liberation Organization) 190
PMCs (private military companies) 220, 222, 228–9
policy 85–7, 88, 103, 239, 268, 271
policy/politics vi, 2, 5–6, 9, 19, 23, 40, 59, 69–86, 107, 164, 165, 166, 178, 185, 197, 203, 205–8, 229, 258, 269, 271, 277, 289–93, 306
political aims and objectives 11, 67, 71, 84, 90, 92, 100, 101, 102–3, 142, 149, 157, 201–2, 203, 294, 306
political leadership 130, 277
political persuasion 160–1, 162
politics 7, 9, 12, 27, 33, 43, 134–5, 189, 262
  control of the military 60, 278–81
  and enduring peace 160–1, 162
  ideal/real war 257–8
  limited war and 289
  multilateralism of 84–5, 87, 88
  offence and defence 172–3
  organized violence and 268–72
  primacy of 99, 201–2, 266, 270–1, 278, 279
  strategy 95, 142–3
  war as subset of 53, 54
post-Westphalian order 8, 9, 34, 39
Powell, Colin 34, 43
power:
  balance of 69, 134, 191, 193, 272, 292
  concept of 84
privatization of war 11, 219–30, 285
probability 45, 46–7, 52–3, 77, 79, 81, 88–90, 204, *see also* chance
professionalism 275
propaganda 154, 215
Prussia 14–15, 19, 29, 42, 99–100, 135, 157, 170, 180
  battle of Jena 66
  growth of militarism 18
  mobilization of the population 146–7
  national liberation of 189, 192
psychology 51, 84, 105, 140, 145–6, 168, 169, 174, 176, 211, 234, 246

'public good' 71
public opinion 145–7, 150, 236, 256, 280
Punic Wars 240
pure reason 77, 79, 82–3, 90
purpose *see* aims and objectives; means, war as a

Qaeda-al 1, 105, 187, 209, 210–11, 212, 214, 215, 230

racism 152
Ranke, Leopold von 200
rationality 11, 41, 77, 79, 81, 82, 85, 86, 204
Reagan, President Ronald 155
real war 2, 66, 67, 69, 164, 165, 194, 253–9, 262–3, 264–5
reason 77, 79, 82–3, 90, 95, 110, 112–14, 117–19, 127, 135
rebellions 87, 183, 187, 193–4, *see also* revolution
reciprocity 37, 55, 225, 253
reconstruction (contestability) 184–6
reductionism 196–7, 286
religion 39, 44, 78
religious wars 294
resistance 168, 169
retreat 168, 174
revenge 118, 213, 265
revolution 30, 87, 92, 103, 251
  French 9, 14, 43, 101, 134, 135, 146
  in military affairs (RMA) 231–50
Richelieu, Cardinal 93
Ritter, Gerhard 25–6, 32–3, 71
RMA (Revolution in Military Affairs) 231–50
Robertson, General Sir Brian 160
Roeder, Karl von, correspondence with Clausewitz 96 n., 99–100
Roman Empire 240
Romanticism 40, 45, 55, 132
Ronfeldt, David 235, 246
Rosinski, Herbert 28
Rothfels, Hans 28
Rühle von Lilienstern, Otto August 2, 201
Rumsfeld, Donald 233, 235, 299
Russia 15
  Napoleon's invasion of (1812) 5, 36, 101–2, 157, 190, 244
Rwanda 299

Saddam Hussein 97–8, 158, 216
Scharnhorst, Gerhard 14–15, 16, 19, 37, 38, 188
Schelling, Thomas 55, 156–7, 261

Schering, Walther Malmsten 30
Scheurer, Michael 217
Schlieffen, Alfred von 20, 23–4, 25
Schmitt, Carl 289, 305
Schubert, Klaus von 287–8
Schuhmann, Dirk 302
Schwarzkopf, General Norman 237
science 45, 46, 87
  genius 131
  non-linear imagery 48–56, 74
  physics 45, 47, 51, 79, 124, 126
secession 103, 155
Seché, Alphonse 151
Second World War (1939–45) 32, 247, 255
  annihilation 152–3, 240
  attritional warfare 242
  German people's mobilization in 1944–5 159
security 5–6, 155–6, 224, 287–8
Sedan, battle of (1870) 150
Segal, David 279
self-control 118–19
self-defence 25, 99, 146, 167, 256, 292 n.
self-preservation 193, 290, 292, 304, 305
Senghaas, Dieter 286–7 n.
September 11th terrorist attacks (2001) 4, 210, 211, 229–30, 242, 256, 284, 305
Serbia 294
Seven Years War (1756–63) 23, 24, 40, 144
Shaftesbury, Anthony Ashley Cooper, third Earl of 55
Shannon, Claude 46
Sharm al-Sheikh terrorist attack (July 2005) 212
Shatt al-Arab waterway 97, 98
Sherman, Jason 233
Shy, John v
Silesia, invasion of (1740s) 97
Simmel, Georg 302
SIW (strategic information warfare) 237, 238, 242, 245, 246–7, 301
Slav peoples 152
small wars 11, 182–95, *see also* people's wars
Smith, Adam 45
Smith, Hugh 177
Social Darwinism 150, 152
social science 123, 136, 137
society 103, 122
  civil-military relations 277–82
  communal self-preservation 290
  mobilization of 146–7, 151
  public opinion 145–7, 150, 236, 256, 280
  understanding of 127

society (*cont.*)
　violence and suffering 102
　war and 98–9
Sofsky, Wolfgang 302
soldiers 271
　ambition and competition 116
　bravery 12, 23, 114–17, 168, 264
　concept of the ideal 12
　democratic control 281
　diplomats 275–7
　elementary tactics 141
　mission command 117
　obedience/disobedience 120–1
Somalia 214
sovereignty 34, 43, 69, 210
Soviet Union 285
　Chechen war 243–4
　Cold War 153–4
　collapse of 156
　German invasion of 244
　nuclear proliferation 203
　*On War* 30–2
　Yom Kippur War 98, *see also* Russia
Spain 138
　insurrection in 183, 187
specialization warfare 272, 274–5
Spinoza, Benedict 108
Stalin, Joseph 32, 279
stand-off warfare 236, 240, 241, 242, 243, 248, 255, 259
state 7–8
　attackers 186
　civil-military relations 277–82
　control of violence 267
　counterinsurgency 190
　decline 267
　disintegration 220–1, 226
　international system 267–8
　interstate wars 6, 186, 219, 229, 253, 267, 268, 270, 275, 294
　monopolization of warfare 134, 219, 220–1, 223, 225, 267, 291
　policy decisions 205–6
　privatization of war 228–9
　professionalization of war 223–4
　self-preservation 193, 290, 292, 304, 305
　small wars 193–4
　terrorism against the 187
　Westphalian system of 76, 224–5, 270, 291–2, *see also* government
Stauffenberg, Claus von Graf 120
Stern, Jessica 217
Stevenson, David 26
Strachan, Hew 142

Strange, Susan 267
strategic debate, ideal or real war 253–9
strategy 11, 138–62
　aims of 67, 148–9
　of annihilation 23, 26, 32
　of attrition 24, 26
　core elements of 239–45
　culture and 12, 253, 255–6
　definitions of 140–3
　dialectic nature of 41–3, 75, 245–6, 249
　dimensions of 6, 148
　and policy 24
　tactics and 22–6, 40, 189
　terrorism 230
　two Clausewitzian interpretations of 140–1, 148–9
　unconditional surrender 247
*Sturm und Drang* movement 40
subordination 7, 41, 77, 79, 82, 86, 204, 208, 272
Suez Canal 98
suicide bombers 222–3, 285
Sumida, Jon 12
Summers, Colonel Harry 34, 43, 80–1, 251
Sun Tzu, *The Art of War* 37, 122, 123–4, 232
Svechin, A. A. 31
SWAPO (South-West Africa People's Organization) 190
synthesis 41, 42, 44, 59, 75, 204, 275

tactics 22–6, 40, 105, 139, 140, 141, 142, 159, 189
*Takt des Urteils* 113–14, 129, 130, 132, 134, 137, *see also* judgement
Taliban regime 105
Tartar warfare 203, 206
Tauroggen, convention of (1812) 15, 121
technological innovation 46, 123, 222, 225, 226, 239, 241–2, 244, 255, 274, 305
technology 31, 50–1, 119, 137
terrain 42, 173, 186, 243–5, 249, 256
territory:
　abandonment of national 179
　boundaries 155, 301–3
　defence of 175, 281
　gain 93, 97–8
　occupation 159, 166
terror, war on 104–5, 136, 194, 196–218, 299
terrorism 4, 12, 92, 136, 183, 184, 185, 187, 193, 209, 229–30, 284
　containment 287, 288, 299–300, 303
　ideal war criteria 256–7
　Iraq 159, 209

terrorism (*cont.*)
  leaders 161
  occupied territories 159
  principal causes of 216–17
  psychology of 246
  RMA and 242
theory of war:
  continuation of *Politik* (policy/politics) by other means vi, 2, 5–6, 9, 19, 23, 40, 59, 69, 75, 107, 165, 178, 185, 197, 203, 205–6, 229, 269, 271, 277, 289–93, 306
  imposing one's will on the enemy 29, 144–5, 147, 148, 149, 154, 159, 192, 197, 229, 234, 255, 277, 291, 300, *see also* Trinity
Third World countries 221, 226
Thirty Years War (1618–48) 30, 39, 209, 211, 220, 270, 294
Tilly, Charles 272
time-space 41–2, 50, 256–7
Tirpitz, Admiral Alfred von 27
Tito 276
Toffler, Alvin 238
Toffler, Alvin and Heidi 232
total war 30, 32, 64–5, 67, 72, 151, 264, 271
totalitarianism 279, 284, 293
translation problems v–vi, 74–90
Trenchard, Hugh 152
Trinity 3, 7–8, 11, 12, 29, 41–4, 71, 213, 251, 264, 290, 292, 307
  amazing vii
  fascinating 77, 233
  miraculous 72
  paradoxical vii, 271–2
  remarkable vii, 44 n., 166, 179
  strange 3, 44
  translation problems 74–90
  wondrous vi, 44, 79, 197, 204–18, *see also* commanders; armed forces; government; state, people
Trotsky, Leon 31
Truman, President Harry S. 271
trusteeship 103, 104, 205, 277
Tunisia terrorist attack (April 2002) 209
Tyrolean uprising (1809) 183, 187

UCAVs (unmanned combat air vehicles) 255
Ulam, Stanislav 50
Unamuno, Miguel de 160
uncertainty of war 20, 52, 116, 127, 143, 149, 168, 202–3, 209, 216–17, 274, 298
  information technology 233–4, 236, 238, 247–8, 259, *see also* fog of war; unpredictability of war

unilateralism 85–7, 211–12, 305
United Nations 134, 158, 229, 262, 299
United States 5, 287
  AirLand Battle 158
  atomic bombing of Japan 152–3
  citizen soldier 273
  conflict management 156–7
  counter-terrorist policy 215–16
  defensive/offensive strategy 181
  definition of strategy (Joint Chiefs of Staff 1989) 142
  immigrant soldiers 222
  invasion of Iraq 4, 34, 105, 137, 158–9, 220, 233, 284, 305
  military supremacy 137
  minimization of losses 222, 236, 244
  nuclear weapons 153, 154–5, 203
  PMCs, use of 220, 228–9
  Revolution in Military Affairs (RMA) 248
  self-limitation 305
  September 11th attacks on 4, 210, 211, 229–30, 242, 256, 284, 305
  strategic culture of 12, 86, 255
  technological innovation 222
  unilateralism 211–12, 305
  *On War* 34–5
  war on terror 104–5, 210, 213, 215–16
  Yom Kippur War 98, *see also* Vietnam War
United States Marine Corps, doctrine manual of 231–2
unlimited war 164, 165, 167, 179, 289
unpredictability of war 53, 79, 81, 204, 234, *see also* uncertainty of war
urban warfare 243–4, 248

Vatry, Lieutenant-Colonel de 19, 21, 22
Vega, José Fernandez 12
Vendée, rebellion in the (1811–12) 183, 187
Versailles, Treaty of (1919) 29, 150–1
victory 99, 105, 138, 139, 142
  definitions of 143–8
  First World War 150–1
  guerrilla resistance 159
  information warfare and 240, 242
  military history 148–61
  small wars and 186, 191
  textbook example of Desert Storm 158
  war on terror 299, *see also* peace
Vietnam War (1964–75) vi, 34, 35, 71, 80, 96, 157, 160–1, 190, 228, 243
violence 91–2, 102, 137, 246
  autonomous 254, 270, 302
  containment 12, 263, 282–307
  controlled/uncontrolled 270

# Index

violence (*cont.*)
  economy of 96
  modern strategic debate 253–65
  monopoly of 286–7 n.
  non-instrumental 104–5
  and order 266–8
  political goals and 268–72
  primordial 7, 77, 79, 82, 204–5, 208
  privatization of 11, 219–30, 285
  strategy and 247
violent emotion 77, 79, 82

Walzer, Michael 296
war 41
  as art 125–37
  art of 140
  and *bellum* 109–10
  chameleon metaphor 1, 54, 56, 77–8, 133, 203
  changes in 2–3, 219–30, 236–7
  climate of 245–50
  dualism of 31, 35–6, 41, 93, 94, 99, 163–4, 306
  extended duel metaphor 185, 186
  future of 236–50
  industrialization of 274, 294
  just 292, 294–5, 301
  nature of 8, 35–6, 77, 93, 94, 198–208, 233–5
  new forms of 183, 192, 236, 240, 241, 242, 243, 248, 255, 259, 285
  non-linear nature of 45–56
  objectives in 91–106, 196, 240
  privatization of 219–30
  proliferation of 283, 288, 293
  rhetoric of 105
  rumours spread during 109
  semantics of 109–10
  small 11, 182–95
  state organization and 272
  for territorial objectives 41, *see also* theory of war; Trinity; violence; *On War*
war criminals 160
War of the Austrian Succession (1740–48) 94
war on terror 104–5, 136, 194, 196–218, 299
Warden, John 255, 261
warlords 6, 10, 11, 221, 223, 226, 229
Warsaw Pact 154, 156, 157
Waterloo, battle of (1815) 5, 36, 289
Watts, Barry D. 234, 262
weather 244
Weaver, Warren 46, 47, 50, 52, 53, 55
Weber, Max 185, 287 n.
*Wechselwirkung* 55–6
Weinberger, Caspar 34
West Germany 280
Westphalia, peace of (1648) 6, 34, 270, 291
Westphalian system 76, 224–5, 270, 291–2
Wilkinson, Spenser 20, 21
willpower 150, 179, 191, 192, 202, 257, 300
Wilson, President Woodrow 43, 293
WMDs (weapons of mass destruction) 242, 243, 245, 246, 284, 297, 304
women, in armed forces 281
Wood, General Leonard 273
world order 212, 221 n., 230, 285, 303–7
World Wars 4, 60, 294, *see also* under First World War; Second World War
Wylie, J. C. 240, 246, 249

Yom Kippur War (1973) 98
Yorck, General Hans von 15–16, 120–1

*Zeitgeist* 40, 207, 269
Zhukov, Marshal 160